Mr. and Mrs.
Laurence T. Paddock
525 - 13th St.
Boulder, Colorado 80302

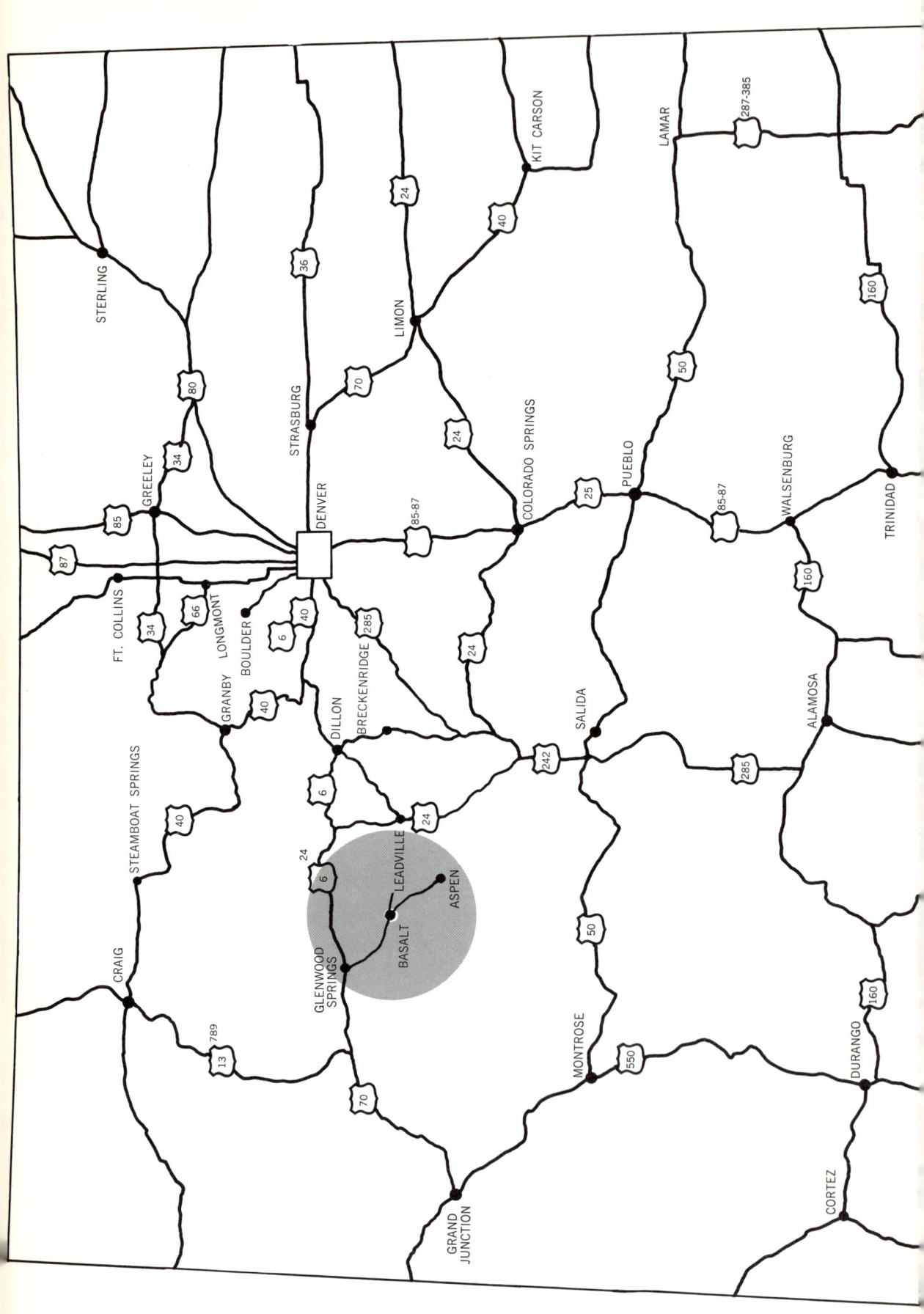

BASALT:
Colorado Midland Town

Clarence L. Danielson
and
Ralph W. Danielson

Published by

Pruett Publishing Company
Boulder, Colorado

Copyright © 1965, 1971
by
Clarence L. Danielson
and
Ralph W. Danielson

Library of Congress Catalog
Card Number: 65-22871
ISBN: 0-87108-038-9
Printed in the U.S.A.

Acknowledgements

A partial list of those who have graciously taken time to write or talk or furnish pictures follows; we hope that the people whom we have omitted inadvertently will please forgive us. Persons furnishing information for the family biographies have been given credit in the manuscript.

Those in Basalt who have helped are Mr. and Mrs. James Hurtgen, Robert Terrell, Emery Arbaney, (deceased), M. C. Newberry, Ruby Gold, Wayne Anderson and Lydia Newkirk. Our special thanks go to Walter and Eva Hyrup, Bramblet and Dorothy Willits, Anna Sloss, and Leonis Usel, who have spent many hours answering our queries.

From Glenwood Springs we have had assistance from Claude Crowley, Lena M. Urquhart, Elizabeth Elliott, the Forest Service Office, and John Schutte. Aid has come from Peggy Cable in Aspen, D.R.C. Brown in Carbondale and Howard Dearhammer and Mr. and Mrs. Allan Craig, of Meredith, as well as India Reeves Luchsinger (deceased) and Dan German, of Rifle. Ronald Bogue, of Snowmass provided his manuscript. Dudley Mitchell and the Grand Junction *Sentinel* gave information. We had informative visits with Orel Clark and James Larsh and letters from Terrence Cannons of Leadville. Gene Luby and Thomas McBreen of Eagle assisted greatly.

The Denver helpers were many: Arthur and Georgina Bates, Clarence and Ethel Dearing, Virgil and Blanche Holcomb, Dr. Donald Turner, Rev. Martin Rist (Iliff School of Theology), Earl Kibby (deceased), Len Shoemaker, Mrs. Earl Carter, Earl Mosley, Clarence Batcheller, Frank Cook, Harvey Sethman and Gladys Wachob.

Maurice Frink, Agnes Wright Spring, Laura Eckstrom, Alice Wallace, Enid T. Thompson, William E. Marshall, Harry Kelsey and John Cleaver of the staff of the State Historical Society have given much assistance. At the Denver Public Library we have had valued help from Alys Freeze, Jim Davis, Ramona Wright, and Opal Harter and others. Rose Rathbone of the Brand Recording Department of Colorado went far out of her way to provide material. The Department of Education of Colorado graciously allowed us to get the names of the former teachers; Ethyl K. Pitton of the State Game and Fish Commission kindly answered our queries. E. J. Haley of the Railroad Club has assisted.

Active and corresponding members of the Denver Posse of the Westerners who have given information and encouragement have been Don L. Griswold, William S. Jackson, Numa L. James, John Lipsey, Fred Mazzula, Forbes Parkhill, Robert Perkin, Francis Rizzari, Richard Ronzio, Fred Rosenstock, and Charles Ryland.

Other helpers around the United States have been Leo Heller of Cheyenne, Arlington Cuthbert of Derby, Prof. Omer Stewart and Dean Philip Worchester of Colorado University, Carrie Hall of Laramie, Wyoming, Dr. Lois Borland of Gunnison, D. H. Gerbaz of La Mesa, California, John R. Smith of Minturn, and Robert Richardson of the Colorado Railroad Museum at Golden. Bert Barton of Seattle has given added information. Philip Danielson of Boulder helped with abstracts. Typing of manuscripts has been done by Katherine Otis, Vivian Langley, Maxine Langley; Jean Killgore and May Edwards helped arrange the manuscript. Robert F. Wilson was responsible for maps and drawings. Fred Pruett, the publisher, has provided valued guidance in the preparation of the book.

United States Government employees in Denver who have cooperated fully have been H.S. Varner, Director of Reclamation Bureau, D. G. Crossen, Regional Director of Post Office, and Henry S. Shyrock, Jr., of Bureau of the Census, and Marion Martin, Cartographer of the Geological Survey.

Jack O'Conner of *Outdoor Life* and George Goodwin of American Museum of Natural History provided needed information.

We are grateful to Katherine Otis for typing much handwritten material, to May Edwards for suggestions as to arrangement, and to Fred Pruett, publisher, for nursing along some novices in the publishing field.

And finally, we owe the most gratitude and thanks to our wives Lucy and Luverne. Lucy Danielson provided much information and many names. Luverne Danielson has done a large amount of typing and has been of assistance with the biographies and in proofreading, but above all, she has allowed the dining-room table to be covered with papers, for many months. We are grateful to both of them for their encouragement when we have been tempted to throw the whole thing in the waste basket.

Foreword

Inspired by a quilt embroidered with 400 autographs of residents of their home town, Basalt, the authors have spent every "extra hour" for several years in collecting hard-to-find and hitherto unassembled historical data for this book.

Basalt, at the junction of the Frying Pan River and the Roaring Fork in Eagle County, Colorado, has always been a small town. It has never had a population of more than 400 at any time. But it has grown from tents and cabins to a substantial town of comfortable homes, stores, schools, and other structures. The place originally was a railroad town with the Colorado Midland track running down the center of the main street. It continued as a railroad town until 1918 when the Midland ceased to operate and the rails were torn up.

In their book, Dr. Ralph Danielson and Mr. Clarence Danielson convincingly show Basalt as a close-knit community, with their chief interest centered around the railroad. Both brothers, sons of a Midland locomotive engineer, did some railroading themselves. From their father they learned the meaning of every train whistle blast and they could tell without hesitating the difference between "highball" freight and "drag." Both have been intensely interested in collecting and helping to preserve the story of the Frying Pan country.

This book does not follow the usual chronological arrangement of a matter-of-fact history. Instead, it centers around personalities—the personalities known by the Danielsons. The authors painstakingly compiled about 70 biographies and have assembled the names of 600 families who have, at one time or another, lived in the Basalt area. Whenever possible they included the names of the children and the names of persons who married into the families. With some families having as many as ten to twelve children, the number of names on the list is staggering! From official records the author also has compiled names of teachers, county superintendents, ministers, postmasters, storekeepers, members of lodges, railroad employees, and many others.

"As we remember—" is an expression often found in the work which includes many vivid memories of such things as carrying lanterns on the streets of Basalt at night to see the way to church or social activities; the setting out on a sidetrack of a Rio Grande box car so that farmers could donate potatoes, cabbages, onions and the like to the little "begging nuns" from the Queen of Heaven Orphanage in Denver; the big snow of 1899; wild flower excursions on the Midland; and the youthful joys of the authors as they successfully fished the holes and riffles of the Frying Pan and gathered wild roses for their mother.

With characteristic vigor and thoroughness Clarence and Ralph have searched out and present here many rare photographs. Through the enthusiastic research of themselves, and their wives, they have aroused much interest among the former and present residents of Basalt in the permanent preservation of historical materials.

To enable others to know the interesting story of how Basalt was built and to recreate with words their boyhood days along the Frying Pan has been the authors' motivating desire.

The book should serve as an excellent reference tool for everyone interested in Western Slope lore. It gives a vivid picture of life in a small, pioneer, western railroad town where the citizens shared each others joys and sorrows and relied upon their neighbors for daily friendliness and help in time of sickness or financial trouble.

The authors have incorporated a number of important paragraphs from the work of other authors who have written about the Roaring Fork or the Midland, but they have been exceedingly careful to give credit for every work quoted.

With the Frying Pan project and the Ruedi Dam becoming realities, there is now nation-wide interest in the Basalt area. Hence, this new work should prove exceedingly interesting and helpful.

Agnes Wright Spring
Colorado State Historian Emeritus

Preface to Second Edition

In view of the rather surprising but wholly gratifying response to *Basalt: Colorado Midland Town*, published in 1965, we decided to bring out a second edition, adding a list of errata from the first book, a new map, some color photographs, and a chapter of interesting family histories and miscellanea received since 1965.

We take pride in our small effort to preserve this bit of Americana for posterity, a pride best expressed, in part, by one of the stanzas in Will Allen Dromgoole's beautiful poem, The *Bridge Builder*.

> ". . . There followeth after me today
> A youth whose feet must pass this way.
> He, too, must cross in the twilight dim—
> Good friend, I am building this bridge for him."

The first edition was hurried through production because we wished friends, some in the twilight of life's span, to have an opportunity to read the book. Sadly, many of them will not see this second printing. During these last five years we have lost, among others, Arthur Bates, Mrs. Lucy Clarke Danielson, Myron Danielson, Mrs. Eva Letey Hyrup, Mrs. Christine Genner Lucksinger, Earl Mosley, Mrs. Lydia Henning Newkirk, Rye Ould, Mrs. Irene Clarke Ould, Mrs. Anna Wilson Sloss, Alvin Sloss, Bramblet Willits, Philip Danielson, and Mrs. Laura Danielson Carey.

Friends who have helped us are Howard Dearhammer, Walter Hyrup, Mrs. Maude Elmont, Jake Lucksinger, Jr., Hal Benson, George McLaren, Jack Smith, Mrs. Caroline Smith, Mrs. Nellie Hurtgen Carpenter, Len Shoemaker, Mrs. Dorothy Willits, Bob Terrell, Virgil Holcomb, Mrs. Lena M. Urquhart, Dudley Mitchell, Mrs. Georgina Bates, Clarence Dearing and many others. We are particularly grateful to Luverne Danielson, Gerald Keenan and Fred Pruett for advice and encouragement. Thanks are also due to Lawrence Strand who prepared the map for this second edition. To all who have aided us, we express our sincere thanks.

Ralph and Clarence Danielson

Ralph Wesley Danielson, co-author of this book, passed away on October 8, 1970, while this second edition was in preparation. Ralph Danielson was a gentleman of the highest order, and a man who had a life-long love affair with his native Basalt, and Colorado, as this volume testifies. Pruett Publishing wishes to express its deepest sympathy to family and friends.

Preface

A few years ago, in reading the admirable articles about various villages in the *Colorado Magazine* of the State Historical Society, the thought occurred to us that "our home town" had been overlooked. It is true that Basalt had been mentioned as Frying Pan City by the Griswolds in their exceedingly interesting book "Colorado's Century of Cities", and by Shoemaker in his admirably written book, "The Roaring Fork Valley." It seemed to us that an article should be written about Basalt also for the magazine, and we started to prepare it. However, as we began to get material and photographs, and our interest in the project grew, we realized that we had enough material for a book.

This book has several purposes. In the first place, it is primarily a record of the people in a railroad town of the past. And yet, perhaps it is even more an attempt to recapture for future residents of Basalt and for our own descendants, the manner in which we lived in our youth. In our generation there have been more significant inventions and discoveries than in all previously known history. We are in a position not only to enjoy them, but to appreciate them also.

In view of the desire to leave a record for our own grandchildren and those who may follow, we have perhaps given too much attention to the Danielson family, and we hope the reader will understand our reason for this emphasis.

Ray Brandes, in an editorial in Arizoniana says the following: "Every family is highly encouraged to preserve its records which might include correspondence, legal documents, photographs, or genealogies. Such record keeping is vital but there is a step beyond this—these papers should be brought forth and deposited in some state agency which is in the business of record-holding where they can be permanently preserved and made available to anyone interested in the study of their region or state." In writing this book we have compiled much source material which we are leaving to the Colorado State Historical Society.

The cooperation of many people has been spontaneous and wholehearted, in marked contrast to the expression of opinion we heard from an "old timer" while we were camping on the South Fork of the White River near Budges a few years ago. He said, quite heatedly, that he didn't intend to give valuable information on the early history of the region to the "history fellers" unless they paid him for it. If he only knew the balance sheet in time, effort, and money in writing a book of this nature!

We also feel that we have only scratched the surface and we hope that our start will stimulate others to go into more detail, and to make corrections of any mistakes that we have made. We would suggest projects in writing or engaging in other endeavors such as:

1—A project for preserving land marks such as historical cabins, Indian camps, and short sections of old railroad grade.

2—A complete list of people buried in the Fairview Cemetery.

3—More detailed maps of Basalt.

4—A supplementary list to ours of those once living in Basalt.

5—More facts about the charcoal ovens.

6—Study of the bands of Indians that inhabited the Basalt region.

7—Origin of names of local towns and mountains and valleys.

8—Maps of location of old bridges, trestles, and ditches.

9—More family biographies.

We have tried to make the history accurate, but if we checked every fact about Basalt, the book would never be written. This dilemma has been well told by Robert Frost in his poem "On making certain anything has happened." The last stanza reads:

"To make sure what star I missed
I should have to check on my list
Every star in sight
It might take me all night."

Actually much of this book has been written in the middle of the night.

We hope to portray that Basalt was a living town. A few years ago at the Circle S Motel, in Laramie, Wyoming, we saw a bronze plaque on a stone monument which read "In 1880, when the Indians roamed this country, right here on this very spot, nothing, absolutely nothing happened." To this amusing and facetious statement, we can only say that in our town things happened.

And finally the preparation of this book has exemplified to us the perils and pleasures of serendipity. The perils are the many interesting publications and situations that one encounters that tempt one to get off the main track of writing the book. On the other side of the ledger, one of the most rewarding by-products is that it has offered us such an excellent opportunity to renew old Basalt friendships and memories, and to meet so many interesting and gracious people.

Contents

Page

Acknowledgments

Foreword

Preface

Dedication

Chapter

1	History of Basalt	1
2	The Colorado Midland	41
3	Clarence's Memories	81
4	Ralph's Memories	109
5	Basalt at Work	135
6	Community Activities	149
7	Families of Basalt	187
8	Newspapers	321
9	Residents of Basalt	337
10	Geology of the Basalt Area	351

Reunion—1964 357

Memorabilia 361

Chronology 370

Bibliography 373

Errata 381

In Memory of our Parents

CLARA HILLGREN DANIELSON

AND

ANDREW MALCOLM DANIELSON

"Breathes there the man, with soul so dead,
Who never to himself hath said,
    This is my own, my native land!
Whose heart hath ne'er within him burn'd.
As home his footsteps he hath turn'd
    From wandering on a foreign strand!"

Sir Walter Scott
from *The Lay of the Last Minstrel*

CHAPTER 1

History of Basalt

Frying Pan Junction and Aspen Junction

Frying Pan Junction (or just Frying Pan), was the name given to the original settlement, because of the Frying Pan River, the naming of which is discussed later. At any rate, this name has been most appropriate because of the millions of trout that have been caught out of that nationally known river in the last eighty years, and have eventually ended up in the frying pan.

This town of Frying Pan was largely a tent village, although a few cabins were built. Shoemaker says, "Dennis Barry opened a tent store and Red Duggan had one of several tent saloons." That their location was in the region of the school house is well attested to because Clarence Danielson, Art Bates, and Walter Hyrup all well remember the broken pieces of glass that were present near the coal house on the school grounds—obviously from the ever-present saloons.

Though squatters in the valley started settling on land as early as 1880, the first settlement town of Frying Pan, built primarily to house and entertain the men working in the nearby charcoal ovens, was built in 1882.

The ovens were used to produce charcoal for the smelters in Aspen and Leadville. There were charcoal kilns also at Aspen and in the Crystal River Valley. Later some were built at Sellars. The charcoal was transported on the backs of horses and mules. The usefulness of the ovens faded after coal was found at Spring Valley and near Carbondale and the railroads reached Aspen, for then it was much cheaper and more efficient for the smelters to obtain the coke from the coke ovens near Cardiff and up the Crystal River.

A family by the name of Arbaney later purchased the land on which the brick charcoal ovens stand. On Emery Arbaney's place

Basalt, about 1900. Taken from the hill northwest of town. Looking up the Roaring Fork Valley toward Aspen, showing the charcoal ovens (extreme left), the Emory Arbaney farm, the Sam Cramer farm and the school house. (opposite page)

Courtesy of D. H. Gerbaz

R. W. D. Collection

The charcoal ovens, built about 1882.

they have used them for many years to house machinery and to shelter cattle and horses in severe winter months. There is no history available as to whether the bricks were made locally or were brought in.

About the same time as the construction of the charcoal ovens on the south side of the Frying Pan River four years before Emma Shehi's newspaper contribution, Gabriel Luchsinger and his wife, Julia, built a "half-way" house nearby for accommodation of travelers over the rough trails and crude roads from the lower portion of the Roaring Fork Valley to Aspen and Leadville. No doubt some of the more prosperous men working at the charcoal ovens chose to stay at the large guest cabin of the Luchsinger's rather than rough it in the flimsy, cold tents of Frying Pan Junction.

Last summer his fourteen-year-old grandson, Luke J. Danielson, and R.W.D., while engaged in the project of photographing Black Mountain, were climbing around the north face of Red Mountain from White Hill. They came across the old road which apparently was used by workmen getting wood out to the charcoal ovens years ago. The pine trees in that area were prized for the making of excellent charcoal. Many of the stumps are still visible. No doubt this trail had also been used to some extent by the prospectors and the ranchers farther up the valley, for there was then no wagon road up the Frying Pan River. For many years these old carts that had been used to haul the pinon trees were stored between Gabe Luchsinger's and the ovens, but have now disappeared.

It gives one an eerie feeling to be following this abandoned road which has not been used for almost 80 years and is almost indistinguishable in many places. We are looking forward eagerly to taking this trip again and going even farther up Red Mountain to view Black Mountain, Sloan's Peak, the Frying Pan Valley, the Amphitheatre, and the Elk Mountains.

And now we shall take up the next step in the evolution of Basalt, the town of Aspen·Junction.

The beginnings of Aspen Junction have been described in a colorful and pungent letter written by Emma Davis Shehi, from Emma, Colorado, to the *Kansas Agriculturist* in April 1887: "A little town started up last summer within a half-mile of our ranch. It was really a railroad camp. In about three weeks there were a boarding-house, a little store, a restaurant or two, and fifteen saloons. The boarding-house and store are still there; happily for the surrounding community the saloons have dwindled down to three; not from any element of reform, but because the navvies have gone, and there was custom enough for only three."

The interesting word "navvies" may be new to some readers as it was to us. The dictionary supplies the meaning, "common laborer." Her reference to the number of saloons at Aspen Junction is probably somewhat exaggerated. Mrs. Shehi was obviously an ardent prohibitionist, as confirmed by comments made to

Luchsinger half-way house as it looks today.

R. W. D. collection

us by her nephew, Bramblet Willits. The number of saloons can be accounted for when we remember that the original towns were almost entirely "men's towns", and the saloons provided a meeting place, not only for drinking, but also for sociability and gambling.

It may be of interest to quote some more from the same letter: "In Aspen you will see almost as many of the white-aproned gentry about the streets as anywhere else, at least they are much more conspicuous than any others. Always bareheaded, their hair shiny with oil, and combed as slick as if they were just going out to be hung; their step as brisk as if all the officers in the city were after them, and their air is tremendously business-like. But what of the hereafter? I wonder if any of them think of that. Perhaps not, but if they do, no doubt Satan is ever ready with the salve for their conscience, 'Never mind! If you did not sell rum someone else would'."

The early day settlement of the town consisted essentially of purchase of the property by the homeowners, business men, and the railroad from the Luchsinger brothers.

The land office records show that tracts No. 45, 47, and 48 were purchased at $1.25 an acre from the United States Government from land within the limits of the late Indian Reservation. Tract No. 45 issued to Otmar Luchsinger was dated November 8, 1890. The acreage was 157.68. Tract No. 47 was issued November 20, 1891, to Gabriel Luchsinger and consisted of 160 acres. Tract No. 48 of 160 acres was granted to John Ruedi, May 19, 1892. Eagle County records can be consulted for exactness. It can be seen from the maps that the northwest part of Basalt was formed by the Otmar Luchsinger tract and the northeast and eastern part of Basalt by the Gabriel Luchsinger area. The kilns, the cemetery, and the south school house were in the John Ruedi ground. The dividing line between the two Luchsinger properties ran north and south and lay not far from an alley that went from John Smith's residence down south to the post office on Railroad Avenue. An interesting fact is that these men sold rights to the railroad and lots for houses for the town before they had actual title to the ground. This was done by squatter's rights, presumably. They had, of course, made application before that.

Eagle County was established in 1884. Otmar Luchsinger made application for land March 18, 1885, from Ute Series No. 7. He sold a right-of-way to the Colorado Midland on May 4, 1886, but he was not granted a deed to the property until April 2, 1889.

D. R. C. Brown, owner of land in the Basalt area and of the original water supply.

photo from D. R. C. Brown III

Gabriel Luchsinger sold a right-of-way to the Colorado Midland on May 4, 1886. Our father and Uncle Albert bought lots number 36, 37, and 38 for $225.00 on October 22, 1890.

D. R. C. Brown sold property to the Colorado Midland on June 30, 1894 and September 26, 1899. W. P. Bates bought several lots from Gabe Luchsinger November 22, 1890, and resold one lot to Michael McCaffery on May 7, 1892. Dan German bought what is now tract 51 on April 6, 1897.

Otmar Luchsinger soon sold part of his tract at Basalt to his Brother, Jacob, who had also taken up some land nearby. After Otmar sold his remaining ground to Jake Lucksinger and John Ruedi, Otmar and John moved up the Frying Pan to the present site of Ruedi.

The post office at Aspen Junction was established February 13, 1890, but the name was changed from "Aspen Junction" to "Basalt" on June 19, 1895. In an essay written for his high school paper in 1942, Randel Bogue says that this was done to avoid confusion in the mail with Grand Junction. He apparently got this information from Mrs. Enoch Olson or El Gray, both now deceased.

Just as an experiment on June 4, 1962, I sent a letter to Walter Hyrup addressed to Aspen Junction. To my pleasant surprise, some employee at the Post Office Department in Denver took the trouble to look it up instead of sending it back. He readdressed it to Basalt and Walter Hyrup returned the envelope to me. I then tried my luck even further on October 31, 1962, by sending a letter addressed to Frying Pan Junction. This time, to my amazement, and to my admiration of the post office department, the

6 History of Basalt

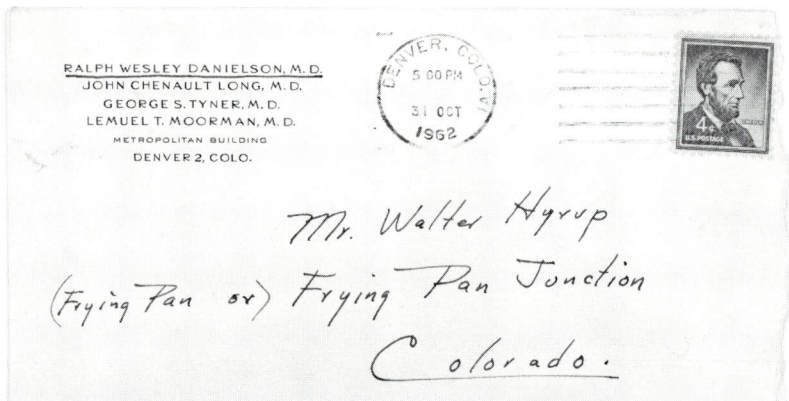

This letter was delivered without question although the town of Basalt has not been known as Frying Pan Junction for over seventy-five years.

letter was promptly delivered without even having the name on the envelope changed to Basalt. I have a hunch there is an ardent Frying Pan fisherman, or Aspen skier, or Colorado historian among the mail sorters.

INCORPORATION OF BASALT

The town of Basalt was incorporated August 26, 1901. The first mayor was Engineer William Conerty.

The town records show that the first ordinances were passed on October 9, 1901, and had to do with a town seal, animals at large, ditches and parks, dogs, licenses (for peddlers, businesses, and saloons), beating of animals, vagrants, town officers, borrowing money, curfew, poll tax, privileges to telephone company, trees, and waterworks.

An interesting note in the town records dated in the year 1912 was that "minors, Indians, idiots, women, and habitual drunkards are not allowed in the saloons."

The size of Aspen Junction and Basalt have remained approximately the same throughout the years. (Frying Pan Junction was only a tent town for a couple of years and had only a few inhabitants working in the charcoal ovens). The size changed little because the number of railroad men and the number of ranches remained about the same. Following the abandonment of the railroad there was, of course, a rather marked slump in population and stores, but due to the fishing on the Frying Pan and Roaring Fork, the motels, filling stations ,and highway workers, the town gradually picked up so that the houses were soon all filled. Recently there has been considerable pick-up in building because of the overflow from Aspen and the inflated prices paid for property there. Several people live in Basalt and commute to work in Aspen. Now that the Askansas-Frying Pan Project is beginning at Ruedi, Basalt will undoubtedly be a center of operations and will stimulate building even more. Recently a new post office has been built there.

Mr. H. S. Shyrock, Jr., of the Bureau of the Census has kindly supplied us with the population figures of Basalt—these seem too low to us, but these are the records:

```
1960..................213
1950..................173
1940..................212
1930..................148
1920..................185
1910..................235
1900..................382
```

The elevation of the town has been officially given to us by Marion Martin of the United States Cartography Department as 6,625 feet.

Now that we have brought the history of Basalt up to the incorporation of Basalt, we shall in the following pages retrace our steps to discuss the earlier history of the region.

EXPLORERS, COUNTIES, VALLEYS

Now that we have had some discussion of the origin and development of Basalt, we felt it would be well, for a matter of interest and perspective, to have some description of the history of the nearby valleys and counties.

There has been so much interesting material published about the state as a whole that one is tempted to go afield in this Basalt history and spend too much time on what has already been recorded. Suffice it to say that the state is derived from land originally owned by France, Spain, England, and Mexico, and was part of several territories.

This history has been well delineated by Hall, Corfutt, Goodykoontz, Perkin, Frazier, the Hafens, and many others. Those interested in the Colorado story would do well to read Leroy Hafen's article in the *Colorado Magazine* of 1932, where he sums it up by saying:

"Many flags have flown over Colorado soil. International boundary lines have cut the territory and national claims have shifted back and forth across the map. After United States jurisdiction was achieved the constant changes in Territorial boundaries have placed various portions of present Colorado within

8   *History of Basalt*

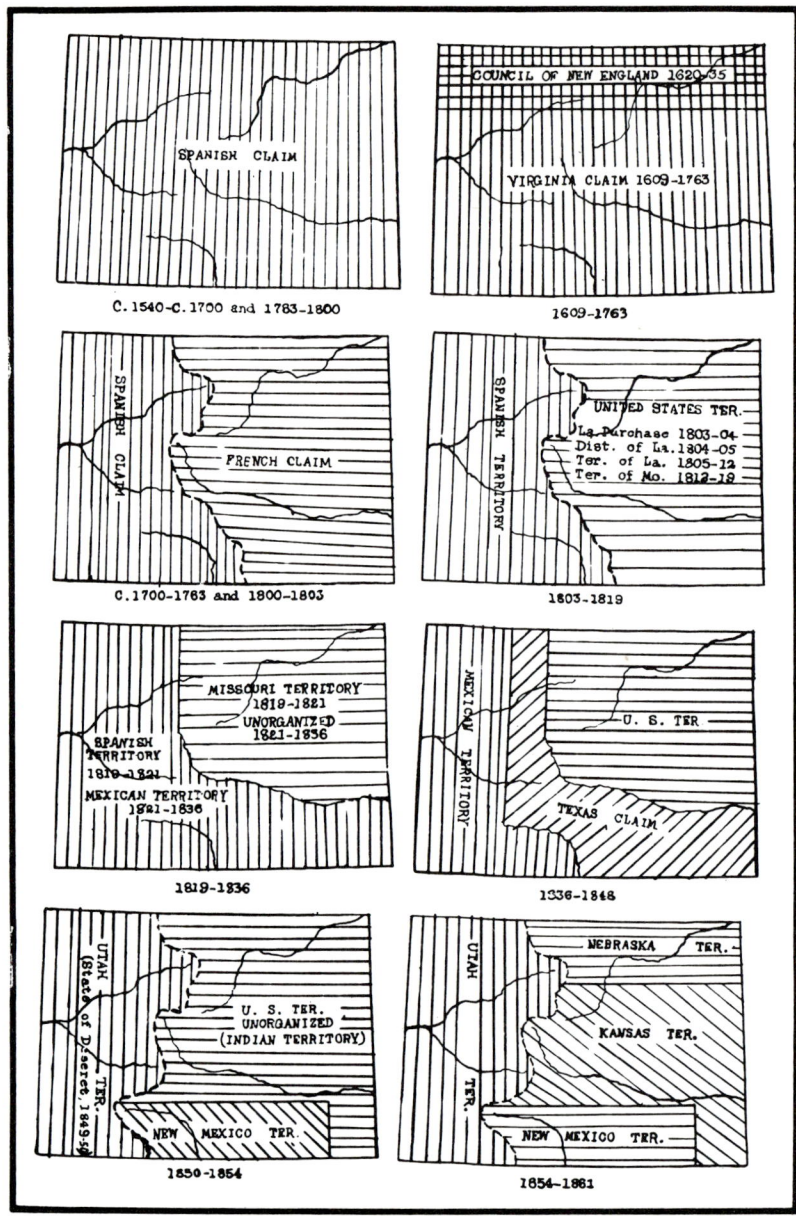

CLAIMS AND JURISDICTIONS OVER COLORADO TERRITORY

from LeRoy R. Hafen article

the domain of a surprisingly large number of different Territories."

He goes on to say:

"The gold discoveries of 1858 inaugurated the Pike's Peak gold rush of 1859 and brought about the permanent settlement of Colorado. Inasmuch as the gold area was far removed from the seats of existing territorial governments, the pioneers of

Colorado decided to form a government of their own and to secure its recognition by Congress. The territory of Jefferson was accordingly created in 1859 and continued a precarious existence until 1861. The boundaries of Jefferson Territory included not only all of Colorado of today, but extended north to the 43rd parallel and west to the 110th meridan, thus including portions of present Nebraska, Wyoming, and Utah. When Colorado Territory was created by Congress on February 28, 1861, it was given the boundaries of the present state."

Roaring Fork Valley

Historically, the Roaring Fork and Frying Pan Valleys were late in the settlement of Colorado. The early explorers came in search of gold and game, not grass. These valleys were not easy to get into in the early days over Taylor Pass, Independence Pass, the Arkansas-Frying Pan (later Hagerman) Pass, and around the Eagle River route by way of Tennessee Pass. The impetus that

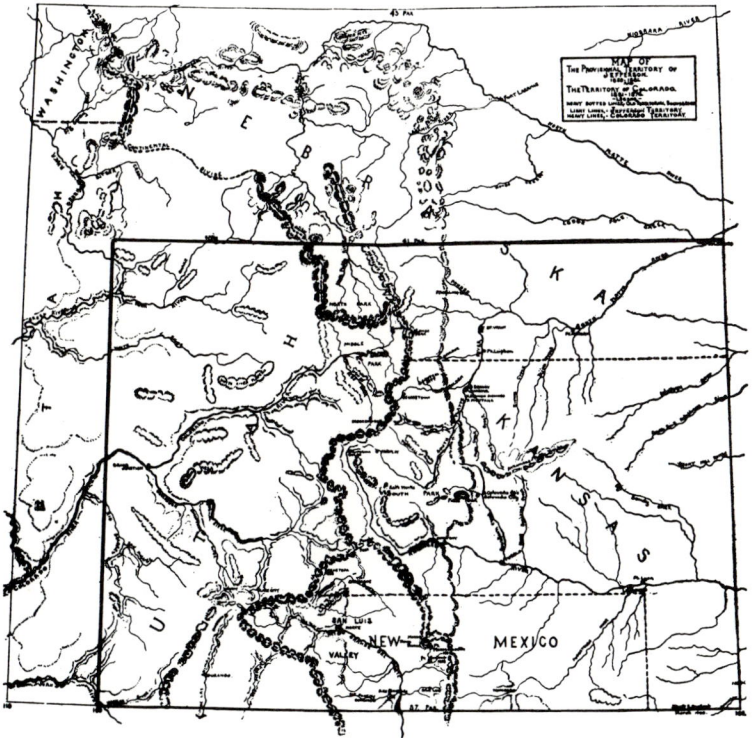

"JEFFERSON TERRITORY," 1859-1861

This provisional Territory, formed by the pioneers of the Pike's Peak country, embraced parts of the existing Territories of Nebraska, Kansas, New Mexico, Utah, and Washington. The dotted lines indicate Territorial boundaries. The smaller rectangle bounds the territory of present Colorado.

from LeRoy R. Hafen article

got men into the region was the finding of gold and silver ore in Independence, Ashcroft, Aspen and Leadville districts.

This story of the early settlement of the area has been excellently written up by Shoemaker in his book, "The Roaring Fork Valley," and it should be read by everyone interested in the history of the region. He also discusses Basalt and the Frying Pan Valley so well that we have left out of our history much that might have been otherwise included. He is now preparing a manuscript entitled "Roaring Fork Pioneers" which should be equally good reading.

Ranchers

Walter Hyrup has kindly given me the names of some of the early ranchers up the Roaring Fork near Woody Creek. They were:

August Clavell	Ashbys
Sam Letey	H. W. Boyce
Bourg Brothers	Alex Arbaney
El Gray	Eli Cerise
Jerry Gerbaz	Fournier
Alexis Arbaney	Vevie
Fred Stockman	Laurent Arbaney

Near, and west of Basalt, were:

Sam Cramer	J. G. Hough
Joe King	Billy Phillips
Gabriel Luchsinger	Clark Chatfield
Jake Lucksinger	Jack Dooling
J. G. Grace	Tom O'Connor
Fred Light	Ed Jacobs
M. L. Shippie	Ollie Jacobs
Sam Harvey	Tom Houston
O'Dwyer	Ob Cain
August Naefe	Henry Gillespie
Fred Nash	Bramblet Willits
Ted Nash	Lee Willits

As a matter of record, Walter Hyrup informs us that the ranches with which we were familiar are now owned as follows:

Pug Gilbert .... Mr. Joe Fiori
Dan German - Phil Smith .... Mr. and Mrs. Armstrong
J. A. Smith on Toner Creek .... Fish and Game Department
Alfred Sloss .... Mrs. Delbert Bowles
Price Sloss .... Miller Nicols Greg, of Kansas City
Ollie Jacobs at El Jebel .... Kelley Cerise sold to U. S. Forest Service for a Nursery

Otto Hyrup at Seven Castles	Phil Sterker, from Texas
Lee Willits (near El Jebel)	Bramblet Willits
Murray Mallory place	Arthur A. Weidman
Gabriel Luchsinger	Zella Luchsinger and Bob Smith
Sam Cramer	Guido Myers
	Also owned at one time by Mr. King and previously Mr. Sherritt
Emery Arbaney	Frederick Arbaney
Fred Shehi - Chris Hyrup	Dr. John S. Schweppe
Kelly Place on Basalt Mountain	Emery Arbaney and now Frederick Arbaney

View of Mt. Sopris from above and northeast of Basalt, showing the Gabe Luchsinger farm and the Big Tree, a childhood landmark of the authors.

Courtesy of Irene Ould

12   History of Basalt

BRANDS

Particularly for the present and future rancher readers we thought it would be interesting to have a record of the cattle and horse brands of the early residents of the Roaring Fork and Frying Pan Valleys.

This has been prepared by information from Mrs. Rose Rathbone of the State Brand Department and from local Basalt ranchers.

C. E. Bogue
Z TRIANGLE

Clara V. Bogue
REVERSE HALF CIRCLE X

William Bogue
Y

Sam Cramer
REVERSE S AND C OVER BAR

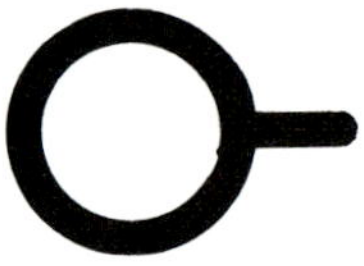

Bob Dwyer
ENDGATE ROD

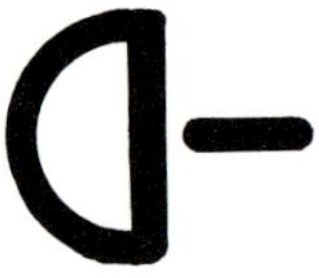

Dan German
REVERSE D BAR

Gus Grace
GGG

Charles Harris
BAR H

W. H. Harris
H K CONNECTED

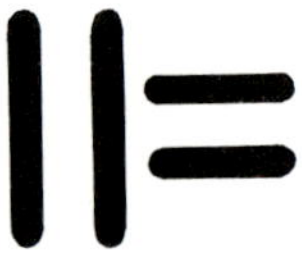

Ralph Harris
ELEVEN TWO BARS

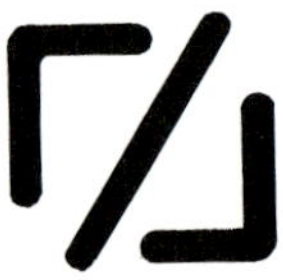

Vern Harris
REVERSE SEVEN SLASH REVERSE L

George Hotz
K O FIVE

Anna Hyrup (1909)
Otto Hyrup (1925)
QUARTER CIRCLE TRIANGLE

Chris Hyrup
C H OVER QUARTER CIRCLE

Walter Hyrup
S L SLASH

Walter Hyrup
REVERSE F OVER HALF CIRCLE

Yvonne Hyrup
FOUR BAR B

Eddie and Ollie Jacobs
THE WHEEL OF WONDER

El Jebel Ranch (Gillespie)
J L OVER SEVEN

Fred and Leo Light
Box L

Christine Lucksinger
L LAZY U

Gabe Luchsinger
G L

Jake Lucksinger and sons
J L

Otmar Luchsinger
L X B

Fred Nash
NASH (Covered Whole Side of Cow)

John Ould
RAFTER F

Alfred Sloss (1903)
L X B

14   History of Basalt

Alfred Sloss (1908)
T OVER V

Alvin Sloss
THE I X I BRAND

Price Sloss
CIRCLE

W. B. Sloss
A S IN LEANING BOX

Clifford Smith
Y REVERSE L

John A. Smith
J DIAMOND A

John A. Smith
J DIAMOND J

Phil Smith
DOUBLE QUARTER CIRCLE

Bramblet Willits
Lee Willits
K HANDLE

Lee Willits
TEXAS HAT

John Wheatley
Arthur Bates
(by transfer)
REVERSE C AND REVERSE J

The Italian Colony

Soon after the building of the Colorado Midland through Basalt in 1887 a group of people emigrated from Aosta in the province of Aosta, Italy to the Roaring Fork Valley. Numerous families settled on ranches from Woody Creek to Carbondale and some of the men worked in the mines in Aspen. Leonis Usel of Basalt believes that the first of the group to arrive was Fred Clavell, who reared a large family at Woody Creek.

The Arbaney, Cerise, Gerbaz, Usel and Dumoz families were included in the colony, as were Fred and Pete Glasier. The latter ranched across the river from the Willits ranch. The Italian emigration continued for some time after the turn of the century. All of them were very hard-working and thrifty people, forming a most valuable addition to early settlers who developed the valley. The wives and children did their part of the farm work. Bramblet Willits remembers seeing one wife walking behind a hand-plow and watching her baby who lay in a small hammock swung from the handles of the plow.

These people from Italy were Roman Catholics, but they had very little opportunity to attend mass, for at that early time there was no Catholic church in Basalt, and it was a long trip by horse and buggy to Aspen or Glenwood Springs.

Few of the group worked for the railroad; but later on Laurent Arbaney, and Alex Arbaney and his son, Emery, all worked for the Midland. Today a number of the group live in the town of Basalt, and many attend St. Vincent's Church there.

Eagle County

Brief accounts of the establishment of Eagle, Pitkin, and Garfield Counties can be found in the *History of the State of Colorado* by Frank Hall and the *Encyclopedia* by the State Historical Association. Hall said in 1895 "This county was named after Eagle River, which rises in the mountains north of Leadville and traverses the entire length of the county.—It was organized by an act of the General Assembly February 11, 1883. It is bounded on the north by Grand and Routt, south by Pitkin and Lake, east by Summit and west by Garfield.

"The first authentic account of the Eagle River country appears in a book written by Captain Rudolph B. Morey who traversed the Eagle River region in 1858."

In the *Encyclopedia* Marilla McCain says "Although tradition claims a party from the Colorado Expedition first passed through

photo from George McLaren

First Street in Basalt, about 1890.

the present Eagle County in 1840, the first authentic account of white man's presence in the Eagle River Valley goes back to the Fremont party, guided by Kit Carson.

"Another known early white explorer in the county was Army Captain Randolph Mark, who made a trip up the Eagle River in 1858.

"The valley remained unexplored and undeveloped until the early 1870's when Leadville became a booming mining town."

The county of Eagle was carved out of Summit County in February 1883.

A detailed history of Eagle County is now being prepared as a thesis at Western State College at Gunnison.

Grant Crosson in the Denver Post Office Department has given the dates of discontinuance of the post offices in the villages as follows: Sloss, July 31, 1931; Sellars, August 10, 1918; Ruedi, November 15, 1941; Ivanhoe, August 10, 1918; Nast, August 10, 1918; Norrie, August 10, 1918, and Thomasville, August 10, 1918.

Pitkin County

Regarding Pitkin County, Hall says in 1895 "This county, segregated from the northern part of Gunnison was organized under an act of the Third General Assembly approved February 23, 1881, with Aspen as the county seat. It is bounded on the north by Eagle and Garfield, south by Gunnison, east by Lake,

from George McLaren

A view of Basalt, about 1905, looking southwest. The Hyrup house is in the lower left-hand corner, the Danielson house next to it. The printing office is in lower right.

and west by Mesa and the N. W. corner of Gunnison. Its area is 950 square miles. By the census of 1890 its population was 8,929. It was named for Hon. Frederick W. Pitkin, then Governor of Colorado.

Pitkin County's main city is now Aspen, but at one time Independence and Ashcroft were much larger. The history of Aspen has been well covered by Caroline Bancroft.

The history of Carbondale has been written but not published by Edna D. Sweet and Anna Olson. The townsite was plotted in 1887 and incorporated January 30, 1888. The first post office was started at Satank, now a suburb of Carbondale, on June 27, 1883. The town was named for Chief Satanta of the local Indian tribe.

Interestingly, the town of Emma was named for the lady who did the cooking for the construction crews on the Spring Gulch-Carbondale-Emma toll road.

The small post offices in the county were discontinued as follows: Redstone, February 15, 1943; Ashcroft, November 30, 1912; Gerbazdale, August 8, 1918; Placita, October 31, 1934; and Watson, June 28, 1918.

Garfield County

Source material about Garfield County and Glenwood Springs has been obtained largely from Virginia Crowner in her article, "Reminiscing."

The precursor of Glenwood Springs was the town of Defiance, which was located about ten miles east on the north side of the river. A fort was built there in 1879 to protect the town of Carbonate, then the leading settlement on the Flat Top. Carbonate City was incorporated in 1883 and was the first county seat of Garfield County, but was moved to Glenwood Springs in October of that year.

In the winter of 1882 Isaac Cooper organized the Defiance Town and Land Company and on February 21, 1883, the town of Defiance was laid out. However, on March 15, 1882, James M. Landis had made a declaration of occupancy of 160 acres of land, now the present site of Glenwood Springs, on the east side of the mouth of the Roaring Fork. On October 5, 1882, he sold this place, known as the Landis Hot Springs Ranch, to Isaac Cooper, who had great faith in the commercial value of the hot springs nearby, which had been frequented for so many years by the Indians for the supposed curative powers, particularly for arthritis. Glenwood Springs was incorporated in 1885.

The first post office was on the north side of the river, the mail coming from Aspen by stage. L. B. Maw was the postmaster, to be followed by Martin Van Buren Blood, H. E. Eaton, and Olie Thorson.

It is recorded that the earliest travellers into the district did not go down the difficult Glenwood Canyon. Instead they went over the Cottonwood Pass from Gypsum on the Eagle River to Cattle Creek Junction on the Roaring Fork.

Basalt Post Office and adjacent buildings.

Courtesy of Fred Carlson

El Jebel Ranch, about 1895.

photo from Bramlet Willits

The name of Dotsero at the head of the Glenwood Canyon reportedly got its name because the area somehow was designated on the surveyor's maps by a dot and a zero. (The town on the other end of the Moffat cut-off is spelled backwards, "Orestod".)

A book about Lake County is now being compiled by the Griswolds.

Early Explorers

The early explorers of the Colorado region were Coronado, Juan De Onate and Juan Maria Rivera, and the friars Escalante and Dominguez about 1540. Purcell and other fur traders came in 1803, Zebulon Pike in 1806, Maj. H. S. Long in 1819-20, the Mormons in 1842-43, and John Fremont in 1942-43. The Lewis and Clark expedition in 1805-06 went up the Missouri and Yellowstone Rivers into Montana and did not touch Colorado. Then in 1858 the flood of gold seekers began.

As for the explorers in this particular region, there is little on record. It is possible that the Juan de la Rivera expeditions, and the Friars Escalante and Dominguez in 1776 may have traversed the Roaring Fork Valley. It is known that Pike reached the headwaters of the Arkansas River near Leadville in 1806. There is mention that a few fur traders, trappers, and mountain men came to this area as early as 1825. Captain Gunnison went into the re-

gion named for him in 1853. The most notable expedition into the Roaring Fork area was made by Sopris in 1860 and some discussion of it is warranted.

Mount Sopris is named for Captain Richard Sopris whose great granddaughter, Mrs. Louise Woodend, lives in Denver.

He came from Indiana, reaching Auraria March 15, 1859. He represented Arapahoe County in Kansas Territory Legislature, and had many elective offices in Denver. Mayor of Denver 1878-1881. As Park Commissioner, started City Park in Denver between 1881 and 1890.

One of his exploits for which he is famed is described in the *Portrait & Biographical Record* as follows: "In 1860 he headed a large company of gold seekers to explore the then unknown regions west of the Snowy Range; the party left Denver July 1, crossed South Park to where Beckenridge now stands, went down Blue River and Eagle River, from there to the Roaring Fork of the Grand, and up Willow Creek to the foot of the mountain they named Sopris Peak, which is a part of the Elk Mountains, near Glenwood. They came to the hot springs (now famous as Glenwood Springs), where they camped and cut pine trees, constructing a boat in which they crossed Grand River. Just below the cave stood a large pine tree, which they blazed and inscribed with these words: 'These springs were discovered on July 23, 1860, by Captain Sopris, and party of prospectors.' After a week at the springs they crossed the river and went via Cochetopa Pass into the San Luis Valley, thence to Fort Garland and Denver, reaching this city after an absence of three months. The prime object of their journey had been to prospect for gold, but they failed to find any trace of the precious metal. However, the notes made and measurements taken were of great assistance to Governor Gilpin in preparing his first map of Colorado."

Dr. Hayden, the geologist, and his illustrious entourage, including William H. Jackson, the photographer, made their famous surveys of the Elk Mountains from 1867 to 1879. Shoemaker in his book tells of the Hayden expedition and relates what little interference they had from the Indians, probably because of the influence of Chief Ouray. He also describes the less friendly treatment of the Graham party, who had intruded on the Ute Reservation in 1870 and had prospected extensively, living

A view of Basalt, about 1900, showing the houses along First street, the roundhouse and engines, and the railroad cars on the wye. Taken from the back of Smith's Store looking toward the Carl L. Gilbert farm.

Courtesy of Gladys Hough Wachob

largely on the game they killed. However, in 1874 they were discovered by the Utes and were driven out.

There were undoubtedly many isolated travellers and prospectors into the Basalt region as soon as Aspen and Leadville were started, but, unfortunately, almost no one took time to write any diary. Most of what is known appeared in the Leadville and Aspen papers.

Frying Pan Valley and Ruedi

Some idea of the early exploration of the Frying Pan Valley has been well told by the Griswolds in their exceedingly interesting book *Century of Cities*, and we have permission to quote the following:

"One of the routes to the Defiance Mining District, which was located west and north of today's Glenwood Springs, was the Frying Pan—Roaring Fork Trail. William Markt took this route, much to his discomfort and displeasure, in July of 1880. On leaving Leadville, he headed in a northwesterly direction and had no trouble in finding the toll gate some eighty miles out. After paying fifty cents apiece for his two pack animals at the gate, Markt was able to follow the trail for a block, perhaps two, and then the trail simply was no more; nonetheless, he made his way over the northerly ridge of Mount Massive without too many hardships. Then, descending westward along the Big* or West Frying Pan River, Markt encountered "multitudinous rocks" on the pathway and on the footbridges. Of the canyon trail, he reported, on his return to Leadville, as follows: . . . steep rock-steps often two feet and more high, crevices in which there is hardly room enough for a horse's hoof, impede and endanger progress; the terminus of the canyon is called Devil's Gate, a most appropriate name, and a good many who pity their animals, carry the loads down it on their shoulders, as they, in case of a slip, can throw the load off, which an animal could not do.

"After crossing a swamp through which Markt again had difficulty in keeping to the trail since there were no markers and where an animal's hoof left 'no imprint on the mossy elastic soil', he came to 'of all things a city!' This mining camp which Markt said was located one-and-a-half-miles from Lime Creek and which consisted of 'one double cabin without doors or windows', bore the name of Massive City. From there Markt continued on down Big Frying Pan Gulch to its mouth. This part

---

*There was also a tributary of the Arkansas River known as Little Frying Pan; to avoid confusion the name was changed to Rock Creek.

of his journey took him two days and during those two days he did not meet one man. His comment was that this lack of travel showed 'the trail is evaded by all who know it.' The remainder of his journey down the Roaring Fork to its junction with the Colorado River and on to the Defiance district was not tedious; but, needless to say, Mr. Markt returned to Leadville by way of the Eagle River-Battle Mountain-Tennessee Pass Trail."

The authors have explained to me that the name Massive City was misleadingly given because the explorers thought they were still on the west side of Mount Massive. Massive City was the forerunner of Calcium and Thomasville.

Roaring Fork was apparently named such in their language by the Indians. The naming of the Frying Pan, however, is a matter of conjecture.

Various stories have been told of the naming of the river and valley. According to one, a party of Missouri trappers encamped along the stream were set upon by the Indians, who killed all but two. One of the survivors, seriously wounded, was hidden in a cave by his companion, who started across the mountains for help. To mark the spot, he tied a frying pan to the limb of a pine. Soldiers returned with him, to find the trapper dead but the frying pan still dangling from the tree.

Two early gold prospectors, according to a second story, lost much of their equipment while fording the river and used a frying pan to wash sands along the stream.

In the W.P.A. project book called *Colorado: A Guide to the Highest State* there is this paragraph:

Miss Elizabeth Elliott, who has owned an historic cabin at Norrie for many years, has provided another possible derivation of the name. She says that "Old Man Wilson" of Glenwood Springs told her that some prospectors were about to make camp on the upper part of the stream near Ivanhoe when they noticed evidence that Indians had been there recently. They, therefore, decided to get out of that area by climbing over a mountain (probably toward Aspen to the south). To their consternation, when they reached the top and looked down the other side, they actually saw a band of Indians camped there. One of the members of the party is reported to have said, "We are just going from the frying pan into the fire." Whereupon, they decided to call the first valley and stream "The Frying Pan".

Miss Elliott tells us that the Forest Service has agreed to let her use her cabin as long as she lives. It is unfortunate that such

Allan Craig collection

Cabin of Miss Elizabeth Elliot at Norrie.

a building could not be set aside as a historical landmark instead of being torn down, as it probably will be.

Howard Dearhammer of Meredith has said that the cabin was originally built by Oliver Hook and his wife and her sister. Hook hauled logs and lumber for Scott Sawyer and Ed Keough. Following them the cabin was occupied by a large family by the name of Allison. Swan Nelson and wife and children then resided there, to be followed by Will Price and Mr. Jameyson of Wichita. The next resident was Hobert La Mont who gave the cabin to Miss Elliott.

Miss Elliott also tells two interesting tales of the area. The first concerns Charley Thias who came into Norrie from Chicago about 1899. The story goes that he courted a girl near there and when they became engaged he not only bought a ring, but also a piano. She then jilted him and he became a woman hater for life.

Then there is the story of Miss Dorothy Faulk, a nurse from Kansas City who had lost her fiance by death. In order to relieve her grief she came to Norrie in 1900 and took up a homestead two miles above there on the Norrie-Aspen trail where she could get a good view of Hagerman Peak. There she built up a large herd of fine goats which she herded down to DeBeque in the wintertime, pitching her tent each night as she went. It is rumored that one winter she herded them all the way to Denver, and sold the milk to a tuberculosis santarium.

Now that the Ruedi Dam is to be built, we thought it would be interesting to get some data about the town and John Ruedi for whom the town was named. Gladys Wachob and others have provided information and a diagram of early ranches has been drawn for us by John Smith. Luverne Danielson has gone to considerable effort to get the information for her write-up of John Ruedi in the chapter on family biographies.

Some of the ranchers who lived up the Frying Pan Valley were Dan German and sons Lewis and Dan, J. A. Smith and sons Phil and Clifford, Peter Hyrup and sons Chris, Otto, Walter and Alfred. Price Sloss and his boys Alvin and Alfred, Dan Shehi, Chub Downey, John Ruedi, Lige Thompson, J. T. Hough, Fred Jakeman, John Nelson, John Henderson, A. J. Dearhammer.

UTE HISTORY

We should remember that the original inhabitants were Indians. All of the original abstracts of the land upon which Basalt is located go back to the Ute Reservation. All the land was purchased from the United States Government. Mrs. Emma Shehi described the Indians most graphically in her inimitable letters to the *Kansas Agriculturist* of her old home state. She and the other early settlers saw much of the Utes.

The Ute Reservation was created in 1868 by an act of Congress and the signature of President Grant. This act is a document which makes most interesting reading, and is the cornerstone of all the history of the Utes. Kappler documents the signing of the treaty by representatives of the various bands of the Ute tribe. In this treaty Congress agrees to allot a certain territory to the Ute tribe, the boundaries of which are as follows:

From the four corners area eastward on the southern Colorado Territory line to the 107th meridian, then north to a line 15 miles north of the 40th meridian, then west to the Colorado-Utah border and south again to the four corners area.

From the map, it is clear that this barely takes in Meeker on the north. The eastern boundary (107th meridian) extends from near Toponas down between Dotsero and Gypsum on the Eagle River just a mile or two east of Basalt on the Frying Pan, and near Snowmass on the Roaring Fork. It then goes south near Gunnison, Creede, and Pagosa Springs.

The great tract of land thus given to the Utes was soon to be turned over to the white man through sale. The Indians were simply moved to other reservations. (That the justice of the dealings with the Indians by Congress, largely determined by pressure from the settlers, was debatable, has been the basis for a recent lawsuit against the United States Government.) By 1873 the San Juan became United States territory, and by 1882 the Indians were all moved out to the Uintah Reservation in Utah.

The Ute Bill for exclusion of the Utes from Western Colorado was signed by the President on June 15, 1880. The Uncompaghre Utes had all left by August 28, 1881, for Utah. The event which precipitated the exclusion of the Uncompaghre and White River Utes from Western Colorado was the Meeker massacre in the fall of 1879.

On August 10, 1882, the former reservation was declared public land. At the time there was no homesteading; it was sold for cash for $1.25 for agricultural land and $5.00 for mineral land.

The names of the bands of Utes in this huge Ute Reservation, which originally comprised about one-fifth of the land area of the Colorado Territory, were the Tabaguache, Muache, Copote, Weeminuche, Yampa, Grand River, and Uintah. The various bands, of course, intermingled, but it is thought that the bands that were in the Basalt area mainly in the summer were the Tabaguache from the Grand Mesa, and the White River Indians from that region. The names of the representatives who signed the treaty of 1868 from the Grand River tribe are interesting. They were Sac-we-och (white lock of hair), Tah-nach (granite), Pah-ah-pitch (sweet herb), Tab-y-ou-souck-en (sun rise), Shou-wach-a-wicket (rainbow), and Pe-ah (black-tail deer).

The many conferences between the Indians and the white men are most interesting, and have been recorded by many writers.

The main Indian leaders were Ouray, Shavano, and Colorow.

O. C. Stewart, Professor of Anthropology at C.U., has written me that he knows of no information dealing exactly with the Indians in Basalt. He says there is an article in the Glenwood Springs paper about 1885 which discusses visits of Chief Colorow and his demands for a bath in the resort hotel and his participation in horse races in the area. There are many references extant to Colorow's travels to Denver and to Leadville. Inasmuch as he was assigned to the White River Reservation, he almost certainly made more than one trip up and down the Frying Pan and Roaring Fork.

That these Indians did not stay on their reservations is well known and it is doubtful that they even knew the boundaries. They undoubtedly went far up the Frying Pan and Roaring Fork, for arrow heads have been found there. Most of these have been found near Basalt. Bramblet Willits has picked up many artifacts on his ranch near El Jebel just west of Basalt.

I have often marvelled at the ability of the Indian to get food. The fish hooks were crude and what did they use for a line? They probably missed 99 out of every 100 shots with arrowheads, and most of these heads would then be lost. Think of the tremendous labor with crude tools that it took to fashion these arrowheads—only to lose them! Think of the contrast of a few cents for a bullet, which is so infinitely more effective than an arrowhead! When the Indian acquired a rifle, his living came much easier.

From a letter received from Robert Terrell, game conservationist at Basalt in 1961, we have this interesting item:

" . . . we found quite a few arrowheads just back of Basalt, some in our garden right here in town. I believe the most we found were over on Cattle Creek, but we have found them all over, up the Frying Pan and the Roaring Fork rivers. This past summer we found several right on top of the divide above Ivanhoe tunnel and some on top of Independence Pass. One real good one was located on Independence.

"I believe the Indians came in here during the summer and hunted and fished, as it was much cooler weather than below. Then they would follow the game herds from summer range back down to winter ranges. We find lots of places below here or down on the main deer winter ranges where Indians no doubt camped all winter. We have found a lot of Indian stuff in caves that we would screen, some real good arrowheads and beads."

So many arrowheads and other artifacts could not possibly be found unless the Indians inhabited this region for thousands of years. For every arrowhead that has been found, there are undoubtedly hundreds of them still lying around unnoticed or covered up. Many a deer probably carried an arrowhead to remote places when he died from his wound, or later, if the wound was non-fatal.

It is also interesting to think of the millions of years when this area existed with no human being present at all. The forest fires, started by lightning, the periods of heavy snows when the deer perished by the thousands, the grasshopper plagues which robbed the wildlife of their food, the floods, the droughts, all altered the landscape temporarily, but the view of gorgeous Black Mountain, (Basalt Mountain) and Mt. Sopris has been the same for an inconceivably long time.

INTERESTING FACTS ABOUT BASALT

Water Works

A history of the water supply of Basalt is worth outlining. Originally, of course, for a short while, everyone got water from the Frying Pan River by buckets. Mrs. Stores used to work for Mother and they would let the water stand overnight if it was muddy. Soon, however, a ditch was built from the same spring, which even now is being used, to a reservoir on the hillside just north of Basalt. The reservoir was built by Gabe Luchsinger. The spring is located further east on Basalt Mountain, and the overflow runs down to the Frying Pan through Whitenack Falls. In addition, many people had a rain barrel to catch water from the roof.

At one time a very unusual thing happened when the water from the ditch soaked the hillside and it gave way below the ditch sending a large amount of mud down the draw just west of the present Forest Reserve house. Clarence well remembers seeing the section men clear the mud from the railroad track by hand.

This spring was originally on the Gabe Luchsinger ranch, but Gabe at one time when in financial difficulty sold the water rights to this spring to D.R.C. Brown, who later sold them to the town of Basalt in 1902. This water was brought from the reservoir to the houses in Basalt by ditches which would often freeze in the winter. Arthur Bates recalls that when the ditches froze he hauled water in barrels to some of the residents of town, getting water from the river or a small spring from near the Rhodes residence where Anna Sloss now lives, for which he received 25 cents a barrel.

Our father and Pete Hyrup got their water from a well dug on the line properties by Henry Freiler. This well was cribbed with cedar posts.

In the *Basalt Journal* of August 9, 1902 it was announced that on the Tuesday before, the Basalt Town Council accepted the bid of J.E. Hurd of Glenwood Springs for the construction of the Water Works for the sum of $11,000.00. Payment was to be made in town bonds. He was to pipe water directly down from the spring instead of through the reservoir. Engineer Rosenberg of Glenwood drew up the plans, but the construction was subcontracted to Mr. Ikeler, also from Glenwood. Mr. Edward Taylor, an attorney from the same city, did the legal work. The Basalt mayor at that time was Mr. William Conerty.

A news item in the *Basalt Journal* of January 1, 1903 stated that the water works would be soon completed. All the ditches to lay the pipes in were four and five feet deep to keep them from freezing, and were dug manually by pick and shovel. The ones most interested in these ditches for pipe-lines were the Burgins and the Trowbridges and others who had short independent pipe-lines from a barrel or box up on the hill to irrigate their lawns. Our family had a barrel on the hill below the Nelson residence.

On April 6, 1902 the rate for water was set at $4.00 a quarter year. Although water rents have always been one of the main sources of revenue, this amazingly low rate for use in homes, on lawns, and on gardens is only very slightly higher today. The spring is still as wonderful!

The Colorado Midland originally pumped the water for their water tank from the Frying Pan River, but later they connected it with the town water supply when it was installed. The railroad, in their first general plans, had picked a site near El Jebel instead of Basalt for a terminal. Fortunately that plan was changed. They realized that Basalt spring water would be a much better supply than any available at El Jebel. It is of the highest quality and purity. Walter Hyrup never loses an opportunity to brag (rightfully) about his town's water supply.

Ditches, Roads and Bridges

It would be a wonderful literary and historical project for someone who knows the Basalt region to write up a complete

Swinging bridge at the junction of the Frying Pan and Roaring Fork rivers.
Denver Public Library Western Collection

history of the location and organization of the irrigation ditches in that area.

The first district to be considered is the Frying Pan. There have been two ditches on the south side of the river from very early times: they both have their inlets just below Thorough Cut. When fishing up the "other side" during high water time, getting from one hole to another was difficult, and we fishermen frequently waded in these ditches to get to the next fishing hole.

Regarding these two ditches Walter Hyrup has this to say, "The lower ditch was built by Gabe Luchsinger. The upper, or King, ditch was built later and possibly by old J. B. King. He used to own the ranch over by the school house, which is now owned by Arbaney. The ownership of the Gabe Luchsinger ditch was ¾ Luchsinger and ¼ Mallory. The King ditch irrigates part of Arbaney's and part of Weidman's (the old Mallory Ranch). The Gabe Luchsinger ditch irrigates part of the Mallory Ranch and all of Gabe's. Weidman has city water for domestic purposes only. The Cramer ranch and other ranches get all their water from the Roaring Fork."

The original wagon road from Glenwood Springs to Aspen followed the Roaring Fork River on the north side to near Satank where there was a bridge to Carbondale. From there it went up past Emma and recrossed the river at the Stockman bridge, continuing on the north side to Aspen. Part of this right-of-way, from Carbondale to Emma, was later purchased by the Rio Grande railroad for its tracks. Indeed, Voyle Tennis of Basalt told me that those who built the road did it not so much for revenue from wagons as for priority rights so that they could sell it at a handsome profit to the railroad.

However, before either the Midland or the Grande came in, the main wagon-road was changed to the north side of the river by building down from Wheeler to the bridge at Satank, and then in the fall of 1884 from Wheeler east around the base of Black Mountain to Frying Pan Junction. The road below Wheeler was built by the ranchers in that region. That from Wheeler to the north side of the Hook bridge and then around the foot of the mountain was built by a group organized by the Harris brothers primarily to get their hay to Aspen where it was bringing more than $100 per ton at that time. Travelers were thus enabled to go all the way from Aspen to Glenwood on the north side of the river. The highway utilized part of the toll-road that extended from Emma to Spring Gulch to send coal to the smelter at Aspen. Prior to this the fuel for the smelter was obtained from charcoal ovens at Basalt and Aspen.

Inasmuch as Aspen became a little city a few years before Glenwood did, the road-building was done down the valley except for the Wheeler-Frying Pan Junction segment already mentioned. The only portion of the highway that was a toll road was from Carbondale to Emma. Part of it below Emma traversed a very narrow passage-way. When it was taken over by the Rio Grande in 1887 the farmers would cross over at Catherine on the Stauffacher bridge to the north side of the river, and then return to the south side over the Hook bridge. This caused no inconvenience to the through traffic because the main wagon road was by then on the north side of the river.

The wagon road from Basalt to Ruedi was finished about 1905.

The early-day bridges were built before the railroads came in, in 1887. The Hook bridge just south of El Jebel and the Willits ranch was constructed in 1882 and 1883, as were the Stauffacher one at Catherine and the Satank bridge at Carbondale. About the same time the Glenwood Springs-Cooper Avenue bridge was moved up nearer Cardiff.

The county bridge just above Frying Pan Junction was originally constructed in 1884, but when it was rebuilt some years later, it was named for Mr. Stockman, a rancher and county commissioner in that area. The bridge across the Frying Pan river was erected in the spring of 1885 and replaced by the present cement one in 1907. Another across the Frying Pan just south of the Midland eating-house was finished in 1890. The Basalt-Emma bridge became a reality in 1899.

A very early picture of Basalt, about 1892, showing the old pump house where water was obtained for the engines. This also shows the ditch for the water works running from the reservoir on the hillside.

For more detailed information about roads and bridges in the area one should read the two books by Len Shoemaker who was kind enough to check my brief account.

The Glassier ditch, traces of which can still be seen on the north side of the foothills south of town, had its origin in the Snowmass Creek and ran down to the Emma region. It was not a success because of seepage and the failure of the redwood tubes to siphon water across the Sopris Creek gulch. It now supplies only a ranch or two near the intake. It was built by Fred Glassier, father of Pete Glassier, who still lives near the Willits place. Fred was the son-in-law of the first Mr. Clavell of Woody Creek. The ditch was built primarily to irrigate an area near Emma which is known as the Crown. You will notice that there are no willows or trees on the hillside along this old abandoned ditch, which there would be if it were carrying water. Up on top of the long foothill one can get a magnificent view of the Elk Mountains to the south.

Later in the book we shall tell about the ditch from Jake Lucksinger's pond to the Peterson ranch, built so laboriously by Charles Peterson. The Robinson ditch south of El Jebel was built by a group of men headed by E. Winchester Robinson.

The two Harrises, Charles and William, and Cyrus Reed built the Harris and Reed ditch between the years 1881 and 1884. It should be realized that all of these ditches were largely built by hand work with pick and shovel.

Power Line

The Public Service Company electric power line was built through the Basalt area from Shoshone to Denver about 1908. We well remember the four and six-horse teams dragging and hauling the metal stands and the wire up on to the ridges where there were no roads. The erection of this line through this area was under the supervision of Earl Mosley, now with the Denver Water Board. Many of the laborers were Chinese and on one occasion quite a commotion was stirred up in Basalt because "Japanese spies" were seen camping on the Missouri flats between Shoshone and Basalt. Men with guns even went out to investigate.

George Lucksinger told me last summer that inadvertently considerable dynamite was left on their ranch and not picked up by the construction men. One day his horrified father, Jake, caught several of the boys running pell mell down the mountain

Allen Craig Collection

Mrs. Hanthorne by the Old Well House (left) near the Nast Lodge (now the Horseshoe Bend Guest Ranch) with "Old Bob, and (right) on the bridge in the same vicinity.

side with their pockets full of this old dynamite—fortunately no casualties.

Hunting

In recent years we have been wondering why the hunting near Basalt was no better than it was when we were boys. We remember that our father used to go with a party of hunters down to Piceance Creek near Rifle and then have to go to all the trouble of getting the deer back by wagon and train. Why didn't he hunt right at home?

By asking and reading we now know the answer. The men in Aspen and Leadville and on the railroad construction crews needed meat. As yet, there were only a few cattle in the area and it cost money, and effort, and discouragement to raise them. The result was that many men made their living by killing deer for the restaurants and hotels and made extra money on the hides. There are many stories of how elk were killed merely to get the teeth and antlers.

The professional hunter's depredations were aggravated also by the few families, particularly among the ranchers, who lived almost all the year round on deer and elk and saved their cattle to sell. Indeed, we have heard it from more than one source that the early settlers also killed game and caught fish in order to throw the carcasses into their hog pens and thus transform venison and fish into pork.

This uncontrolled slaughter was widespread throughout the state, but it was particularly flagrant in the region of the mining camps such as Aspen and Leadville. Because of poor transportation and no refrigeration, it was only natural that the greatest devastation should be right nearby. For a description of this wild meat traffic, one can do no better than to read the interesting diary of Frank Mayer as written up in the 1961 *Brand Book* of the Denver Posse of the Westerners by Charles B. Roth.

The attitude of the times has been well summarized by James Grafton Rogers who says, "Another thing is worth remembering. In some respects the beginnings of law and order here in Colorado were very unusual. Both really began spontaneously. The first comers did not recognize any authority but their own. The United States at Washington and the territorial governments supposed to be at the Missouri River were far away. Weeks of travel intervened. The first settlers considered themselves independent. They set up their own government, their own officers and their own ideas. They met and passed laws as if they were on the moon. — The people did not declare independence. They simply assumed it."

The decline in the game population has been well outlined by Keith Hay, an employee of the State Fish and Game Department, who has said, "Vast herds of buffalo, elk, deer and antelope roamed the territory, beaver were everywhere, and fish and fowl were found in great abundance. The primitive hunting methods of the aboriginal Indians made little inroads on their numbers, but then came the fur trappers, the market hunters and the trophy hunters to tap this 'inexhaustible' resource. The herds began to dwindle under the relentless and unrestricted spree of profit and pleasure killing.

"In 1864 and 1866 a grasshopper invasion swept the Rocky Mountain region destroying practically all vegetation. Despite this disaster, the slaughter of game animals continued until 1867, when the Colorado Assembly finally declared a closed season in Colorado territory on all game animals, wild turkeys, quail, Mexican pheasants (road runners) and prairie chickens.

A view of the Frying Pan Valley from Basalt schoolhouse

Lava Slides on Basalt Mountain

RWD Collection
Charcoal ovens at Frying Pan Junction (Built about 1883)

John Schutte
View of Mt. Sopris and Roaring Fork Valley near Carbondale

"In 1869 the season was opened on game animals and wild turkeys, but due to the hoppers it remained closed on insectivorous birds, quail, Mexican pheasants and prairie chickens. Grasshoppers came again in 1875, leaving disaster in their wake, necessitating federal-aid relief for farmers. That year the English pheasant was imported to make war on the grasshoppers and was later followed by the Chinese pheasant which is today one of the major upland game birds.

"When the First General Assembly convened in 1877, the enactment of our first state laws to protect wild animals was made. The first law pertained to fish and held it unlawful to possess or sell fish from November to March. The position of fish commissioner was created at a salary of $100 a year, and $1,000 was appropriated to buy fish to stock depleted waters. This initial concern for fishing and fish propagation dominated the statutes and the conservation activities of the state for many years to come. Big game and birds were officially protected by closed seasons during portions of the year; but as with fish, no bag limits existed during open seasons. And game could be killed for food at any time . . . 'governed in an amount and quantity by the reasonable necessities of the person or persons killing such animals.' Wildlife protection and law enforcement existed in name only, and hunting and fishing licenses did not come into existence until many years later."

Another factor that I think has been overlooked is that after the Indians were able to procure rifles they killed tremendously more game than by their primitive methods.

Even after laws were passed, little attention was paid to them, we remember this even in our days as boys. Hay goes on to say, "The changing force of politically appointed game wardens rendered the enforcement of early game laws nearly impossible. In addition to the evils of the spoils system, local wardens were reluctant or refused to enforce game laws, especially against their friends and neighbors. No law is stronger than the public sentiment behind it, and laws that protected a man's life or his cattle were justified in the minds of the early settlers; but game laws impeded the basic heritage of the pioneer existence—the right to live off the land. It was not until years later, with the passing of the buffalo, bighorn sheep, beaver, deer and elk from abundance to scarcity, that the public began to fully understand and accept restrictions in game harvest. This recognition came too late, however, for the mountain goat, grizzly bear, wolf, otter and wolverine as they were virtually, if not totally, exterminated."

The first state law to protect wild animals was made by the First General Assembly in 1877.

What we have been quoting about hunting applies equally well to fishing. There is this one difference; the fish had no enemies except disease (rarely heard of), and the exceedingly few fish caught by the Indians by primitive methods, and by the bear, the otter, and the weasel. One would have to recognize, of course, the cannibalistic habits of trout. The deer and young elk, however, have always had a potent enemy in the cougar or mountain lion. It has been estimated that each full grown animal kills another deer almost every day—they prefer the fresh meat and blood to the older carcass. The cougar, on the other hand, until the advent of the white men with rifles and dogs, had no enemy, and the wonder is that they did not multiply to almost wipe out the deer population.

To get back to a brief description of elk, Borden has written up an excellent account of their disappearance, "In the 1880's, when settlers and prospectors first started coming into the Eagle River Valley, it is estimated that there were 6000 to 8000 elk in this one valley alone; they had all disappeared by 1903. There were also large herds on the Frying Pan, Roaring Fork, and Crystal rivers, but they disappeared also because of the methods described. The last bull elk was killed in 1895 on the Frying Pan by Nelson Downey on the divide between Otto and Downey Creeks."

In 1912, however, the Elk Lodge of Aspen and other residents of Pitkin County obtained sixteen head of elk from Wyoming which were released on Smuggler Mountain near Aspen and another herd of thirty-three head were turned loose in the same area. The third herd was released at Meredith, in the Frying Pan on March 17, 1915. These few elk have now increased to many thousands and the annual elk harvest is quite considerable. In fact, the elk and the deer have become so numerous in some areas that they are a menace to crops, and strong fences have to be built by the ranchers in those areas in order to conserve the hay for their cattle, horses, and sheep. The wild life not only gives employment to many men in the Fish and Game Department, and a tremendous source of recreation to thousands of people, but it is also a veritable gold mine for the sporting-goods merchants in all parts of the state.

Horses

It is hard for us today to realize to what extent the horse entered into the early settlement of the region. He (along with burros and mules) carried the supplies and transported the people. It has been told how valuable the horse turned out to be for the Indians, but the white man was even more dependent. It has been said that a man's very life on many trips and expeditions depended on a horse, and R.W.D. can easily believe it after taking an eight day pack trip in the Elk Mountains in the Maroon Bells area south of Aspen this summer with his grandson, Luke Danielson. These trips are sponsored and supervised all over the West by the American Forestry Association and are the most thrilling experience one can imagine if one likes horses, adventure, wild flowers, and scenery.

On this trip—and other similar pack trips in the mountains—one never ceases to marvel at the stamina and strength of a horse. A few times, due to snow slides and dangerous trail at the elevation of 12,000 to 13,500 feet near the top of passes, we would have to get off our horses and go on foot—only to get out of breath and strength very easily. And yet our horses carried not only themselves but one tenth to one sixth their own weight without puffing unduly.

A sorry chapter in the history of the horse is, however, in the abuse and cruelty often imposed on him. In several places in the *Basalt Journal* are descriptions of men beating horses. Hildreth, the editor, commented "A merciful man is merciful to his beasts." The drivers would get drunk and lose their judgement, or would be so weary walking along a plow for hours that they became easily irritated when a horse did not behave and perform as they thought he should. I remember my revulsion at seeing several such horse beatings.

And to have missed seeing the fire horses and fire wagons run in early Denver days—when we went there on visits—is to have missed much excitement. At the signal of a fire the horses jumped into their places and the harness which was held by overhead apparatus would be dropped on the horses and fastened in place by the firemen who slid down the pole through a hole in the floor from the bedrooms above.

In smaller communities there were fire fighter brigades which pulled by hand and foot a hose cart—and which were the source of much competition at one time in the mining camps. We had such a hose cart in Basalt which would be manned by anyone

available when the men at the round house would create a din of whistling on the engines there in order to warn everyone.

We have lived in a most interesting period of history in seeing in our lifetime the almost total transition of use of the horse, and mule, and burro to the automobile and truck. Young people of today may enjoy cars, but they are totally incapable of *appreciating* them as one can who went out into the mountains and country by foot or horse or didn't go at all. Fortunately, cars cannot feel pain, fatigue, and starvation. A person may take pride in ownership of a car, but it can never approach the affection and friendship of a person and his horse.

Looking west on Main Street of Basalt, as it appears today—(opposite page).

CHAPTER 2

The Colorado Midland

It has not been our purpose in this book to give a comprehensive history of the Colorado Midland. Our hope is to present a viewpoint and material not found in other writings about the road.

We have presented the events in the lives of the men and their families who operated the trains in the Grand Junction—Leadville division of the railroad, and in particular, those living in Basalt. This is the history of the employees as we knew them, rather than the management.

The original organization, the description of the promoters and officers, the detailed discussion of the building of the road, along with the vicissitudes and events that led to its closure, have been admirably delineated by Morris Cafky, Carl F. Graves, Earl Mosley, Lucius Beebe and Charles Clegg, John J. Lipsey, William S. Jackson, Robert G. Athearn, E.T. Bollinger, Frederick Bauer, Len Shoemaker, Robert M. Ormes, and by Lemassena, Ronzio and Ryland. Furthermore, Morris Cafky and the Colorado Railroad Club have just finished their excellent book on the Midland.

Thumbnail Sketch

For those unfamiliar with the Colorado Midland history, we feel we should give a thumbnail sketch of the main highlights and events in the relatively short life of the road. The road was built at a time, as described by Ormes, when many railroads were being planned, built and discarded almost everywhere in Colorado. The road reached from Colorado City (near Colorado Springs) to Grand Junction, both in Colorado. At that time nothing gave men and their wives social status quite as much as owning and managing a railroad.

The Colorado Midland was organized November 23, 1883, not only to get to the silver mining at Leadville and Aspen but also to transport lumber from Woodland Park and Manitou Park.

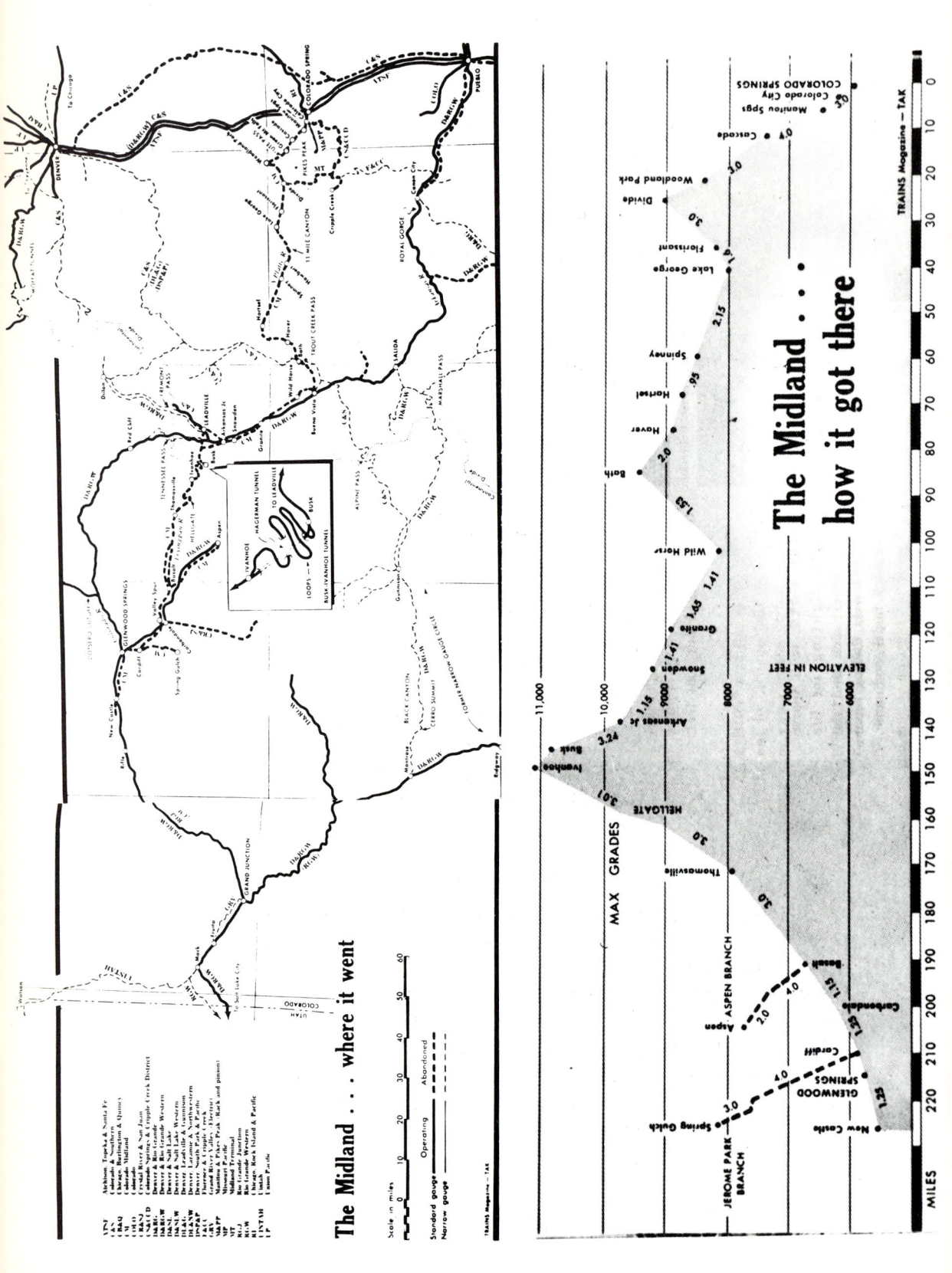

Allan Craig collection

An early emblem of the Colorado Midland Railroad.

Until that time, all the railroads in the mountains had been narrow gauge, but this railroad was conceived as a broad gauge from its inception. The Rio Grande, the rival railroad which raced with the Midland to build into Aspen, was also forced to broad gauge.

Shoemaker quotes President James J. Hagerman's annual report of April 4, 1887 as follows: "On June 1, 1886, the Colorado Midland Railway Company entered into a contract with the Colorado Midland Construction Company, whereby the latter would construct the road. However, prior to that date, under a preliminary agreement, work had already started on May 17, 1886."

The railroad was first built up the Ute Pass from Colorado Springs. However, soon afterward, by getting supplies in over a rival railroad at Bath, building extended both ways from Leadville toward Buena Vista and Aspen and not long thereafter building was done three ways from Aspen Junction (1) up the

Frying Pan to meet the downcoming builders, (2) up the Roaring Fork toward Aspen, and (3) down the valley to Glenwood Springs.

After going up the Ute Pass the railroad crossed the south end of South Park, then down Trout Creek Pass to the mountain north of Buena Vista. The rails then stayed on the north side of the Arkansas River to Leadville. From Leadville the road went west on the south side of the Arkansas River around the north side of Mount Massive to a place on the side of the Sawatch (Saguache) Range, known as Busk. From there the route turned back to the north over a series of switch backs up to the east entrance of Hagerman Tunnel (also known as Saguache Tunnel) at Douglas City. This was a relatively short tunnel going under the Continental Divide at Sugarloaf Mountain to the west portal known at Hagerman. The road then went down to Ivanhoe Lake. From there on the building of the road down the Frying Pan valley to Aspen Junction and on to Newcastle was much easier, except for the treacherous Hell Gate area about ten miles below Ivanhoe.

The promoters from Aspen Junction intended to build on to Rifle, and then on up Piceance Creek to Salt Lake City. However, because of a pinch in finances, the Midland effected an agreement to use Rio Grande tracks to Rifle, and then build a joint track down the Grande River through DeBeque Canyon from Rifle to Grand Junction, there to connect with the Rio Grande Western.

Old Midland advertisement on side of recently demolished building in Denver.

R. W. D. collection

Basalt, Colorado Midland Town 45

THE CONTINENTAL DIVIDE—HAGERMAN PASS, COLORADO.
Copy of an engraving. Original Painting by Charles Graham

The planning and construction of the railroad over the mountains and up the rugged valleys was a drama unequaled in railroad construction, and it is to be regretted that more pictures (and movies) could not have been made. As previously stated, the construction began May 17, 1886. The trains were running to Buena Vista by July 13, 1887. The road reached Aspen Junction November 5, 1887. By December 1887, the first Midland trains were delivering passengers by transfer to Aspen.

The Midland lost out by several months getting into Aspen before the Grande (which had built up from Glenwood Springs) due to the considerable delay in building the high and difficult Castle Creek and Maroon Creek bridges over the deep gorges on the south side of the Roaring Fork near Aspen. By

James J. Hagerman, the man from Milwaukee whose capital and influence turned a bold dream into the first standard-gauge railroad in the Colorado Rockies.

Denver Public Library Western Collection

February, 1888, however, the trains ran on in to the Aspen depot and railway yards. The roadbed construction three ways from Aspen Junction was begun in late 1885 and early 1886, but the rails did not reach there until about November 5, 1887. The land for the right of way and the buildings at Aspen Junction was purchased from the Luchsinger brothers and D.R.C. Brown.

Thus in the incredibly short time of about 20 months, many miles of railroad had been built through some of the most difficult terrain anywhere, and it was done by pick and shovel, hand drilling for blasting, and making of roadbed by hand scrapers drawn by horses and mules. Ormes says, "By midsummer of 1887 the Midland had put in 100 miles of track; in 1888 there were 242 miles in operation from Colorado Springs to Glenwood Springs, and a nineteen mile spur up to Aspen." The road was then soon extended down the river to Newcastle and on to Rifle over the Denver and Rio Grande tracks. It is reported that at times a mile of track was laid in a day. The branch to Aspen was originally considered main line.

In addition to the Aspen branch, others were soon in operation. The Spring Gulch branch was built fifteen miles south from Cardiff to get to the coal in that region for the railroad and the Cardiff coke ovens for the smelters at Pueblo and Leadville. Also in 1892 was incorporated the Midland Terminal Railway Company to operate from Colorado Springs to Cripple Creek over the Midland tracks to Divide and from there to Cripple Creek over a branch line. The line was finally completed, and train service to Cripple Creek began December 19, 1895. There was also a short branch from Arkansas Junction to Leadville.

The owners of the Midland originally pondered whether to build a parallel line with the Grande River Valley from Newcastle or to construct the railroad from Rifle up Piceance Creek and then across to Salt Lake City. The two roads finally agreed to operate a joint track from Newcastle to Grand Junction.

The ups and downs of this 335 mile railroad over the next thirty years have been ably chronicled by several writers. Suffice it here to say that the Midland defaulted on its bond interest due July 1, 1912 and the road was in financial difficulty. On February 12, 1917 the first mortgage of 1897 was foreclosed. At the sale of April 21, 1917, Mr. A. E. Carlton and associates of Colorado Springs purchased the property and for a short while,

W. H. Jackson photo, Denver Public Library Western Collection

Horseshoe curves on the Colorado Midland showing trestle and snowsheds. This is a view of the east side of Hagerman Pass showing the town of Busk in the lower left corner.

due to transportation of war materials, the success of the Midland was phenomenal. However, disaster was soon to follow, for on December 28, 1917, the United States Railway Administration took over the nation's railroads and soon ordered that the business should go by the Grande because the Midland had difficulty in handling the traffic. Even produce from Mr. Carlton's properties in Utah was diverted to the rival road, over Mr. Carlton's strong protest.

Inasmuch as there was now negligible shipping of ore from Leadville and Aspen, and the local fruit, coal, and livestock business could not keep the road going, it was again placed in receivership in July 1918. The court, furthermore, ordered the railroad to cease operating, and the final scheduled passenger train left Grand Junction for Colorado Springs on August 4, 1918. Freight service stopped soon after.

However, Carlton and others made a valiant effort to reopen the road, but to no avail. The tracks were needed from Colorado Springs to Divide to connect with the Midland Terminal in Cripple Creek. The rails were finally removed from Newcastle to Divide in 1921. Much of the roadbed has been used by the State Highway Department, especially up the Frying Pan Canyon.

We can do no better to sum up our brief account of the Colorado Midland than by quoting Morris Cafky, an authority on the Colorado Midland, who says in the September 1957 issue of *Trains*: "The Colorado Midland has been dead for nearly four decades, yet, strangely enough, it lives. Today it continues to stimulate the imagination of thousands who never heard the bark of a Midland stack, never heard the wail of a Midland whistle, and never rode a Midland train. Rail fans, historians, devotees of Western Americana takes pleasure in collecting old photos, blueprints folios, public and employee time tables, or thrill to hikes over the crumbling roadbed. This interest, far from diminishing, seems to increase with each generation. Perhaps this is the Colorado Midland's triumph—in death it has become immortal."

INTERESTING ITEMS

Tunnels and Snow Blockade

Now that the thumbnail sketch of the building of the Midland has been written, we may return to the discussion of a few items of interest regarding the railroad.

photo by W. H. Jackson, Denver Public Library Western Collection

The great trestle near Hagerman Tunnel.

50 The Colorado Midland

Denver Public Library Western Collection
The east entrance of the Hagerman Tunnel as it appeared in 1960.

No write-up, however brief, of the Midland would be complete without a discussion of the building of the tunnels over the Continental Divide and the snow blockade from the big snow of 1899. We presume we are tempted also to write about the tunnels because our father ran an engine through both of them, and an uncle, Mr. Riebel, was caught in the blockade.

In the fall of 1886, only a short distance from the planned east entrance of the proposed Hagerman (or Saguache) tunnel, the Midland built a construction camp of logs and tents, known as Douglas City, to house the workers. The Griswolds say, "By early summer of 1887, this camp, only a rock slide away from the mouth of the tunnel, had eight saloons and at least one dance hall made complete with a few 'faded attractions' from Leadville's State Street, and music furnished by a 'Professor' and one violin virtuosa." They go on to record other interesting data about the temporary camp, including the description of a bone knuckle fight in detail. In their book they are writing about Lake County; they intend to discuss the building of the Midland from Leadville to Douglas City in considerable detail. Douglas City was named after the Douglas Construction Company, later supplanted by the Cooke Construction Company.

There has been, as far as we know, almost nothing written about the village of Hagerman, at the west portal of the Saguache Tunnel. The Grand Junction *Sentinel* says the name was appropriately called Hagerman. The Griswolds believe it was called Hagerman Camp. This western portal camp was supplied by materials transported over Cooke Pass, later known as Hagerman

Old bakery at Douglass City.

Old ruins at Douglass City.

Ruins near west end of Hagerman Tunnel. Lake Ivanhoe in background.

Bob Terrell at Red Tables.

Pass, from Douglas City. Equipment was also moved by mule back down to the camp building the tunnel at the Hell Gate area. From each road camp, not only were the men building the tunnel, but they were also engaged in constructing the railway grade.

Last summer, Allan Craig, of the Horseshoe Bend Ranch above Meredith, took Philip, Luke and Carrie Danielson and the authors in his truck over the old roadbed up to the west portal of the tunnel. Never in our lives have we had a more interesting day observing the remains of the log buildings, the evidence of a side track, the rock dump from the excavation of the tunnel, the pieces of iron junk lying around, the view of Lake Ivanhoe and the Frying Pan Valley, and the peek into the almost caved-in entrance to the tunnel. We hope to go back every summer to repeat the thrill. Perhaps we can figure out why there were about a dozen five gallon tin cans arranged in a horseshoe-shaped fashion near one of the broken down cabins. Do you suppose some lady cook thus had a small flower garden for the gorgeous columbines or other flowers? What is your guess?

The Hagerman tunnel was not very long, only 2,164 feet to be exact, and was bored only 500 feet below the summit. It was blasted out of solid rock so that no cement needed to be used. The tunnel was straight without curves, and entered the side of Sugarloaf Mountain at 11,530 feet on the east side. The western portal was about a mile and a half east of the siding and telegraph office at Ivanhoe, at the side of Lake Ivanhoe. There was, of course, only a single track which ascended westward on a grade of 1.5 per cent.

The digging of the tunnel was begun at both Hagerman Camp and Douglas City in late 1886, and they holed through in August 1887, with engines and cars going through on rails by September 1887. There were snow sheds at each end and apparently some short side tracks. No special orders were given for operating the trains through the tunnel other than train orders, the same as elsewhere. It cost $2,000,000 to build.

A description of the approach to the tunnel is given in the flowery language of a Colorado Midland promotion pamphlet in 1887 and reads as follows:

> "Leaving the city of Leadville on the west, crossing the Arkansas Valley to the Lake Creek, following up Lake Creek a short distance, and the Colorado Midland train is at the foot of Sugar Loaf Mountain, a hill of immense proportions, an offshoot from the Saguache range. After circling around the foot of this mountain, the locomotive begins to climb the great hill to the summit of the Snowy Range. Crawling along the monstrous

Exterior view of the west end of the Hagerman Tunnel, taken in 1952.

D. H. Gerbaz collection

Interior flash shot of the west end of Hagerman Tunnel, taken in 1952. The photographer was forced to dig his way in to take this picture. The water is about six feet deep.

D. H. Gerbaz collection

54   The Colorado Midland

from John R. Smith collection

Train with three engines above Ruedi in winter.

ridge, climbing up the mountain side, higher and higher, gradually leaving the valley and the creek far below until they are hundreds of feet beneath the train, which keeps going up, and up, and up for several miles, when the locomotive appears at the head of the gulch, making a horseshoe curve apparently at the base of the craggy, snow covered peaks, and yet almost to the summit of the great range. In coming up the mountain to the Horseshoe Curve, the scenery is grand and awe inspiring. The traveler is on the side of a great mountain, almost above the timber line, and yet among the thickest of the tall straight pines. In front of him are the snow-capped peaks, the summits of which are now and then visible through the clouds that sometimes touch the train, while on his right, hundreds of feet below the train is the green valley with Lake Creek running through it as the ostrich runs, from side to side, and with here and there a little pond; the waters of the creek and ponds glistening in the sunlight, and resembling a beautiful necklace of sparkling gems, laid out on a strip of green velvet for show. Leaving the Horseshoe Curve the road winds around among the rugged hills above timber line and the scene changes from grandly beautiful to grandly wild. The iron horse with his train of magnificent carriages climbs up among the rocks, round about like a serpent, making several big curves and marking out three or four lines on the mountain side, one above the other, in all of which an increasing elevation is being gained. After passing over a deep gulch on the great "Mountain Trestle" and around the hill and past two or three lakes, in deep basins in the rocks, the engine soon appears to be bent upon butting the top of the mountain off the track when it enters the great Hagerman Tunnel."

The cost of getting up to and down the mountains from the 11,000 foot level to the 11,530 foot of Hagerman Tunnel was expensive enough in fair weather, but in the snows of winter the cost was almost prohibitive. Therefore, on July 25, 1890 contracts were let to build a tunnel at a lower level from Ivanhoe on the west to Busk on the east side. Graves says that the projected tunnel itself was 9,394 feet long, but with approaches was

Denver Public Library Western Collection

Train with snowplow emerging from snowshed on Hagerman Pass.

2.9 miles. It was 15 feet wide and 21 feet high. The Busk-Ivanhoe Tunnel eliminated 6.9 miles of distance, 581 feet of elevation and 1,958 degrees of curvature. By December 17, 1893, the trains began running through.

This lower tunnel was named after the man who was largely responsible for its construction, Mr. J.R. Busk. At the Ivanhoe end were extensive snow sheds which housed the turntable and the dispatcher's office, and later the Y. The running of the trains through the tunnel was largely by train orders, but there was an additional safety arrangement to prevent two trains in the tunnel at the same time, by the use of staffs which were removed on entry and replaced on exit at the other end.

The Busk-Ivanhoe Tunnel has been known as the Carlton Tunnel since 1918. For a while after the rails were taken up in 1921 the tunnel was used for automobile traffic, but was soon closed because of the danger. There are now rumors that it is to be opened again as a tourist attraction and as an aid in building the Ruedi-Arkansas project. The tunnel has carried water from the western to the eastern slope of the Rockies for many years.

photo from Orel Clark

Track-walker cabin at Hell Gate.

The builders of the Busk Tunnel Railway (an independent company) decided to charge twenty-five cents for each passenger and each ton of freight moved through the tunnel. This worked well for a while, but when the Midland tried to get the rent reduced, this was refused. They, therefore, decided to go back to the upper Hagerman Tunnel. The rails were relaid and the ice was removed from the bore. This worked well until 1899 when the huge snow of that year blocked the railroad from January 24 until April 14, or a total of seventy-eight days. After this, the Midland and the Busk Tunnel Railway came to terms. Later the Midland bought the tunnel and the upper route was permanently abandoned. The description of this tunnel building by Earl Mosley is superb.

Basalt Journal Items

Jan. 21, 1899

The coal famine in town had become a serious matter especially to those who are in the habit of buying coal. Had not Supt. Bryant of the Colorado Midland come to the rescue and let Mr. Hull, the genial dispenser of black diamonds, have a car, many of us would be well frozen.

March 10, 1899

Engineer Hyrup and Fireman Fields arrived home from Hagerman first of the week over D & R G. The boy's whiskers had

Courtesy of Orel Clark

Train in Hell Gate.

grown entirely out of our knowledge. They tell of a thrilling story of their experience, while imprisoned in snow shed No. 9 about 44 days. The snow shed is 32 ft. high. The snow on top of the shed was 15 or 20 ft. making it 37 to 42 ft. deep.

The boys made two trips daily through the tunnel to Pepper's boarding car.

April 20, 1899

One of the most welcome sights around Basalt was the evening of April 15, 1899, when the snow plow came into town with red fuses burning, everyone shouting, and, I think, some guns fired after there hadn't been any trains over the hill since January 27, 1899.

Loyalty of Employees

It may be mentioned in retrospect that the Midland paid very little in dividends or profits to the stockholders—many Englishmen and Easterners—in its entire lifetime. Its main value for the relatively few years that it ran was in opening up the district to the mines and to agriculture and stock raising, and to furnishing a livelihood to the employees. Part of the pay of the owners was the pride of ownership of a railroad.

This provision of jobs by the railroad was, however, amply repaid by the loyalty and pride of the employees in seeing to it that the trains went through, and cannot be overestimated. They often performed their tasks under unbelievable hardships and in the face of great danger. Indeed many men who were killed were buried near the place they died, in unmarked graves, and all their relatives knew was that they heard a rumor that "Uncle Jim" was killed in a railroad accident in the Rockies.

Tom McNeil, the oldest engineer by seniority on the second division, and who had the prize job of helper on passenger runs out of Basalt, tells in his diary how proud he and Farquahar were that they were never responsible for the death or injury of a passenger or other employee.

When we recall how our father would go on a trip to Ivanhoe in blizzards in winter time and would often go without sleep or rest for interminable long periods, we cannot but revere his memory. We are grateful and humble as we realize that part of that effort, and exposure and fatigue went into helping us with an education and a much easier life.

We well remember running down the street to the round house to meet our father when he returned from a trip, and to carry his lunch box home when he would be so tired that he would drop on his bed unable to eat or even undress.

One of the most difficult and exhausting chores for him and his fireman was to turn an engine on the turntable at Ivanhoe, particularly in subzero weather. The location of this turntable is still plainly discernible at Ivanhoe. Later when the helper engines were larger, it was necessary to put in a Y (wye) for turning the engines.

Most of the time, however, the men were not, of course, exposed to such hardships and they enjoyed their work. They took intense pride, not only in the work but in their engines, particularly in the day when an engineer and fireman were assigned to

View of railroad installations at Basalt about 1900.

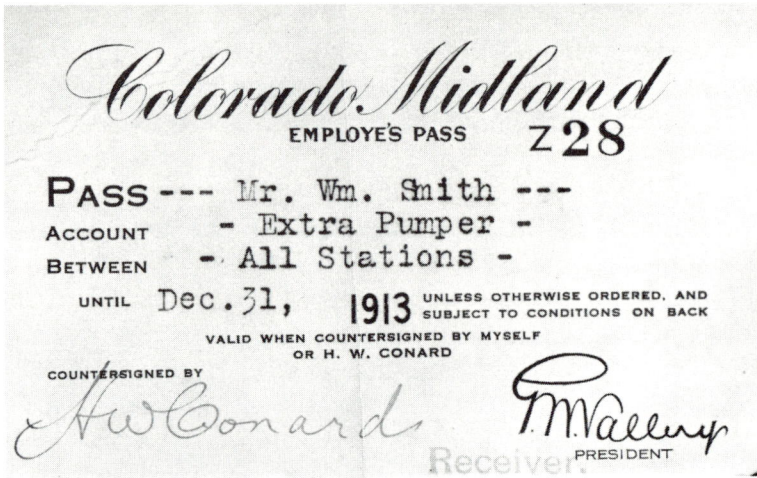

loaned by John R. Smith

Employee's pass.

a certain engine. Between trips they spent many hours doing light repairs and cleaning up their engines without additional pay.

The cab of an engine was not a very comfortable place, as it was frequently entirely too hot or too cold. It could not be closed off in winter; it was necessary for the engineer and fireman to keep their windows open to see ahead and to the rear for signals, and to watch for things on the tracks. This cold at

Relics of the Colorado Midland collected by the authors from the west end of Hagerman Tunnel.

R. W. D. Collection

the high mountain altitudes had to be endured for hours and hours, much to the damage of health in many ways, we are sure. In the summer when the train was not moving, again the heat was almost unbearable. Furthermore, these engines were very rough to ride and many times were very noisy. In addition to the exhaust "puffing" of the engine, there was often the clank-clank of a loose driving rod.

The engineer and fireman on the Diesel locomatives today ride on the front end of the locomotive well protected from the elements—a far cry from the rigors that our father endured.

The Blairs

Two people who were as close to the hearts of the trainmen as their house was close to the railroad tracks were Mr. and Mrs. Frank Blair who lived at Hopkins Spur between Sloss and Ruedi. There was a sandstone quarry nearby where Frank worked. At night he "walked the track" for the railroad up toward Ruedi. Anna kept boarders from the quarry and also sold meals to fishermen.

Because of the lack of space between the river and the cliffs at Hopkins Spur, their long frame house had been built not more than fifteen feet from the tracks. In addition they had chicken houses and a cellar to keep things cool; keeping food fresh was a problem since no ice was available.

Frank and Anna Blair at Hopkins Spur.

Courtesy of John R. Smith

The engineers would whistle loudly and long on approaching the place in order to give Mrs. Blair a chance to shoo her chickens off the track; for them to go by Hopkins without waving to her was unthinkable. Because of the Blair's location it was difficult for them to obtain coal, and besides, it was expensive. Peculiarly some large coal chunks would pile up on the left side of the tenders just before the engines going up the hill would reach Hopkins Spur, and then, of course, to keep the engines from toppling over on the curve in front of Blairs' house the firemen would push the chunks over the side in order to prevent a disaster. Then the couple would be forced to clear up their yard by putting the coal in their coalhouse.

When the helpers were returning about six hours later, the enginemen would stop just long enough to receive a generous piece of wild-raspberry or apple pie from the smiling and gracious Anna Blair. Often there was coal in the gangway of the engine, and there was no better way to clear up the messy place than to shovel it off into the Blair buckets. The same enginemen would often get a big drink of buttermilk from the Slosses when they went into the siding there. The trainmen were very friendly with all the people along the tracks, particularly with the Dearhammers at Meredith, the Lige Thompsons at Thomasville, and John Ruedi at Ruedi.

Often groups would go for a picnic up to Hopkins Spur. It was from there that Clarence remembers taking thirteen people back to Basalt on a light engine. Mr. Scandlan and Ralph missed getting on and had to get back by borrowed handcar. On a few occasions our mother stayed and visited several days with her friend, Mrs. Blair.

After the Midland closed Frank and Anna were left stranded with hardly any income. Then the friendly ranchers came to their rescue with gifts of milk, beef, and venison. There were still a few fishermen to buy the never-to-be-forgotten meals at Blairs.

The Blairs' best friend of all was probably Virgil Holcomb, who remembers them with great affection. At that time he was in the Forest Service, and he saw to it that they had a telephone and many necessities.

The couple came originally from England. They had no children, but Mrs. Blair had a nephew, John Cronin, who worked as a fireman. Frank and Anna now lie in Basalt Cemetery. Never in the history of railroading has there been a closer friendship between railroad men and people living beside the tracks!

Handcars

Between 1918 and 1921 one of the most valuable and prized pieces of property was a railroad handcar that had been used by section men. As Walter Hyrup says, "The reason people used the handcars instead of the Basalt-Ruedi wagon road was that they could put ungodly loads on the cars and move them easily. There were no bumps. The railroad, too, was much shorter than the wagon road. So that was quite a common mode of transportation after the railroad quit operation and before the rails were pulled up."

John R. Smith, of Minturn, who formerly lived at Ruedi, writes in part: "As to the horse-drawn push cars, the mail man, Fred Williams, used this combination three days per week—from Meredith to Basalt, Monday, Wednesday, and Friday; return from Basalt to Meredith, Tuesday, Thursday and Saturday. No mail on Sunday. He would carry any passenger who might want to go to Basalt. The fare was one dollar. Several of the natives also had this kind of transportation when the Midland first stopped operation. A couple of motor cars were used but got in trouble with the horse cars. I remember one occasion when Mr. S.P. Sloss and I were coming up the track with five saddle horses when one of the motor cars came around a curve. The man on the car jumped off with his small son, the car went on down the track. Another man coming up roped the car and that ended the motor cars.

"When the rails were taken up the people joined in and pulled the ties, graded the road bed, and thus began the highway up the Frying Pan.

Handcars were still used after the closing of the Midland. This picture was taken at Ruedi.

photo from Ford Gilbert

Handcars loaded with personal possessions, including old style trunk.

"The first winter after starting the horse drawn car they came as far as Sloss ranch and sledded from there to Meredith. This was the mail service.

"There was one death during this period, Mr. McLaren. His body was taken to Basalt on one of these cars and shipped to Aspen for burial.

"Another stunt that took place was Mr. Williams had one hundred twenty hogs he wanted to market. He took four horses to Basalt and pulled an empty railroad car to his ranch, loaded the pigs and at first was letting the car down by hand brake. This was O.K. for first ten miles. Then at Castles he had to put the horses on and pulled it the rest of the way with hand brake partially set. He unloaded the pigs across the bridge at Basalt, then herded pigs to Emma and shipped them to Denver."

A colorful description of the push cars written to me by Walter Hyrup is as follows:

"I recall an incident with one of those push cars. My mother bought a grain drill from J. F. Sloss & Son. I came down from the ranch at Castles to get the drill. I had brought a saddle horse and the push car. This horse had been tried out for work but was as balky as h---. He would turn his head around to see what he was hooked on to and if it was a wagon or anything that looked large, well, that was it! He wouldn't even tighten a tug. So we boys used him as a saddle horse.

"I was using him the day I was to bring the drill home. Marvin Sloss helped me to load the grain drill, which was all set up, on to the handcar. I tied my lariat rope to the car and got on the horse. Boy, oh boy, - what a time I had! The horse took one look around and I had one h--- of a time even getting him to tighten up the rope. But once he gave the car a small pull and it started to move it was O.K. I sure was more than mad at him. He had just looked and figured it was too big, even though I had a saddle and not a harness on him. Sometimes a horse must be awfully smart!"

One of the features of the Midland was the running of special trains for various purposes. Very early, before the railroad was completed even as far as Buena Vista, the management began to run Sunday wild flower and sightseeing trains up the Ute Pass to the South Park district. Many pictures have been published of the passengers lined up beside the trains holding arm loads of wild flowers. Some were interested more in rock collecting and in digging for fossils at Florissant. (Once R.W.D. was caught behind a wreck at Florissant while returning to school at Boulder and found a fossil of a fish that is still in the University of Colorado Museum). Because a shortage of passenger cars, and because some of the vacationers preferred the open view and air, they rode on flat cars.

While the East End had its flower excursions, the West End had its fishing expeditions out of Leadville down the Frying Pan. Many fishermen also rode the regular passenger trains over in the morning on No. 3 and went back on No. 6. Clarence recalls one night when he was firing passenger up the hill, a group of fishermen were standing on the track at Nast expecting to be picked up, but, because they did not actually flag the train, the engineer did not stop and went off without them, leaving them to spend the rest of the night there, to wait for No. 4 the next

D. H. Gerbaz collection

Private car on the Colorado Midland, "The Cascade". Photo taken about 1898. This car is now in the possession of D. H. Gerbaz.

morning. The complaints that went in to Supt. Vallery were reported to have been long, strong, and heated, and the engineer probably received some demerits.

The cooperation of the employees and management of the railroad for fishermen was well told by Cal Queal a couple of years ago in the *Denver Post* supplement as follows:

"Fishing and railroading, surely two of the most romantic pursuits ever invented by man, were happily combined in Colorado back in the early 1900's. A Leadville passenger agent named Carter decided he should have more customers on the old Colorado Midland, and, being a fisherman himself, started promoting a sort of angler's express.

"Colorado Midland went out of business in 1918, and Sam Phillips of Glenwood took the last No. 6 into Leadville. It was Sam who told us about the fisherman's express.

"A fishing customer simply told the conductor where he'd like to get off. Then, as though it were the angler's private train, the Colorado Midland would roll to a stop beside some likely looking hole on the Frying Pan or its North Fork. The angler would jump off with his gear, and the train would roll on its way.

"That afternoon, his creel usually filled with rainbows and natives, the fisherman would simply go to the track, flag down the next train, and head back home.

"Phillips said the train crews got into the spirit of the thing, would pick up cans of fish at the Leadville fish hatchery, dump them at scheduled points along the Midland route.

ABOARD THE CARS.—PIKE'S PEAK ROUTE.

Denver Public Library Western Collection

This picture was taken from the Colorado Midland publicity folder, "Heart of the Rockies", 1890.

"We can't help but wish the Colorado Midland was still operating, and that Mr. Carter was calling the shots as passenger agent. To us, it sounded like a helluva nice way to run a railroad."

Other excuses for running specials were Race Day and Strawberry Day in Glenwood Springs. On Race Day the bicycle riders would compete for prizes in riding from the Peterson Place between El Jebel and Basalt to the finish line on Grand Avenue.

The train from Aspen and Basalt would stop opposite the starting place and then follow the riders to near Carbondale, when the engineer would speed up and get the passengers to Glenwood Springs in time so that they could get off at the station and hurry over to see the riders come in one by one, often to collapse at the end. John Clarke and I once made the trip by bicycle and were indeed exhausted boys when we arrived.

On Strawberry Day, too, the excursions were gala affairs and have continued almost uninterruptedly until the present. The free strawberries and cream and cake are wonderful, but the real attraction that brings people from miles around in droves to this celebration even today is meeting everybody sometime during the day. Ruby Clarke (Hubbard) was the first queen in 1913, and in 1963 they honored her again by making her honorary queen.

In the old days, too, there were many attractions; for some of the young and older blades the entertainment up on the hill in the 700 block on Parmer Avenue. Many of the boys walked by to get the thrill of being near the houses of suspicion and glamour, especially the one known as "The Brick."

George Hayes, in his book *Rock Hound of the Rockies,* tells about the red light district of Glenwood (in Leadville on State Street and in Aspen on Durant Street). He tells an interesting tale of a W.C.T.U. convention held in Glenwood once, when, either

The Midland depot at Basalt about 1900.

Courtesy of George McLaren

for a devilish joke or for lack of housing facilities, the person in charge of arrangements had several of the delegates put up for the night at "The Brick." When the ladies found out what had happened, they wanted to bring suit but could not get a lawyer to take the case.

It was on one of the excursions, also known as "laundry trains," because everyone dressed up, that the terrible catastrophe happened on the Y at Basalt when, in a collision, many persons were scalded to death by the steam from one of the engines.

RAILROAD JARGON
(The language we learned on the Midland)

While we were writing this book, it occurred to us that a discussion of railroad jargon or slang might be interesting and we have spent much time in getting together the terms we knew and used. At first, we could find no such lists and we believed we were first in the field in this regard. But, after three years of work on this book—as might be expected—we finally found dictionaries by Berrey and Van Den Bark, and by Weseen which give quite engrossing compilations of railroad jargon which are recommended to railroad buffs.

However, we find that we have numerous names they do not mention. Furthermore, we thought the newcomer in railroadiana

Water tank, hotel, railroad station and coal shutes in Basalt, 1920.
Denver Public Library Western Collection

might like to have a brief introduction to whet his appetite for more railroad terms. We have, therefore, decided to leave this chapter in the book and combine it with a short discourse on bums and hoboes.

The peculiar variations of language as applied to railroad terminology might be called vernacular, lingo, jargon, cant, argot, or slang, but jargon seems to fit best the non-standard words used by the railroad men. We believe a discussion of these words will be of interest, particularly when they do not appear in ordinary dictionaries or even in the special volume by Partridge on slang and unconventional English.

After we had written this chapter on jargon, we have had our attention called by Marranzino, to the excellent glossary of railroad terms in the Beebe, Clegg, and Fogg volume entitled *Mixed Trains Daily*. We were surprised to find in their list that a caboose is also known as a palace, louse cage, parlor, shanty, way car, bouncer, cage, hut, buggy, hearse, crib, hack, and chariot.

A *boomer* was a person who took a job for just long enough to get a little money ahead and then move on to another job elsewhere; also known as a *floater*. Many trainmen were boomers.

A *hoghead* (or hogger*) was a non-affectionate term for a locomotive engineer (not to be confused with *hogshead*—a unit of measure). The term *hog* was used to apply to any regular employee who never laid off his regular run in order to give a man on the extra board a chance to make a trip. When business was not too brisk, the extra men often had a very difficult time to make a living *bucking the extra board*. When such an extra man became too desperate financially, it was not uncommon for such an employee to ask to be demoted from engineer to fireman, or fireman to round house worker, or conductor to brakeman, in order to hold seniority and regular work, at a lower classification and lower rate of pay; this was known as *bumping* the man below him.

We had many reasons to respect our parents, but one thing we hold in our memory was having our father look over the extra board, and, if an engineer had not had a trip for a considerable time, he would voluntarily lay off a trip to give that man a chance. That may in part account for the fact that our father was the local secretary of the Brotherhood of Locomotive Engineers for many years and was repeatedly chosen to be the delegate to the national convention that was held every four years.

---

*A helper engine, particularly the consolidate type, was also sometimes known as a *hog* or *hogger*.

Courtesy of Charles Ryland, Golden, Colo.

Railroad station and telegraph office at Ivanhoe at the west end of the Busk-Ivanhoe Tunnel.

I can still remember our trip to Columbus, Ohio, about 1908. Our father was presented a large lounging chair as a gift from the other engineers at the end of his long term of office; we kept the chair for many years after his death.

Some of the terms seem to make little sense, but I suppose an expert on railroad lore may know the derivation. As examples, why should a fireman have been termed a *tallow-pot*, and a conductor called a *Big O*? Why should a brakeman have been known as a *stinger*, and a switchman a *snake*?

The place where engines were repaired was the *roundhouse*, even though, as at Basalt, the structure was rectangular. The word "roundhouse" is used because so many repair houses were actually built round, with the engines pointing in from all directions and with a turntable in the center. Each of these places had a pit underneath so the workmen could get under the engines for repair.

Marranzino, in his January 27, 1964 column of the *Rocky Mountain News,* in discussing the razing of the Rio Grande Burnham Shops, under the heading of "Famous Pigpen Being Razed," says that *pigpen* is railroad jargon for *roundhouse*. He adds "a *pig* is the uncouth designation of what aesthetically is called a beautiful locomotive."

Pie books were scrip issued by the company on a man's next check, so that he could get something to eat. Many a time the

D. H. Gerbaz collection

Thomasville, on the Colorado Midland.

employee would get these pie books and then sell them at a discount to get cash or would turn them in at a saloon to get liquor.

A *car whacker* was a car repairman who would go along beside trains in stations, particularly at terminals, to check on defective equipment, such as leaks in air lines, broken brakes, worn brake shoes, and hot boxes. The engineer would check his own engine and confer with the car whacker, especially in checking out the air brakes. As the car whacker would walk along the train, he would often hit (or *whack*) something with his hammer; hence, his name. He was also known as a car repairman or car *tonk*. R.W.D. worked for a short while at this job in early summer 1918. Brake shoes were made of iron and would wear out and need to be replaced. Have you ever marvelled at how long automobile brakes can be used without replacement? *Hot boxes* would develop in the journal when the grease was deficient.

A car inspector was known as a *car toad*. His work was to check whether cars were properly labeled and securely locked. This work was similar to that of a seal clerk.

A *caller* was the person who notified trainmen when they were to report to take a train out. There were no telephones so the caller would walk from door to door and the employee had to sign his name in a book stating that he had received the call. We remember many times my father would be asleep and one of us would take the book into his bedroom for him to sign. The distances were not so great that this was any burden for the caller in Basalt, but even in large cities, until recently, the employee had

C. L. D. collection

Helper engines in the Basalt yards.

to live near enough to the roundhouse that he could be contacted personally. There was rule against calling a man out of a saloon so the caller would send someone in to have the man come out in order to sign the book. If the trainman was engaged in a poker game that he didn't want to leave or if he was intoxicated, the caller was asked to call the first man on the extra board.

The caller was usually a boy—often under age—who thus started at the bottom of the ladder to work himself up through the ranks at the roundhouse on his way to becoming a trainman.

Section men were the laborers who worked at maintaining the tracks and right of way (discussed elsewhere). They were so named, I presume, because they cared for a section of track. The section house housed these men. The men who constructed track were known as *gandy-dancers*. Subsidiary classifications were *spike maulers, tong gang,* and *adz gang.*

The *trackwalker* was a man who at dusk would start out walking up or down the track from the section house. His duty was to examine the track for defects and for the presence of obstacles on the track. In the canyons many rocks would come down the mountain—especially after a rain—and would lie on the track or actually bend or break a rail. He also looked out for livestock that had gotten through the fences.

The *ties* referred to the logs flattened on two sides to tie or hold the rails the proper distance apart. Many of these were of pine and would be cut along the right of way as the railroad was being built through. The ideal tie, however, is made of oak.

The rear brakeman was called a *hind shack.*

The *hostler* was the man who took care of getting fire boxes clean, getting supplies on the engines, and switching the engines in and out of the round house. A *firenocker* was the man who removed the clinkers and ashes from the firebox, and built up a clean fire.

Called up on the carpet was an expression used when an employee was called before some official (generally the superintendent) to explain what the employee knew about a wreck or some violation of rules.

Rule G applied to the intemperate use of liquor by an employee.

The *catwalk* was the boards laid down on the top of box cars. These were used to walk on and were aptly named, for it took the nimbleness of a cat to walk them on a moving train, especially in icy weather.

Some of the terminology for the trains and engines is interesting. When a train went into a side track, it was referred to as *heading in* or *backing out*. When cars were left on spurs and sidings, the breaks would have to be set and this was referred to as *tying them down*. When an inferior train took the siding for a superior train, it was referred to as *going in the hole*. Any number of cars switched from one place to another was spoken of as a *cut*. The side track near the saloon at Basalt was known as the *whiskey track*.

To *high-ball* meant to give the signal to start the train. This signal was given by hand during the day and by lantern at night. *High-ball freight,* consisting of perishables and livestock, would move faster because fewer cars were put on a train. A coal train however, went slowly because of the maximum loads, and was known as a *drag*. Onlookers said a fireman had a *white feather* when the full head of steam caused frequent releases of steam from the safety valve.

An engine whose boiler was generating steam efficiently was said to *steam well* and that the fireman had the engine *hot*.

To switch meant to transfer cars from one track to another and to assemble a train. In switching, to *hump* a car meant to give it a push and turn it loose down a siding or into other cars. This can cause much damage to the contents of a box car and accounts for signs seen on the side of railroad cars "Do not hump." Today there are large *hump yards* on railroads for sorting cars in making up trains; there weren't any on the Colorado Midland.

The driving wheels of the locomotives had steel tires, and if the brakes were not properly controlled, would become so hot that they expanded and became separated from the wheel. This was known as *slipping a tire* and could cause a reprimand or a discharge for an engineer.

To be promoted from the *left side* of an engine to the *right side* meant to be elevated from the rank of fireman to that of an engineer. An engine could mean the whole locomotive or just the motive part.

To those youngsters who have never seen a steam locomotive, (*engine* and *tender*), it might be explained that the *cab* was the structure at the back part of the engine where the engineer and fireman could sit or stand, as they wished. The head brakeman often rode in the cab also. In fair weather he often rode the *cow catcher*. The cow catcher was an angled protruberance designed to push wandering cattle off the track instead of letting them go under the wheels. There was a narrow passage known as the *gangway* where the men could walk back and forth from side to side just back of the firebox opening. The rear brakeman rode with the conductor in the *caboose* at the end of the train. The caboose was constructed with beds, and a stove to cook a meal.

Bums

In those days, there were many *bums* going through Basalt. Nowadays, the panhandler asks for "a dime for a cup of coffee", but in our time as boys, the favorite expression was "Lady, can I chop some wood for something to eat?" Usually there was no work to do (our mother had three boys for that), but only rarely did our mother fail to put up some sandwiches and we recall the tears in the eyes of the bums as they were handed the sacks. Often several bums would be working separate houses for assigned items of food and would rendezvous later to have their mulligan stew. They often asked for *toppings* (old bread).

A group of bums hitting a town would congregate at the rookery, a jungle, where they would eat and sleep. In Basalt, it was located near the railroad bridge not far from Mrs. Clarke's house yet her daughters recall that they never locked their house— the same as all the other people in Basalt. A group of us boys would occasionally get up our nerve to go visit these friendly people. When a bum asked for money, it was known as *stemming*.

It is reported that these bums who were known as *chronickers* had a secret way of recognizing a house where the people were soft-hearted. A certain mark in chalk on a fence was supposed to be the payoff sign.

76   The Colorado Midland

Officials of the railroad have always frowned on bums riding the trains and have rules against it. But the trainmen themselves did little about it and in the case of coal passers actually encouraged their presence.

Bums have as yet not entirely disappeared. Last summer, while waiting in a car for a train to pass on the old Moffat Road, we saw almost a dozen of these "fellows of the road" riding flat cars, standing in the coal cars, and sitting in the doors of the empty box cars.

Bums are a dirty, ill-kept lot, but the ones we knew as boys were friendly, affable, and almost meek. We never heard of a bum who attempted to hold up or rob a trainman. Robberies and burglarizing in Basalt were almost non-existent. Possibly this was due to the lack of quick "get-away"; no bum ever owned a horse. They had to get from place to place by walking or by

In the picture below is a model of a Colorado Midland locomotive in the Denver Public Library's Western collection. It was built by C. E. Harris (opposite).

train and could easily be apprehended. They weren't anxious to have the train stopped and be put off and stranded a long way from a town; on the desert or in the high mountains this could be a real hardship. There is a law in Nevada that a person cannot be put off a train except at a station.

It has been reliably reported that, during the panic of 1893, there were many bums hanging around Basalt. They became such a nuisance, that a dummy was hung in effigy on the water tank to give warning for them to get out of town. Hardly a way to cure social ills on a national scale, but police do, to this day, give notice to "characters" to get out of town or go to jail.

There were various ways of bumming a ride on a train, either as blind baggage, riding the rods, hiding in reefers or empty cars, or as a coal passer.

On freights, if the weather was not too severe, the bums rode on flat cars or on loads of coal. In the winter they would try to get into an empty box car, but this was hazardous because a trainman might close a door and seal it shut. One of the more dangerous ways was to lie crosswise on the truss rods under the cars and was known as *riding the rods*.

While most of the riding was done on freights, there was some done on passenger trains also. One way that took a lot of guts was to hide in the false vestibule on the end of a baggage car. The rider had to stand, had little to hold on to, and could easily be thrown between the cars. In that case, if the train was moving, he would be killed by being run over by the wheels and by being dragged by the under structure of the cars; he would then be inelegantly and heartlessly described as having *greased the rails*.

The technique of avoiding the trainmen and detectives was to hide somewhere along the side of the train until it started and then swing in between the cars on the iron steps to hide until the train had built up considerable speed. They would then get out into the open on the cars to ride in style. Often, however, their fate was to be put off at the next train stop.

A *coal passer* was a unique bum. Many bums in those days rode the trains free; it was on the railroads that the term "bum a ride" originated. But to get back to the coal passer. He was a bum who, especially in cold weather, would hide on the rear part of the tender. When the engine left on a run, the coal would be piled so high that the engineer and fireman would not be able to see him. When the tender was full, the fireman in the gangway did not have to reach far to get the coal with his shovel. However, on many runs, as from Basalt to Sellars (the next coal chute station), the coal would be fairly low and hard to reach. This meant a lot more work for the fireman.

Then the coal passer would appear to the fireman and offer to pass this coal forward if part of the time he would be permitted to ride in the cab or near the fire box to get warm, discreetly getting out of sight at stations. It was a rare engineer and fireman that did not share their lunches with him.

Some day someone with an imagination and a flare for writing might compose an interesting article on how to differentiate between a migrant, bo, bum, coal passer, transient, moocher, boomer, floater, beggar, loafer, bindle stiff, tramp, vagrant, hobo, cadger, bird of passage, box-car tourist, gray cat, barrel stiff, bundle bum, dingbat, druid, weary Willie, panhandler, or a grease ball. A wobbly, a holder of the I.W.W. union card, was sometimes thusly classified, but really was a man who worked when he had the opportunity.

One might start an essay with a quoted statement by Irwin, in Patridge's dictionary, to the effect that "Bums loafs and sits. Tramps loafs and walks, but a hobo moves and works and is clean."

In looking up railroad jargon in Weseen's *Dictionary of American Slang,* we spent a highly interesting couple of hours perusing the chapter on slang of hobos and tramps and a classification of first, second, and lowest class bums. They mention that the word hobo probably derives from "hoe boys", men who took temporary jobs hoeing out weeds for farmers. It was certainly discouraging to find that in their language the name Ralph was used to designate a fool.

Facilities

A list of the facilities in Basalt in 1917 has been obtained from the State Historical Society through the courtesy of Morris Cafky. In brief, the structures consisted of a frame station and telegraph office, a two-story eating house, locomotive engine house, cinder pit, coal chute, water tank and stand pipe, sand and oil house, store and ice house, section house, bunk house, two cottages, a tool house, coal house, and the handcar house.

There was a wye for turning engines. Tracks and sidings had a capacity of 220 freight cars. For a complete description of the motive power and equipment of the Midland, one should consult the article by Graves and the book by Cafky.

A Midland publication of 1905 lists originating shipments at Basalt of 32 cars of stock, 152 cars of hay and grain, 6 cars of sugar beets, and 66 miscellaneous loads.

Quarries

When the Midland was first built, the sandstone quarries between Seven Castles and Ruedi did a very thriving business furnishing the stone for many buildings and sidewalks in Aspen, Glenwood, and Leadville.

Probably the most active quarry was run by Mr. Wilson at Peachblow, between Sloane and Seven Castles, the siding being named by the railroad, and the stone from there acquired that trade name. There was also a quarry at Hopkins Spur between Sloss and Ruedi.

In the early days of the railroad, whole trainloads of stone were taken to the eastern slope. There would be an unusual consist leaving Aspen Junction composed of three engines and a caboose which would pick up the stone at the quarries and take the loaded cars up to Ivanhoe, for transport on east. When cement became more popular as building material, the quarries folded.

Bogue Tale

Perhaps we might end the discussion of the Midland with an interesting tale.

Lucile Maxfield Bogue tells a story of her relative, Maria McCarthy, wife of Dan McCarthy. She writes of Maria's not only feeding so many strangers, but also states rather colorfully, "Maria says they used engines to make mercy calls. She would board an engine with Bill Bates as engineer and Father Servant firing the boiler and would answer a call for mercy and sickness." We have found no one who could confirm this story.

The Peachblow Quarry, just below Ruedi, where much of the sandstone for sidewalks and buildings in Denver and Colorado Springs was quarried.

Denver Public Library Western Collection

View from the top of the Continental Divide overlooking the east side of the Hagerman Loop. Taken in 1952.

CHAPTER 3

Clarence's Memories

BOYHOOD EXPERIENCES

Trapping

Art Bates and I were pals in many adventures in our boyhood. None, however, was more exciting than helping Art get two bears down to Basalt from where he had trapped them in the Kelly reservoir region. Anyone who knows horses knows that they get panicky when they even smell a bear at a distance. We had to snub the horse's head to a tree and then pull the bear up by a rope over a limb. It took tremendous effort for us boys to lift the bear on the horse in this manner.

Art bagged seven bears altogether in his boyhood—six by trapping and one he shot out on the lava bed on the south side of Basalt Mountain. Unfortunately, the bear, in falling, wedged in between the lava boulders. Furthermore, it was impossible to get a horse even near the carcass because of the terrain. He had killed the bear in the late evening, so he went back the next morning at 4:00, skinned out the carcass and cut out the front quarters, leaving the rest where the bear fell. Until nightfall that day he spent carrying these two quarters of bear meat down the mountain to his home.

On another occasion Art went to his bear traps on Black Mountain after school and found one of them dragged away. He knew he had caught a bear, but he didn't dare to stay on late in the evening for fear the bear might attack him in the dark. Therefore, the next morning his father and three other men took their horse, Bill, up to the spot and found to their surprise a four hundred pound cinnamon bear in the trap. It took all four men to get the bear on the horse, only to have the horse lie down on the way down, presumably from fear and the extreme weight of the bear. Old Bill never permitted another bear on his back.

The thrill of catching and hauling bears was increased by the selling of the hide, then making additional profit from the meat sold to the butcher, who, in turn, offered it for sale to his customers.

We also trapped many bob-cats, coyotes, skunks, and weasels.

We remember another experience,—this one with bows and arrows made by his father. Once, when we were quite small Art and I went out back of Stiffler's rooming-house to play with our bows, to see if we could shoot some chipmunks, snakes, or birds. When a long time passed and our worried mothers could not find us, they had the whistles of the engines blown at the roundhouse which was the signal used in Basalt to alert the people to any kind of an emergency.

Contagious Disease Prevention

I recall with some amusement and yet with affectionate remembrance our mother's employing the time-hallowed custom that prevailed in old Basalt school days of wearing "medicinal necklaces." Most of the mothers in town and in the country prepared little bags containing both camphor and asafetida for their boys and girls to wear to school in wintertime.

They were fastened at the chest to our long underwear with a safety-pin or else tied to a string and worn as a necklace under our clothing. These malodorous gums were held in high repute for their supposed power to ward off diphtheria, scarlet-fever, and other contagious diseases as well as colds and "grippe" we might catch from our school-mates. I venture to say that the preventive action, if any, was in the fact that others, well and sick, kept their distance from us who wore the smelly bags.

Before the discovery of "shots" for babies to make them immune, there existed a real and terrifying worry over whether an epidemic might come to our town which most certainly would have brought death to a number of children and adults.

Waving

Our house faced what was variously called Main Street, Railroad Avenue, or Front Street. It was less than a hundred feet from the railroad tracks, so that the noise of trains going through was very loud. What I remember most vividly, however, was when my father would leave town after dark on a pusher before we went to bed. As the train passed our house, his fireman, for illumination of the cab, would open the fire-box door, so we could see him waving to us. Then, while we slept, he would take the trip to the top at Ivanhoe, often in extremely cold weather, and be back as we were getting up in the morning. It was Mother's job to keep us boys from yelling and fighting while Father got his sleep. Often, of course, in the winter, the trains would be stalled in drifts and he would not be back for a day or two. During his lifetime the sixteen-hour law was passed, making it illegal to keep a man on the job longer than that.

Inasmuch as I was also a fireman and engineer, I, too, was many times on the waving end of this departure. In the daytime we stood in the gangway or leaned out of the cab and showed our greeting with outstretched hand.

Entertainment

The main form of entertainment was the dances. Especially popular were the so-called barn dances held in the Odd Fellows Hall. There were always programs filled in with names as the couples traded dances. It was customary to trade all but two or three dances; of course, the "Home Sweet Home" waltz at the end was with one's partner. The affairs were for both the teenagers and older people. At one time there was a definite program of teaching the youngsters the steps.

These dances would often last until four or five in the morning. Quite a night when one considers that many rode horses five or ten miles to get there and then the same distance back.

When the firemen gave a dance, they would decorate the hall in appropriate fashion by using the green, white, and red flags of the engines and the tools of their work, such as clinker-hooks, scoop-shovels, and coal-picks.

On election day a dance would be held and a wire would be strung from the telegraph office to the hall to report the returns.

Often the affair would be pleasantly interrupted with an exhibition by Pete Frison as a clog dancer and black face comedian.

The musicians who played were Clint Benbow on the clarinet and Genie Hyrup at the piano. Sometimes the McHugh sisters, Sis and Maggie, would come down from Aspen. Hugh McCabe often played, also. The square dance callers were Mark Shippe, Van Gilbert, and Pete McCabe. Georgina Bates remembers one of Mark Shippe's calls as "swing that girl, that pretty little girl, with a hole in the heel of her stocking."

Another unique form of entertaining girls was to take them on railway handcar rides. The men would push the cars with the girls on them up the Aspen branch to No. 2 bridge and then coast back. They had to brake the cars with a club to keep them from going too fast and jumping the track. This unusual

Minstrel Show
By Basalt Dramatic Club
I. O. O. F. Hall, Basalt, April 7

PART 1

CHORUS

Madge Cadwell, Emma Carlson, Sopranos
Mrs. G. R. Jarvis, Contralto.
Mrs. Scott Williamson, Alto.
E. E. Kennedy, Tenor
Harry Brawner, Will Oulds, Baritone
G. R. Jarvis, 1st Bass   Van Gilbert, 2nd Bass
Miss Edith Bailey, Pianist

E. E. Kennedy, Interlocutor
Harry Brawner   Bones   George Jarvis
Van Gilbert   Tambo   Will Oulds

PART 2

Reading — Miss Ina McMahon
Duet — Mrs. S. Williamson, Harry Brawner
Banjo Solo — Harry Brawner
Comedy Sketch:
George Jarvis — William Oulds

AFTERPIECE

"THE COMING MAN"

CAST

Mr. Gates - - Ace Harris
Mrs. Gates - - Mrs. G. R. Jarvis
Mark Anthony - - H. Brawner
Joacamus Hardbeck - Van Gilbert

Admission— Adults 25c   Children 15c
ITEM PRINT

photo from Ford Gilbert

BIG TURKEY SHOOT
Basalt, Colo., SUNDAY, Nov. 20th 1910
100 BIG TURKEYS.
Young Shoats, Geese & Ducks.
ONE 100 Yard RANGE
ONE 200 Yard RANGE
Under Management of
Bill Bogue and "Pug" Gilbert.
Hot Coffee and Sandwiches
•••••••• Served Free ••••••••

photo from Ford Gilbert

A mess of three to eight pound trout caught in the Frying Pan river in the early days.

photo from George Luchsinger

way of riding was, of course, too dangerous to be attempted on the main tracks. It was only for the branch line where they knew exactly when trains were coming.

The cowboys, mostly of the Capitol Creek region, provided what was entertainment to some, but a source of great irritation to the "city fathers." Lucy and I remember how these cowboys would ride recklessly and rapidly through the town yelling and shooting off their "six-shooters." Once the town marshall put one of them in the "cooler," but in the night the other cowboys came back and released him. These escapades were often the cause of an outburst of editorial ire in the Basalt *Journal*.

When marriages occurred the charivari was the source of entertainment to principals and spectators alike, and did not end until the bridegroom handed out treats of candy and cigars. At one marriage where ice cream was to be served the boys sneaked in on the back porch and stole the full freezer, carting it off elsewhere for consumption by non-invited wedding guests.

A few people in town had gramophones with the round cylinder records and would entertain guests on Sunday afternoon or evening.

Fishing

It was not uncommon for us boys to go fishing right in town as soon as school let out for the day and catch enough trout for supper or breakfast for the family. Sometimes after a cloudburst the river would be so filled with mud the fish could not breathe. Then we could throw them out of the water with a shovel.

In my opinion, some of the best fishermen on the Frying Pan were my friends Forest Newkirk, Jake Freiler, Chris Hyrup, Rye Oulds, Arthur Bates, and Dave Hall. Many an evening we saw Dad Sherward or Otmar Luchsinger going up the railroad track shouldering the longest straight bamboo pole they could find. Otmar once took the prize in the *Denver Post* Contest for the largest trout caught that week in Colorado.

The co-author of this book, my brother Ralph, was keen on fishing at an early age, but his outburst of temper and disappointment when a trout got away would have made his Sunday School teacher feel that her work was in vain if she had heard him!

School

We were no angels in school, yet strict discipline at home kept us pretty much in line. One teacher, in order to maintain quiet

C. L. D. collection

Basalt Baseball Team, about 1902. Standing, left to right: Flavine Arbaney, Jim Nelson, Bramlet Willits, Levi Chatfield and Ernest Dwyer. Seated: Bill Ould, _____, Glen Dooling and Jim Tierney.

in the class-room, and to stop any whispering, put the boys and girls together in double seats. I was full of anguish; I well remember, having to sit with Ophelia Miller. Another teacher smacked the palms of our hands with a rubber ruler as punishment. Father made it clear to us that if we misbehaved in school he would follow up with another spanking at home.

I can remember only one act of vandalism in our school. When I was about ten and in the fifth grade, two boys broke into the school-house and did a great deal of damage. They tore all books except those belonging to their sister. Then they threw horse shoes at the breakable slate blackboards, ruining many.

Three Drinking Episodes

Arthur Bates recalls two comical incidents that merit telling. Two prominent ranchers from the El Jebel area arranged to go to Basalt together to buy groceries, each furnishing a horse to make a team to draw the wagon. When ready to go home with their heavy load of purchases they decided to stop by a saloon for a drink first. Well, one drink led to another and then to an argument. One of the ranchers left abruptly, unhitched his own horse from the team, and rode it home harness and all, abandoning the loaded wagon and other horse to his companion. We are still wondering, "Who got the groceries?"

On another occasion one of the same men who enjoyed a drink or two when in town stayed in the saloon too long to suit his impatient son. After waiting a while and urging his father to get going home, the boy with mischief in his head turned the saddle around on his dad's horse, then left for home on his own mount. Finally when the father came from the saloon, somewhat befuddled by his imbibing, he walked around and around his horse, utterly bewildered. Then he asked someone to help him on. The horse, anxious to get home and be fed, started out at a brisk gallop—the rider clinging to the saddle-horn sitting in the backward position all the way. Needless to say, there were loud cheers and laughs from the amazed by-standers.

One drinking incident, however, did not turn out so well, in fact, tragically. Everett Carlson told me that he and my brother, Myron, and Alfred Hyrup witnessed an unusual event. One day a man came by in front of our house and produced a bottle of whiskey from his pocket. He then began to regale the boys with his drinking prowess and bragged that he could drink the entire contents of the bottle within a few minutes. He lived up to his boast, but paid for it with his life, by quickly succumbing before the startled eyes of the youngsters.

Whitenack Falls

Anna Sloss has reminded us about the Whitenack Falls which once was marked by a sign just above Basalt near the railroad track. At one time as a diversion Mr. Whitenack built a few wooden seats and an overhead shelter for picnics at the location where the water from the Basalt water-supply spring came down the hillside over the falls. With the wear of years and vandalism this structure has disappeared.

Fourth of July and Firecrackers

In our boyhood there were no restrictions on the sale of firecrackers. We had almost the same types as today—skyrockets, Roman candles, torpedoes, snakes, and firecrackers of all sizes. Anyone could buy them. Believe it or not, some were almost a foot long and over an inch in diameter; one young man lost a couple of fingers by shooting one. The skyrockets were set off by our father and the neighbors in home-made v-shaped wooden shutes, usually up by the Bates residence or at the

Basalt picnic grove. Once Father lit a firecracker in the house intending to throw it out the door, but the screen was locked, and he ended up with a burned hand.

The picnic grove where the Fourth of July celebrations were held was just south of the cement bridge, between the river and the hill. There was also a horse-racing and bicycle track in this area, as well as high swings for the children.

The baseball field was between the hotel and the river. The boys played the Aspen and Carbondale teams; more games would have been played except for the transportation problem of the time.

Threshing Machines

One of the first threshing machines I remember was being used at Sam Cramer's. The power was generated by four or five teams of horses going around in a circle. A man with a long whip stood in the center and kept urging the horses along. Later, an upright steam boiler pulled by horses generated the power. The first steam tractor outfits were owned by George and Ben Hotz. The Williams brothers of Snowmass also had a steam outfit. Eventually, they bought an oil-powered tractor and Ralph and Raymond Harris operated it for a while. It was called a Rumley Oil Pull.

Helping with Washing

Early each Monday morning before going to school it was our job to run the manually operated washing machine our mother owned. The washing machines of the day were of the rotary, stick, or cradle type, but all took "elbow-grease". We also filled the copper wash-boilers with water and put them on the kitchen range to heat. Water for the wash tubs was carried in from the hydrants and later it had to be carried out again.

Before the day of insecticides our mother would sprinkle the sudsy water on the rose bushes with a small whisk broom—and it apparently worked, judging by her yellow rose bush.

All garments we hung on the line to dry; there were no dryers then.

Carnival

One time a carnival came to Basalt, and as one of the attractions the barker offered fifty dollars to anyone who could ride their prize bucking mule. Newt Henry offered to try and was successful. The manager attempted to renege, but when the roundhouse boys, the cowboys, and other volunteers showed up like a small army, the money was handed over "pronto". This vigilante group also retrieved a lantern that had been stolen from Charles Fouse by one of the roustabouts.

Hand-powered Machines

A chore with a happy reward on Sundays, birthday parties, and holidays was to turn the handle of the freezer for home-made ice-cream. In spite of discoveries and inventions in ice-cream making, there wasn't then and there isn't today any comparison between the home-made and the "boughten" product.

In addition to hand-run machines, we had foot-machines. My mother had a well-deserved reputation as a seamstress and made many articles of clothing for our family and her friends. This was all done, of course, on a sewing-machine run by foot or leg power. And it might be mentioned that the dentists then not only held the drill, but provided the motive power with their feet.

Another interesting hand-operated machine was the milk-shake apparatus which turned the container. These we watched with eager anticipation when our father treated us at Stiffler's, Carlson's, or Zimmerman's.

Knitting and Underwear

Our mother knitted many pairs of stockings and socks. We used to hold the skeins on our hands while she wound the yarn up on a ball. (I have often wondered why the stores didn't sell the yarn already wound into balls.)

There was one reason we rather hated to see winter come. It was because of the woolen underwear which caused our skin to itch so annoyingly. We didn't have the non-itchy long cotton-lined underwear of today. In warm weather we wore "B.V.D.'s", a combination garment, not the two piece suits of today.

Smith's Ranch and Mountain Climbing

Our family from time to time would take trips to the Smith ranch, going by wagon sometimes up around the county road, or on foot up Toner Creek from the Midland tracks. On one such visit to the Smith Ranch, when our cousin, Clara Danielson, was visiting us from Iowa, we took her on a climb to the amphi-theatre. As we were crossing a place of loose shale, Lucy and

Clara began to slide. If we had not had a rope to throw to them, they would have fallen at least one hundred feet.

Miscellaneous

Once when two sheepherders were accompanying their flocks on a stock train they went walking about in the town for exercise, when their interest in the people of Basalt was interpreted by one of the engineers as making improper advances to his wife; whereupon he shot and killed them both. Although the townspeople felt the murders were unjustified, the railroader was cleared at the trial and received no sentence.

At one time William Conerty believed someone was stealing the coal from his shed and, in his anger, he set a bear trap in the door entry. Mrs. Conerty, however, hearing of this, insisted that it be removed and her pleadings prevailed.

When the weather was very, very cold and the snow was on the ground, one would hear the high-pitched creaking of the iron tires as the wagons passed down the street. Many times one's own feet would give the same sound in a lesser degree.

At one time it seemed that everyone was raising Belgian hares. I believe Colonel Stiffler introduced them into Basalt. I had thirty or forty and was careful to cover their cages with wire netting. One morning I found a cat in with my rabbits that had killed most of the young ones. You can be sure that cat did not live to get into any other pens.

Lucksinger's fish pond below town was a fine place for us kids to get cattails. We would soak them in kerosene and carry them at night as torches.

Two neighboring ranchers got into trouble over the cattle running over the other's property. They were having many arguments about it and one day Mr. Caine pulled out a gun and shot Tom Houston. Later Nash and Swartz, who owned the Houston ranch, gave Caine a right-of-way if he would fence it.

There used to be lots of trouble over water-rights, but I can't recall any particular cases of violence.

WRECKS AND ACCIDENTS

This section of my memories will deal largely with accidents, wrecks and other events on the Midland, as experienced not only by myself, but also by my father, uncles and fellow employees.

Arthur Bates

We can start the record in no better fashion than by telling some of the things that happened to Arthur Bates. All of these events are unusual, but two in particular seem almost unbelievable.

As his engine was crossing the Lyle Creek bridge going up toward Ivanhoe, while shoveling coal into the firebox, Art slipped on the apron in the gangway between boiler and tender. He fell off the engine on the upper left side and landed on a steep slope of ice and snow, with the result that he slid under the bridge to the hillside below the track. Fortunately, Engineer Stiffler happened to be looking that way and saw his fireman where he least expected him to be. Automatically, he pushed in the throttle, stopped the train and permitted his uninjured partner to board the engine. If he had fallen on either side of the bridge, he would have been thrown from the wall of snow on the upper bank against the tender wheels, and would have been killed.

Another time when Art was firing Engine 5 for Engineer Dooling on a trip up the hill from Arkansas Junction to Busk he had an equally miraculous escape from death. As he was standing in the gangway the draw bar between the boiler and tender broke allowing him to fall between. This occurred on a drag going only seven or eight miles an hour. The breaking of the connection automatically set the brakes on the rear of the train, but the engine, having steam brakes, kept moving. This left a space so that when Art fortunately landed on his feet, he spryly jumped out of danger off the track. He must have held a charmed life!

A similar narrow escape happened to Andy Wilson. He was shaking the grates when the shaker bar broke and caused him to fall off the engine out the side of the gangway. Fortunately, they were traveling over a fill and he fell onto the soft cinders, so that he just got a good roll instead of a possible serious impact with large boulders immediately ahead of or behind the fill.

Denver Public Library Western collection.

Hoodoo Engine No. 22 as it appeared after a wreck.

Hoodoo Engine No. 22

Nearly all railroads had an engine that was considered a hoodoo; on the Midland this was the No. 22. It was involved in three of the worst wrecks on the line.

Once Conerty turned her over at Wheeler on No. 3 when a freight train was not in the clear on a siding. Another day when someone left the stub switch lined up for the roundhouse at Cardiff, the No. 22 left the rails and ditched. Bill Bates was engineer that time. He was also running her the time a large boulder came down the hillside near Emma and threw the track out of line. Again the No. 22 went onto her side and almost down into the Roaring Fork river.

Our father had several harrowing experiences. The worst occurred near Rifle when two freights collided because the dispatcher made a mistake and let a train out of Newcastle, which should have been held there for the Midland freight going east. Fred Stiffler was on the No. 32 as the head engine helper and father was on the Hoodoo 22 on the train engine. The impact shoved the No. 22 back onto the floors of the tender and the first stock car. It seems impossible that this could be true but we are showing pictures as proof. This is one of the most unusual railroad pictures ever taken. The No. 22 was pulled back into Rifle that way before being let down on the rails.

Miraculously, our father was only slightly injured, but the

(PRIZE-WINNER.) REMARKABLE DOUBLE-ENDER RAILWAY COLLISION AT RIFLE, COL.—*Garrison, Rifle, Col.*

from Frank Leslie's **Illustrated Newspaper,** Dec. 25, 1902.
Denver Public Library Western collection.

The result of the collision of two freight trains at Rifle, Colorado. Engineer Andrew Danielson escaped injury but his fireman, Thorpe, was killed.

engineer of the second engine, Fred Stiffler, was badly hurt and so affected by the memory of the horrible experience that he quit railroading and never went back to it. Father's fireman, a man named Thorpe, was killed. Richardson, the other fireman, missed serious injury.

Andrew Danielson

Arthur Bates tells of the time that he and my father got a train down from Ivanhoe to Sellar in an unusual fashion. After leaving the top of the hill and the train had picked up some momentum, father set the moderate amount of air on the brakes in the customary manner, but the train did not respond by slowing down. He therefore signalled to the brakeman the customary

A closer view of Engine No. 22 taken at the same time as the above picture.

C. L. D. collection

D. H. Gerbaz collection

Tender of Colorado Midland Engine No. 303 below Hell Gate, 1963.

warning consisting of one long blast of the whistle. The head and rear brakemen then, at great risk to their lives, started to walk on top of the fast moving cars. Getting from car to car, they began setting hand brakes by turning the brake wheel on each car with the heavy club they had for this purpose. There is a picture of this operation in Beebe's book, *Mixed Trains Daily*.

At the same time father gave the air brakes the "big hole"; that is, a sudden release of all the air available. For several miles it was a race of courage and strength by the brakemen, and expert air handling by Engineer Danielson as to whether the train would be a runaway or would be successfully stopped. Fortunately, it was finally stopped, but to get started again some of the hand brakes had to be released and some of the air allowed to leak off. Then the combination of hand brakes and "big hole" on the engine had to be enacted repeatedly until the train was down the hill. A helluva way to get a train down a mountain grade!

Albert Danielson

Two major accidents involved our Uncle Albert; one in which he had a close call, and the other resulting in his death.

The first was when Engine 35 blew up at Basalt while waiting on the siding for passing another train. No sooner had Engineer

C. L. D. collection

Wreck of Engine No. 33, in the Roaring Fork river, one fourth mile below Basalt. Engineer Andrew Danielson and his fireman both jumped to safety.

Albert Danielson gone to have a soda at the drug store and Fireman Rhodie Hyrup had gone to the storeroom for some supplies than she gave way with a mighty roar, breaking many windows on Main Street and bringing all the inhabitants on the run to the site of the accident. Charlie Peterson, who was working in the roundhouse, and an unidentified girl up by the Odd Fellows Hall, were struck by debris, but neither was seriously injured. The boiler, firebox, wheels and tender all went in different directions. While there has been some intimation of carelessness in letting her go dry, the Interstate Commerce Commission, in its investigation, found over thirty adjacent stay-bolts broken which could easily account for the explosion. This occurred on August 15, 1896.

Uncle Albert was killed about a mile above Lime Creek on January 2, 1897. Sometimes, in order to facilitate meeting of trains, two light helper-engines on their way back from Ivanhoe would couple together and the lead engineer handle the air for both. Also, the engineer or fireman on the second engine could then take a nap. On the fatal day Uncle Albert was the lead engineer and was evidently working the water-injector. In looking out of the gangway—as was the custom—to see whether any water or steam was coming out of the exit-pipe near the rails, he apparently forgot about the rock banks that were so close to the track on the upper side. It is presumed that he struck his head on a protruding rock, for he was found dead in the snow from a skull fracture. His fireman, Gert Rhodes, missed him from the cab when he noticed that the boiler was getting too full of water.

In similar accidents, three firemen, Ray Trout, Joe Barrett and McManus, were killed on the bridge over the outlet of Turquois Lake. As this bridge was not very far out of Arkansas Junction, a fireman would be just getting his fire built up. The bridge did not have the usual clearance and could be easily overlooked when he looked out of the gangway. Barrett was firing for Mike Walsh and had helped a train to Ivanhoe. When Mike went to get his orders at Arkansas Junction, he found Barrett dead in the cab. He had been hit on the head. This was on January 28, 1914. Ray Trout was killed there on December 29, 1910. He was married to Jessie Harvey. The date of McManus's death is not known; the information was given to me by Leo Heller.

Clarence Danielson

One time a freight train had a wreck near the Old Maid's Ranch just east of El Jebel, caused by a broken wheel. Along with other merchandise, two cars of oysters never arrived on the west coast. We kids took a large number home in buckets and put them in the rain-barrels used in that day. In the new environment, they did not survive long.

The old water stand pipe at Thomasville, formerly used for helper engines, once came in mighty handy. Art Bates was on a rotary snow plow and I had the engine pushing the rotary. When the pilot attempted to raise the ice cutter and flanger for the switch at Meredith, he did not get them high enough and the flanger went into the ditch. We were there so long trying to get the flanger out that we were getting low on water in the tank. We went to Thomasville and tried out the obsolete stand pipe and, to our great satisfaction, it worked, saving us a trip to Ruedi.

One wreck where I almost got mine was at the old Humphrey switch. The pony trucks on Engine 6 jumped off above Hell Gate and we were unable to detect it because of ice on the track. We had slowed down to meet a train at Mallon and when we hit the frog at Humphrey, the 6 spot left the rails with a car chasing Conductor Shanks over boulders by lantern light. I jumped out of the cab and landed in the snow up to my waist.

The engine didn't turn over, luckily for me. The No. 6 had been reported by Engineer Jim Fahey several times as not having enough weight on the pony trucks. Father was on a helper engine at Mallon on the train we were to meet and he and a section boss walked back to find only six track bolts broken. It was evident that Jim Fahey knew what he was reporting.

A similar wreck occurred at Newcastle when the pony trucks split the switch when taking the Colorado Midland lead. The pony trucks went up the Denver and Rio Grande main track. When the engine turned over Bobby Walters was crushed to death between the engine and the tank and a porter was scalded. Fred Willis, the engineer, had his boy on the engine but both were uninjured, as was Clarence Dearing who was deadheading.

Late one spring I was firing for Farquhar on No. 3 and the Rotary was called to go with us to Busk. When we got to Arkansas Junction we were coupled together with a three engine freight. Thus we had one engine on the rotary plow, one engine on No. 3, and three engines on the freight. There had been about a foot of heavy wet snow and the sun had come out and there was no wind. The plow threw an arc of snow about two-hundred feet down the hill and it looked like a great ostrich plume. I wish I had a moving picture of that trip; that combination of rotary, freight and passenger trains would be an historic photographic gem.

One thing that the firemen and engineers got into their contract was that they could mark up rest when they got in from a trip if they didn't feel able to go out again. It was not unusual to be on the road twenty-four hours between Basalt and Grand Junction. We would be four or five hours switching and unload-

ing freight from several cars (peddlers) at nearly every station. Then, before we had had sufficient rest, we would be called to go back. When the sixteen-hour law passed it helped a lot but, at the last, the dispatcher would give a man a message to proceed, regardless.

Other wrecks in which our father was involved are mentioned elsewhere.

I was on one train involved in a costly wreck that started at Sellar at night. We had cut off our train above the wye and had backed in on a cut of refrigerators on the passing track. The brakeman had not set the hand brakes tight enough and when the air leaked off they ran by us and left the track between there and Nast at about the same place where the 301 blew up. If I remember right, there were three cars of merchandise, two cars of shelled corn, one car of gasoline, two cars of beer, and two cars of cement among the eleven cars. The rear truck of the caboose was the only thing left on the rails. You can be sure all the men working on clearing up the wreck made good use of the wrecked beer cars. The gasoline took fire and burned the hillside down to the lower track and lit up the whole country as bright as day.

At a time when the men were usually assigned to a certain engine, they really took pride in it and kept it shined. Later when the men were assigned to a pool they were not so interested and finally got an agreement with the railroad to have wipers do this work. We remember that our father ran the No. 302 and the No. 53 for long periods. On the "alkali run" (Basalt to Grand Junction) Bill Bates had the No. 23, Bill Conerty the No. 25, and Fred Willis the No. 24.

Once in a while passengers from the train would get permission to ride an engine. It always gave the engineer and firemen a thrill when some of these passengers were ladies and sat beside them in the cab. Some of the whistles weren't made by the engine, and the specifications for the girl's construction were often noted. The throb of the air pump was, I fear, sometimes confused with the fireman's pulse. A reference to being "well-stacked" didn't apply to the engine.

On one occasion when four ladies got on at Sellars and rode to Ivanhoe on a Shriner's Special, Dave Cuthbert and I were very envious of the "rocks" worn on the fingers of these ladies. We found it difficult to stay in front of the firebox door shoveling in the coal to keep the engine steaming, when the girls in the cab were so much more interesting.

Collisions

Three major collisions occurred on the west end of the Midland. One was near Akin, one at Newcastle, and one at Basalt.

In the early '90's the Colorado Midland ran excursions from Leadville, Aspen, and the Grand River valley to Glenwood for a day in the pool and at the Hotel Colorado. They were known as "laundry trains" because people were all dressed up in their best bib-and-tucker.

On July 17, 1890, when I was only three years old, one such train was on the wye at Basalt, when an engine being taken from the roundhouse sideswiped the coaches. A boiler check was broken off the engine, releasing live steam under great pressure into one of the coaches, scalding and suffocating to death fourteen passengers and injuring many others. One was a sister of Jim Phelan. In the voluminous correspondence we have had with many former Basalt residents the one thing most often mentioned has been the memory their parents had of hearing the agonizing screams of those being scalded. Our parents, too, frequently told of it.

Another ghastly collision occurred in September, 1897, when a Midland stock train struck a Rio Grande passenger train head-on near Newcastle. Engineer Ostrander and Fireman Hynds were both killed. Of course, the cattle were almost all lost but the real tragedy was due to the demolishing and burning of the wooden coaches on the passenger train. The estimated death list varies

A type of helper engine. There were six of this class used on the Colorado Midland Railroad.

100 Clarence's Memories

C. L. D. collection

A wreck just below Seven Castles.

The wreck of Engine No. 2 at the edge of Lake Ivanhoe.

from John R. Smith, Minturn, Colo.

from twenty-five to one hundred people. The hoodoo Engine 22 figured in this wreck also.

A major collision at Akin was described by Andrew Danielson. Jack Clegg and Bill Bates collided there due to the fact that Clegg had placed a flag brakeman on a train ahead to hold Bates on No. 4 at Akin. The brakeman failed to get off and tell Bates that another train was following and when Clegg started to leave they hit head-on. A few years ago in the *Green Light,* published by the Denver and Rio Grande, there was an article reporting the finding of an engine truck in the Grand River at Akin at the bottom of DeBeque hill. No doubt it was left there at the time of this collision.

In another wreck Victor Biglow was killed November 24, 1906 in a collision at Hell Gate. Two light engines in some way overlooked No. 6. Joe Hall and George Norris were the engineers on the light engines and Art O'Neil and Reed were the firemen. Tom McNeil and Victor Biglow were on No. 6. Biglow and O'Neil were brothers-in-law.

An explosion that resulted fatally for Jack Clegg and Clarence Augustine destroyed Engine 301 about a mile above the Horsheshoe tank. Augustine's widow, formerly Miss Kniphausen, taught school in Basalt after his death.

Mud Slides

When the cloudbursts of summer would arrive, the mud slides in the cuts on the Midland would occur in mild degree, or heavy enough to block the tracks.

On one occasion there were several cloudbursts between Ruedi and Basalt, and several big slides resulted. I was coming down on a light helper and had stopped at Hopkins to pick up thirteen people who had sought shelter with Mr. and Mrs. Blair. Fishermen, wives and children filled the cab and gangway, and sat on the coal in the tender. Fortunately, I was able to get them to Basalt just in time.

My brother, Ralph, tells us elsewhere how he and Mr. Scandlan, both avid fishermen, stayed out on the Frying Pan too long, missing my engine, and had to get back to town by hand push-car and on foot. They were fishing one day on the south side of the river at Seven Castles when a big mud slide came down and dammed up the lower end of the Stillwater. They sized up the situation hurriedly and ran across the river bed below the dam of mud to get to the tracks,—a dangerous and foolish thing to do.

The account of our father's experience in hitting a mud slide just below Basalt on Engine 33 appears elsewhere under excerpts from the Basalt *Journal*.

Another mud slide was caused by a dam break instead of by rain. An earthen dam of the Smith Reservoir on Toner Creek on the east side of Black Mountain gave way allowing a wall of water to come pouring down the canyon. It tore out the earth in the fields of Smith Ranch and deposited it on the Midland rails. It happened on a clear day so that Engineer McNeil naturally was not alert to any danger of this sort. His engine was light after helping No. 4 and he struck the slide before he could stop, throwing the locomotive off the rails.

Tunnel Accidents

The Hagerman tunnel blockade was partly due to a broken blade on a snowplow, but primarily to one of the heaviest winter snowfalls on record. A whole trainload of cattle froze and starved to death, but no men were killed or injured, although trainmen and the laborers trying to clear the blockade endured terrible hardship and cold. Our Uncle Oscar Riebel was one who fought his way out through the snow. Some of the trainmen went to Leadville and then back to Basalt via Glenwood Springs and Emma on the Grande.

Sometimes the helpers from Basalt would need to go through to Leadville. Once, on the way back, due to smoke from their own engines and that of a previous train, our father and his fireman, Rube Hammond, were barely able to get to the exit at Ivanhoe. They were taken to Basalt on a caboose and had to remain in bed several days because of terrible headaches and nausea. It is reported that Dr. Kennedy resorted to the stomach pump several times to aid them in their distress.

Although the Hagerman tunnel was too short for gas fatalities, Hancock and McFarland died due to gas in the Busk-Ivanhoe tunnel. They were on the helper engine on the front of No. 5 going west. Somehow their engine broke loose from the train engine. Farquhar, the engineer, managed to get the angle cock on the pilot closed and to back the train to Busk. Hancock and McFarland, however, had inhaled so much smoke that they were unable to proceed to either end and perished in the smoke, largely from their own engine. A freight was

Following the explosion of Engine No. 35 at Basalt. The engine blew up just after Engineer Albert Danielson had gotten off.

Courtesy of Mr. Newberry

following No. 5 up the hill and when it reached Busk, Engineer Crawford and Fireman Bates volunteered to take their engine into the smoke-filled tunnel. They found Hancock and McFarland lying dead beside the track and had to leave them there, but were able to couple onto the helper engine the first time they tried and to back both engines to the east entrance. After the smoke had cleared somewhat, the section men took a push car into the tunnel and brought out the bodies.

Switching Accidents

Bill Bogue first went to firing and then transferred to braking later. He was on an east bound freight and was braking behind and they had a short time to make Bryant for No. 3. He had gotten out of the caboose and crossed over the refrigerator car to turn the angle cocks on both cars. He was attempting to uncouple them so the refrigerator car could be set out on Sweet's Spur for potato loadings. He evidently fell between the cars, for Art Bates, who was on the helper engine behind the caboose, saw him fall out from under the train. Bates tried to stop the train but was helpless because Bogue had the air cut off.

Ed Brown lost his life at Cardiff when caught between the couplings when trying to adjust them to make them lock.

While taking an engine around the wye at Basalt as a hostler helper, one of the Gregory boys, after throwing the switch, started to step on the pilot but slipped and went under the engine. Both legs were cut off by the wheels and he died soon afterwards from bleeding, shock and pain.

Between Nast and Sellars, a fireman by the name of Cran was thrown from the slick running board of a rough-riding engine when he went to start the air pump which had stopped. He was fatally injured. Farquhar was the engineer.

Pete Frison was killed in the Aspen yard. He was riding the head end of a cut of cars on a heavy grade when the engine began slipping. This gave the cars such a jolt that it threw Pete off. Before he could recover and get to his feet the cars ran over him.

A brakeman by the name of Hopfinger was watching a hot box by hanging out on the iron step of a freight car, when he hit his head on the bridge at Bigelow, killing him instantly.

Runaway Trains.

The most notable train runaway was the one on the coal branch out of Cardiff in the early morning of November 24,

1899, when Pete Hyrup was killed. Hyrup had been up there only once before and had some brakemen who had never made the trip on this four-percent grade. When Pete whistled off at the Spring Gulch tank, the brakemen let off the retainers and also released the hand-brakes. The train was soon out of control and miraculously ran nine miles before leaving the track a mile and a half above Cardiff near the Dearing ranch. When Engine 32 hit the bank, the boiler blew up. Clarence Dearing was then only a small boy but he recalls the loud explosion and remembers how he and his mother and brothers and sisters took a lantern and walked across the valley to view the wreckage after telephoning to Cardiff that something terrible had happened. Hyrup's fireman, a man by the name of Peryean was killed, also. The brakemen and conductors had jumped off in time and were not seriously injured.

Walter Packard was killed in a runaway on the Moyer Branch at Leadville.

Another big runaway of a freight train started at Busk on January 17, 1910. Harry Forrest was the engineer. The train got out of control just after they left Busk and ran about four miles before leaving the track. Forrest was in the hospital for a long time and they never found all of Fireman Marshall Rich's body. The rear brakeman, Hugh Fair, and Smith, the conductor, were found dead in the caboose. It was supposed that they had tried to cut it off but were unsuccessful. The head brakeman, Langlois, was found in a daze down by the creek. Of two hobos who were riding the train, one was killed and the other walked to Arkansas Junction to report the accident to Edwin Johnson, the telegrapher there, who later became Governor and U.S. Senator.

When the Colorado Midland was being built, a car full of rails got away and left the track at Brockway. Several laborers lost their lives at that time.

A car of coal once got loose at Basalt and ran all the way to Cardiff where it was turned up the coal branch. An engine was ready to follow it so that it would not then come back as a runaway in the opposite direction. Fortunately, there had been no trains on the main line.

SIGNALING

A discussion of signals is given on Page 56 of the February, 1964 *Train Magazine*. One can also find information in the

Rules and Regulations of the Operating Department of the various railroads.

It may be interesting to non-railroad people that those "in the know" could tell just which engineer was whistling his engine by the manner in which he did it. An engineer was particularly apt to whistle in a special way when he was coming into or going out of a town where his family lived and some engineers were prone to whistle a great deal more than others.

To those not familiar with the signals of an engine's whistle I will explain: one blast means "stop"; two long ones mean "start the train" (used particularly when there is more than one engine on a train); two short toots signify to the brakeman or conductor that the engineer has received the signals given him. Three whistles mean "back up"; four, "call in the flagman from the west or south" (who has been out on the track to flag any oncoming trains); and five, "call in the flagman from the east or north." To get the brakeman to protect the train at an emergency stop the engineer used one long and three short. Several repeated toots meant that the brakes were not releasing properly. One long blast, when traveling, indicated that the brakes were not holding and help was needed from the brakeman on the hand brakes. It was also used coming to a station.

One long and one short blast meant whistling for a curve, but two long and two short was the whistle used out on the open road and to indicate to people farther down the track or at crossings that a train was approaching. It was particularly in this last signal that the engineer would indicate his individuality by the manner in which he varied the length and intensity of the whistles. My mother and we boys always knew when my father was coming in by his own manner of whistling, and I would be able to tell which engine to flag when we were waiting for my father to take us back after a day's fishing.

This latter whistle has since been modified to be two long, a short, and a long; the last one to be prolonged until the train enters the crossing. It is, also, the whistle used repeatedly when trains are passing through heavily populated areas.

Having been an engineer myself, I know from personal experience that the manipulation of the whistle gave us as much pleasure as the listeners.

It was told to us by one Basalt resident that their dog even knew his master's whistle, but perhaps he only knew when to expect the engine back from a helper trip, as many a dog knows when school is out and goes to meet the children.

D. H. Gerbaz collection

The last passenger train leaving Basalt on Aug. 4, 1918. Original photo by R. O. Strong.

THE TRAGEDY OF THE CLOSING OF THE MIDLAND

The railroad's closing in 1918 was the cause of a reverse trend of "rags to riches" for many families. A few months previously everybody seemed to be prosperous. Business was booming; in 1917 Carlton and Penrose had just recently gone to great expense for improvements such as new locomotives and cars, oak ties, heavier steel rails, and, in October, a new coal chute for Basalt costing $50,000.

Never before had the Midland carried so much freight. Consequently there was a shortage of crews and of engines to move it. The son-in-law of President Wilson, William G. McAdoo, was given control by government order of all railroads for the war's duration and for some months after its expected end. He was Director General, and his authority seemed to go to his head. Instead of lightening the freight burden of the Midland to solve the dilemma, he suddenly ordered all freight to be routed over the Rio Grande in major part, with smaller amounts over the Santa Fe and the Union Pacific. The Midland business was ruined. It was left with only local hauling; not enough to justify its survival. There was hope by many that after the war was ended it could be given new life, but that was only wishful thinking and a dream on the part of the people and the region it had so benefitted. The last scheduled train left Grand Junction on the 4th of August, 1918, and on it were a number of saddened Basalt families leaving their homes for the hope of finding work in Colorado Springs or elsewhere, and transported at the railroad's expense.

Although the blow was tremendous to the owners and the stockholders, the real tragedy was to the employees. They had been well-paid and happy in their work. Men with long seniority found it difficult to find other jobs; young men had not had time to build up funds to tide them over. There was no other payroll to fall back on other than the income from the farms and ranches, and these people up the Frying Pan had great hardship in getting their produce to market. Most of the employees went eventually to other railroads; some stayed to work on ranches near Basalt; others migrated to Aspen, Glenwood Springs, and Leadville. At that time the ski business was unheard of in Aspen or anywhere else in our mountains.

Although the Midland was generous in transporting household goods and men and their families, no severance pay was granted. To top off the despair, a conductor on the East End took up a collection for hiring a lawyer to force some monetary settlement, then he absconded with the money. It took a long time for our town to recover. Today, however, because of the Aspen Institute, the Ruedi Dam, and good fishing, Basalt is larger and more prosperous than at any time in its history.

CHAPTER 4

Ralph's Memories

Fishing

This chapter describes events of my boyhood which impressed me. Among the most interesting of such adventures were experiences with trout fishing.

One of the highlights of my young life came with my graduation from the eighth grade at the age of thirteen. Up until that time I had used my brother's and father's second-hand split bamboo rods. I had at an early age ceased using a cane fishing pole, which was used so commonly by the old-timers. They used poles, partly because rods were unavailable and expensive, but partly because of their advantage in bait-fishing in high-water time.

As those who have done bait-fishing know, there is a secret in getting fish in this manner. With the long twelve-to-fifteen foot pole, one could get the bait behind a rock even in the middle of the river. One could also, except in brush, (where the pole was a disadvantage) reach the fish in a hole at the side of the stream. When the river is high in the spring, the fish just can't stay in swift water and will migrate to the holes, whereas in summer the fish get out in the riffles. Almost no hole is too small to catch a fish on bait in high-water time. Many, many times I have crawled through the brush, shortened my line to no more than twenty-four inches and then dropped the bait straight down in a pool not much more than a foot across and pulled out a beautiful eight-to-ten inch trout.

For a graduation present my parents promised me a complete fishing outfit, a rod, automatic reel, basket, flybook, leaders, and flies. At that time fishing coats were unheard of and a fisherman would have been ashamed to wear one. Fishing boots and waders, too, were used by no one around Basalt, and it was just as well, because in my eagerness, many a time, while wading in the river, I slipped and fell and got wet from head to foot. Without boots you can swim or work your way out; you are apt,

with boots full of water, to drown. (Only a fool wears boots in a boat on a lake.) It is well that my mother did not see how many times I fell in the river. My clothes had usually dried out before I arrived home.

To get back to my graduation gift—on the first day after I arrived home from my buying spree at the George Tritch Hardware Store, in Denver, I rose early, picked up a lunch prepared by my mother, and went forth to try my luck. I chose to fish "the other side" from Gabe Luchsinger's up past Mallory's below the ditches still in use for irrigation, and on up to "Thorough Cut." This terrain was difficult and rough for a boy to negotiate, but the beautiful holes were wonderful, especially the big hole in the bend at the upper end of my trip. There was usually not another fisherman on the river. I did not have to compete for holes, or find others scaring the fish ahead of me.

By a most unusual bit of luck, I chose a day when the trout were really hungry and waiting for my Royal Coachman and Yellow-bodied Grey Hackle. From hole after hole I pulled out beautiful fat fish; it seemed that I just couldn't miss. When I was about halfway along on my trip, I could tell that I was going to get my limit, which was twenty in those days! I therefore changed my strategy and did what I had never done before and have done on very few occasions since, namely, to throw back all those under nine or ten inches so that I would not go over my limit and I could fill my creel with larger fish (now unlawful). The result was that by the time I finished fishing the big hole I had the most beautiful mess of half- to three-quarter-pound speckled beauties you ever saw. They filled my basket without any of the usual wet grass put between. And they were all caught without benefit of a net. This manner of fishing is more sporting, for it gives the fish more of a chance, there is added excitement in it for the fisherman and it is a test of his fish-landing ability. What does it matter if one does get away once in a while?

The next job was to get home, but first I had to get this heavy basket, filled to the brim, back across the river or go back the way I came—which would have been exceedingly tiresome. Therefore, with a stick to steady me, I slowly waded the river, arrived at the north side, and climbed up on the railroad tracks. I was much more interested at the time in saving that basketful of fish than saving my life. I could have cleaned them and lessened the weight by two or three pounds, but the thought of detracting from the beauty of these trout couldn't be accepted. Carrying the heavy fish was really a burden, but even their weight added to my happiness.

Catching them was an ecstatic experience, but the best was yet to come. After fishing trips I always looked forward to showing off my catch to my mother and father when I arrived home, but on this particular occasion I was in seventh heaven. As I picked each Rainbow, Native, and Brook trout out of the basket and placed it in the dishpan, I was the happiest and proudest boy that ever lived. I remember that several were quite dark, and there is nothing prettier than a dark trout with bright red spots on the sides.

Five years later, when a freshman in the University of Colorado, at Boulder, I described this event so vividly in a theme in my English class for Miss McKeehan that I received the highest grade I ever had on an English paper in college. She even asked me to read it aloud to the other students. I wonder if class-mates Amy Pitkin Stearns and Ruth Colestock remember; they were in Miss McKeehan's class with me.

Just for memory's sake I repeated that trip again in the summer of 1962 and caught three puny fish about eight inches long. By some odd chance, in one of those holes a nearly two-pound rainbow came up and curved out of the water for a bug, but he wasn't near my fly and wouldn't take it later, even after prolonged trying with several changes of flies. Was he laughing at me for not having caught his grandfather when I was a boy?

In talking to Dr. Duane Lahey, of Denver, I find that he and his father have also discovered this magic two miles of the Frying Pan, as I am sure many others have done.

Fishing was the occasion of many other memorable experiences. My brother Clarence and I had one novel manner of transportation to fishing waters, that I doubt has been shared by more than a handful of people in the whole United States. Our father was an engineer on a helper engine from Basalt to Ivanhoe for twenty-five years. The freight trains out of Basalt going east consisted of about sixteen to twenty-two cars, depending on the nature of the cargo. To get this train to the top, three engines were required, one smaller on the head end and two larger helpers, one in the middle and one on the rear. The grade varied from one to three percent. It ordinarily took about eight hours for the round trip on a "drag" (coal train) and about seven hours on "highball" freight (stock and fruit). The helpers would come back light (that is, without any cars), sometimes singly and sometimes coupled together, with the head engine setting the air brakes for both.

In the summer days when we boys were not working at a job and when a freight was scheduled to go up the hill in the morning, we would get on the engine with our father and ride up the Frying Pan. There were several fills in the track where there was relatively soft dirt with many cinders, but no boulders. Just before we would get to such a "jumping-off place," two to ten miles above Basalt, our father would push in the throttle on his engine, with the result that the other two engines would have to pull not only the train but his engine also up the steep grade. As a result, the train would slow down perceptibly—the other engineers knew why, because they had seen us get on my father's engine down in the yards in Basalt. As soon as the train had slowed down sufficiently, we would get down on the step on the side of the gangway on the engine and jump—often tumbling down the slope. As soon as my father saw we were safely off, he would throw our rods and baskets to us, and we were soon busy fishing by ourselves. This chance to fish with no one else near—almost unheard of in the crush of fishermen today—was a wonderful experience. Often only one of us went at a time, so he would fish all day alone.

Then, when we estimated that our father would be coming back light, we would stand out at the lower end of a long stretch on the railroad and wait. We could hear him whistling his engine a long way up the canyon; when he saw us he would stop and pick us up. We would then show off our fish to our father and the fireman. The day was complete after we had displayed our catch to our mother and given her a bunch of wild roses. This experience was shared by both my brothers, Clarence and Myron. Cal Queal tells of trains stopping anywhere, but actually only at stations. Perhaps trains stopped for employees "on the inside," but usually not for the general public.

While reminiscing with Walter Hyrup recently, we recalled two of our experiences together. One concerned the first fish I ever caught on a fly when a very small boy. I well remember the lure, a California hackle with the tricolor body. I also recall vividly the place and the hole just a short distance above Basalt. This ten-inch brilliantly colored Native was such a milestone in my fishing career that Walter says I ran all the way home to celebrate.

On another occasion, when we were a little older, we decided to fish all night in the Stillwater, a long, deep, quiet stretch of the Frying Pan at Seven Castles, hoping to catch a big one on bait. We built a fire beside the stream, in order to attract the fish, and then sat down holding our rods and anticipating a bite. Alas, we were to be sadly disappointed, for we had none at all— only mosquito bites. Finally at three in the morning we gave up and went to bed at his mother's cabin on her ranch. (Incidentally, in my boyhood, I never did catch a fish weighing over a pound. I have caught three-pounders since, one during a heavy hail storm on the Conejos River in southern Colorado, and without a hat. That was quite an experience.)

While I was a small boy I used to hear about the fabulous fishing at Trapper's Lake. In those days it was not easy to reach and the report was that one caught a fish every cast and three fish if you had three flies on. Much to our regret, Clarence and I never had the opportunity to go there. What a memory that would have been! Trapper's Lake is no longer quite such an excellent fishing place, because there is a car-park nearby.

Two years ago, however, I took a pack trip with the Sizemores, of Buford, Colorado, to Marvine Lake and helped my grandson, Luke, then twelve years old, land a two-pound trout from a boat. Fortunately, I was able to take some excellent color slides of the exciting action for us both to enjoy. The scenery in that area is incomparable!

Although I had no qualms of conscience as a boy in using bait, I have long ago joined the snobbish crowd of fly-fishermen; I still teach my small grandchildren how to use bait. In my boyhood days the only fish put in the river were small fry or fingerlings. Most of these were shipped from Leadville and put in the river by the trainmen rather than by any game warden. The present practice of fishing with bait for fish that have been

R. W. D. Collection

Clara Danielson with her favorite yellow rosebush.

raised to legal catching size in a fish hatchery, and conditioned to feeding, seems hardly a sport. It is just plain murder.

The story has been told so many times that there must be some truth in it that there are people who now watch for fish trucks to go out from hatcheries—or in some other manner find out when they are to leave—and then go and clean out a hole immediately after it has been planted. Perhaps fishing in a planted area should be restricted for one to two weeks or at least the fish placed very thinly over long distances. The game and fish department has no doubt given much thought to this problem; I don't know what their plans are. Incidentally, another practice that irks me is the use of salmon eggs; they ought to be prohibited for many obvious reasons.

As I look back on it, I am amazed how my parents let me, as a very small child, go fishing alone in the rushing Frying Pan and Roaring Fork—which I am sure I would fear to have my own boy do. An interesting sidelight on this is the memory of my inability to understand at the time why Art Bates and Clarence never wanted me to tag along when they went fishing. I realize now, of course, that there was no more devastating robber of a good time for Clarence, in fly-fishing especially, than to eternally have to keep his mind on whether his small-fry brother was falling in the river. Even worse, a little boy sees no reason at all why he shouldn't skip flat rocks across a nice quiet pool of water. When a daddy or granddaddy takes a small child fishing, he should make a business of it and leave his own rod at home.

Flowers

Mention has been made of taking wild roses home to my mother. Perhaps a rabid fisherman shouldn't become sentimental about anything other than fish, but part of my joy was to stop along the river and drink in the sight and scent of these roses! They were irresistible to me, and often my creel would be filled with more roses than fish. I can still picture my mother as she placed them in water. Perhaps I imagine it, but I seem to remember noticing that her eyes were moist. At any rate, I am sure that the gift of wild flowers really meant more to her than looking at my fish, although she was always a most appreciative audience as I would take the fish out of my basket, one by one.

Other wild flowers gave me great pleasure, also. Most of them were on the Gabe Luchsinger and Mallory Ranches. That was one reason why "the other side" was my favorite place to fish. The bluebells (blue beardtongue, *Penstemon unilateralis*) and the pasque flowers *(Pulsatilla hirsutissima)* were more numerous up beyond the Cramer place toward Aspen. The flowers I remember best were the Rocky Mountain bee plant *(Cleome serrulata)*, the Indian paintbrush *(Castilleia miniata)*, the rose thistle *(Carduus undulatus)*, the mariposa lily *(Calochortus gunnisonii)*, the small evening primrose, the sessile and dwarf red and pink small-flowered "bread and butter," and the wild rose *(Rosa acicularis)*.

The bluebells we picked by the armload, and the pasque flowers (we called them anemones) we gathered in big bunches. In those days the few people who picked them made not the slightest dent, but now increasing numbers of people visit the open spaces and gather the blossoms. Unless something is done, they will be virtually eliminated. The danger in the "population explosion" is not that we won't be able to feed and house people, but that we will crowd out our recreation areas to the extent that we can never be quite alone and will see fewer wild flowers and wild animals as we travel. Although I once picked as many flowers as I cared to, (only a fraction, however, of those I stood and admired), I now cringe at the thought of such a great number of them being picked and pulled up by the roots by vacationers. Happily, most drivers refuse to slow down to pick a flower.

The lavender columbine—the state flower—was not abundant

at the Basalt altitude, but I saw many of them because the trainmen would pick them along the line from Nast to Ivanhoe when they stopped for a siding—or the light engines would stop long enough, if they were in the clear, for the men to pick a few to bring home. The cowboys, in riding for cattle in the upper ranges, would also bring down many of them.

I remember that I did not overlook the beauty of the few garden flowers around our house. We had a wonderful big yellow rose bush, golden glow, pansies, tulips and crocuses, and, above all, tiger lilies, which held a special fascination for me. The pleasure they gave me has been somehow considerably diminished since these flowers are to be seen in such profusion in parks and gardens. I can't recapture the joy I had in these familiar flowers in our yard. As a boy one flower I had an aversion to was the carnation, for we never saw it except at funerals, where it was much in use because it stood shipping from Aspen and Glenwood Springs better than any other. This dislike has, fortunately, been overcome because of the exquisite new color variations now produced by Colorado growers.

Mountains and Mountain Climbing

The residents of countless villages and towns in our country would feel very fortunate if they had even a small hill to look at and to climb near their homes. How lucky then are the people of my birthplace to have the ever-present view of two majestic mountain peaks of totally different conformations! Basalt has this setting in addition to a lovely wide green valley panorama in the foreground. I would dread to see houses take the place of the farms there.

By walking a short way above town to the north one can see in the southwest the symmetrical and lofty Mount Sopris with its granite gray color above timberline and forested slopes below. It was named for the early explorer, Captain Richard Sopris, great-grandfather of our Denver neighbor, Mrs. Clinton Woodend. During most of the year the summit remains snow-covered. It is unfortunate that the craggy 14,000 foot peaks in the Elk Range on the border of Pitkin and Gunnison Counties are hidden from view by the foothills to the south. However, they can be viewed by driving on the readily accessible automobile road from Emma to Snowmass which passes by the famous Trappist Monastery where the monks raise hay and cattle on their extensive holdings.

R. W. D. Collection

Box to discourage hens from setting. Photo taken on Lucksinger farm.

Just over the Frying Pan near Gabe Luchsinger's place, or near the school-house, one looks up to the northeast at Basalt Mountain, which is also known as Black Mountain. It is so named for the black volcanic lava (basalt) with which it is covered. It is topped by a sheer cliff and below that is a long sloping lava bed. One can see an eroded red and white scooped-out area above the old Dan German place, and below that some small foothill out-croppings also red and white in contrast to the lava. This view is ever interesting to me, and it becomes more so every time I see it.

When I was a boy I was unaware that there was anything higher than Basalt Mountain, but not long ago I took one of the most delightful trips of my life when I drove on the Red Tables road built by the U.S. Forest Service from the summit of Cottonwood Pass east almost to Wood's Lake. The road was built to fight the spruce-killing beetle by spraying the trees. From up there one can see, a long way down, the top of Black Mountain at the head of Cattle Creek, and the high ranges and lush valleys in great number in all directions. It is a view one can never forget.

When about thirteen, I took a trip that not many youngsters have made alone. One day, my mother packed my lunch and I started out and climbed the hill north of town almost to the old Kelly reservoir up on "little" Black Mountain, just west of Black Mountain. I then turned east and climbed over the lava bed at the foot of the cliff on Basalt (Black) Mountain, went on, and dropped down into the Smith ranch in the evening. The view was magnificent, but the trip was dangerous and my sense of triumph was keen. One thing struck me as peculiar—the presence of grouse out there in the bare volcanic rock. Then I realized they were there drinking out of the water pockets in the lava boulders.

Soil and Gardens

Although the hillside back of Basalt is largely yellowish clay, right in town the soil is very black. This blackness is due partly to the mountain earth of decayed leaves, and partly to volcanic ashes from nearby Basalt Mountain. Nearly every family had a vegetable garden in this wonderful black earth, even as the residents do today. The soil of the fields south of town and up the Frying Pan Valley is a rich beautiful red, which is ideal for raising Red McClure potatoes and it seems to have a special value for growing alfalfa. (See the Geology report by Dean P. G. Worcester elsewhere in this history.)

Drowning

About half a mile below Basalt, just below Jake Luchsinger's old place, was a side stream near the Roaring Fork. Across this and the main river was the Emma bridge; just below the bridge on the side stream was a deep hole where we boys used to go swimming. No one used swimming suits; we just hid under the bridge when people drove across.

One day, when I was just a beginner, I tried to swim across there but couldn't make it and went under. Only quick work by the other boys and Bill Hall got me out of the water in time. I still remember the fright and the terrible headache I had later.

The awful feeling of going down and not having enough strength and ability to come back to the top is frightening in the extreme; it probably accounts to this day for the fact that I am never at home in a boat on a lake. I am always happier when I get back to land. Later I did most of my learning to swim at the shallow end of the Glenwood pool.

Another favorite swimming hole was at Flat Rocks on the Frying Pan, just above the present Ranger Station, used mainly in late summer when the water is warmer.

Animals

We boys had the pleasure of keeping a variety of animals in our back yard. In the summertime we would catch chipmunks under a box, using a figure-four contrivance to trip it. (This figure-four would be whittled out by our father or ourselves.) When the chipmunk nibbled at the bait on one of the sticks, the box would fall down on a board. Then the real work began, to get the chipmunk out from under the box; sometimes he got away or gave us a good bite for our trouble.

Once my father heard of a large squirrel cage for sale in Leadville. He purchased it and brought it back on his engine for our yard. The cage contained a wheel and bars, and a nest so that young chipmunks could be raised. As we fed them, they became quite tame. We caught both the larger and the smaller types.

As we raised guinea pigs, we learned a good deal, noting the behavior of the male and female and the birth of the young. Some of the boys also caught and caged magpies, while some had rabbits.

We had from a dozen to two dozen chickens most of the time. This was quite a profitable venture since our parents bought the eggs from us, and we had no expenses for feed. Not only were the scraps from the table available for the hens, but our parents would buy wheat for them as well. We also had many pigeons in the upper part of our coal house.

As in most early towns, burros roamed the streets, seeming to belong to no one. We used to catch them and—I was about to say, ride them,—but those who know burros know that often, although you could get on them, they would have their own ideas about the ride, bucking you off or refusing to move.

Peddling Milk

Clarence and I both peddled milk for Gabe Luchsinger. We carried two cans, one of which had a quart measure as a cap. The customer would leave a covered five or ten-pound lard can at the door, and we would measure out the milk, taking in return a blue, red, or yellow ticket, according to the amount. The milk usually sold at twelve quarts for a dollar when I delivered, and sixteen when Clarence worked at an earlier date.

In addition to carrying the milk, we helped herd the cattle up on the south side of Black Mountain. The trail we took around the hillside below the Bates residence can still be seen. Cattle would often range up toward the spring on the mountainside, from which Basalt gets its water. The dairy cattle would be turned out on the hillside during the day and brought in in the evening.

We remember how Julia Luchsinger, Gabe's wife, used to pour the milk out into large pans and then skim off the cream after twelve hours. The butter, of course, was made in a churn worked by hand.

Section House

Opposite our house on the other side of the tracks was the house for the section men — all single, of course, except the boss, who lived close by. There was a heating stove in the center and bunks were all around the walls. Of course, there were no such things as sheets, and the blankets and quilts went months on end without being washed. Once in a while on Sunday, (they had six-day weeks then), the men would build a fire under a tub and a wash boiler and proceed to do their washing down by the river. Mrs. Danielson and I recently found marigolds growing in one of these old copper wash boilers at a filling station at the west boundary of Carbondale.

One interesting habit of these section men was that on pay day they would settle their board bill at their eating house and would then take the remainder of the money to the saloon and buy bottles of whiskey. Many would then lie in their bunks dead drunk until the liquor was gone, with the result that there was never any work done by the section gang for two or three days after each pay day.

Much to the embarrassment of our parents, we boys would go and pick up the empty bottles that were thrown out in the brush or left in the bunks, clean them inside and out, and take them back to the saloon to sell for a few cents a bottle. Needless to say, we usually avoided letting our parents know we were doing this.

Clara Danielson, mother of the authors.

R. W. D. Collection

One story I heard several times as a boy—possibly it was only a legend—was that one of these section men in the early days, while in an alcoholic stupor, fell through the poorly-built toilet floor or open seat and became almost entirely buried; only his head and arms were sticking out. When he was finally discovered, a rope was put under his arms to pull him out. He was then taken to the river by some good Samaritans for a thorough scrubbing.

Coasting and Skating

A thing in which the children in Basalt were fortunate was the coasting, sledding, (and even sleighing and bobsledding). We not only had our small sleds, but the older boys made bobsleds, using a plank to hold two sleds together. The riders sat on the plank with side sticks for their feet. The one in front did the guiding with ropes.

The coasting in Basalt is better than in eastern Colorado because there is more snow there. Furthermore, the hills are excellent, and in our day there were no automobiles to be a hazard. The danger was largely to pedestrians and sometimes to the teams of horses. There were even editorials in the paper about the carelessness of coasters. We coasted on the Bates hill, the Fahey hill, the White hill, and even down from Smith's residence to the post office. Skating was done on the few ponds available.

The big ski industry of the area had its preliminaries in the barrel staves that we fastened on our feet which allowed us to slide down the north side of White Hill in our amateurish, but happy, fashion.

Work Schedule

One of the first odd jobs I remember was when I was about eight years old. Miss Grace Hallock and Miss Irene Willits, two school teachers living next door to us, hired me to bring in coal and kindling for their stoves, to bring in water from the hydrant outside, and to carry out ashes, for which I received five or ten cents a day. They did not cheat me; that was what was usually paid at the time. At the end of the week I would put the dimes in a dime bank. Then when it was filled, I would give it to my father, who kept track of it in a book for me. There has never been a commercial bank in Basalt.

Also at a very early age I picked strawberries at two cents a quart box for the Gilberts and the Harveys, at a time when berries were much smaller than the varieties now grown. There was always rivalry between the country kids and those of the town for this job. One day Mr. Harvey fired me for putting green berries in the bottom of some of the boxes; but I had not done it. They had been sneaked in by the country kids, and Mr. Harvey believed them instead of me! I walked home, indignant, and with a heavy heart; the injustice of it was quite a blow to a small boy.

When I was entirely too young for such work (about fourteen), I picked potatoes on the Ollie Jacobs ranch near El Jebel, (now the U.S. Forest Service tree nursery.) Lifting half-bushel buckets of potatoes into the hand sorter was exhausting; if my parents had known how tired I was at bedtime, I am sure they would never have permitted it.

The summer of 1913 found me hoeing weeds for the Rhynes at Carbondale. An unusual attraction of working there was the presence of a cold spring in their underground milk and vegetable house. Here they fed beautiful large trout that would come upstream from the Roaring Fork River.

Also, I weeded the strawberry patch for Pug Gilbert and drove the horse-drawn delivery wagon for the grocery store.

For a while I sold the *Saturday Evening Post* and the small magazine *Grit*, but became discouraged when I found that, in order to push me to sell, they would frequently send me more copies than I ordered.

During the summer of 1915 I went back and worked at the Otto Hyrup ranch at Seven Castles, putting up hay, weeding potatoes, and grubbing out sagebrush and wild oak with a mattock, a combination cutting and prying instrument. Only one who has tried it knows how tough a sagebrush root can be!

During another summer vacation (1917) I worked for Alfred Sloss. I irrigated alfalfa, milked cows, put up hay, and drove cattle into the Woods Lake area, up Lime Creek from Thomasville. Sunday afternoons were set aside for trout-fishing in the Frying Pan, and I made good use of the time, the reader may be sure.

In the summer of 1918, the year the Midland ceased operations, I worked on the railroad with the "car-whackers" in repairing freight cars and in clearing up wrecks before I was drafted into the Army. There were many wrecks at the time because the roadbed had not been kept up. We would often work twelve to eighteen hours at a stretch on a wreck in order not to delay the trains any more than necessary.

Our Father's Nickname "Leaky"

Shoemaker has done a superb job in writing his book *The Roaring Fork Valley,* but he was incorrectly informed about one item. He states that one of the engineers was called "Leaky" because he took a cup and held it under a car of liquor that had been in a wreck. We boys well remember that our father was called "Leaky", but for a very different reason, which is verified by Walter Hyrup. Clarence was known as "Young Leaky".

Pledge of the Anti-Saloon League.

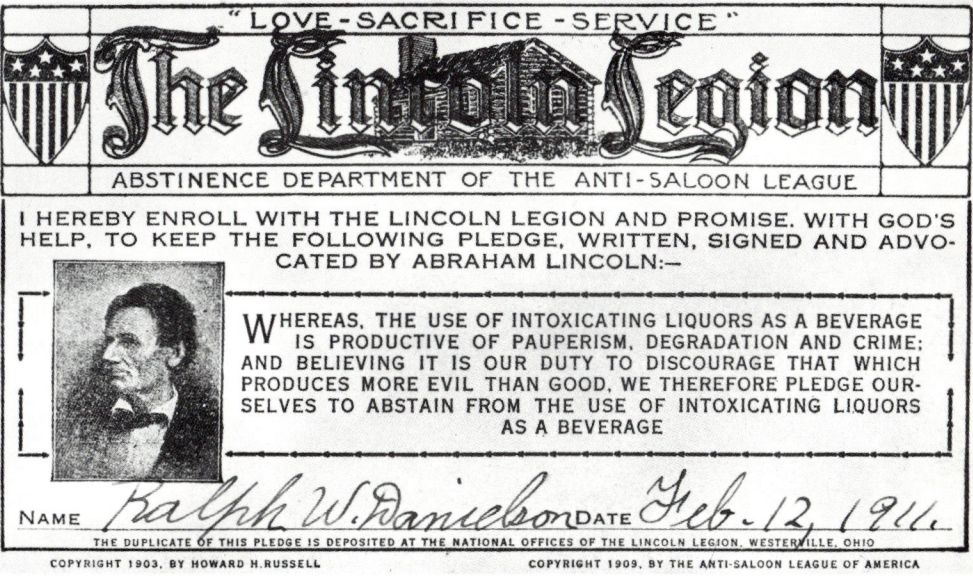

Father was given that nickname by Conductor Max Stiffler because he always insisted that the air brakes be tested for leaks before he took a train down the hill from Ivanhoe. After the engine or train once started down the grade, if the air brakes weren't working, it was usually too late to prevent a runaway, for when the train got going fast the brakeman could not walk on top of the freight cars to set the hand brakes. Hand brakes weren't very good anyhow. Perhaps it is a small point to others, but we'd like to put the record straight, since our father was a prohibitionist and a teetotaler.

Saloons

Father was a bitter enemy of the saloon, for he saw how many married men would cash their pay checks there each month and let the grocery bill go unpaid. He was on the City Council almost constantly for twenty-five years and during that time many of the elections hinged on the issue of local option. The two parties were called the Citizens and the Independents, more commonly known as the Drys and the Wets.

As a result of the feud with the saloon group, our father was once led into an altercation. One day, as we were waiting in front of the post office for the sorting of the mail after the train came in, a man walking nearby said loud enough so Father and others could hear it, "Danielson drinks just the same as the rest of us, but he just doesn't patronize the local places; he buys his liquor in other towns". The immediate result was that Father walked over and hit the talker so hard that he had to be carried to a nearby building to recuperate. Needless to say, I, a youngster, was elated, but somewhat scared, to see father so strongly uphold his cause.

In those days local option (that is, the decision as to whether or not there would be saloons) in a village, meant something, for to get a drink other than at home one had to walk, or ride a horse, or take the train to other towns.

In spite of our father's strong feelings about saloons, we know from hearsay and personal knowledge that most saloon-keepers were responsible, public-spirited individuals who took considerable interest in the welfare of the community.

Work for Our Mother

Part of our boyhood was spent in helping Mother. One of the jobs was to get down on hands and knees to scrub the linoleum each Saturday morning. In those days it was more difficult to keep houses clean because there were no paved streets and much mud was tracked into the house. And there were, of course, no vacuum cleaners, so that twice a year the carpets had to be taken up from the floor, hung on the line, and beaten with a wire apparatus on a handle—a dusty job indeed!

This work was more than compensated for by the weekly batch of fresh bread made by Mother. When we would come from school at noon, the aroma of the new baked bread and the melted butter on top was a never ending source of pleasure and delight for us boys—and I am sure for our father also.

Books and Magazines

Andrew Danielson was a voracious reader of magazines, particularly the *Review of Reviews* and the *Saturday Evening Post*. I remember how he would read aloud for hours to Mother while she did the ironing or other work.

In common with all other homes in Basalt, ours had very few books, but I remember we had a set of small books by Theodore Roosevelt that I read avidly. (My father was a great admirer of Teddy). The books that were popular, particularly with young people, were *The Winning of Barbara Worth,* by Harold Bell Wright, and *Riders of the Purple Sage, Lone Star Ranger,* and *Under the Tonto Rim,* by Zane Grey.

Wild Raspberry-picking Trip

One trip taken by our whole family was an unforgettable event. Just above Hopkins, where the Blairs had a quarry, were two large wild raspberry patches on the mountain side south of the river. My father, being an engineer, arranged with the trainmen on a freight train to let him load our tents and other equipment on a flatcar going out of Basalt. Our family and a few friends climbed on also. The train stopped at a camping site between the north side of the river and the railroad tracks and we hurriedly got our camping equipment off. Then for a delightful week we lived in tents, our father and we boys filling ten-pound cans with wild raspberries in the morning, and fishing for trout in the afternoon. No combination on earth can ever beat fried trout and biscuits with wild raspberry jam, washed down with coffee or milk.

In the afternoon my mother and the other ladies put up the fruit on a small camp stove fired by wood furnished by my father. At the end of the week she had canned whole berries and also made jam enough to fill sixty-five quarts. Then the Mason jars were placed into galvanized wash tubs and we made the trip home on another flatcar on another freight.

It was while we camped on these occasions that my father used to rouse us every morning with his cheery call of "Wake up! Wake up! Bear in the berry patch!"

Although wild raspberry jam is one of the ultimates in taste for gourmets or just plain eaters, there is one preserve recipe that in my opinion has it surpassed. This is a mixture of wild raspberries and service berries. This combines the distinctive tart and tangy taste of the raspberry with the sweeter, blander service berry—what we used to call "sarvis" berries. There were many service berries up along Toner Creek and the side of Basalt Mountain. In my opinion this recipe would take the prize hands down if ever offered in a national jam-making contest. Gladys Hough Wachob would vote for her mother's squaw-berry and wild cherry jelly.

My mother also put up many glasses of wild choke-cherry jelly every summer. I used to pick the cherries and sell them for twenty-five cents for a ten-pound lard bucketful, finding most of them over by August Naefe's.

Incidentally, in connection with "putting up" things, I remember how we used to make our own root-beer. We would prepare it in a clean copper washboiler, bottle it ourselves, and keep it in our cool cellar. The taste was always far better, for some reason, than the "boughten" variety.

Smith Ranch

Among my most pleasant recollections were the many trips I took on weekends with Clifford Smith, two years my senior, to feed the cattle in the winter on his father's ranch on Toner Creek. His parents and brother, Mr. and Mrs. J. A. Smith and Phil, would move to their home in Basalt in the winter, but they went

up to feed the cattle and horses each day. On Friday night after school, we would hitch Dan and Bell to a bobsled and drive to their ranch about four miles above town, on the road that was built around the hillside from Basalt to Ruedi along the Frying Pan. This ranch is now owned as an experimental acreage by the State Fish and Game Commission and is closed to traffic except during deer and elk season. Then on Saturday and Sunday we would be a welcome sight to the cattle as we fed them the hay and checked the creek to be sure water holes were open in the ice.

It would be dark when we arrived at the ranch-house and we would need to build a good wood fire to get the place warm and for cooking our supper. In the evening we would play "pitch" and then go to bed in cold beds and listen to the coyotes' "singing bark" outside.

The following incident is reported in the *Basalt Journal* for May 19, 1906:

> "Ralph Danielson accompanied Clifford Smith to the ranch last Friday night, staying over until Sunday. The two boys had quite an experience Saturday morning up on the ranch and the only wonder is that their eyes were not knocked off in the brush. They were strolling up the gulch and ran a deer into the corral, but while they were going for a rope, the animal made its escape to the hills. This is no fish story, either."

The fact that neither of us stayed at the gate or closed it will always be a sad commentary on our thinking.

Clifford Smith and I also made several overnight trips to the Smith reservoir at the head of Toner Creek to hunt grouse out in the forest to the east toward Shehi Park—a beautiful sight from the edge. With much pleasure I retraced this trip on horseback in 1962 with Dale Terrell, a pleasant and accommodating companion, the son of the game conservationist at Basalt. This reservoir was used to water cattle from the headwaters of Cattle Creek and to impound water for late summer irrigation on the Smith ranch.

Before we started on one such trip, Clifford came to me and put smoking and chewing tobacco in my pocket with the comment, "My parents will search me before I leave, but they won't search you." After we had eaten our lunch that evening up on the mountain beside our bedrolls, Clifford suggested that I take a chew of tobacco—the taste of which I really liked for about three minutes. Then I began to get dizzy. I was soon so sick to

R. W. D. Collection

The authors seated on an old sled on the Smith Ranch, 1963.

my stomach that I lost the meal just eaten and I believe several meals before. I thought I would die out there on top of Basalt Mountain; for a while I hoped I would. There at an early age I found out I was sensitive to nicotine; even now I can never smoke a cigar or more than one cigarette without nausea.

I was very fond of the Smith horses (mostly quarter horses), but three in particular stand out in my memory: Dan, the tall, strong gelding; Bell, the beautiful brown mare; and Rattler, a small saddle horse that belonged to Clifford. Mr. John Smith used to say he was ashamed the way he worked Dan, for he could be used as a saddle horse, as a buggy or sled horse, and as a work horse. He was a magnificent bay and it is too bad that he had not been kept as a stallion. When the Smiths told me later that Dan had died of colic in his stall, and how he had looked at them pleadingly, as much as to say "Can't you help me?" before he died, I felt the loss almost as much as if a human friend had passed away.

Bell, the mare, was a typical quarter horse, dark brown in color and of beautiful contour; in addition to doing road and heavy-duty work such as plowing, she presented them each year with a fine colt.

Rattler was rather large for a pony, probably a cross with a quarter horse, and was an excellent saddle horse for Clifford. On a couple of occasions when money was a little tight, the Smiths sold him, but each time, a few months later they would look out some morning and see him back, standing at the gate waiting to be let in.

R. W. D. Collection

Old hay wagon on the Smith Ranch.

Being a cowboy has been glamorized, but it was largely hard work, dangerous, cold, and fatiguing. Bob Cormack in the December 1962 issue of the *Denver Westerners Magazine,* in his article about Will James, has this to say: "Will James once said, 'It must be great to be a cowboy!' That's what a feller says to me one time. Ther'd a been only one way of answering: a chance for him to be a cowboy for a year or so."

Snow Slide—Aspen Branch

One winter we boys in the seventh and eighth grades heard that the rotary snow plow was going to clear out a big snow slide on the Aspen branch. We suddenly had a big desire to play hookey to see how it worked. We went down to the railroad yards and were just about to climb on a flat-car next to the plow when I looked ahead and, to my great consternation, saw my father was the engineer on the engine that would push the plow. I could tell that he saw me too, so there was nothing to do but go and speak to him. Imagine my pleasant surprise when, instead of reprimanding me, he merely said, "Well, if you want to go, you might as well get up in the cab here with me." This was only one of the many times I, as a child, rode with him, although theoretically it was against the rules.

Fannie Freiler

A death that occurred when I was only nine years of age affected me profoundly. Fannie Freiler, small granddaughter of

Mr. and Mrs. Gabe Luchsinger, and daughter of Henry Freiler, died of appendicitis on April 21, 1906. This was the first death that I remember well. I just couldn't believe or think of knowing that a girl I had gone to school with had died; and we all missed her acutely.

Barney Flynn

Above Basalt, because of the falling rocks in the canyon, trackwalkers would patrol the track at night. Regarding one such worker, the *Basalt Journal* had this to say on August 11, 1906, "Barney Flynn, an old timer in Basalt, is lying quite ill in a dugout back of the section house. It would be well for our charitable people to look into his condition and surroundings." I was only nine years old then, but I vividly remember my mother having me take a five-pound lard-pailful of soup to him every day until he died. This is the man Clarence remembers as being so apologetic when, by mistake, he gave us some Roman Catholic literature; he had intended it for the Hyrups.

Trapping

For a couple of winters when I was about thirteen or fourteen years old I set traps for coyotes and bobcats on White Hill and on the side of Black Mountain up near the spring, the origin of the town water supply. For bait I would use scraps of meat from the grocery store, or, better yet, I would kill a porcupine or a rabbit and hang it up over the trap. After once setting the trap, one would, of course, avoid going any nearer to it on subsequent investigative rounds than would be necessary. If the animal gets the human scent, he will not go near. When I think now about how I used to climb (almost run) up those mountains and not even stop to rest, it seems incredible.

As well as trapping, I used to set snares which were loops of wire fastened to the lower wire of the fences in the path made by the rabbits, but I can't recall ever catching any bunnies in this manner.

One spring, when making my last rounds to pick up the traps, I had a highly exciting experience. As it was the last trip and I would have the heavy steel traps to carry home, I decided to leave my single-shot 22 rifle at home. To my surprise, I found I had caught a lynx cat. To kill him, I hunted up a club and hit him solidly over the head, avoiding his savage lunges at me when I came close. (Good thing my mother wasn't watching!) I then put him on my back and started home, holding his hind feet around my head and neck with my hands. I hadn't gone far when his movements indicated that I hadn't really killed him, so I had to put him down and finish the job. I was lucky not to have a big chunk bitten out of my behind.

One bad part about the trapping was that somehow my mother didn't like the idea of the fleas leaving the dead animals and taking up a new habitat on her boy as he carried them back home. I would skin the animals in the back yard and sell the pelts, shipping them away by express after drying.

Weather

In the *Empire of Eagle,* an early-day promotional pamphlet of Eagle County, the statement is made about Basalt that "the climate of the place is perfection itself, many winters being free from snow; mild and sunshiny."

But that is not the way I remember it. We had lots of snow and cold, perhaps more than in recent years. Probably we noticed it more because, although it was customary and necessary for trainmen and others working in the open to wear overshoes, somehow the children didn't use them as often. To keep our feet dry, instead of using rubbers and overshoes we used to oil our heavy shoes at intervals. This did not help our mother in keeping the house clean, however.

Neither did this keep our feet warm. On the four block walk to school many times our feet became so cold that we frequently huddled about the stove in the schoolroom before classes started. This frequent occurrence of getting our feet cold led to a condition that is seldom heard of today, chilblains. This was a thickening or redness of the feet resulting in such severe itching that it interfered with studying.

Some of the winters were extremely severe and accounts in the early newspapers indicate this. There is an item in an Aspen paper telling that the winter was so severe that the deer at Woody Creek were so hungry, weak, and emaciated, because of the heavy snow, that you didn't need to hunt them. You merely walked up to them and pushed them over. It also mentions that this same winter the snow was so deep that there was no food for the burros, and that a Frenchman camping at the confluence of Frying Pan Creek with the Roaring Fork kept his animals alive by feeding them venison all winter.

Christmas Presents and Trees

Christmas was then, as now, a big time for children. We hung our long black stockings behind the heating stove in the parlor (front room we called it); no one had fireplaces in the frame houses, but somehow Santa got down the chimney. Inasmuch as, after Uncle Albert was killed, there was only one Danielson family in town, most of the presents were from relatives elsewhere. The gifts for the children, therefore, came by mail, and going to the post office before Christmas was an eager and expectant daily performance. Then waiting to open the presents was a difficult time indeed.

I recall that a relative, forgetting that I had grown up to the age of about six years, sent me a tin watch. I was furious that they would send me something that would not run.

The other pleasant part of Christmas, in addition to getting presents, was the decorating of the tree at home and in the church. There were no purchased trees; everyone just took the liberty of going up on the hillside and cutting down his own. A couple of years our father took a hatchet with him on his trip and when coming back light would stop somewhere up around Nast and he and his fireman would cut a fir or spruce and bring it home on the tender.

A dangerous practice was the use of lighted vari-colored candles clipped on with a metal holder, instead of the light bulbs in use today. This was particularly perilous in the church with the big tree. Our parents would place presents for each of us children at the church. One year my parents put some money anonymously in a package for the minister's family.

The decorations were largely cranberries and popcorn strung on thread with a large needle. However, we did have ornaments, and the best tree in town by far was the Hyrup's; people in Basalt looked forward to being invited into their home to see the display. The reason for its excellence is explained by Walter in a letter in this manner:

"Yes, Ralph, all the trimmings on our Christmas trees of my youth came from Germany. We had an Aunt Amelia in Germany and each year she sent a package of gifts for each of us. Boy! O! Boy! How the Hyrups looked forward to receiving it. Most of the time there was a new decoration to add to our collection. My Aunt Mary had brought some with her when she came over to live with us. Our Christmas tree was one of the best and believe me my memories go back to boyhood days each year. I would like to see the colored candles and the smell of them when blown out."

On New Year's Day the men would go to the roundhouse and pull the whistles loud and long on all the engines that were there.

The Games We Played

There was no end of games that we could play unimpeded by speeding automobiles or limited space. Marbles had their season, but we had the advantage of a dirt ring where a marble could be made to drop and stay, rather than always roll off as in a chalk ring on asphalt. Tops, too, were a cheap and interesting form of individual competition.

Other contraptions which we made for ourselves were beanies and sling-shots. The beany is made from a forked branch of a tree or a willow. A rubber band is attached to each end of the V and these in turn are fastened by strings to a leather holder or pocket. By holding the handle with one hand and pulling back with the other, we could shoot a rock at a target, tin can, bird, or chipmunk.

Another device was the sling-shot, used in various forms by many peoples throughout the world. It consists of two strings attached to a leather pocket containing a rock. This is swung around in a circle and then one string is turned loose which allows the rock to go in the aimed direction.

Kick the can, a variation of hide and seek (also known as "shinny-on-your-own-side") was our favorite game; hard on shoes but good for leg muscles. The few who had air rifles had room to shoot them. Skipping rocks on the river never ceased to interest us.

And because we had much snow, we had the traditional snow men. Then we would lie down in the snow and move our arms up and down and our legs sidewise to make the bird figures. Fox-and-geese was a favorite pastime for us, which the children of today seem to have forgotten.

Sloss Horse

One of my fondest memories occurred while I was helping drive the Sloss cattle up Lime Creek to summer pasture near Woods Lake. Price Sloss had a tall, big-boned buckskin gelding that he used for his personal riding; he needed a large mount for he weighed about 200 pounds. For some reason, Price wanted someone to take it home and asked me to do it. This was the best saddle horse I have ever ridden; the trip was marvelous and to get to ride the boss' horse was exciting beyond description.

The town of Basalt today.

R. W. D. Collection

CHAPTER 5

Basalt at Work

Altho the names of many people appear elsewhere in the text, we thought it worthwhile to group them in the various occupations at which they worked.

The lists of trainmen of the Colorado Midland Company have been prepared from two sources. The names of the engineers and firemen working at the closure of the railroad have been furnished by Dave and Arlington Cuthbert. Clarence Danielson, Arthur Bates and Clarence Dearing have not only added to the engineer and firemen lists but have also compiled the names of the conductors and brakemen.

RAILROAD EMPLOYEES

Second District Engineers   *Date Hired*
1. McNeil, Thomas B.   *R   3-18-1887
2. Farquhar, D. B.   R   4-27-1887
3. Conerty, Wm.   R   5-3-1887
4. Switzer, Wm.   1887
5. Fay, Walter   1887
6. Nelson, John   1887
7. Kalfus, J. W.   1887
8. Bates, W. P.   R   9-22-1887
9. Dibble, W. N.   R   10-1-1887
10. Fahey, James   R   10-8-1887
11. Willis, F. B.   R   10-24-1887
12. Nelson, Chas.   11-1-1887
13. Danielson, A. M.   1888
14. Bossinger, Charles   1888
15. Sebring, A. H.   1888
16. Trowbridge, E. C.   R   12-19-1888
17. Hall, Joe
18. Hedges, Wm.
19. Goff, Walter
20. Cahill, Wm.
21. May, John and Jim (brothers)
22. Ostrander, —
23. Hollingsworth, Ross   R   12-19-1891
24. Wright, Wm.
25. Mead, John
26. Hyrup, Pete
27. McCarty, H.
28. Sheppard, J. B.

*R — working at time of closure of railroad in 1918
T — traveling engineers

29. Dooling, John	R		6-15-1892
30. Marsell, Ernest			
31. Chidester, C. W.			
32. McMahon, Mike	R		8-20-1895
33. Andrus, C. C.	R	T	8-30-1895
34. Phelan, J. E.	R		8-31-1895
35. Weaver, James			
36. Clegg, John			
37. Stiffler, Fred			
38. Hancock, Thomas			
39. Riebel, Oscar			
40. Rutherford, John			
41. Ramsey, George			
42. Johnson, Jack			
43. Reed, Andrew	R		10-9-1898
44. Horrell, M. F.	R		10-13-1898
45. Burgin, B. F.	R		10-15-1899
46. Lathrop, Carl			12- -1899
47. O'Brien, J. T.	R		9-10-1900
48. O'Brien, W. L.	R		9-12-1900
49. Fraser, James E.	R		10-5-1901
50. Hollingsworth, Walter			1902
51. Hammond, Rufford			
52. Rhodes, O. G.	R		11-11-1902
53. Omar, E. W.			
54. DeGroot, D. T.			
55. Valiquette, J. R.	R		
56. Howard, Gean			
57. Hyrup, Rhodie			
58. Bowler, Wm.			1905
59. Haggbloom, Alfred			1906
60. Crawford, H. C.	R		9-5-1906
61. Walsh, Mike			11-7-1906
62. Lydick, Clay			1906
63. Hilton, John			1906
64. Mills, Fred(?) or Ed(?)			1906
65. Fouse, Charles			1906
66. Norris, George			1906
67. Packard, Walter			1906
68. Denton, Walter			1906
69. Fuller, C.			1906
70. Norstrum, Arthur F.	R		1906
71. Howie, James			1907
72. Truggles, C.			1907
73. Buffer, Charles			1907
74. Murray, Charles			1907
75. Dunn, P. A.		T	2-19-1907
76. Kinney, Frank			1907
77. Suttlemyre		T	1907
78. Cuthbert, D. A.	R	T	10-17-1907
79. O'Neil, Arthur			11-21-1907
80. Atwater, C. E.			
81. Forrest, H. A.			10-10-1909
82. Downey, Dave			1909
83. Mayhew, B. L.			1909
84. Kelley, J. J.	R		1909
85. Danielson, C. L.	R		1-17-1910
86. Kellerup, J. M.	R		2-10-1910
87. Sawyer, Tom			
88. Chatfield, Clark			
89. Luzi, John	R	Yard	3-22-1909

Photo from Bramblet Willits and Harlan Harvey

Railroad employees of the Colorado Midland. Fifth from left, top row, is Clint Benbow, machinist. Center row, from left to right, are Sam Harvey, Jim O'Brien and Sam Gordon, engineer. The second, third and fourth men on the bottom row are Dean Sutcliff, hostler; Clay Lydick, fireman; and Dick Griffith, roundhouse foreman. The rest of the men's names are unknown.

90.	Rothe, Bert		
91.	Bates, A. L.	R	7-6-1912
92.	Decker, J. H.	R	8-26-1912
93.	Baker, John	R	8-31-1912
94.	Newkirk, F. D.	R	9-3-1912
95.	Dearing, C. A.	R	9-6-1912
96.	Heller, L. O.	R	9-7-1912
97.	Hartson, H. H.	R	9-30-1912
98.	Walsh, John	R	9-10-1914
99.	Hoffman, Wm.	R	7-15-1917
100.	Harris, C. E.	R	7-15-1917
101.	Daywalt, Frank R.	R	7-17-1917
102.	Phillips, S. C.	R	7-21-1917
103.	Drake, R. M.	R	7-31-1917
104.	McDonald, T. M.	R	8-3-1917
105.	Williamson, J. S.	R	8-7-1917
106.	Heid, L. A.	R	8-17-1917
107.	Denson, G. C.	R	8-19-1917
108.	Pottinger, B. W.	R	8-29-1917

no hiring dates known

109. Sawyer, Tom	117. McGonagle, —	
110. Hickman, Jack T.	118. Barton, Bert	
111. Paddock, Fred	119. Hartson, Claude	
112. Bedford, Fred	120. Danielson, Albert	
113. Law, Charlie	121. Colligan, Tom	
114. St. John, Louie	122. Packard, Fred	
115. Burton, Fritz	123. Frison, Jake	
116. Hall, Joe	124. MacLain, A. K.	

SECOND DISTRICT FIREMEN

1. Randall, J.	Basalt	*9-22-1909
2. Kniphausen, R. N.	Basalt	11-7-1909
3. Arnold, C. P.	Leadville	9-28-1911
4. Shay, J. M.	Basalt	10-7-1911
5. Quist, Oscar	Basalt	3-3-1912
6. Hall, W. E.	Cardiff	5-31-1912
7. Frieler, J. W.	Basalt	6-7-1912
8. Paddock, Fred	Basalt	7-11-1913
9. Rumley, Bert	Cardiff	7-22-1913
10. Brewer, Roy	Cardiff	8-24-1913
11. Cain, J. A.	Leadville	8-24-1914
12. Frieler, Harry	Basalt	9-1-1915
13. Hyrup, W. J.	Basalt	9-1-1915
14. Bergstrom, C. A.	Leadville	8-8-1916
15. Hyrup, C. A.	Basalt	8-24-1916
16. Hartson, C. H.	Basalt	8-27-1916
17. Young, Ralph	Basalt	9-2-1917
18. Gale, Wm.	Cardiff	9-11-1917
19. Lightner, F. A.	Basalt	9-13-1917
20. McCall, L. G.	Leadville	10-18-1917
21. Erickson, E. A.	Cardiff	12-4-1917
22. McEnroe, Chas.	Leadville	12-4-1917
23. Downey, C. A.	Basalt	12-4-1917
24. Reed, O. L.	Cardiff	12-10-1917
25. Rosa, Pete	Cardiff	12-11-1917
26. Hines, W. P.	Cardiff	12-20-1917
27. Woodruff, W. W.	Cardiff	1-18-1918
28. Opie, H. R.	Basalt	1-30-1918
29. Coe, S. D.	Basalt	2-1-1918
30. Minchey, W. B.	Cardiff	2-13-1918
31. Cronin, J. J.	Cardiff	2-17-1918
32. Geilenfeldt, H. R.	Cardiff	2-20-1918
33. Manis, J. E.	Cardiff	2-20-1918
34. Gunn, O. C.	Cardiff	2-21-1918
35. Gregston, E. L.	Cardiff	2-22-1918
36. Clark, J. W.	Cardiff	2-24-1918
37. Roberts, H. W.	Cardiff	2-25-1918
38. Thomas, Robert	Cardiff	3-5-1918
39. Huse, Wm.	Cardiff	3-8-1918
40. Wheeler, E. F.	Basalt	3-8-1918
41. Kinnisch, J. R.	Cardiff	3-8-1918
42. Downey, P. R.	Cardiff	3-16-1918
43. Shehorn, E. A.	Cardiff	3-17-1918
44. Stiffler, W. E.	Leadville	3-19-1918
45. Zeiler, H. J.	Leadville	3-19-1918
46. Geary, J. E.	Leadville	3-20-1918
47. Barkley, A. M.	Basalt	3-20-1918
48. Burrell, S. S.	Cardiff	3-22-1918
49. Hickox, R. L.	Basalt	3-23-1918
50. Stone, C. E.	Cardiff	3-24-1918

*Earlier firemen became engineers.

Firemen who worked for Midland at some time, but not listed under roster of those still working in 1918.

- Andrews, Ted
- Biglow, Keith
- Bigelow, Dick
- Brickel, Lou
- Clark, Orval
- Chatfield, Art
- Chatfield, C. Parke
- Cope, Henry
- Denman, —
- Fields, Milt
- Giffen, Archie
- Hall, Dave
- Hammond, Rube
- Hancock, John
- Howard, Gene
- Hynes, Bill
- Larsh, Jimmie
- Lumsden, John
- McFarland, —
- Mills, Fred
- Packard, Fred
- Randall, John
- Reed, Oscar
- Rich, Marshall
- Riley, Pete*
- Ross, Bert
- Schmeuser, Jim
- Shidler, Grover
- Smith, Bill
- Thornbull, —
- Valiguette, Joe
- Watson, —
- Woods, Lewis

SECOND DISTRICT CONDUCTORS

All time — no hiring or promotion dates known.

- Andrus, Josh
- Askins, —
- Blyth, William
- Burke, —
- Cole, Charles
- Collins, Pete
- Dentner, Charlie
- Eckerman, Ed
- Ecrema, —
- Fagan, Barney
- Gilbert, Pug
- Gillette, —
- Glen, Fran
- Glenn, Chesty
- Godfrey, —
- Golden, —
- Gum, Chester
- Hamilton, A. V.
- Hartley, Frank
- Jones, Davie
- Kinney, —
- Lake, Earl
- Lee, Walter
- Lorry, —
- Lynch, James
- Mallon, Jim
- Manning, Jack
- McCall, —
- McPherson, —
- McGill, —
- Mead, William
- Meal, Billy
- Miller, Riley
- Mitchell, Ira
- Neadham, Daniel
- O'Neal, Art
- Phipps, Bud
- Rickard, Otto F.
- Robertie, Ed
- Rogers, —
- Sanborn, Howard
- Schurr, —
- Shanks, William
- Smith, Vet
- Spahr, Jesse
- Stiffler, Charlie
- Stephenson, —
- Stiffler, Max
- Terry, —
- Walker, Tom
- White, Willis
- Willis, Ed

SECOND DISTRICT BRAKEMAN

All time record — No hiring dates known. (Many promoted and listed later as conductors.)

- Bogue, Bill
- Brown, Ed
- Davis, "Sunny Jim"
- Dillon, Jim
- Dorthy, Jack
- Fair, Hugh
- Frison, Pete
- Green, Chester
- Hall, Billie
- Hartley, Frank
- Hawkins, —
- Kennedy, Charlie
- Kennedy, Rod
- Kopkey, Charlie
- Kopkey, Gus
- Lake, Rollie
- Mallon, Ed
- Mallory, Murray

*Traveling Firemen

Neal, Billy
Phelps, Lou
Stager, Fern
Stahr, Rufus "Rube"

Stiffler, Charles
Sweeney, Bum
Tarbell, Ed
Thomson, —

ROUNDHOUSE MEN

The roundhouse is a term applied to the repair shop for the engines. It was originally called roundhouse because it was built in that shape with the turntable in the center so that engines could be put in various stalls to make repairs. Under each engine was a pit so that the repairmen could get to the under side of the engine. Some repair shops, such as Basalt's, were oblong, but were still called roundhouses. There were large stacks in the roof to carry off the smoke. Large stoves were placed to keep the workmen warm. Men who aspired to be firemen and engineers would start work at various jobs in the roundhouse and then be student firemen for a period. Of course, some men, such as machinists, had permanent jobs there.

The roundhouse employees were in various categories. The foremen were James Ryan, George Bancroft, and Clint Benbow. The machinists were George Thompson, Al England, Scott Shafer, and Jess Bogue. Hostlers included Dean Sutcliffe, Dick Griffith, E. M. Monks, Asa Harris, Billie Smith, and Perry Sprague. Some of the car inspectors and repairmen (car whackers) were S. H. Miller, Tom Weir, Newton Barnes, J. H. Johnson, Matt Hanson, August Johnson, Lester Henning, F. C. Barker, R. Hazleton, John Eckwall, Charles Peterson, and Louis

Clifford Rhodes in delivery wagon, with Sam Drake, in front of the Sheward Pool Hall.

Photo from Jake Lucksinger

Courtesy of Clementine Cramer Bryant

Sam Cramer in his Potato Commission office.

Valiquette. For boilermakers they had Ed Stockton, Frank Fullman, and George Liddle. A. M. Gonzales and Albert Stobbs did the boiler cleaning and boiler washing.

We remember the Kastelic brothers and Shorty Arbaney as the coal chute shovelers. The pump house man was — Davis. The section foremen were Mike Shay, Dan Connell, and John and Tom O'Connell.

DEPOT EMPLOYEES

Depot agents and assistants were Charlie Law, A. T. Folger, Arthur J. Kibby, W. C. Fleming, — Borneman, Clark Kinney, Edwin Hilliker, Ben Johnson, B. G. Phares, John Johnson, L. G. Campbell, D. E. Heyward, J. F. Peck, Fern Stager, Pat Shannon, and Will Shanks.

An interesting tale about Hilliker is that when he heard a caboose had broken loose and was rushing loose down toward Basalt he had to make a decision whether to turn it into some other cars on a siding or up the Y toward Aspen. In one case the caboose would be demolished; in the other case the car might jump the track and plow into the railroad station. He chose the former with disastrous results to the caboose but kept it from going on through Basalt down toward Glenwood and possibly hit some train coming from the opposite direction.

Dick Mizer, blacksmith.

Photo loaned by Jake Lucksinger

Clerks were John Johnson, Jimmy Ryan, E. F. Collier. Night operators were George Viverka, L. G. Campbell, John Scandlan, — Glass.

Two of the brass pounders (telegraph operators) we remember were Slim Ellis and — Holder.

PROFESSIONAL PEOPLE

The physicians and surgeons located for varying periods in the town were Pemberton T. Rucker, Arthur Gill, M. McNeilan, Erlo E. Kennedy, E. M. Phelps, J. C. Thompson, and E. S. Corbin. It is interesting that one advertised in the paper "Night calls and home calls cheerfully made." Calls were made by foot, horseback, buggy, or train. Doctors often came from other towns, particularly Dr. A. J. O. Lof, from Aspen, and Dr. LeRossignol, from Rifle. The latter cared for our mother at the birth of R. W. D. on March 6, 1897; it was the doctor's birthday also. Dr. Clagett, whose son, Dr. James Clagett is a distinguished surgeon at Mayo's, at times came to Basalt.

The dentists were all on a visiting basis from Leadville, Aspen, and Glenwood Springs. Dr. J. H. Setzler was there more than the others. In addition, some dentistry was done by the physicians.

Much of the law work for the region was done by Edward Taylor, of Glenwood Springs, who was also a member of the U. S. House of Representatives for many years.

One of the most interesting men in Basalt was a blind pianist by the name of Hugh McCabe. He not only gave music lessons, but gave professional concerts in Aspen and Leadville and other towns.

The visiting oculists were Drs. E. S. Corbin and J. C. Thompson.

No graduate veterinarian was ever located in Basalt, but John Smith graciously helped with advice when consulted by fellow ranchers.

TRADESMEN

The storekeepers and others are listed in the interesting reproductions from the Basalt Journal. The dates people were in Basalt can be gleaned from that publication. Dennis Barry had the first store in a tent at Frying Pan Junction.

The Pinger Mercantile operated at both Basalt and Emma. The Collins Mercantile was run by L. L. Collins. John Smith and B. L. Smith had one of the first stores, first on Railroad Street and later under the Odd Fellows Hall on First Street. For a short while A. M. Danielson and George Bancroft were in partnership with the Smiths. The store was later run by L. R. Tucker and even later by Arthur Simmons. William Tierney had a store near the drug store, but, on his death, his widow, Ella Tierney, built the brick building later purchased by J. P. and Marvin Sloss, and which has now been converted into the American Legion Hall. John Nelson ran the Basalt Mercantile Company.

Dunn and Company were succeeded by Fred Paddock in the candy store and tobacco business. Clark and Hanson had a store for shoes and dry goods; Carl Rother originally repaired shoes for them, but later had his own store. Walter W. Frey operated a general store on Main Street next door to Carlson's Drug Store. W. A. Simmons and Dan Denton ran the Basalt Mercantile for a while, originally owned by the Smith Brothers. L. R. Tucker also managed the same store. Col. Stiffler ran a small candy and sundry store.

The first drug stores were owned by Frank Waite, Mr. Tandy, and R. H. Zimmerman. Later, for many years, the proprietors were Anthony and Victor Carlson. There was never more than one drug store at a time, always in the same building as of today.

The bakeries were operated by Col. Stiffler, May Burch, and Mrs. Lapham.

There were several tent saloons at Frying Pan Junction, but the only proprietor remembered was quoted by Shoemaker as Red Duggan. The other owners of saloons at Aspen Junction and Basalt were E. B. Kelly, Magnall Brothers, James F. Lunt, Benedeck and Benedeck, Kendrick and Salisbury, S. H. Miller, Lupton Brothers, and Mr. Epperson. Old timers mention that the Lupton Brothers ran a very respectable establishment, not permitting gambling as did some of the others. The bartenders recalled were Ben Darien, Al Clegg, Mr. Priest, and Shuford Reynolds (nephew of Mrs. Kelly).

Pool halls were run by Fred Paddock and Col. Stiffler. For several years Sam Cramer managed a commission house for purchase and sale of potatoes in carload lots. Ice was sold by the barber, John Ould.

The restaurants and boarding houses were run by Mrs. Edith Clarke, Maggie Simpson Mattingly, Nell Smith, William and May Burch, Mrs. Lapham, Oscar Venettish, W. L. Fitzgerald, and P. F. Nott. Proprietors of the Midland Hotel were Dr. Thompson and Mr. Bear. In 1907 the hotel was turned into an emergency hospital for out of town patients. Mr. Hazleton operated the hotel as a "Santa Fe" Harvey House for a time.

The main barber for many years was John Ould. He also had a place for baths which was operated for ladies by his wife one day a week. Another barber who was there for a while was J. W. Tansy (or Tandy?).

The blacksmiths who repaired farm equipment and shoed horses were A. W. Chatfield, Dan German, Sr., S. H. Miller, C. D. Mizer, and C. Van Deventer. These men often allowed us boys to watch and we could actually help them by running the blower which was propelled by hand or foot pedals.

The painting and paperhanging was done by H. E. Boyce and John Bureman.

The carpenters remembered were John Auld and Dave Hall who built many houses. They gave their help to the building of the church. Early there were a few log houses (especially the Gabe Luchsinger halfway house), but the first settlers and workers lived in tents. Later the houses were (and are today) of the frame type. The Tierney and John Smith residences were largely prefabricated.

Dairies were operated at various times by Jake Lucksinger, Sr., Gabe Lucksinger, E. G. Mallory, Ray Jones, Dan Denton, and Gus Grace. Many families, in addition, especially early, had their own cow which made up the town herd. We well recollect the cows coming from Gabe Lucksinger's each morning and going back each evening, over the cement bridge and around the trail below the Bates house.

Smith's Store was the first in Basalt. Below is a view of the store interior. Both photos were contributed by Blanche Stager Holcomb.

Slaughter houses were operated by John Smith, Daniel Lupton, and Dan Denton. The ranchers did their own butchering.

The patrolmen for the Public Service Company power line usually lived up the Frying Pan Valley in the region of Ruedi or Meredith, but often came to Basalt for supplies or to enter into the affairs of the community. The patrolmen whose names we have been able to obtain are Sam Phillips, John Lumsden Ray Jarvis, Virgil Holcomb, H. B. Biglow, Harold Perkins, Ray Jones, Ed Hartzog, Wallace Duzenberry, Russell Craddock, and Kenneth Baillie.

The man who superintended the construction of the towers and stringing of the wires from Shoshone to Leadville in 1908, Mr. Earl Mosley, still lives in Denver. Clarence and I recently had the pleasure of having dinner with him, and a most jovial, intelligent, and interesting man he is.

The forest rangers we recall were Kenneth Baillie, William J. (Bill) Barber, Virgil Holcomb, George McClaren, and Russell Craddock.

The game wardens were Chub Downey and E. B. Kelly.

POSTMASTERS

The list of postmasters was furnished by the Post Office Department. Most people then had boxes at the post office and it was a daily get-together there after the morning trains came in. The post office at one time was located in the Smith Store. Later it was located in several places on Railroad Street.

Post Office at Basalt, Eagle County, Colorado
Established as Aspen Junction on February 13, 1890*
Name changed to Basalt on June 19, 1895.

Names of Postmasters   *Dates of Appointment Before 1929*

Aspen Junction
    M. B. Louthan .... February 13, 1890
    Arthur J. Kibby .... June 21, 1890
    Basil L. Smith .... January 12, 1894

Basalt
    Miss Jennie Shryock .... December 8 ,1897
    John P. McMillan .... March 26, 1898
    Mattie Stiffler .... March 2, 1901
    Bernnard F. Stager .... January 16, 1905
    William H. Hildreth .... March 31, 1906
    Roaldo D. Strong .... January 13, 1908

*There was never any official post office at Frying Pan Junction.

Charles W. Gilbert .... June 11, 1918
Ina E. McMahon (declined) .... July 15, 1918
Anna Bogue .... February 5, 1919
(Still serving in 1929)

Part of the time during the storm of 1899 the mail was routed by the D. and R. G. narrow gauge via Gunnison to Grand Junction.

TOWN OFFICERS

The town officials elected at the incorporation of Basalt on July 18, 1901, were William Conerty, Mayor; John A. Smith, John Auld, B. W. Burgin, J. T. May, C. L. Benbow, and W. W. Frey, Councilmen. Lupton and A. M. Danielson were soon elected as councilmen.

Ira H. Mitchell was the recorder in 1902, to be followed by J. P. McMillan.

The mayors who have held office are William Conerty, 1901-1903; McMillan, 1903; Dr. Erlo Kennedy and E. B. Kelly, 1909; C. C. Andrus, 1904; Ed Trowbridge, 1910; John Scandlan, 1911-1918; Lamb, 1918; and more recently, Renshaw who has been mayor for many years.

The councilmen who were elected from 1901-1918 were E. B. Kelly, John Dunn, Dan Lupton, A. T. Lydick, Jake Lucksinger, Henry Stiffler, Ed Trowbridge, W. V. Hall, E. D. Whitenack, Emery Arbaney, A. E. Waller, John Smith, M. P. Sloss, Sam Drake, L. R. Tucker, George Jarvis, Claude Hartson, Asa Harris, Mike McMahon, J. P. Mattingly, James Lamb, A. M. Danielson, Walter Frey, Beulah Burgin, John Auld, John Nelson, R. Hazleton, W. P. Bates, B. Johnson, W. A. Irwin, O. G. Rhodes, W. H. Bogue, and Matt Hanson.

The clerks and recorders have been R. D. Strong (many years), Asa Harris, J. P. McMillan (1903), W. H. Hildreth (1907), P. T. Rucker (1903), George Liddle (1904), M. P. Sloss (1914), H. W. Landin (1917), and W. E. Reid (1918).

Justices of the peace were J. P. Jones, John Sloss, John Auld, W. H. Harris, H. Van Deventer, W. V. Hall, and F. O. Barker.

It was jokingly reported in the *Basalt Journal* that, at his first wedding ceremony, J. P. John Sloss said "Do you each solemnly swear that you will obey the constitution of the U. S. and of Colorado, and to perform the duties of your office to the best of your ability, so help you God?" The couple nodded assent and the squire continued: "Then by the power vested in me by the strong arm of the law, I pronounce you man and wife, now and forever, and you will stand committed until the fine and costs are paid, and may the Lord have mercy on your souls."

Town marshalls have been C. D. Mizer, John Eckwall, John Ould, and Walter Hyrup.

CHAPTER 6

Community Activities

The organizations to be discussed under this heading are lodges, churches, schools, and cemetery.

There are several social societies also, the list of which can be culled from the copy of the Directory, as published in the *Basalt Journal,* and from the names on the unusual friendship quilt made by the Ladies Aid and described elsewhere.

It was pointed out to us by Bramblet Willits that lodges in those days had a dual function, social and financial. It must be remembered that very few people in those days had any insurance. Furthermore, while it was the custom if a man was killed on the railroad for the management to make some kind of payment to the family, nevertheless, there was no certainty of it and the amount given was minimal. The result was, with ordinary death, the family was usually left penniless unless there was the benefit from a lodge. This feature was a great help in gaining members. In some cases, fortunately, the trainmen had additional insurance through their unions.

The most active and flourishing lodges with the largest membership were the Odd Fellows and their auxiliary, the Rebekahs. The fact that about forty members of the Odd Fellows in a town of four hundred would appear in one picture would attest to their popularity.

LODGES

The early history of Lodge No. 83, I.O.O.F., has been well written up by Bramblet Willits from whose account I get the following information. He and his father were always ardent members in a lodge that is still quite active. Bramblet tells that on March 28, 1895 the original eight members were obligated, their names being William Harris, A.M. Danielson, August Naefe, William Tierney, M.L. Shippee, Orvin Maylin, and Joshia Reeves. The lodge was instituted by J.A. Brockway and E.D. Tandy from the lodge at Carbondale and Aspen. On the following two days, March 29 and 30, in all-night sessions, 21 more

The I.O.O.F. Lodge at the time of the funeral of Albert Danielson, January, 1897.

members were initiated. The first meetings were held above the Frey store on Railroad Avenue, but, realizing the need for a larger meeting hall for themselves and other organizations, the trustees, Willits, Danielson, and Bancroft, soon arranged with J.A. Smith to build a two-story structure, the upper part to be used by the Odd Fellows and others, and the ground floor to be used as a general store by John Smith. By March 28, 1899 the structure was paid for.

On July 6, 1895 the minutes were headed Aspen Junction, but at the next meeting, July 13, they were headed Basalt, Colorado. At the 50th Anniversary in 1945 there were three men present who had been members 50 years, namely, Charles E. Bogue, August Naefe, and E.H. Gray.

At no time has there ever been a Masonic Lodge, although one was organized in Carbondale about 1890, and is still active. Known Masons were A.M. Danielson, John Scandlan, William P. Bates, Charles E. Bogue, John Smith, and probably Andy Wilson, J.P. McMillan, and Wm. Tierney.

In addition to other lodges, the locomotive engineers and firemen and their auxiliaries were also very much alive. The *Basalt Journal,* of January 10, 1903, says "The Tuesday Evening Musical met at the home of Mrs. A.M. Danielson."

The Sorosis Club of Basalt, still going, is one of the first five in the State of Colorado. This summer the club dedicated a plaque at the park at Basalt in honor of George Washington.

There was also a group known as the Chautauqua Club, whose picture is given.

CHURCHES

Basalt Methodist

The Basalt Methodist Church was the only active house of worship in the town for many years until the organization of St. Vincent's Roman Catholic Church, comparatively recently.

The first services in Aspen Junction were apparently held in the school house. Mr. Earl Kibby, who passed away in Denver in 1961, told the authors that his father and mother, Arthur J. and Ellen Kibby, were the organizers of those first meetings. They first asked the Rev. Cornine to come there from Aspen. Later the Rev. John R. Wood from Leadville was invited on several occasions. Beardsley, in his book on western church history confirms this and says, concerning Mr. Wood: ". . . his next appointment was Leadville, 1890, where he had an almost continual revival. While there, Mr. Kibby, agent of the Midland at Aspen Junction, invited him to come down there to preach for them, which he did in May 1891. After the sermon he gave an opportunity for any to testify, when seventeen persons spoke for Jesus. This was the first service of the kind in that locality and led to the formation of the Aspen Junction (now Basalt) Circuit."

An account of the formation of the church in this area has been written by the Rev. Walter J. Boigegrain, now the pastor of the Westminster Methodist Church near Denver. His book, entitled *The Methodist Church in the Eagle-Colorado River Valley in Colorado 1880-1906,* was compiled in 1961. Everyone interested in the church history of the area should read this superbly prepared and illustrated document.

The Basalt church and that of Carbondale shared pastorates in the early days; in recent years the arrangement has been with Aspen and the present pastor is the Rev. Keith Merriman. The Methodist church was organized under "The Aspen Junction Circuit." First appointment to this circuit was the Rev. Sherwood A. Webber in 1892. The Aspen Junction church building was started under the supervision of the Rev. W.R. Ashby in 1895 and finished under the administration of the Rev. H.M. Law in 1896.

Mr. Boigegrain regrets that he has been unable to find any record of a dedicatory service after the Basalt Church was finished. We keep wondering if perhaps a reader of this book may find a copy of such a program. He states that the church and the parsonage were largely built by the pastors themselves

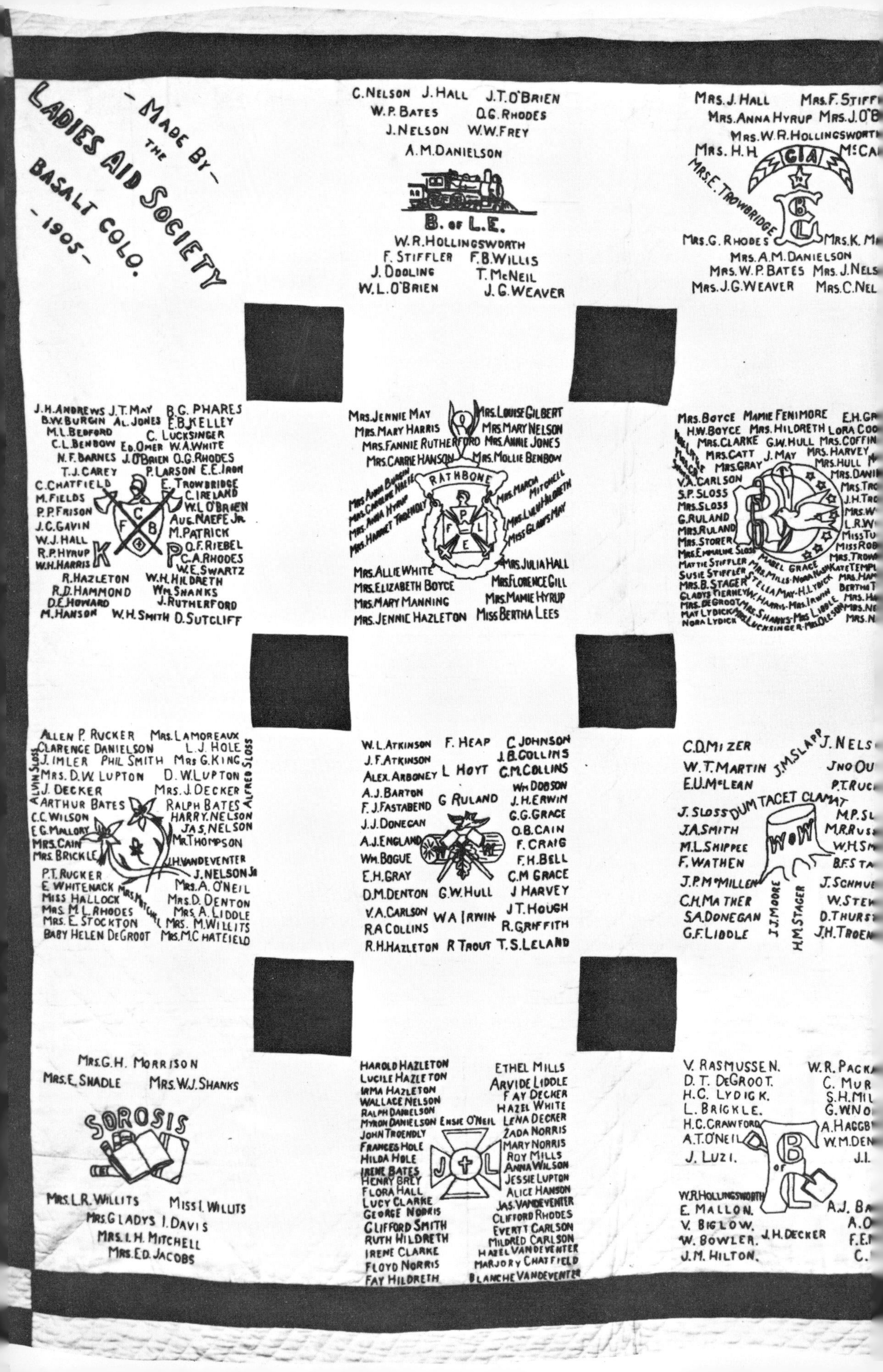

Made by the Ladies Aid Society, Basalt Colo. — 1905

Top center block (B. of L.E.)
C. Nelson J. Hall J.T. O'Brien
W.P. Bates O.G. Rhodes
J. Nelson W.W. Frey
A.M. Danielson

B. of L.E.

W.R. Hollingsworth F. Stiffler F.B. Willis
J. Dooling T. McNeil
W.L. O'Brien J.G. Weaver

Top right block (G.I.A. / L.E.)
Mrs. J. Hall Mrs. F. Stiffler
Mrs. Anna Hyrup Mrs. J. O'Brien
Mrs. W.R. Hollingsworth
Mrs. H.H. McCa...
Mrs. E. Trowbridge
Mrs. G. Rhodes Mrs. K. M...
Mrs. A.M. Danielson
Mrs. W.P. Bates Mrs. J. Nelson
Mrs. J.G. Weaver Mrs. C. Nelson

Middle-left block (K. of P.)
J.H. Andrews J.T. May B.G. Phares
B.W. Burgin Al. Jones F.B. Kelley
M.L. Bedford C. Lucksinger
C.L. Benbow Ed. Omer W.A. White
N.F. Barnes J. O'Brien O.G. Rhodes
T.J. Carey P. Larson E.E. Iron
C. Chatfield E. Trowbridge
M. Fields C. Ireland
P.P. Frison W.L. O'Brien
J.C. Gavin Aug. Naefe Jr.
W.J. Hall M. Patrick
R.P. Hyrup Q.F. Riebel
W.H. Harris C.A. Rhodes
W.E. Swartz
R. Hazleton W.H. Hildreth
R.D. Hammond Wm. Shanks
D.E. Howard J. Rutherford
M. Hanson W.H. Smith D. Sutcliff

Middle center block (Rathbone)
Mrs. Jennie May Mrs. Louise Gilbert
Mrs. Mary Harris Mrs. Mary Nelson
Mrs. Fannie Rutherford Mrs. Annie Jones
Mrs. Carrie Hanson Mrs. Mollie Benbow

Mrs. Anna Burgin Mrs. Marda Mitchell
Mrs. Caroline Naefe
Mrs. Anita Hyrup Mrs. L.W. Hildreth
Mrs. Harriet Troendly (?)
Mrs. R.W.
Miss Gladys May

Rathbone

Mrs. Allie White Mrs. Julia Hall
Mrs. Elizabeth Boyce Mrs. Florence Gill
Mrs. Mary Manning Mrs. Mamie Hyrup
Mrs. Jennie Hazleton Miss Bertha Lees

Middle right block (R.G. / Star)
Mrs. Boyce Mamie Fenimore E.H. G...
H.W. Boyce Mrs. Hildreth Lora Cook
Mrs. Clarke G.W. Hull Mrs. Coffin
Mrs. Catt J. May Mrs. Harvey
Mrs. Gray Mrs. Hull M...
V.A. Carlson Mrs. Trc...
S.P. Sloss J.H. Tr...
Mrs. S. Sloss Mrs. W...
G. Ruland L.R.W.
Mrs. Ruland Miss Tu...
Mrs. Storer Miss Re...
Mrs. Emaline Sloss Mrs. Trow...
Mattie Stiffler Mabel Grace
Susie Stiffler Mrs. Mills Nora Nash Kate Templ...
Mrs. B. Stager Stella May H.L. Lydick Mrs. Ha...
Gladys Tierney W. Harris Mrs. Irwin Bertha T...
Mrs. DeGroot Mrs. Shanks Mrs. Liddle Mrs. Ha...
May Lydick Mrs. Lucksinger R. Fields Jos. Ne...
Nora Lydick Mrs. N...

Lower-left block
Allen P. Rucker Mrs. Lamoreaux
Clarence Danielson L.J. Hole
J. Imler Phil Smith Mrs. G. King
Alvin Sloss Mrs. D.W. Lupton D.W. Lupton Alfred Sloss
J. Decker Mrs. J. Decker
Arthur Bates Ralph Bates
C.C. Wilson Harry Nelson
E.G. Mallory Jas. Nelson
Mrs. Cain Mr. Thompson
Mrs. Brickle J.H. Van Deventer
P.T. Rucker J. Nelson Jr.
E. Whitenack Mrs. Mitchell Mrs. A. O'Neil
Miss Hallock Mrs. D. Denton
Mrs. M.L. Rhodes Mrs. A. Liddle
Mrs. E. Stockton Mrs. M. Willits
Baby Helen DeGroot Mrs. M.C. Hatfield

Lower center block
W.L. Atkinson F. Heap C. Johnson
J.F. Atkinson J.B. Collins
Alex. Arboney L. Hoyt C.M. Collins
A.J. Barton Wm. Dobson
F.J. Fastabend G. Ruland J.H. Erwin
J.J. Donegan G.G. Grace
A.J. England O.B. Cain
Wm. Bogue F. Craig
E.H. Gray F.H. Bell
D.M. Denton G.W. Hull C.M. Grace
V.A. Carlson W.A. Irwin J Harvey
R.A. Collins J.T. Hough
R. Griffith
R.H. Hazleton R. Trout T.S. Leland

Lower right block (W.O.W.)
C.D. Mizer J.M. Slapp J. Nelson
W.T. Martin Jno Ou...
E.U. McLean P.T. Ruc...
J. Sloss **Dum Tacet Clamat** M.P. Sl...
J.A. Smith M.R. Rus...
M.L. Shippee W.H.Sm...
F. Wathen B.F. Sta...
J.P. McMillen J. Schmu...
C.H. Mather J.J. Moore W. Ste...
S.A. Donegan H.M. Stager D. Thurs...
G.F. Liddle J.H. Troen...

Bottom-left block (Sorosis)
Mrs. G.H. Morrison
Mrs. E. Snadle Mrs. W.J. Shanks

Sorosis

Mrs. L.R. Willits Miss I. Willits
Mrs. Gladys I. Davis
Mrs. L.H. Mitchell
Mrs. Ed. Jacobs

Bottom center block (J + L)
Harold Hazleton Ethel Mills
Lucile Hazleton Arvide Liddle
Irma Hazleton Fay Decker
Wallace Nelson Hazel White
Ralph Danielson Lena Decker
Myron Danielson Ensie O'Neil
John Troendly Zada Norris
Frances Hole Mary Norris
Hilda Hole Roy Mills
Irene Bates Anna Wilson
Henry Grey Jessie Lupton
Flora Hall Alice Hanson
Lucy Clarke Jas. Van Deventer
George Norris Clifford Rhodes
Clifford Smith Everett Carlson
Ruth Hildreth Mildred Carlson
Irene Clarke Hazel Van Deventer
Floyd Norris Marjory Chatfield
Fay Hildreth Blanche Van Deventer

Bottom right block (B. of L.F.)
V. Rasmussen W.R. Packa...
D.T. DeGroot C. Mur...
H.C. Lydick S.H. Mi...
L. Brickle G. Wno...
H.C. Crawford A. Haggb...
A.T. O'Neil W.M. Den...
J. Luzi J.I.
W.R. Hollingsworth A.J. Ba...
E. Mallon A.O.
V. Biglow
W. Bowler J.H. Decker F.E.
J.M. Hilton C.

Basalt, Colorado Midland Town 153

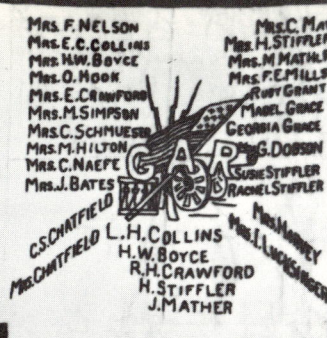

Friendship quilt made by the Ladies Aid Society of the Basalt Methodist Church. The organizations represented are (left to right):

Upper row: Brotherhood of Locomotive Engineers, Grand International Auxiliary (G. I. A.), Grand Army of the Republic (G. A. R.).

Second row: Knights of Pythias, Rathbone Sisters, (Auxiliary of the K. of P.), Independent Order of Odd Fellows (I.O.O.F.), Rebekahs.

Third row: The Columbines (miscellaneous), two blocks of Woodmen of the World (W. O. W.), Women of Woodcraft.

Fourth row: Sorosis, Junior League of the M. E. Church, Brotherhood of Locomotive Firemen, Ladies Aid of the M. E. Church.

Courtesy of Arthur and Georgina Bates, the owners of the quilt.

Photo from Gladys Clavell

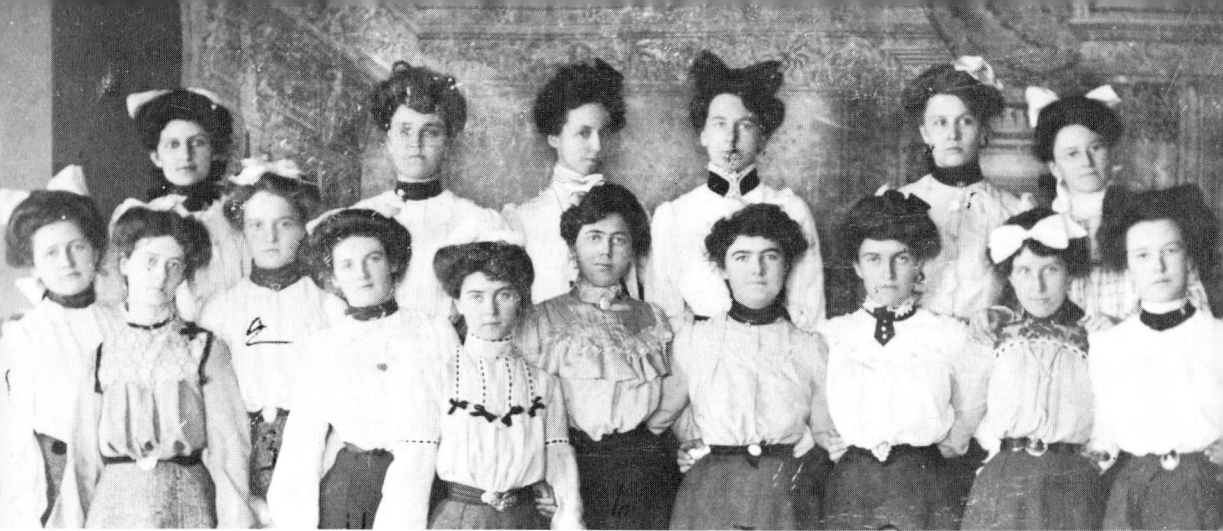

Leap Year Club of 1904. Back row (left to right): ...., Abbie Robinson, ... Cook, Mattie Stiffler, ..., Rachel Stiffler. Front row: ...., Gladys Tierney, Eugenia Hyrup, Jennie King, Bertha Tierney, ..., Mable Tierney, Blanche Smith, May Griffith, Susie Stiffler.

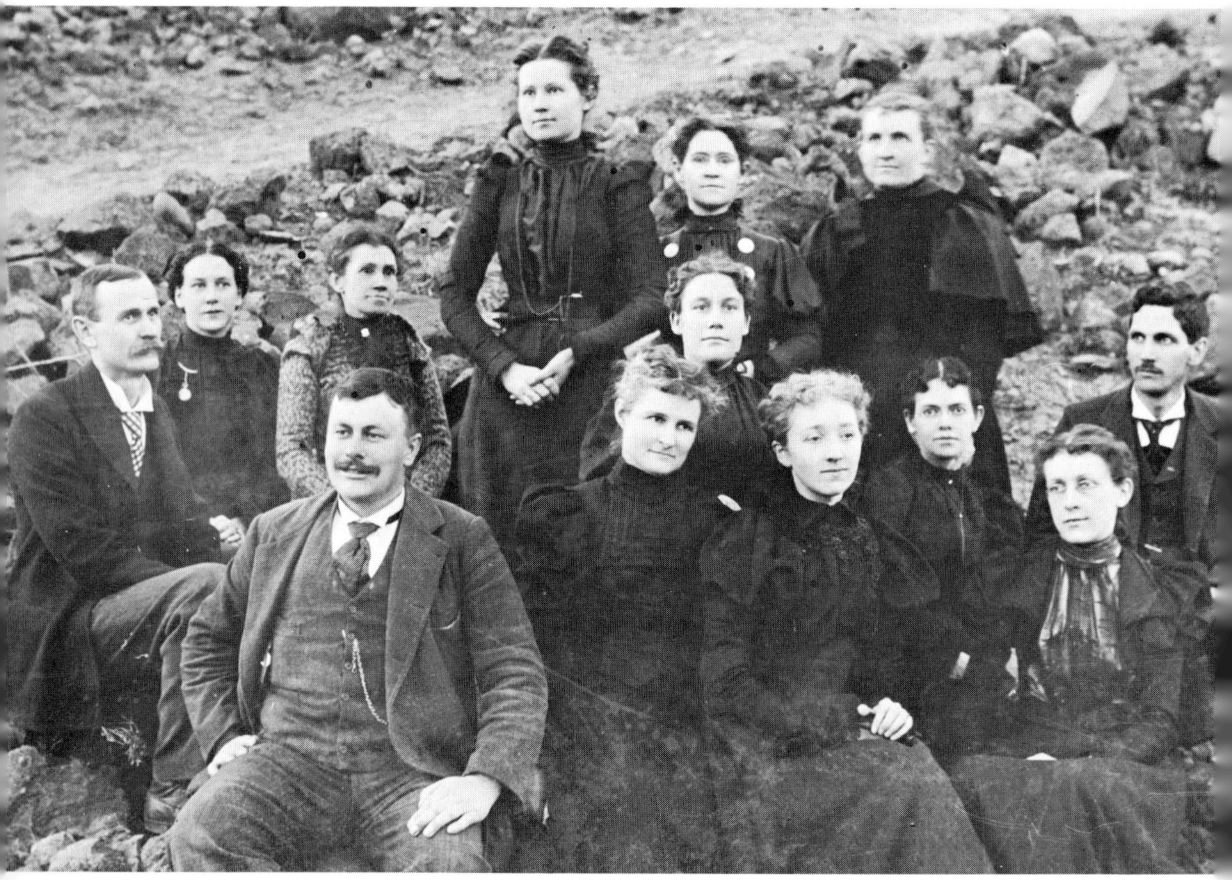

Basalt Chatauqua Club, about 1904. Standing (left to right): Pearl Willits, Mrs. Zimmerman, Mrs. John Smith. Seated (second row): Mr. McMillan, Mattie Stiffler, Mrs. Cornelia Willits, Mrs. Hardcastle, Mrs. Bates, Grant Ruland. Front row: Dr. McNeilan, Mrs. Jim May, Mrs. McNeilan, Mrs. McMillan.

assisted by members of the congregation. Lee Willits has written us the following note about the early years:

"The church was incorporated as the James Bennett Memorial Methodist Episcopal Church sometime during the founding years. We have never been able to find any information on this, and the original certificate of incorporation has been lost. No one we have talked to has ever heard of James Bennett; there are many conjectures.

"On August 5, 1954 the name of the church was changed to the Basalt Community Methodist Church, and the articles of incorporation was issued that day." The Illiff School of Theology has no information about the earlier designation.

Clarence Danielson remembers that our father spent many hours working on the masonry of the foundation of the building and the carpentry. Others remember their fathers doing the same. Improvements to the building have culminated in an enlargement in recent years so that it no longer appears exactly as the little church with the steep steps in front that we knew as children. The unforgettable, impressive, and joyous rededication service took place on February 2, 1964, with a number of past ministers present. Bishop Glenn R. Phillips and Superintendent Hawes performed the "Act of Dedication", and the sermon, "The Church and You" by Bishop Phillips, made a deep and lasting impression on all those in the large congregation. A new rug and electric organ were given as memorials in 1963.

The Rev. Martin Rist and the Rev. Emery Purcell of the Iliff School of Theology most graciously compiled for the authors the list of names of the pastors of the Basalt Methodist Church from 1892 to the present—taken from the conference journals.

One man whom R.W.D. remembers well, even though he was a small boy at the time, was a visiting minister and lecturer only. He was Chancellor Henry Buchtel of Denver University who came to our town at intervals. Many years ago he went from hamlet to hamlet, by train, horseback, buggy, and on foot, to talk about Denver University and to try to get funds for it. Later he was elected Governor of Colorado. I doubt that he ever collected more than small sums from any one community, but I remember that his earnest pleas for D.U. and his interesting lectures won rapt attention and attendance always. To me, R.W.D., as a small child, they were real "tear-jerkers." To hold down expenses he travelled on the chair-car, no fancy Pullmans for him! We were happy to have him stay at our home when he was in Basalt.

Basalt Methodist Church about 1890.

Evangelists who visited our church were the Rev. Rimanosgy and the Rev. McDowell in January 1903. The Rev. and Mrs. W.J. Kalfie came in 1907.

Special mention should be made of the Rev. Harvey M. Law who was born in West Virginia, April 9, 1848. His parents were Andrew and Margaret Law. He married Catherine

Interior of the Basalt Methodist Church, 1961.

R. W. D. Collection

Rexroad, March 18, 1868. They had two children, Charlie Warren and Andrew Dixon.

He was active not only in building the church at Basalt, but also in building those at Carbondale and at Glenwood Springs. His son, Charlie Law, worked first for Smith Mercantile Company and was station agent on the Midland for many years. He married Sylvia Barker, Feb. 17, 1892. They had two daughters, who were born in Basalt. They are: Mrs. Nina Esther Law Corbin, and Mrs. Bessie Myra Law Drath, both now residing in Denver who have given the following information regarding their parents.

Harvey Milton Law received his preacher's license September 29, 1866; traveled a part of two years under the presiding elder

photo from Nina Law Corbin

Rev. and Mrs. H. M. Law. Rev. Law was pastor of the Basalt Methodist Church during the years 1896 and 1897. To the right is Rev. Law in later years.

in the West Virginia Conference. In the spring of 1870 he came to Greeley, Weld Co., Colorado, where he worked as a carpenter for seven years.

In his book Beardsley says about Harvey M. Law: "From 1877 to 1883 he supplied in the Colorado Conference, when he was admitted on trial, having been ordained a local deacon the year previous. His appointments since entering the Conference have been: Rawlins, three years; Lamar and Montrose, each one year; Glenwood Springs, four years, where he built a church valued at $3,500; Del Norte and Gunnison, each one year."

In addition, quoting from the "Record of Colorado Conference of the Methodist Church", he served at Bald Mountain (Nevadaville) three years; at Basalt 1896 and 1897; at Fruita 1898 and 1899. He transferred to the West Virginia Conference in 1902.

The church at Rawlins is still in use in 1963, as well as the one at Basalt. Sylvia Law played the organ in the Basalt church from 1892 until about 1899. The family visited the Basalt church in 1934 when she played the original organ again.

The Ladies Aid and the Junior League played prominent parts in the life of our church. One noteworthy project of the Ladies Aid remains today as a valued historic memento, the unique Friendship Quilt (also known as the Souvenir Quilt and the Autograph Quilt). It is a thrilling experience to look at the many familiar names embroidered on it, and also to realize that much of the lettering and designing was the work of Mrs. W.P. Bates and our mother, Clara Danielson. There is space for each organization in Basalt with its insignia and the names of members. A note in the Basalt Journal of December 16, 1905 says

Envelope in Rev. Law's handwriting, illustrating the fine style of penmanship of the time.

Loaned by Nina Law Corbin

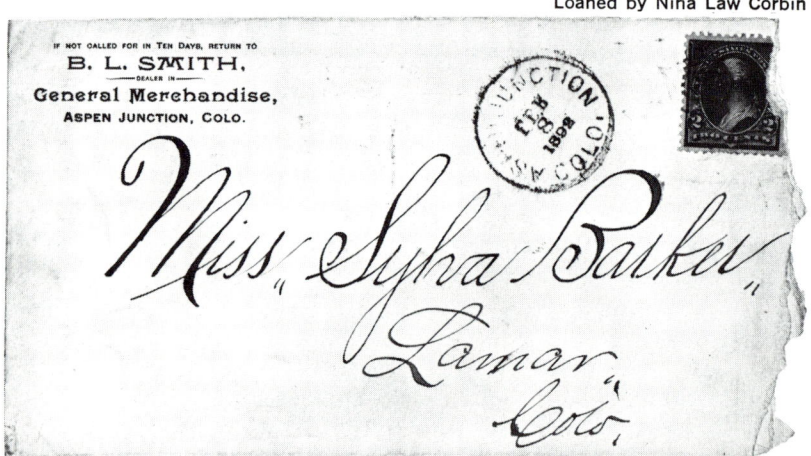

that the quilt was purchased at auction by Mr. W.P. Bates for $11.00 having been "bid in" for him by Mr. E.B. Kelly, as Mr. Bates was out of town. This beautiful quilt of 1905 is in excellent condition and is now the property of Mr. and Mrs. Arthur Bates of Denver. They may eventually put it on exhibit at the State Historical Society of Colorado so that many people may have the privilege of seeing it. The number of names embroidered on it is approximately four hundred. Each person represented paid ten cents for having his name there. The money raised seems small to us today, yet it was quite a sum in those days. The quilt is an excellent source of reference for the lodges and organizations of the period.

A child of a former Basalt pastor told us that her father had been greatly impressed by the good behavior of the children of one of his parishioners. When he complimented the mother she replied that this was because each Sunday she spanked them before they went to church to be sure that they would behave. One wonders how this affected them in later years in regard to church-going.

It is interesting to peruse editorials from the *Basalt Journal*.

Feb. 10, 1900

"No one feature contributes more to the enjoyableness of church going than a pleasant appointed and well furnished church edifice.

"Last fall the building was thoroughly renovated, papered and painted on the inside, and now through the united efforts of the Epworth League and the Ladies Aid a fine new pulpit has been received.

"It is not often that a public lecturer finds his way into Basalt, but we are about to be especially favored in this respect on Saturday evening, Feb. 17. 'The Cowboy Preacher,' Rev. Tom Leland of Rifle, will deliver his famous lecture 'The Cowboy in History in the M.E. Church.'

"Before his conversion and entrance upon the ministry, Mr. Leland was a thoroughbred cowboy, having ridden the ranges of Colorado and New Mexico for years. He has not forgotten how to handle the rope and the gun, but no one need fear to attend the lecture on this account."

Another clipping from the *Basalt Journal* of March 24, 1900:

A Railroad Man's Prayer

An old railroad man was converted, as the story goes, and was asked to lead in prayer. This is the way he worded it:

160 Community Activities

Photo from Mr. Hollenback

Rev. and Mrs. Frank R. Hollenback. Rev. Hollenback was pastor of the Basalt Methodist Church during the years 1899 and 1901.

"O Lord, now that I have flagged thee, lift up my feet from the rough road of life and plant them safely on the deck of the train of salvation. Let me use the safety lamp known as prudence, make all the couplings in the train with the strong link of Thy love, and let my hand-lamp be the Bible, and, Heavenly Father, keep all switches closed that lead off on the sidings, especially those with a blind end. O Lord, if it be Thy pleasure, have every semiphore block along the line show the white light of hope, that I may make the run of life without stopping. And Lord, give us the Ten Commandments for a schedule; and when I have finished the run, on schedule time, pulled into the great dark station of Death, may Thou, the Superintendent of the Universe, say, 'Well done, thou good and faithful servant; come and sign the payroll and receive your check for eternal happiness'."—*Exchange*.

The authors have been exceedingly fortunate in having a son of one of Basalt's former pastors and the two daughters of two others all willing to help us by writing about their families, the church, and experiences in the community. Happily all have a background of literary talent which adds much to the accounts.

The article by Frank R. Hollenback, a consulting engineer and a writer of note who lives in Denver follows. (He is the author of many articles and books on Colorado railroads.)

Frank R. Hollenback

Frank R. Hollenback, pastor of the Basalt Methodist Episcopal Church, once a part of the Basalt-Carbondale charge, was born in Minonk, Illinois, February 16, 1871. The family moved to Gage County, Nebraska, then several years later to a farm near Blue Springs.

In his early twenties, Frank Hollenback served as lay preacher in several small towns near Lincoln while attending Nebraska Wesleyan University. Upon graduation, and marriage to Eva Mable Schock in 1896, he entered Drew Theological Seminary at Madison, New Jersey. While completing the three-year seminary course, he also held a student pastorate at Seaford on the south shore of Long Island, commuting twice a week between Seaford and Madison.

It was a big jump in 1899 from a fishing village on Long Island to the booming town of Basalt in the Colorado Rockies. But when the opening at Basalt-Carbondale was offered, the Hollenbecks accepted at once. It would have been typical of them, upon arrival, to look up and down the Roaring Fork valley and say, "This is our country." They always recalled the two years from 1899 to 1901 at Basalt-Carbondale with the fondest of memories. The Hollenbacks are credited with building the church and parsonage at Basalt during their stay.

From Basalt the Reverend and Mrs. Hollenback went on to Salida, Canon City, and Rocky Ford before coming to Denver, where he assumed the superintendency of the Colorado Springs district in 1909. From 1913 to 1915, he was pastor at Grace Church, Denver. Between 1915 and 1925, he held, successively, the positions of Greeley District superintendent, Denver area secretary, and Denver District superintendent.

In the Methodist church a district superintendent's job is probably nine parts field work to one in the office. Four times a year he must visit and hold quarterly conferences at each of the churches in his district. Fifty years ago his mode of travel was but a step removed from the old-time circuit rider's horse and buggy. He rode the milk trains and narrow-gauge lines between whistle stops, usually late at night after a full day and evening at each town. One week of his railroad routine would probably satisfy today's most avid railroad fan for a lifetime.

From 1926 to 1938, Dr. Hollenback served in Boulder and Longmont Churches and Christ Church, Denver. He retired in 1938.

Two sons who did not survive infancy were born in Carbondale. Another son, Frank Robert, a graduate of the Colorado School of Mines, lives in Denver.

Dr. Hollenback, awarded a D.D. from Denver University in 1911, was on the boards of trustees of the university and the Iliff School of Theology many years. He also held many posts on numerous national boards of the church. He was a member of the Ben Franklin Club, Inspiration Lodge No. 143, Colorado Consistory No. 1, and El Jebel Shrine. At the time of his death, April 7, 1942, he was president of the Colorado Methodist Historical Society.

Eva S. Hollenback was the ideal minister's wife. She entered wholeheartedly into all church and community activities, always making lasting friendships wherever her husband's assignments took them.

As Eva Mable Schock, born near Falls City, Nebraska, October 22, 1873, she received degrees from Nebraska Wesleyan University and the University of Nebraska. She taught at both Falls City High School, where she was also principal, and at the Wesleyan University. She and Frank R. Hollenback were married in 1896 and left immediately for Seaford, Long Island, New York. There, the couple became avid seafood eaters since pay was largely in kind at this fishing village. While her husband was away at school all week, returning only for week-end services, Mrs. Hollenback held an unofficial post as "assistant pastor" during his absence.

This experience, together with a natural aptitude for the job, served her well in assisting her husband during his many pastoral and administrative assignments in the Colorado Methodist Conference, beginning at Basalt-Carbondale in 1899.

Mrs. Hollenback, a very capable administrator herself, occupied many high-level positions nationally in both the home and foreign activities of the Methodist church. This work required considerable travel and numerous convention roles for which she was well suited.

As a hobbyist, she always found time for gardening, women's clubs, and writing; she had a deep interest in the history of Colorado and of Methodism in the state. Throughout her later life, despite a wide acquaintanceship in other Colorado towns and cities, her remarks many times began with, "In our days at Basalt . . . ." Mrs. Hollenback passed away in Denver, March 11, 1951.

Rev. Louis J. Hole

Louis Jacob Hole was born in Salem, Ohio, Sept. 15, 1866. His father and mother were Methodists and he joined the church

Courtesy of Hilda Hole Parmater

Rev. and Mrs. Louis J. Hole. Rev. Hole was pastor of the Basalt Methodist Church in 1904 and 1905.

and became very active in it at an early age. He received his college training at Mount Union College, Alliance, Ohio. He married Miss Cora S. Burford on July 5, 1893, in Salem, Ohio. They had three daughters. Dorothy died at the age of 3 years. Frances is now Mrs. R. L. Underwood, of Riverside, Rhode Island. Hilda (Mrs. Harry) Parmater lives in Denver.

Before entering the ministry he took some training in art which stood him in good stead in chalk talks later. His first charge was at Melbourne, Florida, but, in the hope of alleviating his chronic asthma, he moved west in 1895. He held pastorates in several Colorado towns including Basalt, Carbondale, and Aspen. His last charge was at Highlands Church in Denver where he died during the flu epidemic in 1918.

After his death, Mrs. Hole, during her thirty-two years of widowhood, worked faithfully in many capacities for Trinity Church,

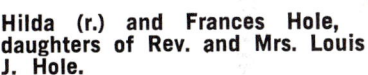

Hilda (r.) and Frances Hole, daughters of Rev. and Mrs. Louis J. Hole.

Ladies Aid Society of the Basalt Methodist Church, about 1915.

Back row (left to right): Mrs. Joe Randall (Jennie), Mrs. Myrtle Randall Dickerman.

Second row: Mrs. John Smith (Adelaide), Mrs. Marvin Sloss (Edna Long), Mrs. Drake, Mrs. Anthony Carlson (Neva), Mrs. Clinton Benbow (Mollie), Mrs. Kennedy, Charles Kennedy, Mrs. Tierney Gray, Mrs. Tucker, Mrs. Phil Smith (Helen Clarke), Mrs. Asa Harris (Birdie), Mrs. Boyce, Mrs. Borneman, Mrs. Hartson, Mrs. Virgil Holcomb (Blanche Smith Stager), Mrs. John Scandlan, Mrs. Strong.

Third row (seated): Mrs. Clarence Danielson (Lucy Clarke) Mrs. Clarence Batcheller (Lois Danielson), Mrs. Edith Clarke, Mrs. Arthur Vaughn (Edith Danielson), Mrs. Rye Ould (Irene Clarke) Mrs. Simmons, Mrs. Howard Shader (Lucy Jane Ould), Mrs. Herman Thelin (Irene Stager), Mrs. Carl Rother (May Lydick), Lucille Rother.

in Denver. Mrs. Hole passed away following a stroke on Nov. 28, 1950. Editor Claudius Spencer, editor of the Central Christian Advocate, wrote as follows: "We first met Louis J. Hole where asthma had driven him to the sunny skies and health-bringing rivers of air flowing from the mountains of Colorado. He was wrestling with his health problem but filled with the wonder and love of life, especially the life of the ministry. He seemed so fragile, and yet there was sweetness, a faith, a buoyancy in his thought that transformed his weakness into strength."

Hilda Parmater relates that before she was old enough to go to school, Rev. and Mrs. Hole taught their small daughter about the value and practical use of money, assuring her it was a waste to spend all her pennies on sweets. One day a generous parishioner gave her a nickel. At her first opportunity she spent it. She could scarcely wait to show her parents her purchase, as proof she had learned her lesson well. To her surprised parents she exhibited a pair of shoe laces, only to be reminded by them that she was wearing button shoes.

The following interesting account by Frances Underwood merits publication.

"Return to Basalt in 1961
(After an absence of fifty five years)
In remembrance of Dr. and Mrs. Louis J. Hole."

"In the summer of 1961 our entire family (my husband, son and daughter and myself) left Rhode Island to fulfill a dream of many years. It was to travel to Colorado and visit each of the eight towns I had lived in as a child and young woman during the time my father had served in them as a Methodist minister.

"Our first stop in Colorado was Denver, the scene of my father's last pastorate, Highlands Methodist Church. We had a few days visit here with my sister Hilda and her husband before continuing our Colorado trip.

"I was especially looking forward to seeing Basalt again, because I have some of the most vivid memories of my life of experiences I had when I lived there. That was the town where I started to school at the age of six years.

"The first place we located in Basalt, in 1961, was the Methodist Church where father had preached. From the outside it looked much the same as I remembered it back in the early nineteen hundreds. I missed the long flight of stairs on the outside leading to the sanctuary. I used to dread that stairway because, as a child attending Sunday School and church, I had to

THE BASALT JOURNAL

W. H. HILDRETH, Publisher.

CHURCH DIRECTORY.

Services every Sunday at 8:00 p. m. Sunday School at 10:30 a. m. Prayer meeting each Thursday evening. Choir meeting Friday evenings.

REV. L. J. HOLE, Pastor.

EPWORTH LEAGUE—Meets regularly every Sunday evening at 7:00 o'clock. All called and business meetings will be announced by the president. Grant Ruland, President; Miss Susie Stifler, Secretary.

JUNIOR LEAGUE—Meets every Sunday at 3 p. m. Mrs Mollie Coffin, superintendent.

LADIES' AID SOCIETY—Meets every other Thursday. Time and place of meeting will be announced by the president through the Sabbath pulpit notices. Mrs. L. J. Hole, President; Mrs. O. G. Rhodes, Secretary.

LODGE DIRECTORY.

KNIGHTS OF PYTHIAS—Eagle Lodge, No. 83, meets every Friday evening in Odd Fellows' hall. R P. Hyrup, C. C. R H. Hazleton, K. of R. and S.

RATHBONE SISTERS—Calla Lily Temple, No. 9, meets every alternate Wednesday at 8 p. m. Mary Harris, M. E C Allie White, M. of R. C.

BROTHERHOOD OF LOCOMOTIVE ENGINEERS—Seven Castles Division, No. 515, meets every Tuesday at 2:30 p. m. James Fahey, C. E.; A. M. Danielson, F. A E.; B. W. Burgin, Ins. Agent.

G. I. A.—Columbine Division, No. 242, meets every first and third Tuesdays of each month at 2:30 p. m. Mrs. Augusta Snell, President; Mrs. Mary Nelson, Secretary; Mrs. Jennie Bates, Ins. Sec.

BROTHERHOOD OF LOCOMOTIVE FIREMEN Mt Sopris Lodge, No. 503, meets every Monday afternoon at 2 p. m. Dan De Groot, Master; H. C. Lydick, Sec'y.

ODD FELLOWS—Mt. Basalt Lodge. No. 83 meets every Saturday evening at 7 o'clock in I. O. O. F. hall. J. H. Troendly, N. G. W. H. Hildreth, Secretary.

REBEKAHS—Free Silver Lodge, No. 47, meets the first and third Mondays in each month at 7:30 p. m. Durinda Turner, N. G. Claudie Ohngemach, Secretary.

WOODMEN OF THE WORLD—Frying Pan Camp, No. 393, meets the first and third Tuesday evenings of each month at I. O. O. F. hall. J. H. Troendly, Consul commander, R. H. Hazleton, clerk.

WOMEN OF WOODCRAFT—Laurel Circle No. 323, meets every second and fourth Wednesdays of each month. Anna Hull, Guardian Neighbor. Jennie C. Hazleton, clerk.

TOWN OFFICIALS.

Mayor—Charles C. Andrus.
Aldermen—Danielson, Nelson, Stifler, Smith, Burgin, Hazleton.
Clerk—W. H. Hildreth.
Treasurer—A. G. England
Marshal—J. H. Vandeventer.
Police Magistrate—H. C. Lydick.
Water Commissioner—J. H. Vandeventer.

OFFICERS OF EAGLE COUNTY.

BOARD OF COMMISSIONERS—Mack Fleck, Avon; A. D. McKenzie, Eagle chairman. John Auld Basalt;
CLERK AND RECORDER—James D. Cooper Red Cliff.
TREASURER—A. S. Little, Red Cliff.
ASSESSOR—N. Buchholz, Eagle.
SHERIFF—Frank Farnum, Gilman
SUPERINTENDENT OF SCHOOLS — Grant Ruland, Basalt.
COUNTY JUDGE—E. Tagne, Red Cliff
CORONER—W. H. Farnum, Red Cliff.
SURVEYOR—W. H. Lea.

A page from the Basalt Journal, September 24, 1904.

pass by all the little boys who lined up on the edge of the stairway and teased and called you names. I discovered later that the stairway had been enclosed in the fine new addition to the church, which may be a discouragement to the modern day boys.

"By chance, as we were looking over the outside of the structure, we introduced ourselves to two women who were picking gorgeous sweet peas at a beautiful modern house next to the church. One of the women proved to be a former close friend of my mother's, as well as a faithful church member when my father had served the church, as well as now. She was Anna Rhodes Sloss. She had the church key in her pocket and offered to take us on a tour of the church. I was not able to go with the others because of being badly handicapped from a serious paralytic shock. They all reported it was a well-planned structure with fine modern equipment. I am sure it would seem much changed from the building my mother and father worked in. I remember the room where the primary class met for Sunday School at the rear of the church sanctuary, which was taught by my mother. I well remember the Sunday when Ralph Danielson announced he had no offering because he had swallowed his nickel on the way to Sunday School. Mother was quite concerned and thought he ought to go home for treatment. But he refused to go with the comment, "I'll be all right. My mother swallows needles and pins all the time and they don't hurt her." (I presume he had seen her with a mouthful of pins while she was sewing. Women used to do that a lot in those times.) He seems to have survived the experience, as I understand he is now a successful doctor in Denver. I also remember the large stove in the rear of the church which was the only method of heating in the winter time. One time, in the middle of the week father took me into the church with him when he was going to start a fire to warm up the church for a later evening meeting. He was amazed to find live coals in the fire box which should have gone out some time previous since there had been no meetings since the previous Sunday. Then he noticed tracks on the floor. We followed them across the church to an unlocked window. On opening the window he pointed out to me men's footprints in the snow under the window on the side of the church near the hill. He decided some tramp had climbed in and had a few comfortable warm days. Altho he did not begrudge the tramp a little comfort, he was fearful that if it became a known retreat some careless tramp might cause a fire. So from then on, he was careful to see that any accessible windows were locked.

"Another thing I recall about the church was the time and work my mother and the other women of the church put into beautifying the clear paper window designs. The women spent many hours pasting these paper designs on the windows. After they had completely adhered to the glass, the sun and light coming through them gave an appearance, at least from a distance, of stained glass windows. They were exceedingly proud of their efforts.

"Whenever I look at a Western on television, I always feel the business section of the town looks like Basalt did back there in 1903 to 1906, with the saloon and postoffice at one end of the block and the fine drug store at the other end, with the long connected one-story building running along in between. In one of the buildings, one of the two doctors had his office. The town had two doctors but no dentist. The two doctors, whose names I do not recall, had no great love for each other in their competitive profession. The dentist would appear every year or so and stay at the hotel near the railroad station. Then everyone who needed dental attention would go to him there. In between visits, the doctors would care for any aching teeth by pulling them with the dentist's forceps which they both had in their medical equipment. There was a favorite story that one of the doctors had an aching tooth and the other, when appealed to, pulled it, or at least so he thought. By mistake, he had pulled not the aching tooth but a perfectly good one. From that day, relations between the two were quite strained.

"It was interesting in 1961 to drive through the streets of Basalt and pick out the places we had known fifty-five years before. I recognized the Smith house where I had often played with Clifford Smith and the other friends at the top of the hill which led down to the postoffice when I was a child. My sister recalled when Clifford caught scarlet fever the same time we did, and how Clifford and his mother came up to the parsonage to be quarantined with us, while father went down to live at the Smith's so he could continue his pastoral work.

"I recognized the Rhodes' home where Anna Sloss had lived and where I used to meet her each day to be taken to school by her. My sister remembered that it was just about here on the road that our mother had been walking up the hill from town when she looked toward her home and saw children flying through the air, as it were, jumping from the top of one shed to a lower shed and then off into the parsonage coal pile. Imagine her relief when, breathless, she reached the top of the hill to find her daughters and several neighbor children still sound of body and limb.

"Altho there were many changes, of course, I could still recognize many of the former homes. The parsonage was still standing. We found Anna Sloss now lived in what had been Professor Troendley's home when he was school principal. I recall one very interesting experience I had with him. His wife was away for a few days so my mother invited him to lunch. Mr. Troendley and my father became engaged in conversation over politics or some other issue and he and I were late getting into my first grade class. We had a school rule that every class which had no late or absent pupils would have a half day holiday the last Friday of the month. I shall never forget the looks of scorn when I walked in late. I was terrified because I was sure the boys would beat me up at recess because that was their method of treatment to late comers. I was very relieved when in the middle of the afternoon Mr. Troendley walked in and announced that since he was late also it would not be counted against me. Was I happy! The schoolhouse was in the same location in 1961 as when I attended it. Altho as I remembered it, it was a very nice brick school, the present one is a splendid modern building. In my time, the school was surrounded by farms which in the fall of the year presented quite a problem because a number of them raised grain. The word would go around school that the wheat was to be harvested and that the threshing machine was at so-and-so's farm. At recess time the daring members of the school would decide to play hookey and go over to the farm and watch the threshing machine. I was always afraid of being punished. So I never had the courage to go. I remember one day, after recess, there were practically none left but just a few of us scaredy cats. As I remember it we were allowed to have a holiday because we had not played hookey.

"My mother thought the road was rather dangerous for a six year old to travel alone. So she had an arrangement with Anna Rhodes, who was six or seven years older, to take me to school each day, since I had two hills to go down, a railroad track and a bridge over a river to cross, as well as climb a hill just before arrival at school. Probably the greatest hazard was the railroad track we had to cross. It ran down the middle of the main street. Often a long freight train would be stopped right across our path. It might mean a wait of at least a half hour, or maybe more, until it moved on. Sometimes many of the children would crawl under the train from one side to the other. Altho we had been

170 Community Activities

warned not to do so. I was sure I had never disobeyed, but in 1961 Anna Sloss told me she took me under once because she remembered how her father scolded her for doing it when she was supposed to be looking after me.

"The drug store was a favorite shopping place for the school children to buy candy. There was a time when a certain kind of chocolates were most popular. I had a bag of them at home one day and father took one. He was very disturbed to find they were filled with wine. Being a minister with a strong temperance viewpoint, he went immediately down to the drug store and asked them to discontinue that line of chocolates. And this they did. I don't recall the attitude of the children, who probably never knew.

"I have many happy memories of Basalt, especially of the night-time thrill of going out in the dark streets carrying lanterns to see our way to church or social activities.

"As we arrived home from our 1961 Colorado trip, one wish kept returning to me — the wish that I could start right out and take the trip all over again."

By Mrs. Robert L. Underwood
(Formerly Frances Ruth Hole)

List of Pastors of Methodist Episcopal Church

Courtest of Dr. Martin Rist, Chairman of the Dept. of New Testament and Christian History, The Iliff School of Theology, Denver.

PASTORAL APPOINTMENTS FROM THE
CONFERENCE JOURNALS UNIVERSITY

Year	Pastor	Year	Pastor
1892	S. A. Weber (1)*	1914	
1893	S. A. Weber (2)	1915	F. H. Rose (1)
1894	W. R. Ashby (1)	1916	J. Andrew Dean (1)
1895	W. R. Ashby (2)	1917	J. Andrew Dean (2)
1896	H. M. Law (1)	1918	J. Andrew Dean (3)
1897	H. M. Law (2)	1919	W. H. Rose (1)
1898	E. P. F. Dearborn (1)	1920	W. H. Rose (2)
1899	F. R. Hollenback (2)**	1921	W. H. Rose (3)
1900	F. R. Hollenback (3)	1922	W. H. Rose (4)
1901	T. S. Leland (1)	1923	W. H. Rose (5)
1902	T. S. Leland (2)	1924	W. H. Rose (6)
1903		1925	
1904	L. J. Hole (1)	1926	J. N. Glazier (1)
1905	L. J. Hole (2)	1927	Ernest Everett (1)
1906	E. N. Mallery (2)	1928	W. E. Bennett (1)
1907	Will E. Bennett (2)	1929	Theo Dowler (1)
1908	Stephen Lumley (1)	1930	
1909	G. F. Brock (1)	1931	(No appointment listed)
1910	C. E. Harris (1)	1932	(No appointment listed)
1911	O. R. Ellmaker (1)	1933	J. M. Glazier (1)
1912		1934	J. S. Brownell (1)
1913	supplied from Grand Valley J. V. Watson		

*a number in parentheses indicates the year of service on the charge.
**a (2) after a name that appears for the first time indicates that the man served a major portion of the preceding year also.

1935 J. S. Brownell (2)	1948
1936 J. S. Brownell (3)	1949 Keith Hamilton (1)
1937 J. S. Davis (2)	1950 Keith Hamilton (2)
1938 R. D. Webster (1)	1951 Sigurd Burch (2)
1939 O. C. King (1)	1952 Sigurd Burch (3)
1940 O. C. King (2)	1953 Bronston Greenwood (1)
1941 O. C. King (3)	1954 Bronston Greenwood (2)
1942	1955 Bronston Greenwood (3)
1943 Norman Babcock (2)	1956 Bronston Greenwood (4)
1944 Norman Babcock (3)	1957 Doyle Hauschulz (1)
1945	1958 Doyle Hauschulz (2)
1946 Minar A. Gerrard (2)	1959 Doyle Hauschulz (3)
1947 Minar A. Gerrard (3)	1960-64 Keith Merriman (1)

Minutes of Ladies Aid

For a nostalgic and enlightening bit of church history one can find much of interest in the carefully-kept "Minutes of the Ladies' Aid Society" for the years and dates: December 10, 1902 to February 7, 1918. On September 17, 1903, for example, "A motion was made that the Ladies' Aid Society devote one hour to business and that this hour be devoted strictly to business. Motion carried." Addie Rhodes, Secretary.

On September 8, 1905, a happy motion was made. "Mrs. Hole suggested we make an autograph quilt and get the names of

Courtesy of Mrs. Lydia Newkirk

BIRTHDAY PARTY.

I. O. O. F. Hall, Monday, May 18, 1896.

A Birthday Party, we're talking about,
And we could not bear to leave YOU out!
So we ask you kindly to come and see
The tip-top time, we'll furnish you free!
We promise to give you supper and song,
So please, dear friend, come right along.
We send you the cutest little sack
And we only ask you to bring it back,
Or send it, if you cannot come,
With as many cents as you are years old.
We promise your age shall never be told!

LADIES' AID.

members belonging to all the different organizations. Appointed to the committee: Mmes. McMillan, Hazelton, Hole and Benbow."

On May 24, 1907, it was noted by the secretary, Electa M. Scandlan, that, "On account of so much work on hand no business meeting was held." On September 16, 1915 the minutes state: "Flowers have been sent to Mrs. A. M. Danielson in her sad bereavement, and a letter from Mrs. Danielson has been received thanking us for the flowers."

Through the years in these minutes one finds how many types of "socials" for raising money for the church were in vogue in those far-off days. The Pie Social, Experience Social, Literary Social, Parcel Post Social, Sewing Social, and Ice Cream Social were some of them. A "Health Lecture" by Miss Wilson is mentioned too, and also a "Night-gown Sale."

The Basalt Catholic Church

Before there was a Church in Basalt visitations were made by priests from Aspen and Glenwood Springs from time to time and for funerals. Our long-time boyhood friend, Walter Hyrup, remembers Father Servant of Aspen; Father O'Begley, Father O'Dwyer, Father Bruner, Father Sugrue, Father Hapet, Father Rivalier, and Father Corrigan, all of Glenwood. He also remembers that Father Joseph came to Basalt for the Fahey funerals. Services were held irregularly in homes of the area.

Most of the farmers from Italy and ranchers of Italian descent were of the Roman Catholic faith. The Midland section men, being mainly of Irish and Italian descent also were Catholics. The one we remember best was the track walker, Barney Flynn. Townspeople of Catholic faith were the Hyrups, Faheys, McMahons, McCartys, Connels, Frisons, Paddocks, Conertys, Willises, Tulleys and others.

In a letter received on October 23, 1962, Walter Hyrup's sister, Eugenia, now Mrs. Charles Murray of California, writes as follows:

"In the early days the Catholic group in Aspen Junction was a tiny part in the extensive Mission of St. Stephen's Catholic Church in Glenwood Springs. Mass was infrequently celebrated in the homes of the faithful.

"The lack of a church inspired an organization dedicated to raise the funds for one. It progressed slowly, and as time went on new members took over.

"At long last a lot was bought, the gift of a 3-room house was accepted, moved and renovated, and became St. Vincent's Church. It was dedicated by Bishop Tihen of Denver, assisted by the Rev. J. P. Corrigan of Glenwood Springs in June 1924.

"The priests of sacred memory who have departed this life, and who served our Mission were: Father O'Begley, Father David O'Dwyer, Father Joseph Brunner, Father Sugrue, and Father Corrigon.

"As for the nuns you saw at our home, they were regular visitors every fall. They were sent out by the Orphange for homeless children, "The Queen of Heaven" institution in Denver, to beg.

"The Rio Grande railroad as an act of charity set out a box car at Emma on the side track so that farmers who donated potatoes, cabbages, onions, etc., to these little nuns plodding through the countryside could deposit their gifts in the cars and thus be delivered free to the orphange in Denver. I can't recall any names, although Sister Mary Clair and Mother Ignatius have been suggested.

"I wish I could have presented these foregoing notes in better form and I hope I've helped a little."

A few additional bits of information we have been able to gather will be of interest.

The building was originally a house owned and given by Mrs. Anna Murmann Hyrup, and was moved onto a lot which also belonged to Mrs. Hyrup. Father Corrigan obtained the bell from the Church in Glenwood Springs and then the entrance vestibule and bell tower were built. It is said that the marble altar came from an old chapel in Redstone.

About 1956 the building was enlarged to double its seating capacity and also, at that time, a new bell tower was build independent of the building itself.

After 1914 priests from Aspen instead of those at Glenwood Springs took over Basalt services. Father McSweeney of Aspen served from 1914 until he died in 1941. Then came Father Charles Sanger who remained until 1944. From that time until 1946 Father Abbott officiated. Father Banigan served from 1946 until 1954. The present priest, Father Joseph E. Busch, began the custom of saying Mass not only on Sundays but on other Holy Days as well.

Today, counting all families considering belonging to the parish, there is a membership of about seventy-five families.

174 Community Activities

Schools

It is recalled by the early residents that there were at one time two schools in Basalt. One was located on the hill north of town and was known as the "High School", whether because it was on high ground, or because of the grades, I do not know. This was a totally Eagle County school, and was closed about 1890-95. One of the teachers C.L.D. remembers then was Miss Minnie Sandusky, although her names does not appear on the official record of the Board of Education office.

On the other hand, the main school was built about on the line between Eagle County and Pitkin County and was a joint venture of the two counties. This school is still located near the original settlement of Frying Pan Junction.

As I look back on it, what a treat we had, as we left home to go to school, in view of snow-covered majestic Mt. Sopris. Then when I arrived at school, I could look back the other way and see the ever-interesting Basalt mountain with its lava bed and amphitheaters. Mr. and Mrs. Arthur Weidman, who have now built a home on the old Mallory place, have a unique location in that from their gorgeous home they see Basalt Mountain one way and Mt. Sopris the other.

Teachers

The teachers I, R.W.D., remember best were Irene Willits, Grace Hallock, Mary A. O'Dea, and Dee Hibner. Miss Willits taught me in the first grade during her three years there. She also taught three years at Red Cliff and one year at El Jebel. She married Dr. Randall, a dentist in Eagle, Colorado, in 1910. Miss Hallock became Mrs. Pike and moved to Spokane, Washington. Dee Hibner was my teacher in the two years of high school and taught all the classes in the two years. He later married Eleanor McCarty and became Superintendent of Schools in Safford, Arizona, for many years.

Through the cooperation of the office of the State Board of Education, we were permitted to go through the old records of teachers and to prepare the following list of teachers and the superintendents of schools of Eagle County.

Teachers and Superintendents—Basalt Public Schools, 1887-1918

Year	Teachers	Eagle County Supt. of Schools
1887-1888	Louisa Morris, Lillie (Till?) Curtis	Edward A. Stinson
1888-1889	Louisa Morris, Fannie Gould	Edward A. Stinson
1889-1890	W.E. Long, Kate M. Corbett, Fannie Gould, Miss M.A. McVey	Edward A. Stinson
1890-1891	B.L. Smith	Edward A. Stinson

photo from Fred Carlson

Miss Grace Hallock.

1891-1892	B.L. Smith, Julia Mitchell, Ida Biller, Mable Laura Cook	Edward A. Stinson
1892-1893	Maggie Mitchell, Mary Andrus, Ida Miller	Edward A. Stinson
1893-1894	Elizabeth Tully, Bertha Johnson	E.M. Scandlan
1894-1895	Elizabeth Tully	E.M. Scandlan
1895-1896	Elizabeth Tully, Grant Ruland	E.M. Scandlan
1896-1897	Elizabeth Tully, Grant Ruland, Frona Abbott	James Dilts
1897-1898	Grant Ruland, Rose Tounard	James Dilts
1898-1899	Grant Ruland, Pearl Willits	Eva Bovea
1899-1900	Grant Ruland, H.G. Stearns, Pearl Willits, Blanche Bancroft, Minnie Bowen	Eva Bovea
1900-1901	J.H. Troendly, Ella B. Crowder, Clara Crawford, Clara Denton	Eva Bovea
1901-1902	J.H. Troendly, Ella Crowder, Clara Crawford	Grant Rutland
1902-1903	W.H. Lowry, Meta Reik, Abbie Robinson, Grace Hallock	Grant Ruland
1903-1904	J.H. Troendly, E. Lora Cooke, Grace Hallock, Abbie Robinson	Grant Ruland
1904-1905	Same as 1903-1904	Grant Ruland
1905-1906	J.H. Troendly, E. Lora Cooke, Grace Hallock, Irene Willits	Grant Ruland
1906-1907	Same as 1905-1906	Stella Ruth Welch
1907-1908	Ralph Ellis, E. Lora Cooke, Grace Hallock, Irene Willits	Stella Ruth Welch
1908-1909	J.W. McKeown, Grace Hallock, Flora Trezise, Mary A. O'Dea	J.H. Troendly
1909-1910	Mary A. O'Dea, Nora Lydick, Irene Stratton, Rachel Stiffler, Mrs. H.K. Beigler	J.H. Troendly
1910-1911	D.M. Hibner, Nora Lydick, Irene Stratton,	

C. L. D. collection

The cast of school play, about 1897. Left to right: Phil Smith, Clarence Danielson, Erle Timberlake, Harry Nelson, Will Tierney, Harry Bancroft, Jim Nelson, Roy Bancroft, Ed Swartz and Arthur Bates.

	Bertha Tierney	J.H. Troendly
1911-1912	D.M. Hibner, Jenny Simmes, Irene Stratton	J.H. Troendly
1912-1913	D.M. Hibner, Jenny Simmes, Helen Tandy	Agnes Quinlan
1913-1914	R.M. Early, Jewell Greener, Rachel Stiffler	Agnes Quinlan
1914-1915	R.M. Early, Irene Augustine, Jewell Greener	Ollie Graham
1915-1916	A.C. Armstrong, Dorcas Fleming, Edythe Bailey, Sue Bowland, Irene Augustine	Ollie Graham
1916-1917	W.E. Reid, Dorothy Sherrett, Edythe Bailey, Sue Bowland, Elsie Lucksinger, Irene Augustine	Ollie Graham
1917-1918	W.E. Reid, Rose Ackerman Dorothy Sherrett, Elsie Lucksinger, Yvonne Letty	Ollie Graham

Experiences — High School

I, R.W.D., had my first two years of High School in Basalt, but to say that it was good is not to tell the truth. All subjects of both classes were taught by one teacher. Adequate lesson assignments were not given and there was no competition to push one. My grades were fabulous, but it meant nothing. In my freshman year there were three in my class, and in my sophomore year, only two. The result was that, when I went to Boulder to school, I had a most difficult time and ended up taking three more years in high school in order to graduate. Clarence had his last two years of High School at the Kearney (Nebraska) Military Academy.

Several young people, of course, went to college. Those who went to the Aggies at Fort Collins were Arthur Bates, Ralph Bates, Alvin and Alfred Sloss, and Will Harris. Gladys Hough, Clementine Cramer, Ione Rutherford, Roland Trowbridge, and Ralph Danielson attended Colorado University at Boulder. Jim Tierney and Will Ould graduated from the Denver University Dental School at Denver. One of the Kalfus boys and Clifford and Chester Reibel went to the University of Oregon. Rachel Stiffler attended Colorado State College at Greeley.

Cemeteries

The Fairview Cemetery Association was organized June 30, 1898 by J.A. Smith, C.S. Bancroft, R.H. Zimmerman, C.L. Benbow, W.W. Frey, F.C. Barker, and R.L. Willits, with August Naefe as notary public. The original land for this cemetery was given, according to his daughter, Clementine Cramer Bryant, by her father, Mr. Sam Cramer, at the time of the death of Mrs. Willis, wife of engineer Willis. This gift must have been a considerable time before 1898, for our uncle, Albert Danielson, was buried there in January of 1897. At a later date an additional plot of ground was purchased from Mr. Cramer. Our father purchased a lot July 21, 1898.

Before this cemetery was used, a few people, mostly navvies killed at the time of construction of the Colorado Midland, had been buried on the north bank of the Frying Pan opposite the Mallory place. This ground was on the south side of the road across from the present Ranger Station and was known as graveyard hill.

Unfortunately, the Fairview Cemetary has never had water available to keep it in the condition it deserves.

Basalt Community Methodist Church Basalt, Colorado

photo from Gladys Clavell

Basalt High School, class of 1897-1898.

Standing (l. to r.): Prof. Grant Ruland, Arthur Bates, Floyd May, ..., Claude Grace, Harry Nelson, Horace Irwin, Lilly German, Blanche Bancroft, Gladys Tierney, Susie Stiffler, Bertha Tierney, Mattie Griffith, Eva Dobson, Grace Taylor.
Seated: Mabel Tierney, Blanche Smith, Nellie Caffery, May Griffith.

Basalt High School, about 1904. (Opposite page.)

First row (l. to r.): Harry Nelson, Clarence Danielson, William Caffery, Jim Nelson, Arthur Bates, Bertha Tierney, Nellie Caffeny, Susie Stiffler, Gladys May, Eula Hardesty, Floy Hardcastle.
Back row: Bramlet Willits, Pearl Wilson, ..., Floyd May, India Reeves, Mabel Tierney, Ophelia Miller, Mattie Griffith, Eva Dobson, Gladys Tierney, Mabel Chatfield, Marcia Willits.

Basalt, Colorado Midland Town   181

School in Aspen Junction, about 1894.

1—Mrs. Tully
2—Harry Nelson
3—Leona Clavell
4—Gladys Tierney
5—Floyd May
6—Newton Baines
7—Clarence Danielson
8—Claude Grace
9—Laura Storrs
10—Bertha Tierney
11—Jim Nelson
12—Gertie Riggs
13—Kate O'Neil
14—Jake Frieler
15—Flavine Arbaney
16—Mabel Tierney
17—Julia Luchsinger
18—Eugenia Hyrup
19—Arthur Bates
20—Blanche Smith
21—Eva Dobson

Basalt School, about 1900.

1—Richard Binnings
2—Oma McCabe
3—Harry Hanson
4—Irene Clarke
5—Isabeline Arbaney
6—Jake Frieler
7—Roy Snell
8—Phil Smith
9—George Mather
10—Claude Hartson
11—Ella King
12—Gladys May
13—Cassie Grant
14—Alvin Sloss
15—Jess Bogue
16—Alfred Sloss
17—Lucy Clarke
18—Ernest Dwyer
19—Bill Bogue
20—Joe King
21—Blanche Smith
22—Olive Troendly
23—Jennie King
24—Mattie Stiffler
25—Eugenia Hyrup
26—Ophelia Miller
27—Essie Bogue
28—Cecily Clavell
29—Flavine Arbaney
30—Arthur Bates
31—Clarence Danielson
32—Dan German
33—John Troendly, Supt.
34—Miss Crowder
35—Albert Harris

Basalt, Colorado Midland Town   185

Basalt School, about 1906.

1—Austin Grace
2—Myron Danielson
3—Johnny Genner
4—_____ Miller
5—Ester Valette
6—Leonis Usel
7—Raleigh Dooling
8—Teddy Lucksinger
9—George Lucksinger
10—Alfred Hyrup
11—Willie Price
12—Jack Daywalt
13—John Clarke
14—Everett Carlson
15—Bessie Weaver
16—Bessie Dobson
17—Virginia Usel
18—Ina McMahon
19—_____ Ogden
20—Pauline Eiswerth
21—Juanita Eiswerth
22—Gerald Grace
23—Willie Luchsinger
24—Teller Hall
25—Carl Gilbert
26—Marie Englebright
27—Julia Usel
28—Hazel Mount
29—Elsie Lucksinger
30—Maggie Shay
31—Steve Miller
32—Blanche Valiquette
33—Walter Hyrup
34—Ralph Danielson
35—Miss Mary O'Dea
36—Mrs. Augustine (Irene Stratton)

160 A. M. Danielson
Monthly R. R. Checks,
Average per month.

Year	Amount	Year	Amount
1879	$46.85	1897	120.60
1880	55.02	1898	143.08
1881	63.48	1899	134.45
1882	66.80	1900	109.34
1883	64.85	1901	140.13
1884	64.96	1902	133.85
1885	86.95	1903	123.58
1886	97.40	1904	115.89
1887	127.20	1905	117.75
1888	60.72	1906	153.10
1889	100.86	1907	149.93
1890	186.57	1908	152.28
1891	175.22	1909	148.00
1892	175.86	1910	118.56
1893	198.78	1911	123.96
1894	127.96	1912	139.99
1895	150.76	1913	143.60
1896	142.96	1914	57.10

R. W. D. photo

The average monthly rate of A. M. Danielson, first as a fireman on the C. B. and Q., and later as an engineer on the Colorado Midland.

CHAPTER 7

Families of Basalt

The people who lived in Basalt are the main reason for writing this book. The early chapters deal with the influence of many families on the development of the town. Here we attempt to give a picture of their personal qualities insofar as information has been available.

Unfortunately descriptions have not been readily obtainable about every family in the list we have compiled. For all errors and omissions the reader's forgiveness is sincerely requested. To prolong further the search for material would postpone the publication date beyond the lifetime of those most interested.

Fortunately there are two published volumes of biographies of prominent Colorado residents. These books make most mention of farmers and ranchers and thus they complement our write-ups dealing primarily with residents of the town and those taking active part in town affairs. In 1905, *Progressive Men of Western Colorado* was published in 2 volumes. It includes biographies of these men of the Basalt area and their families: Alexis Arbaney, Samuel Cramer, William A. Gillespie, Gustavus Grace, Elbert H. Gray, Jerry Gerbaz, William R. K. Hook, Fred Light, Dr. A. J. O. Lof, Enoch G. Mallory, Dan McCarthy, Frederick A. Naefe, Marcus L. Shippe, Sterling Price Sloss, and Edward T. Taylor. All four Harrises, Charles, John, J. M., and William, from below Basalt are also included.

In the more recent *Historical Encyclopedia of Colorado* published by the State Historical Association (not the State Historical Society of Colorado) loaned to us by Leonis J. Usel of Basalt, there appear interesting accounts of the following men and their families: Kelley Cerise, Auzel H. Gerbaz, Harvey F. Gerbaz, Edward G. Gerbaz, Orest A. Gerbaz, and Leonis Usel. This also contains excellent histories of Eagle, Garfield, and Pitkin counties.

ARBANEY

Alex Arbaney's wife's name was Clementine ——. They had five children, Emery, Alver, John, Lena, and Edith. Lena married a Gerbaz, and Edith married a Skiff. Alex had two brothers, Emery D. and Peter, and one sister, Ermine. Their parents were Etienne and Lucia Arbaney, whose ranch was near Snowmass. Etienne and Alexis Arbaney were brothers and, therefore, Flavien and Isabelle Arbaney were first cousins to the four children of Etienne and Lucy.

Alex and Clementine first lived on a ranch about two miles south of Snowmass. They later bought a ranch south of Carbondale, now owned by their children.

Emery D. Arbaney and his first wife, Lottie Clavell, had two children, Lucille and Frederick. Lucille first married Boyd Carlson, who is deceased. She is now married to Albert Nelson; they have one daughter, Sue Ann. Mr. and Mrs. Frederick Arbaney have two sons who now run the home ranch with their father near the school house at Basalt. Emery's second wife was Jessie Miklich. He was killed in a mowing accident in 1963 near the charcoal ovens, attempting to do his share of work even at an advanced age. When we talked to him in 1961 he spoke very fondly of our father, Andrew, for whom he fired on the railroad for a considerable period.

The Laurent Arbaney, Sr., ranch is now owned and operated by his sons, Alex, Laurent, Jr., and Fierman.

(Information from Leonis Usel)

Alexis Arbaney

Alexis, son of John B. and Margaret Arbaney, prosperous farmers living near Aosta, Italy, was born there November 27, 1861. He had finished his stint in the Italian army, and besides that had worked for four years in a cheese factory in his native land. At age 29, he emigrated to Delray, in Wayne County, Michigan. For a short time he worked there in a foundry, and then in lumbering. In October, 1890, he moved to Colorado, where he temporarily became a ranch hand for Charles Harris at Emma. The following summer he rented Sam Cramer's ranch. In wintertime he mined in Aspen.

In partnership with his cousin, L. C. Clavell, he bought a 320 acre ranch two miles east of Basalt; within seven years he purchased his cousin's share and an additional forty acres.

R. W. D. Collection

The W. P. Bates family (l. to r.). Bill, Irene, Ralph, Jennie and Arthur.

His wife, Felicity Gerbaz, also from Italy, was born on July 2, 1862. They married June 17, 1886 in Italy. Their two children were a son, Flavien, called Flalie, born February 28, 1888, and a daughter, Isabelline, called Isabelle, born on December 4, 1890. In 1904, the Usel family purchased the Alexis Arbaney ranch near No. 2 Bridge and operated it until 1958.

The son, Flavien, went to school in Basalt, but left as a young man in 1904 to return to Italy. He became a surveyor. He died the summer of 1961 in Doues, Aosta, Italy. He left a widow there. His sister, Isabelle is living; she also attended school at Basalt.

(Information from Leonis Usel)

BATES

William Pridham Bates was born on a farm in Cavan County, Ontario, Canada, on April 8, 1856. In 1873 at the age of 17, he found work in the United States as a fireman for the Cleveland and Pittsburgh Railway, but the panic that struck the United States that year caused him to lose his job. Returning to Canada, he worked for the Grand Trunk Railway from 1874 to 1881.

Like so many of the young people of that day, Bill was attracted by the West. He came to Colorado in 1881 and went to work as a locomotive engineer for the Denver and Rio Grande Railroad. As an engineer on the work train he helped lay the rails over Marshall Pass.

While working in Gunnison he met the daughter of a pioneer family, Jennie Burpee Herrick. She was born at Mt. Pleasant, Iowa on July 17, 1859, and came West with her parents, Samuel and Myra Herrick, when she was young. Bill and Jennie were married on June 26, 1884. There were great floods in the spring of that year and all the roads into Gunnison were washed out. In order to be on time for his own wedding Bill walked from Grand Junction to Gunnison. He remarked later that it would have been an easier trip if he had not been forced to skirt the Black Canyon since he could not find a way to cross it. The bridegroom had blistered feet, but he arrived at the church on time.

One of the most thrilling moments of his life came in 1888 when he became a citizen of the United States.

In February 1887 he was the second engineer to hire out on the Colorado Midland Railroad at Colorado City (Colorado Springs). Afterwards he transferred to the second district (Leadville-Grand Junction) and lived in Aspen Junction (Basalt) from 1890 to 1909. Railroading in those days was a very dangerous occupation. The safety devices of today hadn't come into being yet. It was quite a common occurrence for a train to come around a sharp curve and be face to face with

from Arthur Bates

another train or a rock slide. Today, as you travel so easily the beautiful highways along the Roaring Fork and Frying Pan rivers which are built on the old railroad beds, it is difficult to imagine the hardships encountered in railroading thru this rough and rocky country in those days. Although Bill Bates was a large, forceful man, over 6 feet tall and weighing more than 200 pounds, he was a gentle man, and took it very much to heart when his fellow workers were killed in the numerous and horrible railroad accidents that occurred. His brother, Edward Bates, was killed in one of these unfortunate tragedies.

In 1909, the Bateses made their home in Grand Junction. Bill Bates had the distinction of pulling the first passenger train on the Colorado Midland when it opened for business, and pulling the last passenger train into Grand Junction on August 4, 1918, when the Midland ceased operation. They then moved back to Basalt where he had loved to fish and hunt. He was an expert marksman and had many trophies to prove it. Every year he took at least one month's vacation to spend hunting. He and his party of hunters would pack in by horse to some of the most inaccessible places in the mountains and make camp. Bill always did the cooking for the group, even to making homemade bread. When not able to spend his time hunting or fishing, his hobbies were woodwork and raising bees. His hands were never idle.

Mr. and Mrs. Bates were very civic minded and were always ready to lend a helping hand in community affairs. Although he was an Episcopalian, and she was a Presbyterian, they were very active in the only church in Basalt, which was the Methodist Church. Mrs. Bates helped make the Church quilt described elsewhere in this book. Mr. Bates won the quilt at a raffle. He was also a Mason, although there was no lodge there. When he became ill with heart trouble Mr. Bates went to Glenwood Springs, because there wasn't a doctor in Basalt; he died there January 11, 1924. His obituary notice included the following comment: "Mr. Bates was a splendid family man. He was unusually thoughtful and considerate of others and was loved and respected by all who knew him. It can be truly said of this good man that he never had an enemy." Jennie Bates died in Denver, November 29, 1932.

The William Bateses had three children: Arthur, born at Salida; Ralph, at New Castle; and Irene, at Basalt.

Arthur Bates followed very closely in his father's footsteps. He attended school in Fort Collins, but returned home when his father was hurt in a head-on collision and was unable to work for months. Arthur went to work in the roundhouse of the Midland in 1905 and was promoted to engineer in 1911. He married Georgina Wheatley, June 28, 1911. After the Midland ceased operation in 1918 he farmed his father-in-law's ranch for four years. The family moved to Basalt when they had a tragic fire on the ranch. Their home was burned to the ground.

After working in California and Wyoming Arthur hired out in Denver on the Moffat Railroad in 1924. After more than 45 years of railroading he retired in 1956, and resides in Denver. He and his wife celebrated their 50th wedding anniversary in 1961. The Arthur Bateses have four daughters: Norma, Mrs. Herbert Minor, of Cucamonga, California; Kathryn, Mrs. Arthur Abbey, of Cheyenne, Wyoming; Barbara, Mrs. Richard Jones, also of Cheyenne; and Esther, Mrs. James Delaney, of Denver, Colorado. The Bates have five grandchildren: Arthur, the 2nd, Linda, and Barbara Ann Abbey; Michael and Daniel Delaney. The six great-grandchildren are: Sharon, Janet, and Gregory Abbey, children of Arthur Abbey, the 2nd. Linda Abbey married Anthony Torsiello, and they have triplet boys, David, Jeffrey, and Michael.

Ralph Bates attended school in Fort Collins, Colorado, and married Edna Wells of Grand Junction, in 1913. He worked a short time on the Midland, but went to work for an abstract business at Grand Junction in 1910 and later worked for abstract companies in La Junta and Pueblo before settling in Colorado Springs. He was president of the Security Abstract and Title Company before his death in 1960. The Ralph Bateses have one son, Ralph William, who succeeded his father as president of the business. Edna still lives in Colorado Springs.

In 1920 Irene Bates married a classmate at the University of Colorado, M. Harry Wilson. They lived many years of their married life in Grand Junction, where he was a pharmacist. They had six children: Donald, of Rangely, Colorado; Mary Jane, Mrs. Alex Rasmussen, of Belmont, California; William, deceased; Ralph, of Ogden, Utah; Barbara Flint, also of Belmont, California; and Arthur, of Ogden, Utah. Harry died a few years ago, and Irene is living in Vernal, Utah.

(Information from Arthur Bates)

CHARLES E. BOGUE

Charles E. Bogue was born March 6, 1856 at Des Moines, Iowa and died at Lakeside, California on February 8, 1946, a month before his ninetieth birthday. His wife, Clara Smith Bogue, was born December 28, 1861 at Des Moines, also, and died on May 1, 1949. Charles belonged to the Odd Fellows and the Masons. They were ranchers south of Basalt.

They had seven children, and of those seven there were two sets of twins. Their first child, Clifford C., born August 10, 1882, married Ollie Foster. They now live at Lakeside, California. William E., born February 1885 married Anna McCarthy. He died in 1916—killed in an accident. His widow married Frank Paddock.

The twins, Jesse R. and Essie M., were born January 21, 1888. Jesse married Prue Templeton who still lives in Basalt. Their children were Viola, Artie, Aloha, Beulah and Buford. When Jesse died August 30, 1955, he and Bramblet willits were the two oldest members of the Odd Fellows Lodge, having joined it at the same time. His twin sister, Essie, married C. N. Kinney, an agent in Basalt for the Colorado Midland for several years. Essie died September 8, 1959 at Gypsum and is buried there. Mr. Kinney died July 22, 1960 and is also buried at Gypsum.

The twins, Josiah C. and Steven H., were born July 8, 1893. They both became bus drivers for the Greyhound Bus Company. Josiah died in San Francisco, California in 1957 after about 30 years with the Greyhound Company. Steven lives with his wife, Mary, at Ocean Beach, California.

Frank E., born February 15, 1906, lives with his wife, Gertrude, at Phoenix, Arizona.

(Information from Prue Templeton Bogue)

Victor and Myra Carlson.

photo from Jake Lucksinger
Everett Carlson.

from Fred Carlson
Victor Carlson, standing in front of his store.

JAMES T. BOWLES

James T. Bowles, son of Samuel and Sarah Bowles, came with his parents from Missouri to Carbondale, in 1887, when he was a boy of eight years.

He married Luetta Jacobs who also came with her parents from Missouri in 1887 and grew up on a homestead near El Jebel.

James and Luetta Jacobs Bowles had four children: Oliver born in 1895, Gertrude in 1900, Adelbert in 1903, and Clarence in 1905. The two youngest, Adelbert and Clarence moved to the Frying Pan area in 1927 and started a resort business at Biglow. They then built a dude ranch—The Diamond J—which they sold to the Riley family in 1945.

The Bowles brothers purchased the well-known Woods Lake from Pete Englebright in 1946 and still operate the beautiful resort. Adelbert passed away in 1958.

(Information from Clarence G. Bowles)

CARLSON

Three Carlson brothers arrived in Basalt about 1900. They were Anthony, Victor and Oscar. They came from Jönköping, Sweden, in 1872, and settled in Iowa before moving to Basalt.

courtesy of Fred Carlson

Oscar Carlson, with son Fred, seated on mower holding Evelyn Ruth, seven months old.

(l. to r.) Fred Carlson, Phil Smith and Charley Hanson, about 1910.

from Fred Carlson

Anthony F. Carlson

Anthony was born on August 9, 1870. In December, 1897, he married Neva C. Cox of Laurel Springs, North Carolina. She was born there on March 16, 1878. Anthony was a large, friendly man, as were his brothers. In partnership with them, he owned and operated the drugstore.

Eight children were born to Anthony and Neva Carlson.

The first, Adolph, born August 20, 1899, married Esther Nyland of Aspen in 1917. Their children are Neville, now a minister in California, and a daughter, Annie. After working for many years for the telephone company, Adolph is now maintaining the television relay station and operating a television repair service in Basalt.

Two daughters followed Adolph. Emma is married to Erwin D. Cramp, Executive Vice-President of the First National Bank of Glenwood Springs. They have a daughter, La Rita (Mrs. James Watson of Denver) and a son, Charles, who is with an oil company in Texas. Eunice died in the influenza epidemic in 1918 and is buried in Glenwood Springs, as is her youngest brother, Boyd (1913-1937).

Anthony, Jr. married Anna Mae Cunningham in Great Falls, Montana, where he was general superintendent of the telephone company for twenty years. He died in August, 1962, leaving six children, Gene, Tony, Jr., Terry, Randy, Maryann and Neva.

Dwight Carlson married Irene Gilkison in April, 1925. He is in the feed business in Fort Collins, and is the father of two children. A son, William, teaches at Colorado State University, and a daughter, Elaine (Dobler) is married to a teacher in the Business School of Utah State University.

Loyal C., a minister in Loveland, married Mabel Krebs of Byers. They have three children, Loyal, Barbara and Wanda.

The youngest Carlson daughter, Cherry, is married to Mike Smullings of Aspen, and has one daughter, Pollyanna, who lives in Denver.

Victor Carlson

Victor was born April 22, 1867. He was in partnership with his brothers in the store, but he was the pharmacist. The authors recall him as an affable person who on occasion would fix up that rare treat, a banana split. We bought our first trout flies and other fishing equipment from him. He belonged to the Modern Woodmen, I.O.O.F., and Rebekahs. When the Midland closed in 1918, Victor stayed on until 1930 when he sold the store to Mr. Waite and opened a drug store in Clifton, Colorado. He died there August 3, 1942.

Victor was a rather small man. His picture shows him standing in front of the store by the wagon scales located there.

Victor married Myra Elizabeth Johnson, March 21, 1893. She was born March 21, 1874 in Georgetown and died June 19, 1963. She is buried in New Castle. Son Everett M. says his mother in all her life was never out of the state of Colorado. They had four children, Mildred Elmira, Everett Melvin, Pearl Margaret, and Lyon. Mildred, who married Merl Bottorff and lived in New Castle, died September 1963. Everett and his wife, Viola, live in Thornton. Pearl, not married, lives with them. Lyon died in infancy.

Oscar Carlson

Swan Oscar Carlson, born 1855, was 17 years old when he came to the United States. He arrived in Basalt in 1901 and lived there for thirty-five years. In 1936 he went to live with his son, Fred, in Montrose, and died there in 1944.

Oscar, as he was generally called, married Ida Ogren in Ogden, Iowa, in 1879. They had five children, of whom two sons, Fred and Everett, came to Basalt. Everett lived only a brief time in Basalt, and died in 1959 in Iowa. Mrs. Carlson died in Iowa when her children were still young; Fred was then about five years old. Other children were sent to live with relatives, but Fred went to Basalt to join his father in 1904, and lived there until 1920. Oscar had been a shoemaker before going in with his brothers in the drugstore in Basalt. Oscar and his son, Fred, lived in rooms above the drugstore.

Fred worked on farms near Basalt, among them those of John Smith, Dan German, and Richard Binning. He also did some farming with Jake Lucksinger. For a year he worked in the Basalt Supply Company before going into the army. Soon after his army service, he took up a grazing homestead on Blue Mesa, near Sapinero, in Gunnison County. From there he went to Montrose in 1921 and rented the farm he now owns and where he has lived for forty-two years. He joined the Carbondale Masonic Lodge in 1919, and has been a member of the Farm Bureau since 1923. He has also served on boards of various other agricultural and community organizations.

Fred married Ruth Snyder of Basalt in 1921. She is an active worker in community affairs. In earlier years she was able

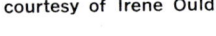
courtesy of Irene Ould

Dr. Virgil Clarke.

to handle any kind of farm work, but as she says, "When Fred went to mechanized farming, I was scared to death of tractors. I quit then and there, except for the hand labor, and driving a truck."

Fred and Ruth have two daughters, Mrs. William E. Bray of Redvale, Colorado, and Mrs. Clyde H. Miller, Jr., of Montrose. There are five grandchildren.

(Information on the Carlson families furnished by Everett Carlson and Mildred Bottorff, Fred Carlson, and Dwight Carlson)

KELLEY CERISE

Ranchers Joseph J. and Emily Tisseur Cerise moved to Basalt in 1912, having come to the United States from Aosta, Italy, with their two boys in 1906. They purchased the Fairview Ranch near Carbondale from the original homesteaders, the Jacobs family.

The two sons, Kelley L. and John, both born in Italy had begun their education there. Kelley, born on February 27, 1897, married a neighbor of the same last name. She is Eva J. Cerise, one of three children of John and Ermine Blanc Cerise of Leadville. They were also from Aosta, Italy and moved into the Basalt area in 1904. The Kelley Cerise family is well-known and are prominent citizens of the town.

Kelley and Eva Cerise had one son, John, who is now deceased. Their daughter, Aleda, was given an excellent musical education. For some time she has been the talented organist for the Basalt Methodist Church where her parents are prominent and faithful members. She married Byron Burns and they have six children, Stephen, Kathy, Jeffrey, Richard, Lisa, and Denise. Mr. Burns works for Porto Mix Construction Company.

Kelley's brother John, married Darphine Usel, sister of Leonis Usel. Their four children are: Ella (Mrs. Francis Stapleton), Alvin, Anita (Mrs. Darrell Hatch), and Denna, who is unmarried and still at home with her parents. John is retired and lives in Glenwood Springs, Colorado.

After Eva's father died, and her sister Georgina became Mrs. Terlianis, her brother, Mela, continued to operate his parent's ranch. His three children are: Reno, Tillio, and Lola Mae (Mrs. Jim Russo of Oregon). Eva's mother still lives in Basalt and is now Mrs. Eugene Chatrian.

(Information from Kelley Cerise and Leonis Usel)

photo from Clementine Cramer Bryant

Sam and Lutie Ruth Cramer.

CLARKE

Dr. Virgil Clarke, a physician, graduate of the Medical School at the University of Memphis, and his wife, Edythe May Willits Clarke, and their five children arrived in Basalt from Bowie, Texas, in August 1897. Within three weeks, Dr. Clarke, who was suffering from tuberculosis, died and was buried in the Basalt Cemetery. The oldest of the children was Lucy, age 10 years. The others were: Irene, Helen, Ruby, and the baby, John, age nine months.

The widow and mother, Mrs. Clarke, a refined and pretty southern woman, reared her family and kept them together. She worked very hard cooking for boarders, washing and ironing, and doing some practical nursing. Her daughters remember when they were small children watching her scrub the many greasy overalls with soap and brush as she spread them out on an old table outside the house. She washed hundreds of them at 25 cents a pair. She was also the janitress at the school.

Her mother, Mrs. Mary (Frick) Willits, affectionately known by the townspeople as "Grandma Willits," helped watch the children and did as much as she was able to help her daughter. As the girls grew older they did baby-sitting and washing, too. When the one boy, John, was big enough, he sometimes took a gunny-sack and picked up coal that had fallen off the railroad engines and coalcars and which was on the ground for anyone to take away. R. W. D. remembers going with John on these foraging expeditions.

Lee and Fred Willits, Mrs. Clarke's brothers, had preceded the Clarkes to the area, and they aided her substantially. The Odd Fellows Lodge of Basalt built her a home near the confluence of the Frying Pan and the Roaring Fork Rivers. At that time, there were a number of houses in the location; now flood waters and changing river beds have almost entirely swept away the land where they once stood.

Lucy Clarke married Clarence Danielson, co-author of this history. Their daughter, Lois, was born in Aspen while they lived there for a short time. Their other daughter, Edith, was born in Basalt.

Irene became the wife of Rialto Ould, son of the John Oulds of Basalt, and they make their home in Glenwood Springs. For many years, Mr. Ould ran a filling station until his recent retirement. Irene and Rye have four children. Lucy Jane (Mrs. Howard Shader) lives in Pocatello, Idaho. Clifford resides at North Plainview, Oregon. Ruth is married to Lerew Stull; their home is in Glenwood Springs. Virgil is employed by the D. and R. G. Railroad at Pueblo.

Helen Clarke married Phil Smith and they lived on the Smith and German ranches for years, until moving to Glenwood a short time before they died. They had no children.

The youngest Clarke girl, Ruby, was graduated from Glenwood High School. She was the queen of Glenwood Springs' first Strawberry Day, an annual festival. Her husband, Erle Hubbard, has held many elective offices in Garfield County and is now County Assessor. Two of their four boys, Jack and Kenneth are now attorneys. Robert is an electronic engineer with the U. S. Bureau of Standards in Boulder, Colorado. Ralph works in the Glenwood Springs Post Office.

John, the only son of the Clarke family, married Hazel Chapman and manages the Glenwood Distributing Company in

R. W. D. collection

Albert and Emma Hillgren Danielson.

The A. M. Danielson family, about 1903. (l to r.) Ralph, Clarence, Myron, Clara and Andrew.

R. W. D. collection

Glenwood Springs. Their son, Conway, is a pharmacist and lives in Greeley. Their daughter, Anna Maude Neil, lives in Denver.

Mrs. Edythe Clarke died February 14, 1945 and is buried in Glenwood Springs Cemetery.

(Information from the Clarke children)

SAMUEL CRAMER

Samuel Cramer, son of Solomon and Mary A. Billiter Cramer, of Muscatine, Linn County, Iowa, was born April 28, 1847. He was educated in the Western College in that county, and served in the Civil War under General Sherman. He was mustered out at Louisville, Kentucky.

In 1880 he came to Colorado and mined in Chaffee County, but, during the silver boom in Aspen in 1881, he moved to Pitkin County. He continued mining for several years and also served as County Commissioner. Later he homesteaded a ranch of 320 acres which lay in two counties, Pitkin and Eagle, just south of Basalt.

By his first wife, Amerzette Ammerman Cramer, whom he married in 1870, Mr. Cramer had two children, Frank and Maude. They preceded him in death.

In 1893 he married Mrs. Lutie Ruth Binning who with her three boys, Ernest, Albert, and Richard, came from Sandstone, Michigan, to live on the homestead near Basalt. They all are now deceased, but a daughter of the youngest son, Richard, Myrna Binning Gorman, who was born at Basalt, lives in Denver.

Mr. Cramer and his second wife had a daughter, Clementine Alice, who is the wife of Earle Bryant, a lawyer of Montrose, Colorado. They recently moved to Denver.

Samuel and Lutie Ruth Cramer sold their extensive property interests near Basalt in 1915 to Sam Letey and reinvested in Florida, and also in Montrose, Colorado, where he died in 1936 at the age of 89. Sam Letey sold the place to Albert Grange about 1940. Guido Meyer, the present owner, purchased it from Mr. Grange in 1961.

Always a public-spirited man and an ardent member of the G.A.R., Mr. Cramer and his wife, Lutie Ruth, entertained frequently at their ranch home. It was he who gave the land for the Basalt cemetery and the right-of-way to it through his property.

The richness of the Cramer farm is one of the authors' boyhood memories. The vivid red of the earth and the equally striking green color of the alfalfa was impressed upon our minds. The potatoes dug in the fall seemed unbelievable in size, yield, and texture. Even today the alfalfa is almost too thick and too high to cut.

(Information from Mrs. Earle Bryant and Leonis Usel).

DANIELSON

Andrew Malcolm Danielson was born August 2, 1858, on a farm in Jefferson County, Iowa. On November 19, 1885, at age 27, he married Clara Louise Hillgren. At that time he was an engineer on the Burlington Railroad. During a prolonged strike on the line in 1888 the couple with their infant son, Clarence, moved to Colorado, where Andrew immediately found work in Leadville as an engineer for the Colorado Midland. Very soon he was tranferred to Basalt to run a helper engine.

It was there that Clarence attended school and his two brothers, Ralph and Myron, were born. In 1914, because of Andrew's failing health, Mr. and Mrs. Danielson and their youngest son, Myron, returned to Iowa to a lower altitude. The next year, September 6, 1915, Andrew died in Creston, their original home.

The one-hundred percent Swedish ancestry of the family has this background: Grandfather Swan Danielson first saw the light of day on a farm, "Hylton," in Våxstorp-Soken, Jönköpings-Län, near the city of Värnamo in Småland, Sweden. The place was very rocky, resembling to a great degree the Maine farms in this country. Born on February 8, 1816, he was thirty-eight years old when he left for America. In Sweden his first wife had died leaving him with two daughters, Mary and Anna. Then he married her sister, Johannah, and they had had two boys and a girl: John, Jacob, and Martha Christina.

It took a certain toughness of spirit and courage for a man nearing forty years with a wife and five children to cross the Atlantic on a long voyage to begin a new life in a strange land. He never learned English; in fact, not one of the four Danielson grandparents forsook the Swedish tongue. The prospect, however, of cultivating the rich black soil of Iowa seemed a dream come true as compared to the soil in rocky Småland.

In 1864 Iowa was a young state. The family settled on a farm in Jefferson County. There three more sons and a daughter were born to them: Andrew, Albert, William, and the little girl who died at age 3½. The mother of the family, Johannah, lived only six years after coming to America. She died February 13, 1870, shortly after the loss of the daughter.

Left with eight children, Swan Danielson married a third time. The kindly new wife, Ella Sofa Hedstrom, is the only "grandmother" the Danielsons of Basalt remember. She presented Swan with three more daughters and a son. The first of the daughters died at age 2, but Ella Mathilda, Hilda Charlotte, and Charles grew up. Before the last two were born the family had left Jefferson County and settled on a farm in the southwestern part of the state, in Adair County near Spaulding.

On June 11, 1893, the year of the great Chicago Fair, Grandfather Swan held a happy family reunion on his farm. His eleven surviving children, together with seventeen grandchildren and eighteen other relatives, making a total of forty-six, spent the day at the old home. He was the center of attention, and with all his dear ones around him, he was indeed a contented man. The next day the whole family visited a Creston photograph gallery and had a group picture taken which is now a treasured memento. Grandpa died February 14, 1895, at age 79.

Danielson men were tall—about six feet—and well built. Andrew's sons remember how unhappy their father felt when, as illness came on, he lost somewhat, the excellent physique he had always had.

From so large a family, one would expect there would be many grandsons to carry on the name. However, the Danielsons seemed to "daughter out," as the saying goes. There are many descendants, but few to bear the name. Andrew's oldest brother, John, who was born in Sweden, and finally made his home in Washington State, leaves two grandsons, Marshall and William. The former is an attorney in Tacoma, and has a son, John, who is a professor at Temple University in Philadelphia. Uncle William's son, Dwight Danielson of Arizona has an adopted son, Richard Danielson. Andrew's grandson, Philip (Ralph's son), now deceased, is survived by a son, Luke, and daughters, Nora and Carrie.

The Hillgrens, the authors' maternal grandparents, emigrated soon after their marriage in 1857 in Rimforsa, Ostergotland, Sweden, to a farm settlement of Swedish people near Salina in Jefferson County, Iowa. Although Ostergotland in Sweden was a much more productive farmland than Smaland where the Danielsons originated, transportation was very undeveloped at that time and it was difficult to make a good living. Charles Hillgren, born Carl Jonsson in 1830 in Rimforsa, and his wife,

Louisa Larson, born Louisa Larsdotter in 1837 in Tjarstad near Linkoping, decided to make their home in America. As a reward for his military service in Sweden, Grandfather was privileged to change his name from the rather common one of Jonsson to one he liked better—Hillgren—and Carl became Charles in the new land.

An excellent cabinet-maker, Charles Hillgren built the altar and the pulpit of the Lutheran church in the village of New Sweden near his Iowa farm. The town is known as Lockridge today. He made their furniture for their new home, and also the wagons for his team of oxen. Every Sunday he hitched up this team and drove his family to the village church. His grandchildren are proud today of the pieces of attractive furniture left of his handwork, including the flax spinning-wheel.

Charles and Louisa Hillgren had seven children, all baptized in the Lutheran church in New Sweden, Iowa. They were Hulda Matilda, Clara Louise, Charles Albert, Mary Ellen, Christina Josephine, Gust Nathaniel, and Emma Charlotte. At age thirty-two the father of the family enlisted in the 4th Cavalry, Iowa Volunteers, fought and was wounded in the Civil War. Uncle John Danielson was in the same unit. We have their tintype pictures in uniform.

The family was an industrious and a religious one. The second child, Clara, our mother, was eleven when her father died, May 3, 1871—age forty-one. Later Grandmother Hillgren married a neighbor, John Eckwall, and they had two sons, John and Harvey, our half-uncles. There are a great many Hillgren and Eckwall descendants.

Two brothers of Andrew Danielson, Jacob and Albert, who were engineers on the C.B. and Q. Railroad, came to Colorado and were employed as engineers in Leadville. Jacob worked only a short time for the Midland, then went to Denver where he opened a fish market. He and his wife, Josephine, had two daughters: Laura, now Mrs. Joseph Carey, born in Creston, Iowa, and Florence, who is Mrs. Charles Means, born in Denver. They now live in Los Angeles, Cailfornia.

Albert married Andrew's wife's sister, Emma Hillgren. They lived in Basalt from 1889 until his death in an accident on the railroad in January, 1897. Their one son, Carl, was a double cousin to the authors. Albert's widow later married Mr. Kleymann and they lived in California. All three are now deceased.

Oscar Riebel and Josie Hillgren, another sister of our mother, were married in a double ceremony with Albert and Emma in

Basalt on May 25, 1893. Oscar and Josie had three children, Chester, Clifford and Iona. Clifford is survived by a wife and children. Chester has grandchildren; he and Iona live on the Pacific Coast. The Riebels moved to Grant's Pass Oregon about 1898, where Oscar was an engineer for the Southern Pacific.

Although Andrew Danielson did not have a college education, he was a great reader. After high school in Creston, Iowa, he attended business college for a short time. We still have his penmanship practice-book. Ambitious to excel in letter-writing and in accounts, after his marriage he took at least one International Correspondence School course.

His pride in a neat appearance is apparent in his photographs. One taken about the time of his marriage shows him in a derby hat. He carried a gold-headed cane which we still have. His eyes were wide apart and blue; his hair, light brown. He always wore a large mustache. He was a firm supporter of prohibition and never drank liquor in our home, or elsewhere. Neither did he use tobacco in any form. James Larsh, of Leadville, told us that our father was "quite socialistic." We know he was an ardent antisaloon man.

Our parents, although brought up in the Lutheran faith, were both active in the Basalt Methodist Church. Father took a great interest in boys' athletic teams, put in considerable time at umpiring, and gave money for uniforms. He was an alderman in the town almost the whole time he lived there.

Mother was short, small, and slender. Her complexion was similar to that of our father. Her gaze was direct, interested, and friendly, and her blue eyes often twinkled in amusement. With a great fondness for growing things she supervised us boys in spading up the rich volcanic earth in our back yard in Basalt and in planting a vegetable garden each spring. We shall always remember, too, her large yellow rose bush and wonderful sweet peas. Do any of you readers recall the bead necklaces women used to make out of flower petals and paste? They were delicately fragrant. Mother made a number of them.

The minutes of the Ladies Aid show that Clara was one of the church women who year after year went calling from door to door to collect money for the pastor's salary. Music and literary societies also held her interest. Notes from the *Basalt Journal* tell of "musicales" held in our house. For such a small woman she accomplished an immense amount of work at home and for the church, and also with her needle. She made many

C. L. D. collection

The A. M. Danielson home in Basalt.

clothes for children of needy families as well as her own dresses and shirts for us boys.

Mother rarely reprimanded us except when we ran noisily through the house when father was trying to sleep in the daytime after an all-night run on the railroad. We were a source of irritation in that we often came into the house with muddy shoes, forgetting to clean them first. Overshoes were not used so much then as now.

Father went as a delegate to the national conclave of the Brotherhood of Locomotive Engineers in Columbus, Ohio, in 1904, and in San Francisco in 1908. The boys were treated to wondrous tours through the great buildings in Washington, D. C., and visits to the zoo and the parks of St. Louis, Los Angeles, and Milwaukee. They saw Buffalo, New York, and the great sight of Niagara Falls. Ralph's detailed boyish diary describes all the wonders of eastern and western trips.

At home in Basalt, although we had our regular chores and were encouraged to earn money at various jobs after school and during vacations, still we led a rather carefree boyhood in many respects.

Andrew Danielson, and his brother Albert, bought town lots for $225 from Gabriel Luchsinger, and had three houses built: the "square house," the "Decker house," and the one on Main

Street where Myron and Ralph were born. After our family left Basalt our home was used as the telephone exchange for a time. Then various families rented it until, in 1961, it was purchased from Chris Hyrup by rancher Leo Light, of East Sopris Creek. Leo had the old house torn down and a modern one built on the site.

After Father's death in Iowa, Mother and Myron returned to Basalt where they remained until 1917 when she married Charles Burdette and moved again to Iowa. When Mr. Burdette died in 1931 Mother came to live first with Ralph and then with Clarence in Denver until she passed away December 19, 1933.

Clarence, born in Iowa January 28, 1887, was brought the next year to Leadville. He obtained most of his schooling in Basalt where his parents moved, and finished high school in Kearney Military Academy in Nebraska—Class of 1906. After graduation he hired out as a call boy in the round house until he was made a fireman that October. He worked on the switch engine in Aspen from 1908 until December 1909 when he went on the extra board at Leadville. He was married on December 23, 1908 to Lucy Clarke, daughter of Dr. and Mrs. Virgil Clarke, in Basalt. He was promoted to the right side of the cab January 17, 1910, and worked for the Midland in Basalt and Cardiff until it closed in 1918.

He was a member of the Odd Fellows and the Brotherhood of Locomotive Engineers. His wife, Lucy, joined the Ladies' Auxiliary and the Rebekahs. She was interested in church work and in literary activities. They had two daughters: Lois, born in Aspen, and Edith Louise, born in Basalt. In 1918 the family moved to Denver and Clarence worked for many years for the Colorado and Southern Railroad as a "clam-shell" operator. He retired in 1952. In 1958 they celebrated their golden wedding anniversary with a large reception.

The daughters married and both live in Denver. Lois and her husband, Clarence Batcheller, have two children: Diane, now Mrs. Robert LeHew, and Kim, who was graduated in June 1964 from the University of Colorado.

Edith Louise Danielson married Arthur Vaughn, a fireman and part-time engineer on the Denver and Rio Grande and they have two daughters: Marlene, now Mrs. Jerry Knudsen, and Janice, who is Mrs. Jerry Forte, both of Denver. The three married granddaughters of Clarence and Lucy have given them seven great-grandchildren.

When Ralph Wesley was born in Basalt March 6, 1897, Dr. W. J. LeRossignol, of Rifle, who was called, arrived too late because he had to come by train. Mrs. August Naefe acted as midwife and nurse. It happened to be the doctor's birthday, also.

Ralph went through the tenth grade in Basalt, then transferred to Boulder High School where he finished in 1915. The first winter in Boulder he lived at his uncle Will Danielson's home. Then on account of his father's death it became necessary for him to work his way. He lived on the dairy farm of Mr. and Mrs. W. A. Groom where he did chores for his board and room. He enrolled in the University of Colorado, summer vacations, returning to Basalt to work. In the fall of 1918 he left for the army and was stationed at Fort Lewis in Washington. Upon his discharge in 1919 he and a classmate, Tommy Wolf, followed the wheat harvests in Kansas as laborers. Ralph reentered the University. The next summer he sold books in Nebraska and found that much more lucrative than his other jobs. He obtained his A.B. degree in 1920 and his Doctor of Medicine in 1923. He married in June, 1922. His wife, Luverne Gove Langley, a classmate at the University, had been graduated in 1921 and was teaching in high school.

Then followed for Ralph an eighteen months internship at Denver General Hospital and general practice of medicine in Grant County, New Mexico. There, two children were born: Philip Andrew, and Marjorie Louise. Ralph obtained a two-year residency in Ophthalmology at the University of Colorado Medical School in Denver. Since 1930 he has been a practicing eye physician and surgeon, and a volunteer on the staff of the Department of Ophthalmology at the University. For seven years he was head of the Eye Department at the Medical School.

Ralph's son, Philip, is a graduate of the University of Colorado. He married Miss Mildred Page, also a graduate of the University. Her father was at one time Chief Commissioner of the Reclamation Bureau at the time of the building of the Hoover Dam. Philip is an attorney-at-law in Denver and commutes daily from Boulder where he and his family live. He serves the University as a Regent. His children are: Luke, Nora and Carrie.

Marjorie, also a graduate of the University of Colorado, holds a master's degree from Middlebury College in Vermont and taught school before her marriage. Her husband is Dr. Leonard Kowalski, a Denver dentist. They have four boys, Daniel, David, Kenneth, and Keith.

Ralph Wesley Junior, born in Denver, November 10, 1938, died of pneumonia at the age of one year.

Myron Custer, youngest of the three Basalt Danielson boys, was born May 25, 1899. An attack of encephalitis—sleeping sickness—when he was a small child, left him without the usual amount of physical vigor. However, his health improved as he grew and he was able to go through grade school and two years of high school in our town. He enlisted in the army in World War I. After his discharge he lived with Clarence and Lucy in Denver while he completed his education and was graduated from North Denver High School.

He married Mrs. Nina Willard who died less than two years later. Myron enlisted in World War II, and after his discharge worked for the Denver branch of the Ford Motor Company. He bought a half-interest in a creamery in North Denver owned by Mrs. Leone Putnam, which he helped operate for three years. Following an accident, his health failed and he has been a patient at the Veterans' Hospital in Knoxville, Iowa, for a number of years.

(Information from Clarence, Lucy, and Ralph;
written by Luverne Danielson)

DEARING

Frank and Mary Virginia Smith Dearing came to Colorado from near Bangor, in the state of Maine and joined in the placer-mining near Alma, later doing farming also. Their son, Clarence was born on a farm near Cardiff, April 13, 1887. Mr. Dearing, a true "down-east Yankee," had learned to be a sawyer in his youth in New England. Even after he bought his farm three miles south of Cardiff he was in great demand in sawmills and was considered one of the best in the west. Mrs. Dearing was a native of Tennessee.

The son, Clarence, was educated in Cardiff elementary school. He became a fireman for the Midland Railroad and in 1911 married a school-mate, Ethel Fipps, daughter of W. M. and Sarah Redmond Fipps. Ethel's parents had come west for the wife's health, first to Denver, then to the Western Slope soon after. Mr. Fipps was a railroad agent at Cardiff twenty years for the Midland Railroad. Mrs. Mary Smith Dearing and Mr. W. M. Fipps both were born in Bristol, Tennessee, near the Virginia border.

In 1912, Clarence was promoted to engineer and was on the extra board. He and his wife, Ethel, lived in Basalt two different times. One year they rented Store's home by the Frying Pan.

In 1918 they moved to Utah and soon afterward to Tabernash on the Moffat Road where he worked as storekeeper and in the train service. About 1930 they moved to Denver and Clarence was passenger conductor between Denver and Craig from 1930 until 1947. Ethel and Clarence Dearing have lived in the same home in Denver for over thirty years and have celebrated their golden wedding anniversary. Howard, their only child, was born in Tabernash and went to school there until he transferred to North High in Denver when his parents moved there.

Howard worked for a time at Hilb and Company in Denver where he met Rose Betting and they were married. Railroading was "in his blood"—he was always a railroad man at heart, so he began at age 21 to work for the Rio Grande. In February 1963, he was transferred to Glenwood Springs as trainmaster. Their two daughters, Caroline, age 16, and Patricia, now Mrs. Gordon Brigham, of Greeley, keep the Clarence Dearings busy with visits. Julie, three-year-old daughter of the Brighams is the great-grandchild of Clarence and Ethel.

(Information from Clarence and Ethel Dearing.)

DOOLING

John William Dooling was born in Shamokin, Pennyslvania, March 31, 1861. He had the distinction of having fired the engine on the first Missouri Pacific passenger train into Pueblo. While working on the building of that railroad he met and married Gertrude Camp in 1888. She was born in Iowa, April 10, 1870.

The couple made their home in Leadville, Colorado for twelve years, moving to Basalt in 1900. He was both a fireman and an engineer for the Midland.

Three boys and three girls were born to John and Gertrude Dooling. Ruth Dooling Forrest passed away in Oakland, California in 1962. Glen died in Cody, Wyoming in 1939, and Jean died in Basalt in 1911. The three who are living are: Gertrude Dooling Maher and her brother, Raleigh Dooling, both of 221 Douglas Street in San Francisco, and Paul Dooling and his wife and family of Grand Junction, Colorado.

At one time the Dooling home in Basalt burned to the ground; all they owned was lost except for the piano which was saved. They later bought a ranch at Emma where they lived five years. Then they moved back to Basalt and purchased a house near the William O'Brien place.

After the Midland closed John first worked at the State Home in Grand Junction. Then he became custodian for the Knights of Columbus Home there. Later he moved to California to stay with his children, and passed away in San Francisco on December 20, 1931. His wife, Gertrude, died in Pueblo on December 14, 1935.

(Information from Paul Dooling)

EISWERTH FAMILY

William Franklin Eiswerth was born in Woodland Park, Colorado, on December 16, 1872. He grew up there and in 1907 married Addie Roberts who was from Cascade, born July 3, 1875. They lived in Basalt where he worked in the roundhouse. Then he leased various farms in the area. He had joined the Odd Fellows in Woodland Park, and belonged to the Free Masons in Colorado Springs.

William and Addie Eiswerth had thirteen children: William Fayette, who married Fern Collins and now lives in Denver; Helen Frances, who married Earl Cain, is deceased; Anthony was killed as a youth in a hunting accident; Bessie died in infancy; Juanita, who married Clavel, is now dead; Pauline Clara Clavel, married a brother to Juanita's husband and they live in Pasco, Washington; Norma, who died in infancy; Beulah, who married first a Mr. Gerhont, and later a Mr. Peterson, lives in Jerome, Idaho; Mary, who married Bill Webb, lives in Woodland Park; Phoebe, who married Charles DeLong, lives at Oakhurst, California; Robert is deceased; Arthur died in infancy; and Vernon, who married Rosella (Zella) Olson of Basalt and resides in Basalt.

In 1921 the William Eiswerths moved to Englewood, Colorado, near Denver. Faye and Fern have three children, William F., Betty Jane, and Addie Fern.

(Information given by Fayette E. Eiswerth)

FAHEY

James Fahey was a locomotive engineer who ran passenger trains most of his life. Born October 2, 1853 in Brasier Falls, New York, he grew up in Huntington, Pennsylvania, where he began to work as a fireman on the Pennsylvania Railroad. In 1878, he came west and found employment with the Denver and Rio Grande Railroad, where he remained for five years, then went to Pocatello, Idaho to work for the Oregon Short Line.

214 Families of Basalt

Toss and John Fahey (above) taken in Sept. 1926. On the right is Stephen Fahey and Mrs. Annie Fahey.

In September, 1887, he joined the Colorado Midland and remained with that railroad until it closed in 1918.

His wife, Anna McCahey Fahey, was born in Ireland in 1864 and had come to Colorado in 1886. They were married in 1890, lived in Leadville, but moved to Basalt in 1897. James and Anna had five children: John, Stephen, Thomas, James Jr. and Mary Rose.

A double tragedy happened to the family in Basalt. James Jr. was drowned in the reservoir north of town—the one which was the original water supply. The only girl, Mary Rose, died in infancy of a skull fracture received in a fall from her high chair.

In 1908, the family moved back to Leadville where Mr. Fahey died on Labor Day, 1929 and was buried in Huntington, Pennsylvania. Mrs. Fahey remained in Leadville until 1938 when she moved to Denver and lived at St. Rose's Residence until her death, March 24, 1947. She also was buried in Pennsylvania. Remembered by all as a tireless worker, along with her friend Mrs. Peter Hyrup, for the establishment of the Roman Catholic Church, St. Vincent's, in Basalt, she was its first treasurer. In her later years she could still say, "The happiest days of my life were spent in Basalt."

John Fahey, called Jack, their eldest child, born in Leadville in 1893 received his early education in Basalt where the family had moved when he was four years old. He was sent to Sacred Heart High School, now called "Regis"—near Denver. He was

from Stephen Fahey

from Stephen Fahey

James Fahey, engineer, and Annie McCahey Fahey.

photo from Mrs. Thomas Fahey

Thomas "Toss" Fahey, taken in 1952.

good at sports, especially boxing, and also an excellent fisherman. He often spoke of his boyhood days of fishing and swimming in the Frying Pan. After graduation, he worked as a railroad mechanic in Salida, Colorado, and also in Nevada, California and Utah. He married Helen Swartz who died in 1938. He passed away in November of 1937 in Cody, Wyoming, and was buried in Basalt.

The second Fahey son, Stephen J., born in Leadville May 14, 1895, attended Basalt grade school. He spent two years in the Army in World War I, stationed in France, then in Germany. He worked for the Western Pacific Railroad for nearly forty years as a locomotive engineer. Twenty years were spent in Elko, Nevada, and fifteen in Salt Lake City, Utah. On December 16, 1928 he married Mae D. Ferney. Their thirty-five years of life together were happy ones. He was a devoted, kind and considerate husband and a beloved and respected friend of many people. Stephen was always willing and ready to help those in need. Mourned by a host of friends, he passed away March 22, 1964 in Salt Lake City. Art and Georgina Bates had stopped to see him the week before he died on their way to California.

Thomas Patrick Fahey, always called "Toss," was born at Basalt, February 13, 1898, and attended school there until the family moved back to Leadville in 1908. He attended St. Mary's, Central and Leadville High School where he was an above-average student and very active in sports. He was sent to Sacred Heart College and finished at the Colorado School of Mines at Golden. He majored in metallurgical engineering. During summer vacations he worked at the Leadville smelter and mines, and one summer at the C. F. and I. in Pueblo. Always active in athletics, including baseball, football, basketball and track, he was named "All-Colorado Half-Back" at Mines in 1918.

In 1922, after traveling and working in a number of states, he began his employment at the Arkansas Valley Plant of the American Smelting and Refining Comany in Leadville with the intention of remaining a few months. Instead, he stayed with that company almost thirty-six years and worked his way up from the sample mill to the position of Plant Superintendent. He retired in 1958 because of ill health.

On June 25, 1924 Toss married Loretta M. Reagan of Denver, sister of his friends, the Reagan brothers of Sacred Heart College days. She was born June 19, 1900 in Butte, Montana, daughter of Michael and Catherine Reagan. The Reagans and their four sons and one daughter had moved to

Denver in 1912. Thomas and Loretta remained in Leadville most of their married life. In April 1930, they adopted a daughter, Mary Adelaide. After retirement and one year in Denver, they moved to Mesa, Arizona. The milder climate was beneficial because he was suffering from emphysema and heart trouble. He passed away on June 18, 1960 and was buried in Mount Olivet Cemetery, Denver. At the time of his death, the Leadville paper devoted considerable space in recognition of his devotion throughout the years to civic, philanthropic, church and organizational affairs of the city. Loretta is living in Boulder, Colorado.

R. W. D., in a letter to Loretta, had mentioned her huband's reputation as a boy pugilist. She answered, "Yes, as a kid, I understand he loved to fight. But as a husband and father he was very gentle and kind. We loved him dearly."

Mary Adelaide Fahey married John W. Vidrik who is a cost accountant with the Sundstrand Aircraft Corp. She is a teacher of English in Arvada High School. Her love for Basalt is inherited from many childhood trips there with her parents. They have two boys.

Mrs. Vidrick recently sent us an autograph book that had belonged to "Toss" in which he had verses written by Annie Fahey (his mother), Flora Hall, Guy Crawford, Walker Hough, Julia Usel, Ina McMahon, Willie Lucksinger, Earle Hilton, Wallace Nelson, Edgar Hilton, Gerald Grace, Clifford Rhodes and Fay Hildreth. Fay wrote: "In the golden chain of friendship, regard me as one link." John Clarke wrote:

> "When you get married and your wife gets cross,
> Come over to my house and eat apple sauce."

(Information from Loretta Fahey and Mary Vidrick)

FRASER-STEWART

James E. Fraser was a locomotive engineer on the Colorado Midland Railroad. He married Ida Louise Murray Stewart, widow of George Hugh Stewart, who had six children.

While the family lived in Basalt, which was about two and a half years, the three younger children, Mary, Bertram and George, went by the name of Fraser in school. They were advised to do this by their teacher, Irene Willits, who thought it would be less confusing in case anything happened to them on the school grounds—it would be easier to remember to contact their mother, who was Mrs. Fraser.

When the division point of the Midland was changed to Cardiff from Basalt, the family moved there. Mr. Fraser died in the terrible "flu" epidemic of 1918. After losing their step-father all the children used their own name of Stewart. The eldest, Winifred, passed away in 1914 before her stepfather died. Bertram, the third child died in 1923. William LeRoy is married and lives in Fort Worth, Texas. George Hugh, Jr. (Bud) married Dorothy Shanks and they live in San Angelo, Texas. Mary M. resides at 900 Lafayette Street, Denver, Colorado.

Mrs. Fraser's first husband, George Hugh Stewart, was a native of Canada, and a farmer. He came very early to Leadville and engaged in mining. In December, 1902, he passed away in Leadville. Their son, John, died in infancy there.

Ida Murray Fraser remained very active and alert and enjoyed life right up to the time of her last illness in 1963. She was a native of Canada and became a naturalized citizen of the United States.

(Information given by Mary M. Stewart)

GRACE

This prominent family, who occupied the farm across the Roaring Fork from Basalt, now owned by Mela Cerise and sons, raised hay, grain, vegetables, and fruit. The history of the Grace families has been so interestingly written up by Georgia Grace Atkinson, a daughter of Gustavus Grace, that we are reproducing it as written.

"Colorado was admitted to the Union August 1, 1876. In an issue of Harper's Magazine of that year was a write-up and pictures of it. Among them was a picture of the Mount of the Holy Cross. A young man from Vermont saw the picture and decided that Colorado was to be his home. He and a friend went to Leadville, a bustling community filled with the spirit of the west. The young man was Gilbert Gustavus Grace and his friend was Henry W. Tabor, who later made history in his chosen state.

"Gus Grace liked what he saw, so had his mother, two brothers, sister and family, and uncle join him. All of the brothers went into the freight business, hauling merchandise from Leadville to Glenwood Springs. Some of the trips were made over Tennessee Pass through Red Cliff. Some were made over Independence Pass through Aspen and Aspen Junction, later called Basalt because of a mineral near there.

"It was on one of these trips that they found the homesteads that they wanted in the Roaring Fork Valley. On their trips to

Auzel Gerbaz, taken at Woody Creek, 1961.

R. W. D. collection

Glenwood, they would stop on Independence Pass and cut pine logs, hauling what they could to the homesteads for their cabins. In the meantime, Gus met Miss Minerva Case, the girl of his choice, in Leadville. They were married October 5, 1882, in Leadville, Colorado. In 1884 their first child, Claude, was born in Leadville. In 1885 they moved on their homesteads; Gus and his family on one, Benjamin, the second boy, and his wife on another and their mother and her brother, a deaf mute, and another brother, Lorenzo, on the third homestead.

"After his mother and uncle died, Ren, as he was called, went to Glenwood Springs and was County Commissioner. On one of their trips up the Glenwood Canyon, the car he was driving hit a boulder, and they went over the bank into the Grand River. One man got out, and one other man was drowned. Ren Grace was in the river six months before they found his body washed out on a sand bar. He was buried May 20, 1920.

"Gilbert Gustavus Grace was born in Burlington, Vermont, July 16, 1854 and died July 29, 1929. Minerva Case Grace was born in Plattville, Wisconsin, September 28, 1858 and died June 28, 1915. Benjamin died September 28, 1928. The three brothers are all buried in Basalt.

"To Gus and Minerva Grace six children were born: Claude, now living in Prescott, Arizona; Mabel Grace Cooper, Seattle, Washington; Georgia Grace Atkinson, in Renton, Washington; Nina Grace Conner, in The Dalles, Oregon; Gerald Grace, Kennydale, Washington; and Austin Grace, Seattle, Washington. All grew up and went to Basalt school. All six are living and in good health."

(Information from Georgia Grace Atkinson)

GERBAZ

The father of Auzel H. Gerbaz emigrated from Doues, Italy, in 1892 to Michigan in the United States. There, in Detroit, Auzel was born on March 11, 1893.

The family moved to Colorado where they leased a ranch on Woody Creek, then bought the A. B. Foster place in 1899.

Auzel attended Colorado Agricultural College in Fort Collins for four years. He married Clonia R. Corbin from Indiana in 1917. They were divorced in 1923; she lives in Texas. Auzel was postmaster at Watson (once called Gerbazville). He still lives there. The Gerbaz family have been active in sheep raising for 23 years, but have also given attention to cattle, potatoes, and grain.

Their son, Delbert, was born in Denver in 1919 and spent the first two years of his life on the ranch at Basalt. After his parents separated, he attended grade school and high school in Indiana. Returning to Colorado, he enrolled in the University of Colorado where he was graduated in 1940. Since then he has been employed at the Consolidated Aircraft Corporation in San Diego, Los Angeles and Texas. The name of the firm is now General Dynamics - Astronautics.

During the last twenty-one years he has made many vacation trips back to Colorado. His hobby has been research on the Colorado Midland and he owns an old Midland officials' private car. He has even hiked some thirty miles along the old road-bed, in the Hagerman Tunnel, and to Wildhorse, Hewett, and Bath.

Brothers of Auzel Gerbaz were Edmund, who married Albena Tekowick—children Cherie and Jimmy; Harvey (Mike), who married Eva Arbaney—children Dolores (Mrs. Stutsman), Douglas, and Jerry; Orest, who married Helen Evans, one child Beverly; Homer (deceased) who married Mabel Hoaglund—children Jerry, Mae, and Epeneter; and Alice (deceased) who married Lena Arbaney—children: Ted, Ernest, and Freddie.

(Information from Delbert Gerbaz)

DAN GERMAN

Dan, a native of England, and Elizabeth Farthing German and their small daughter, Mary, came from England and settled in California in a mining camp called Table Mountain. He was a blacksmith for an English syndicate that owned property all over the world. While there seven more children were born to them: Emma, Lewis, Ena, Lilly, twin girls Alice and Amelia, and Dan John (Dan, Jr.). Emma and the twins, died very young.

As the mines would close, the family moved three times. Finally the company sent Mr. German and his son, Lewis, to Granite, Colorado. A year later the family joined them. This mine, too, closed in a short time. Hearing that Aspen Junction had need of a blacksmith, Mr. German bought a shop there, then homesteaded a place for the family about two miles east of town on the Frying Pan River. He was the first blacksmith and horse-shoer in Basalt.

His shop was a favorite hangout for the boys of the town, for it was fascinating to see him mold the hot iron and apply the shoes to the horses' hooves. A heavy leather apron was the emblem of the trade. Often the blacksmith would allow us boys to turn the hand-blower for the fire in the forge—an altogether pleasing chore. As a boy between six and eight years of age, Clarence once broke the tongue off his little play wagon. He remembers how his mother sent him over to the blacksmith's for repairing it, and he had to drag that wagon all the way by the front of it without a tongue, but Mr. German's repair made the effort worthwhile.

As there was no road, the German children had to walk two miles down the railroad tracks to school in Basalt. Sometimes the boys would hook a ride home on a freight train, jumping off as it slowed down on the heavier grade at the end of their ranch stretch. Lilly walked all the way to Basalt, also, to sell eggs at 25 cents a dozen, and butter at 25 cents a pound. Our mother bought from her regularly. I wish we had a picture of her with her basket on her arm.

When Mr. German grew older, he gave up blacksmithing, and Dick Mizer took over as the Basalt blacksmith. Ena German married Dick. Their three children were: Leo Mizer, now deceased; Lewis Mizer, an automobile mechanic in Riverton, Wyoming; and May Mizer, a beautician, now living in California.

Lewis German bought the Taylor Creek ranch of "Dad" Hall, who moved to Basalt to become Justice of the Peace. Lew married Elsie Steele. Their three children were: John, Ellen, and Philip. Soon after the Midland closed they sold their ranch to Jake Frieler and moved to Whitewater. There his wife lost her life in the burning of their home, and Lew's sister, Ena Mizer, took the youngest child, Philip, only an infant, to her own home and brought him up.

Lewis and Elsie Steele German's older son John, a carpenter, is head of Welfare for the Church of the Latter-Day Saints in

Ford Gilbert photo

The Gilbert's 1914 Buick on the cement bridge at Basalt.

Salt Lake City; Ellen married Leroy Williams who operates tourist cabins at Meredith.

Lilly married Jim O'Brien, an engineer on the Midland. They had one daughter, Ellen, who is deceased. After Mr. O'Brien died Lilly moved to California.

Dan, Junior, born in 1886, married Bertha Hand in 1911. They continued to live on the old home place on the Frying Pan until 1919 when they sold it to Fern Stager. Mr. Stager in turn sold it to E. J. Hawk. The ranch was then purchased by Phil Smith. Now it belongs to Mr. and Mrs. Armstrong. Dan and his wife now live in Rifle.

I (R. W. D.) remember in the summer of 1918 before I went to the army and while I was working on the car-repair gang at Basalt, I was initiated into the Basalt Odd Fellows. Both Lewis and Dan German, Jr., were very active members and went through all the "chairs." For each of the three degrees Lew walked down the railroad track from his place six miles, and six miles back (twelve miles in all) reaching home in the dark after midnight. Dan walked six miles. This life a lasting impression on my mind of their great interest and devotion to the lodge and to me.

Dan, Jr., remembers that his nickname in Basalt was "Germie." He writes, "Those days were happy; not concerned with the whole world as we are now."

(Information by Dan German, Jr.)

"A Gilbert family group on our ranch at Basalt. In the rear are Uncle Will, Van and myself. Mrs. Gilbert is holding Carl's oldest boy. The other two children are Uncle Will's boys, George and Harmon. George is now a doctor at Johns Hopkins." Quoted from Ford Gilbert. Carl L. "Pug" Gilbert is seated on the right.

GILBERT

Carl L. (Pug) Gilbert

Carl L. (Pug) Gilbert arrived in Leadville in June of 1886 and immediately began work with the contracting firm of Orman and Crook in building a 25 mile stretch of standard gauge track for the Colorado Midland. He worked for the Midland for many years and was the oldest man in point of length of service when the railroad was abandoned in 1918.

First, he was conductor on the "through" passenger traffic from Aspen to Colorado Springs. On March 29, 1889 in New Castle, he married Louise Nixon, whom he had known in Leadville. While living in Aspen their two sons were born: Carl Wilson on July 26, 1899, and Ford Lincoln on May 25, 1902. Mr. Gilbert joined Aspen Lodge B.P.O.E. 224.

From 1904 to 1907, the family lived in Colorado Springs, then returned to Aspen. As the base of operations was moved to Basalt in 1909, the Gilberts purchased the C. L. Benbow ranch south of there. Mr. Gilbert's youngest brother, "Uncle Van" Gilbert, came to live with them.

224   Families of Basalt

from Ford Gilbert

Carl and Ford Gilbert with "Lady," about 1910.

Ford Gilbert says "We were at Dinkel's Lake for a three or four day camping trip." (l. to r.) Francis McLaughlin, Hallam Pierce, Ford Gilbert, John Fry, Lewis Mizer, ..., and George Lucksinger.

Ford Gilbert photo

Pug was secretary of the School Board during the years his boys were completing their elementary education and Ford remarks: "It is freely said that, had this been otherwise, the two Gilbert boys would still be in grade school."

During the days of Pug's railroad career, he was always active in the Brotherhood of Railroad Trainmen and Conductors. He acted as chairman of the grievance committee for many years, making numerous trips east to air grievances of the Colorado Midland men before the general committee of the Brotherhood.

Following the abandonment of the Midland in 1918, he went in for politics and was elected to the Colorado 23rd General Assembly in 1920. He was on the committee approving the building of the Moffat Tunnel.

He had made considerable money from the operation of the "Doctor" Mine in Gunnison County—a mine which produced zinc. Partners in this venture were veteran Coloradans George Runtz, Aspen saloon-keeper; Ed Wolf, R. & R. G. conductor; and Frank Hoheisel, mining man and prospector.

In 1924, the Gilberts moved to Long Beach, California where he died in 1942, and Louise survived him until 1952. The Gilberts celebrated their golden wedding anniversary in 1939.

(Information given by a son, the Rev. Ford Gilbert)

Carl Gilbert, Jr.

Carl Wilson Gilbert, born in Aspen, July 26, 1899, was graduated from Basalt Elementary School where the was class valedictorian. After attending high school there he transferred to Aspen High. There he fell in love with Nora Harrington and decided schooling was not for him. They were married at the Gilbert ranch in Basalt on November 29, 1917. Their marriage has been a long and happy one.

Carl began work for the Midwest Refining Company in Casper, Wyoming in 1917. Two sons were born in Casper: Carl W., Jr., and Ralph L. The family moved to Parco, Wyoming where the Producers and Refiners Oil Company established a new distilling process called the Dubbs Distillers. Soon the Shell Oil Company installed the same type of stills at their Dominguez Refinery near Wilmington, California. Because of his experience the Shell Company asked Carl to come to California and operate the Dubb Stills for them. The family moved there on January 1, 1926. When Carl retired in March 1960 he was one of the plant superintendents. Since retiring Carl and Nora have travelled a great deal throughout the United States and Canada.

The sons, Carl Jr., who resides in Long Beach, California, and Ralph L., who lives in Worland, Wyoming, are married and have families.

Ford Gilbert contributed his brother Carl's Valedictory Address which makes one wonder why Carl did not turn out to be an editor:

Valedictory
May 14, 1914
by Carl Gilbert

To the friends gathered here this evening and to the teachers and classmates it is my privilege to give a farewell greeting.

Classmates, this day finishes another year of our school course, and some of us have perhaps come together today for the last time. The more fortunate ones of us may go to High School, and the rest of us may go out into the world to shift for ourselves, but wherever we go or stay we will find abundant cause to remember our school with gratitude.

This event and those of the past school days we have spent together will be remembered and recalled many times with pleasure when we have passed down into the vale of years.

Then the little incident which now seems hardly worth telling will possess a deeper interest, and will linger longer and fondly with us.

Today with its trials and triumphs will be regarded as an epoch in the career of some of us and a day worth remembering by all of us.

But before we take leave of the pleasant associations which have bound us together, we wish to acknowledge the debt of gratitude we owe to our teachers who have labored so faithfully for us, and who have helped us through our many difficulties. For whatever of wealth or honor we may hereafter win in the world, we shall be largely in debt to our school for success.

May we long cherish these memories, and let us tell to those who come after us the pleasures of our school days, our blunders, our failures, and our triumphs, so that they may profit by our experience.

To the school officers and the county superintendent of the present year we return our sincere thanks for their hearty and continued interest in our welfare. And now as the class of this year separates we bid you all a respectful farewell, with the hope that prosperity and happiness will attend us in the future as in the past.

Class Members:

Carl Gilbert
    Ardith Dunn
        James Frey
            Emma Carlson
                Paul Dooling
                    Alfred Hyrup
Madge Cadwell
    Adolph Carlson
        Pauline Eiswerth
            Kelley Cerise
                Austin Grace
                    Myron Danielson
R. M. Early, Principal
Motto: "Energy wins the way."

Ford L. Gilbert

Ford Gilbert, younger son of the Carl L. Gilberts, was born in Aspen, May 25, 1902. He finished grade school in Basalt in 1916 and had the "high distinction of writing and giving the class prophecy." He says no prophecy ever written could have been further from the actual result life's peculiar quirks play. He still treasures this program and also the one in which his brother Carl's name appears as valedictorian. He has loaned us the original copies of both addresses for publication.

After three years in Basalt High School, and his senior year at Colorado Springs, Ford was graduated in 1921 and that fall entered the University of Colorado in Boulder to study engineering. He did not complete the course, but went to California and worked in the oil fields there. He met Frances K. Jensen at the Methodist church and they married in 1928. They had three children: a daughter, Frances Marilyn, now Mrs. Porter; a son, George; and a son, Ford Van Tuyl.

Ford had a call to the ministry and reentered college at the Los Angeles Pacific College. After two years, in the fall of 1927, he transferred to the University of Southern California from which he received both A.B. and Master of Theology degrees. In later years, he studied at Iliff in Denver, and at Harvard in Cambridge, Massachusetts.

One of the highlights of Ford's life in Basalt was in 1914. Hod Nicholson, a rancher, hunter and guide, living in the Snowmass area, was contacted by a professor of physical education at East

Cleveland, Ohio, a Mr. Offinger, who was interested in bringing a group of his boys for a long horseback trip in Colorado. The next summer, 1915, Mr. Offinger and fifteen boys arrived and Hod Nicholson asked "Pug" Gilbert to guide them into the White River country. Carl and Ford accompanied their father. During the trip, plans were made for another the following summer from the Gilbert ranch in Basalt, to Cheyenne, Wyoming. Hod Nicholson was to be guide and Ford the horse wrangler. They left Basalt soon after the 4th of July, crossing the Rockies with the pack train, following trails for there were no roads. After attending Frontier Days, the group headed back by way of Fort Collins. Ford was leading an extremely obstinate pack horse and got a mile or more in the rear of the party. Mr. Offinger turned around and gave Ford a terrific bawling out for his delay. The 14-year-old boy quit on the spot and told the professor he could worry from then on about the unruly pack horse.

Alone and broke, Ford made his way to Denver. After begging for money and even appearing in a rodeo sponsored by the Tishiana Feature Film Company, and borrowing $3.00 from one of his school teachers, he began the long trek to Basalt alone on horseback over the Rockies. The 225-mile journey took him four and a half days. The first night after going over Lookout Mountain, Ford stayed at Empire. Leaving there about 3 A.M., he rode over Berthoud Pass in a bad snowstorm, sleeping the second night in a livery barn in Hot Sulphur Springs. The third day he reached a ranch very close to Gore Canyon. The last night, Ford made the miles to Gypsum and the following day crossed Cottonwood Pass to his home.

Rev. Ford Gilbert served a number of pastorates. The last one was at the Community Church of Henderson, Nevada. When the Second World War broke out, Ford was pastor of the First Methodist Church in Las Vegas, Nevada. He volunteered as an army chaplain and was sent to the European theatre of operations. He remained there during the remainder of the conflict. He had been overseas 27 months of his 32 months of service. At the end of the War, he resumed his work in the ministry.

Frances and Ford recently celebrated their 35th wedding anniversary at their home in Henderson.

Ford was most gracious in loaning pictures, and also the Class Prophecy he wrote as a boy for his Basalt eighth grade of 1916. We pass on this interesting document to the reader:

Class Prophecy
May 18, 1916
by Ford Gilbert

Will you lend me a moment of your time? If so permit me to lead you into the misty valley of the future.

An extract from an old diary of a member of the eighth-grade class of 1916 dated June 22, 1930 reads: I passed over Basalt on my way to Washington, D. C. and was so impressed by the change in the town that I alighted from my aeroplane and sought for some of my old friends. One of the first things I noticed was that the streets had all been paved, and magnificent buildings in place of the old houses which I first knew. The one attracting my attention most was a beautiful new depot and a post office just across the street from it.

Next I walked up the street to my old friend George Ould's home to inquire about George. His mother told me that he had been mayor for several years, and all the credit for these reforms was given to him of whom the people were very proud.

Picking up the Basalt Herald, which, by the way, was published by our old class-mate John Cerise, I noticed in startling headlines: "Noted Soloist Visits Basalt Soon." I carelessly glanced over it, and to my surprise learned it was Doratha Dibble who had graduated from Denver University several years before. So I decided I would stay and hear her sing.

Sunday morning beamed bright and clear. I thought I'd go over to the church as I had often done when a boy, but not very often since. Upon entering the church I seemed to recognize the voice of an old school-mate. Yes, it was Teddy Luchsinger in the pulpit, and a venerable-looking minister he made, too, and seemingly very well-informed, for all I knew. He was graduated some years before from a Methodist College in Utah, and I later heard he had won great fame as a minister. Well, after the service, I walked up to shake hands with him. He failed to recognize me for a minute, then extended heartiest greetings to me. He invited me home with him to dinner. As we talked over our old school days I began to ask questions concerning certain class-mates. He told me that Hortense Hartson had graduated from the University of Colorado with high honors, and was teaching English in Colorado College at Colorado Springs, and had recently married a well-known prizefighter of Colorado Springs. Next I inquired about Pearl Ogden. He informed me that she completed High School and married a ranchman who took her to New Mexico.

Well, by counting them I could remember only one more. That was Raleigh Dooling. I learned that he also was graduated from the University of Colorado in law, and was now a prominent lawyer in Kansas City. He had proven to be very brilliant and also very successful in his line of work. After all this interesting information I was very glad I had stopped off in Basalt It brought back many pleasant memories of our school days and friends.

I hope all of you may be as successful as my class-mates of 1916.

Class:

Doratha Dibble
Raleigh Dooling
Ford Gilbert
Hortense Hartson
Teddy Luchsinger
George Oulds

Motto:
"Perseverance makes success."
(Information provided by Ford Gilbert)

ELBERT HENRY GRAY

Elbert H. Gray, born September 14, 1858, in New Jersey, came to Longmont, Colorado, where he worked on a ranch for four years, saving enough to attend the State Agricultural College in Fort Collins. After a year there he obtained work on the G. W. Gillespie ranch. On April 27, 1887, he married Annie B. Gillespie.

For seven years he clerked in the Charles H. Mather store at Emma, Colorado. On May 31, 1898 his wife died. When Mather sold his store, Mr. Gray bought the Gabory Ranch of 200 acres west of Emma which he sold two years later. He then moved to Basalt.

He became a meat-cutter in the Basalt Supply Company Store. The owner of the Tierney Mercantile Store, widow Tierney, married him on May 20, 1902 and they moved to a ranch on Woody Creek for a few years and then returned to Basalt. His second wife had had five children by her first husband, William Tierney.

By his first marriage he had three children: Ernest, Harold, and Beulah (Woods). Ernest passed away seven years ago. Harold lives in Jerome, Idaho. He and his wife Ethel have three children: Dale, Don, and Shirley (Mrs. Monte Bell). Beulah

Gray Wood is still in Basalt and very active in the Methodist Church there.

(Information from Beulah Gray Woods and Ethel Gray)

GRIFFITH

Richard Griffith was born March 15, 1858, in Quebec, Ontario, Canada. He came as a small child to New Jersey and as a young man worked on the New Jersey Central Railroad. He and Margaret Doherty were married on December 24, 1881, and moved west to Salida, Colorado. He worked for the Denver and Rio Grande as shop foreman and machinist, and later for the Colorado Midland. He was then sent to Basalt as master mechanic. In 1906 he moved to Colorado Springs as superintendent of machinery of the Colorado Midland. In 1909 he worked for the Uintah Railroad as master mechanic and engineer and stayed until his retirement. After his retirement, he went to live with his youngest daughter, Mrs. Nina High, in Arizona. He was very proud of having received his fifty-year pin from the Colorado Springs Masonic Lodge. He was also a member of the Knights Templar and Mystic Shrine. He died in September, 1940, and with Margaret Griffith is buried in the Masonic Cemetery in Grand Junction, Colorado. Eight children were born. John died in infancy.

Martha Hill (Mattie) was born November 5, 1884. She was eight years old when the family moved to Basalt. She lived there until her marriage to Charles A. Graham, a rancher of Eagle, Colorado. They moved to Washington State in 1925 and soon after to California where he continued ranching until retirement. They now live at Colusa, California.

Anna May, born December 2, 1885, spent her early years in Basalt. She married Albert J. Barton, an engineer on the Colorado Midland. They later moved to Three Forks, Montana, where he worked for the Chicago, Milwaukee and St. Paul until his retirement. They now live in Seattle, Washington, where their two daughters also reside.

Grace Irene, born April 2, 1887, died in 1946. She married Scott Shafer, a machinist on the Colorado Midland. They had one daughter, Margaret, and after Scott's death, Grace lived with her daughter until her death. Jeanette Viola, born October 2, 1889, passed away at the age of eighteen in Colorado City.

Marguerite, born in September, 1891, died in 1926. She married Charles Smith who worked for the Uintah Railroad.

Richard Glen Eyre was born in September, 1893. He was the first son born to a member of Glen Eyre Chapter, Order of

Eastern Star of Colorado City after its institution. He served in the Navy in France during World War I, and returned to marry Beulah Lewis, of Three Forks, Montana. He worked for the Chicago, Wilwaukee & St. Paul until his death in 1957. His widow, Beulah, now lives in Spokane, Washington.

Nina Esther, born September, 1895 in Basalt, was the youngest of the Griffith children. She married Sam A. High, who worked on the Uintah Railroad. They had two sons and a daughter. Later they moved to Arizona where he farmed cotton, then to Twin Falls, Idaho. Sam and his two sons are now farming there.

(Information obtained from Martha Hill Graham)

ASA HARRIS

Asa and Bertie (Kennon) Harris were born in the little farming community of Fairplay, Missouri. His birthdate was July 31, 1878; hers, November 20, 1880. A few years after their marriage, worried about his wife's health, Mr. Harris took her and their small daughter, Thelma, to New Mexico where the air was dry and the temperature mild. They homesteaded there in 1907. Later they arrived in Basalt where they believed that the soil was better for farming. Asa found work on the ranch of Sam Cramer.

Later Mr. Harris was employed on the Colorado Midland Railroad as a hostler for several years. They moved into a nice house in town up on the hill near Anthony Carlson's and Boyce's. Another daughter, Wilma, was born in 1910. Dr. Kennedy attended at the birth and Anna Sloss assisted.

Asa was a rather small slender man with twinkling blue eyes and fair complexion. His wife, Bertie, was tall and had dark hair and dimples when she smiled, which was often. They both were interested in community affairs. Gardening and flowers were their shared hobby. Mr. Harris took his turn on the town Council. She was a Rebekah and he belonged to the Odd Fellows Lodge. The family attended the Methodist Church, and Thelma to this day cherishes her "perfect attendance" Sunday School pin.

When the Midland suspended operations they left Basalt on the last train out of town and lived for a time in Colorado Springs where Asa worked for the Golden Cycle Mill. Hearing from his good friend, Clarence Danielson, that there was an opportunity for a job in Denver, he took his family to visit with those old friends until he found a house. Mr. Harris became a "clamshell" operator for the Colorado and Southern Railroad. The families remained very close. Often the parents would have a congenial card game of an evening while the daughters did their schoolwork in an adjoining room.

Mr. Harris retired because of disability about 1941, then did a little general work at the Colorado Christian Home. He and his wife loved children. Some women who still work there and knew him remember how pleasant and helpful Asa was and how he assisted with their programs. He died November 14, 1944. Mrs. Harris survived him nine years, taking care of children much of her time. If they were living today how proud they would be of their two lovely daughters, and also of their three granddaughters who are teachers.

Thelma married Vernon Tiller who worked for the Colorado Fuel and Iron Company for twenty years before his death in August 1958. Since then Thelma has been employed in the personnel office of the Bowman Biscuit Company of Denver.

Thelma and Vernon Tiller's daughter, Barbara Tiller, married John Casson from Elmira, New York. He is personnel manager of the Water Board of Denver. She taught three years at North High School in Denver. Their two little girls are Linda and Cynthia. The second daughter of the Tillers, Janet, who is a teacher at Ashley School, Denver, married Daniel Wolfe, a senior medical student at the University of Colorado Medical School.

Wilma Harris married Walter Shideler of Denver who has been with the Bureau of Reclamation for thirty-one years. Their one daughter, Joan Shideler, was married in June 1963 to Roger Maxwell of Superior, Nebraska. He is a young Denver architect and Joan teaches at Sabin School.

(Information from Thelma Harris Tiller)

C. E. HARRIS

Claude Edelbert Harris, a locomotive fireman and engineer for the Midland, was born in Seymour, Wisconsin, July 24, 1876. His wife's maiden name was Emma Zella Allison and she was born in Pike County, Ohio, November 14, 1875. They were married August 20, 1902.

Their three daughters are: Ethel Muriel, whose first husband was Kenneth Storrs, is now Mrs. Elmer Morihugh; Erma Belle now Mrs. Errol Snyder; and Lois, who is married to O. A. Fosberg.

After the Midland closed the Harrises moved to Seattle, where Claude worked as a stationary engineer for many years at the T.B. Hospital for the city. In 1946 he retired and since then he has been unusually active in writing for the *Railroad Stories Magazine,* and in building model locomotives. He presented one of the miniature engines—the Number 9—to the Western Section of the Denver Public Library where it is proudly displayed and much admired.

Mrs. Harris died in 1962. They had been married for sixty-one years.

The following, written by this 88 year-old man to the authors in August 1964, is quite remarkable:

"I still work half a day in a hobby shop, building locomotive models similar to the one in the Denver Library. It takes a whole year to build one and I get $150 apiece for them. So you see I will never get rich on this job, but it keeps me busy and active in old age.

"I built the models of the two locomotives that were at the driving of the Golden Spike at Promontory, Utah. The Union Pacific bought them from the doctor I sold them to. I visited Salt Lake City last year to see them. They are valued at $1,000 each; I got $100 each fifteen years ago."

Anna Sloss sent us a letter from Claude Harris to Mrs. Frank Paddock, dated March 1940, in which he asked for data about the last crew on the Midland and the list of people who left Basalt on the last train out. (As far as we know there is no list of passengers available.) She also enclosed a clipping from the *Seattle Times* printed about 1938 describing an exhibition of Mr. Harris's models. One of them had brought up a memory of personal experience for Claude; it says, quoting Mr. Harris:

"This engine is a three-quarter-inch scale model of a Schenectady Consolidation of 1887, used in passenger service on the Colorado Midland Railway between Leadville and Cardiff on grades of 159 and 174 feet per mile.

"In sixty-two miles this road went up one mile in altitude. I was firing engine No. 9 one dark night, going up grade and leaned out to get some air—missed the grab irons and fell off!

"I fully expected to hit a rock and roll under the train, but landed on my side slightly below the ties in soft sand and cinders. All of my wrong deeds flashed through my mind while falling that six or eight feet. I waited until the observation passed, then shouted, expecting the flagman would hear, but he was inside and the tail lights of the train passed round a bend, but I heard the engineer shut off, as the steam gauge got lefthanded suddenly.

"Having been looking into the white-hot fire box, my eyes were nearly useless in the dark, and I stumbled up the track. Soon three lanterns showed up, the trainmaster, flagman, and another hand were coming down the tracks. Passengers had told them of hearing my shouts. They would not back up for fear of running over me. I ran up alongside and saw the conductor and engineer examining the trucks to see if I was tangled up in them. I climbed on the engine, got up some more steam and we proceeded on our way.

"I always had a desire to build a model of that engine. That railroad went out of business in August 1918, so no blueprints could be obtained. I figured it down from gauge of track, diameter of drivers, diameter and stroke of cylinders. It has thirteen 5-16-inch flues and is a live steamer, but built it for an ornament for my den."

Mr. Harris writes us now: "I have hardening of the arteries in my feet and legs, and that is why the doctor here advised me to take up *tap dancing*. It sure keeps me limbered up. When I was young I got stage fright, but now it does not bother me any. I have appeared on stage as I have a top hat, tails, and cane."

Clarence and I are quite excited to hear from him that he plans to come to Denver by train to attend a Basalt reunion party we are planning. It seems to us that he will be one of the youngest in spirit at that occasion.

(Information from Claude Harris and Anna Sloss)

CHARLES H. HARRIS

Charles Harris took up a ranch six miles west of Basalt in 1880. He was one of the earliest settlers in the valley. He brought the first wagon and the first cook stove in, packing the latter in pieces on horseback.

In 1884, in company with sixteen other men, he built the wagon road around the hill, across the river from Emma, and just west of Basalt. The road was donated to the county and was in use until the old Colorado Midland grade was made into a road. Those helping Mr. Harris on the road were William H. Harris, Riece Brown, Newton Lantz, Timothy Carey, Frank Dalton, John Cox, Patrick Muney, Edward Stauffacher, John Ruedi, John Cummings, Cyrus Reed, William Hopkins, Walter Vance, and two Luchsinger brothers.

He was a judge of election in the first election held in the region, which was part of Summit County at that time. The election was held in Glenwood Springs and a son still has the check for $2.50 for services rendered.

In 1886 he was married to Miss Rosetta Noble, a school teacher in Aspen. They had four children: Nettie, now living in California; Dora, in Pueblo; Arbrose Vern, four miles below Basalt; and Beth, who is deceased.

(Information procured from Bramblet Willits)

WILLIAM H. HARRIS

William Harris soon followed his brother, arriving in the neighborhood in July 1881. He located a ranch by taking a squatter's claim five miles below the present town of Basalt. He afterwards preempted this claim. He was one of the seventeen men who built the road around the hill opposite Emma, making it possible to get their hay into Aspen without fording the Roaring Fork River. Hay at that time brought as much as $160.00 per ton.

In partnership with his brother, Charles Harris and Cyrus Reed, they built the Harris and Reed ditch, which was started in 1881 and completed in 1884. This ditch was built mostly with pick and shovel labor.

On January 31, 1884, he was married to Miss Mary Carey, the marriage license being the first one issued in Garfield County. Mr. and Mrs. Harris had three sons who reached maturity, several children having died in infancy. The three sons were Albert, Ralph and Raymond. All worked hard on the ranch with their father. Albert was a member of the first graduating class at school in Basalt, with Bertha Tierney and Susie Stiffler. Albert died a few years ago. Ralph and Raymond now live in Glenwood Springs.

Mr. Harris is buried in Basalt. He belonged to all the various lodges in the district. He was always known as Bill.

The ranch is now owned by Mr. Brice Arlian.

(Information procured from Bramblet Willits.)

HAZELTON AND CRAWFORD

Robert Hall Hazelton, of English descent, was born April 15, 1863 in Ireland when his father, a Methodist minister, happened to be preaching there. He was one of eleven children, and his mother died of tuberculosis when he was about twelve years old. He grew up in England. When he was twenty he emigrated to the United States and brought a younger brother who was very ill with "consumption," as they called it then, and took care of him until he passed away. Because of Robert's exposure to the disease, doctors advised him to go west to the mountains.

He first went to Kansas where he met his future wife at Dodge City. But he left Kansas and worked on the railroads in several places—Flagstaff, Arizona; Albuquerque, New Mexico; and Barstow, California. He returned to Kansas and married Jennie Crawford, September 11, 1894. They went to Basalt, Colorado, where he took charge of the Fred Harvey eating house for the Midland. Their children born there were: Harold, September 27, 1895; Irma, July 13, 1897; and Lucile, who was born in the house that Mr. Hazelton built (where Mr. Terrell, the game conservationist now lives) June 30, 1900.

About 1904, the family went to Missouri and then back to Dodge City, Kansas. In 1914 they moved to Chicago. Mr. Hazelton died November 4, 1932 at the age of 69. Irma remembers her father as a very loving and kind parent, a wonderful husband to her mother.

Harold died September, 1944, of a heart attack at age 49. His only son preceded him in death at age 11. His widow survives and also two daughters. There are now two grandsons.

Lucile married Ira C. Jordan and they live in Milwaukee, Wisconsin. They have three sons and five grandchildren.

Irma married Seine R. Brandt in 1928 and has always lived in Michigan. Their daughter lives in Rocky Ford, Colorado and has three little girls. After selling their home in Michigan, Irma and her husband moved to La Sierra, California in 1963, where their son lives.

Two months before going to California, Irma and her husband visited their daughter in Rocky Ford, and the whole family spent two days on a trip to Basalt and Glenwood Springs. She writes: "I was thrilled to see both places again. We ate dinner at the Harvey House (now called Basalt Hotel) where I was born. Mrs. Sloss went with us and pointed out some of the buildings. I was glad to see the old post office, store buildings and the church we attended, and especially the house my father built; the river, and the path to school; the mountains and the little stream that still runs through where Vanderventers used to live and where we used to play. I remember asking my father when he was building our house, "How tall is God? Is he as tall as the highest peak on our house?"

Mrs. Jennie Crawford Hazelton was one of seven children born to James and Jane Crawford of Dodge City, Kansas. All her brothers, John, Abe and Henry Clay, lived for a while in and around Basalt and Aspen. Her sister, Clara Crawford Schmueser, and her husband, Jesse Schmeiser, lived in Basalt and then moved to Newcastle. Mrs. Jennie Hazelton died in Chicago, February 5, 1930 at the age of 61 of heart trouble.

Henry Clay Crawford and his wife, Effie, moved to California about 1914. Both died there in 1940. Their daughter, Margaret Crawford Rasey, widow of Bert Rasey, lives in Manhattan Beach, California. She has three daughters and several grandchildren.

(Information from Mrs. Irma Brandt)

HANSON (HANSEN)*

Matthew Hanson was born in Milwaukee, of German parents. His wife, Carrie Lucinda Clark, came from Massachusetts. They lived for a while at Gilman, Colorado, before coming to our town about 1890. Matt worked both as a master mechanic and as car foreman for the Midland, but soon gave it up to go into business with Mr. Clark (Mrs. Hanson's father). They sold boots, shoes, and dress goods, and Mr. Hanson was the shoe repair man. His son, Harry, writes: "He was quite a hand to progress as he worked in Basalt in the City Council until he got the City water works put in and was after lights but never got them. Walter Hyrup tells me he laid the linoleum in their kitchen over 60 years ago and it is still there and still good."

Mrs. Hanson was born in Massachusetts in 1865. She was very active in the Ladies Aid. She and Mrs. Andrew Danielson were very close friends.

There were two children, Harry, born in 1890, and Alice, born in 1893. (Two other boys died in infancy.) From a house on Main Street, Basalt, the Hanson family in 1905 moved to a ranch on Castle Creek at Seven Castles next to Hyrups. Later after Mrs. Hanson's death in 1912, Matt moved to Salt Lake City with Alice. They sold the place to J. A. Smith. Matt Hanson died in Milwaukee at the age of 85.

After ranching for a time, Harry worked for the Colorado Midland in the round house and for the smelter at Leadville. He went to Salt Lake City, then worked as a fireman for the Rio Grande before going into the Railroad Corps in the Army in World War I. On his return from the Army he went back to firing, then transferred to train service and worked for the Rio Grande in that capacity for 43 years until his retirement. His

---

* Although Matthew spelled his name *Hanson,* his son and other relatives have always used the spelling *Hansen.*

first call as a fireman was to fire for Clay Lydick, a former Colorado Midland engineer at Basalt. Harry and Mrs. Florence Fullmer Taylor were married in 1921. They have one boy, Harold Malcolm, a major in the Air Corps in France.

Alice married her cousin, Charles Hansen. They lived in Milwaukee until their deaths a few years ago. Their children were two boys and two girls.

Matt, Carrie and Mr. Clark are buried in the Basalt Cemetery.

HALL

William V. "Dad" Hall was born in Ohio, December 7, 1838. On February 8, 1861, he married an Ohio girl, Mary Jane Reynolds. Her birthdate was August 12, 1846. Fifteen children were born to them, but as happened in many of the families at that time, several died in infancy.

They moved to Missouri, then to Kansas, and to Colorado in 1888. Mr. Hall had a sister, Mrs. Nelson Downey living near Basalt, so the Halls homesteaded on Taylor Creek in 1889. They remained there until they sold the ranch to Lewis German and moved to Basalt in 1907. After the Midland closed, Lew German sold the ranch to Jake Frieler and moved to Whitewater. At one time, "Dad" Hall was Justice of the Peace in Basalt. He died there in 1922 and is buried in the Basalt Cemetery. His wife, Mary Jane, who survived him ten years, is also buried in Basalt.

Their son, Isaac, born in Ohio in 1864 preceded them to Colorado. While freighting on the Maroon Creek road near Aspen, he was buried in a snowslide and was not found until the next spring,—1887.

Mary (Molly) Hall, born in Ohio March 7, 1869, married John Griffith. They had five children. She died in Pocatello, Idaho in 1929.

David J. Hall, born in Missouri February 5, 1874, never married. He died at Sloss, Colorado in 1936.

Arthur (Doc) Hall born in Missouri January 11, 1877, married Nettie Tatum. He died in Gooding, Idaho May 22, 1960.

William E. Hall, born in Missouri on April 4, 1881 is now the only one of the "Dad" Hall Family now living.

Francina Hall, born in Missouri May 9, 1883 married Paul Noble. They had five children. His wife died in Basalt in 1921.

Edna Lee Hall, born in Kansas April 25, 1888 married Maurice Kramer. They had three children. She died in Glenwood Springs, Colorado in 1941.

240 *Families of Basalt*

Fred A. Hall, born at his parents' ranch on Taylor Creek February 10, 1892, married Hattie Buck. He died in San Francisco, California in 1959.
(Information furnished by Zella Kramer, daughter of Edna Lee Hall Kramer.)

GRACE HALLOCK

One of our most prominent teachers was Miss Grace Hallock. She has written as follows:

"In regard to the history of Basalt, I went there to teach in about 1903 or 1904 thru the influence of Will Craig who was then Ticket Agent for the Midland. George Craig, his brother, was also in the office. I went to board with the Houghs—as did two of the other teachers. Basalt was a very sociable little town—made up of intelligent railroad people. I made many good friends and still think of them as such. I taught there seven years and then moved to Spokane, Washington in 1910. Some of my former pupils still live there — Anna Rhodes Sloss, Tiny Frey, and others. I had lots of fun socially. The dances and card parties were very nice. Some of the "big shot" mining men of Aspen used to make a point of "happening" to be going to Denver on our dance night and stopped over.

"I never missed a Sunday evening in going to church and singing in the choir. Dear Abbie Robinson and I sang together on many occasions. She passed away a year ago.

"I still love you all and you seem very near to me."

Grace Hallock Pike
(Mrs. Frederick Pike)

HELLER

The grandparents of Leo O. Heller emigrated from Holland to America before the Revolutionary War, settling in Pennsylvania.

His parents came by stagecoach to Leadville, Colorado, from Springfield, Illinois in 1879. They brought their four children with them and five more were born here,—completing the family of eight boys and one girl. Leo is the only one left today of this large group.

Born August 25, 1886 in Leadville, Leo grew up there and married Lena Evelyn Decker who was born March 9, 1891 in Superior, Nebraska. He was a fireman on the Colorado Midland. Three boys were born to the Hellers. They were: Leo Francis born in Basalt August 11, 1908 and died in Leadville at age

Basalt, Colorado Midland Town 241

from Gladys Hough Wachob

The Johnston Hough family. (l. to r.) Christine, Walker, Gladys, Ruby and Johnston.

The Johnston Hough home southwest of Basalt.

1 year; Bernard Leroy, born in Leadville December 5, 1910 and died in Los Angeles, California at the age of 13; and Robert Earl, born in Leadville July 26, 1913 and who was killed near Los Angeles February 26, 1950, age 36.

Leo and Mrs. Lena Evelyn Heller were divorced and she moved to California. He married Clara May Galvin on October 20, 1920 and they live in Cheyenne, Wyoming. Clarence remembers him as "one of the finest fellows I have ever known—a man of the highest character." Mr. Heller remains an avid railroad fan and corresponds with his old-time fireman and engineer friends continually.

(Information from Leo Heller and Clarence Danielson)

HILDRETH

William Henry Hildreth was the editor and publisher of the local weekly newspaper, the *Basalt Journal*. He and his wife, Lulu Dean Scudder, were married in Leadville in 1888. They first moved to Aspen Junction with their three children in the year 1894. Two more children were born later. The family first lived in the building in which the newspaper was published. Later they moved to one of the Collins cottages across the river.

William was born in Watsonville, California, Oct. 28, 1865. Lulu was born in Maryville, Missouri, June 22, 1869.

Mr. Hildreth learned the newspaper business on the *Pueblo Chieftain* in 1887, later transferring to the *Pueblo Star Journal* until 1894 when he came to Aspen Junction. For a while the family went to Chama, New Mexico, but returned to Basalt in 1903. Later they moved to Eagle, Colorado. In 1909 the family moved to Soda Springs, Idaho, where Mr. Hildreth and son, William, or "Bill", as he was better known, edited the *Soda Springs Chieftain*. Mr. Hildreth passed on in 1932.

The printing shop at Basalt at one time was on the hill just across First Street north of the Danielson residence. At another time the shop was on the alley behind the postoffice on Railroad Street, where we watched him set type by hand. Mr. Hildreth was the postmaster for a while also.

Arthur Bates, Bramblet Willits, and Clarence Danielson all worked for Hildreth on the newspaper. The boys helped him to get out the newspaper by rolling a large gum roller to ink the type, one sheet at a time. They also pulled the big handle that pressed the type on the paper. It was Hildreth who was editor of the local paper at the time of the snow blockade. Elsewhere in this history is a chapter on his editorials and news items of the *Basalt Journal*.

Of the five children of the family, Lambert died in 1916 and Bill in 1939, leaving a wife and six children. Frank died in 1958. Fay and his wife live in Soda Springs, Idaho, and have three children. Ruth Hildreth Liston is a widow; she operates the printing shop and gift shop that her brother Frank owned in Long Beach, California.

Ruth Hildreth Liston writes: "I think it is just wonderful that you are writing a book about the people of Basalt. Dad would have been very proud to be remembered. He loved the people of Basalt—as we all did. There are not very many of the old timers left.

"Here the children went to school and the family enjoyed the friendship of the wonderful people in this little railroad town."

(Information from Ruth Hildreth Liston)

HOUGH

In the fall of 1889 Johnston Thomas Hough arrived in the Frying Pan valley. Two years of drought in Kansas had forced him to abandon his farm in Gove County there. His wife, Christine Jakeman (whose "Jacqueman" grandparents came from Orsiers, Switzerland), a former Iowa teacher, took another school position while "Jonce", as he was affectionately called by family and friends, went out west to locate a homestead.

Christine's brother, Fred Jakeman, had settled in Thomasville, Colorado, and had written in glowing terms of the abundant rainfall, the fertile acres, the forests of spruce and pine and the tall grasses awaiting those who took up land in his valley in the Rocky Mountains. Mr. Hough filed on 160 acres near the place called Ruedi. Before heavy snows fell he had cut timber, built shelters for his animals, and for his farm machinery, and finished a two-room log house. His wife arrived on the Colorado Midland Railroad in time for Christmas.

The new homestead in a narrow valley northwest of the railroad water-tank station was a lonely place for a woman,— brightened only by the books, magazines, and home-town newspapers from Iowa and Kansas. Their only neighbor, John Ruedi, kind but very quiet, and almost a recluse, picked up the mail thrown from the mail car at the water tank. He enjoyed sharing their reading material.

When five years of "proving up" gave them title to their homestead, the Houghs looked for a new home nearer to a community, a church, and good schools for Gladys and Chauncey, their two children. They found a place with good soil, and water rights for irrigation, although it had not been entirely cleared of sagebrush and was full of stones. Located a fourth of a mile south of Basalt and the Roaring Fork River, it was ideal for market crops, grain, alfalfa, and potatoes, which were grown in rotation. Cattle, driven to the range in summer, wintered in the fields and fed from alfalfa stacks. An ample vegetable garden, small fruits, and dairy cows, and chickens made the place almost self-sustaining.

For Christine Hough there was a wider horizon after the move. The surrounding mountains were not precipitous, and the valley was wide,—about a mile and a half, and it was more than five miles long. Sunlight hours were no longer shortened by the shadows of towering mountains. The community life in Basalt was satisfying. Sunday School and Methodist Church services in the lovely white-steepled building were a new interest, and the Ladies Aid Society, meetings, dances, and the celebrations of holidays in the Odd Fellows Hall made life brighter. There were stores and a post office too, and good near neighbors.

The Gus Grace family on the adjoining farm included six playmates for Gladys and Chauncey. Then across the road to the north lived the Williamses, an elderly couple. He was a crippled Civil War veteran, who limited his farming to a luxuriant vegetable garden, and just enough hay and grain for his own horses, cow, and chickens. Mrs. Williams' flower garden was the pride of the community. The wonders of the Williams' pasture were a constant delight to all the neighborhood children.

The first summer Mrs. Hough surrounded the four-room log farmhouse with a pansy lawn, and made paths outlined by stones. She began making jelly from the wild berries and devised a recipe for a delicious wild cherry jelly which was often complimented. The recipe consisted of: juice of one gallon of wild chokecherries combined with the juice of one cup of bright red squawberries (which grew sparsely on a gray-leafed thorny bush), and a cup-for-cup measure of sugar. It was a task to obtain the squawberries, as their thorns kept most of the pectin-laden fruit for the birds.

The second winter in their new location brought deep sorrow to the Houghs. Gladys caught typhoid fever and pneumonia. As she was beginning to recover Chauncey, then only four years old, contracted the illness and died. The loss of the unusually sweet-natured son lessened the parents' joy in living. He was buried in Basalt's hillside cemetery.

Because the farm was located south of the Roaring Fork River, it was in Pitkin County, while Basalt was in Eagle County. In the 1896 "free silver" election Jonce was the only Republican voter in his county. The district provided a one-room, one-teacher school of eight grades located near the Ren Grace ranch. There were only ten or twelve pupils. The school was near to the tracks of the Denver and Rio Grande branch railroad to Aspen. Gladys had more than a mile to walk through the two Grace farms where herds of cattle were feeding in winter, so she always waited to join the children of the Gus Grace family. Mrs. Grace, their mother, was almost an invalid from rheumatism, and needed a great deal of help in her household tasks from her girls. Mabel, Georgia, and Nina cared for Mrs. Grace and their younger brothers and sisters besides doing much of the housework. For this reason they were often tardy at school, yet they kept up good grades in their studies.

Basalt School in Eagle County was located in the triangle of the joining of the two rivers. It was "on the way to town" for rural children. It had four rooms, ten grades, and four teachers, one of whom taught the upper grades and acted as principal. The Houghs were prime movers in a plan to unite the Pitkin and the Eagle school districts. This proposal was opposed at first by some of the Pitkin County school-board members. However, in 1901 the union was accomplished, and the children from south of the Roaring Fork then had a shorter walk to a better school.

In the 1890s in order to get ahead a farmer had to be a competent "Jack of all trades". Mr. Hough with the help of his hired men, in 1899 built a new nine-room, two-story frame house of "seven gables" which his wife had planned for the northeast corner of their 160 acres. Only the plastering was done by a professional. The family now included another boy, Walker Blaine. Before Christmas in the new home a second daughter, Margaret Ruby, was born.

The family now lived a little nearer to their neighbors, the Benbows, who occupied the farm where the Williams couple used to live. Mr. Benbow worked on the Midland and his farming was limited to vegetables and flowers. Mrs. Benbow's sister, Mrs. May, and her daughter, Gladys, lived with them. They were delightful neighbors. However, by this time Christine Hough had so many duties as a busy farm wife that she had little time or energy left for the community life and neighborly visiting of which she had dreamed when living on the lonely homestead in Ruedi valley. After a few years Carl Gilbert, a passenger conductor on the Aspen branch of the Midland, bought the Benbow farm. The Gilberts' two boys were welcome playmates for little Walker and Ruby Hough.

Country children are blessed with opportunities to learn the ways of nature; they not only know about the swarming of bees but also the life cycle of farm animals and pets.

Gladys Hough also remembers a sudden summer storm when several members of the family and the horse, Nellie, sought shelter under the heavy protective branches of a tree. They had a very narrow escape when lightning struck the treetop and the acrid odor of electricity filled the air. For an instant the horse seemed all aglow with what looked like fire or only a brilliant light. Fortunately it was not injured and the lightning spent itself by breaking an underground drainage pipe.

Every year, soon after school closed, flood waters washed out the north end of the wagonbridge which was used to reach school, and also the footbridge. So, often the farm families were prevented from attending the Fourth of July picnic in the cottonwood grove just south of the Frying Pan River before it joins the Roaring Fork. Veterans of the Civil War and the Spanish American War were honored and patriotic speeches were given. There was usually band music, and everyone joined in singing patriotic songs. All sorts of contests and games delighted the children. Picnic tables were laden with every home's best cooked foods. Small girls wore white dresses made for the occasion or for the earlier Sunday School Children's Day program. In the evening fireworks climaxed the wonderful day.

There were rural pleasures for Basalt farm children too in summer. Mr. Hough built a four-swing merry-go-round in their fenced-in yard. It was powered by Billy, the pet angora goat, hitched near the center. A leafy bough was held enticingly just out of his reach. His reward was usually his favorite food, beets. Ruby had a gentle brown horse, "Fanny", and her love of riding and pleasant memories of Basalt were life-long.

Walker was the active, exploring type of small boy. Once, after a frantic search of the neighborhood, the family found him exhausted and asleep "between the rails" on the railroad tracks. He also had the distressing habit of taking a nap at the side of a deep irrigation ditch. As he grew bigger he found friends to roam with him on his adventures. He and Willie Lucksinger had a brief but successful business venture selling frog legs to the dining-car on the Midland. It ended ingloriously when, after the supply of frogs ran out, they substituted some toad legs.

On the farms hired girls were scarce. Mrs. Hough depended on her eldest daughter, Gladys, for many household tasks. It was only natural, however, that Gladys, like all children, preferred out-of-door play to work. The story is told that she made friends with "Nellie", the horse bought for a buggy-horse who refused to accept the role. Even hired men who attempted to ride her on an errand found themselves taken on a wild uncontrolled jaunt right back to the farm stable. The community's master horse-trader noticed Gladys riding this apparently docile beautiful mount and offered to buy Nellie for a buggy-horse for his wife. Mr. Hough reported the offer at home with a chuckle. Gladys worried as the price rose, for she knew that her father had previously been bested in a trade by this man. After she went away to high school in Aspen the deal went through and Jonce Hough felt the score was even.

People ask, "Were the farms around Basalt successful?" The answer is "Yes! if the acreage was large enough, the location good, and the farmer and his family worked hard." The Hough farm produced bountifully; carloads of Red McClure potatoes were sold to Aspen or Leadville merchants, and also to commission houses in Denver. Carloads of cattle sometimes went to the Chicago stockyards. Neighboring ranchers bought hay and grain; Basalt grocers got butter and eggs. Strong work horses, and the help of two good hired men enabled Mr. Hough to do all the plowing, planting, cultivating, and irrigating, and to care for the cattle. When more help was needed at harvest time it was often recruited from the so-called "hobo jungle" on the north bank of the Roaring Fork River just before it was joined by the Frying Pan River. Except in the coldest part of the winter, every night there were camp and cook fires there and the place was "home" to the "bums" who came through the region. The regular hired men and young Walker Hough were enthralled by the tales of travel and adventure told by these "knights of the road". In fact, when Walker was a small boy and people asked him the question so often asked of small boys, "What do you want to be when you grow up?" In reply he never mentioned rancher, engineer, conductor, cowboy, doctor, or even President of these United States; his answer was always the same,—"I am going to be a 'bum'."

In those days, as now, farms of small acreage did not succeed well and many were bought up by cattle ranchers. The Houghs all felt that the farmers did not rank as high in prestige as did the ranchers and the railroad engineers of Basalt, yet they gloried

248   Families of Basalt

photo from Walter Hyrup

Anna (Mrs. Peter) Hyrup, with Chris and Walter, about 1917.

Walter Hyrup, on left, with John Shay and Charlie Murray, about 1917.

in their independent, hard-working life. Potatoes, at harvesttime sold for 75 cents to a dollar per hundredweight; in the spring the price rose to two dollars or more. The Houghs built a large drive-in cellar on their farm with bins to store the entire crop. This increased their return, and too, the work of sorting, sacking, and marketing was postponed to a less busy season. One day in the fall of 1905 Jonce drove a team with a loaded wagon into the cellar and somehow suffered a serious back injury. He lay for weeks in a plaster cast. Warned by the doctor to avoid heavy work, from that time on he could only direct

Eugenia Hyrup Murray.

The Hyrup boys. (l. to r.) Alfred, Walter, Otto and Chris.

photo from Walter Hyrup

farm operations, and each season had to hire more help. He and Christine realized that they could no longer continue the 16-hour work days that had made their place a success.

Mrs. Hough, as a former teacher, always remained ambitious for her children's education and future. Gladys was sent to Aspen to finish her last two years of High School. The mother always kept in mind college as a goal for her son and two daughters. More and more she dreamed of the opportunity that Denver high schools might be able to give Walker and Ruby, in preparation for college. So, in 1909 they sold the farm to one of the Cerise family and moved to Englewood near Denver, close to South High School.

Gladys was graduated from the University of Colorado. Walker received a degree in engineering from Cornell University in New York. Ruby attended the University of Colorado for two years and then married a classmate, Thomas D. Cole, a successful engineer who now owns a cotton products factory in Lockport, N. Y. Ruby died May 30, 1958. They had no children.

Walker married Kathleen Hagood. He has been a consulting engineer and is now retired and they live in Manchester, Vermont. They have no children.

Gladys married Frank C. Wachob, a prominent attorney in Denver. She had taught school before her marriage. They had a son and two daughters. John F., a graduate of Princeton University and of the Sorbonne in Paris, France, a specialist in international law, unmarried, is now advertising manager of the Paris Edition of the *New York Herald Tribune*; Helen, who obtained her degree in diatetics at Cornell University, was a dietician in Denver hospitals until her death September 21, 1958. Virginia, a graduate of the University of Colorado, is now married to Professor Alfred Tissieres, professor of molecular biology at the University of Geneva, Switzerland. Virginia and Alfred have a small daughter, Helen, and reside in Geneva. So a descendant of the Swiss family of Jacqueman has returned to the land of her forebears!

Gladys Hough Wachob's husband, Frank, died April 10, 1955. She still resides in Denver, Colorado.

(Written by Mrs. Gladys Wachob and Luverne L. Danielson)

HOTZ

The Hotz family came to the area in the early days, settling in Spring Park, the site of the present Missouri Heights reservoir. The father was named Martin and there were three sons, George,

C. L. D. collection

Walter Hyrup, Clarence and Lucy Clarke Danielson and Eva Hyrup.

Ben, Joe and Augustine. There were, also, three daughters but their names are not known. Martin Hotz came from St. Louis, Missouri in 1889.

On the day of Mr. Bates's funeral George and Gus were clearing the snow from the road to the cemetery when George suffered a heart attack and died.

Gus lived in Englewood, Colorado, until December 20, 1964.
(Information given by Bramblet Willits.)

HYRUP

Jens Peter Hyrup

Jens Peter Hyrup, born January 2, 1857 in Denmark, emigrated about the year 1885 to South Dakota in America. He soon moved to the Territory of Montana where he entered the employ of the Northern Pacific Railroad as an engineer. In Helena, Montana, he met Anna Regina Murmann and they were married in January 1887.

Their first two children were born in Helena. They were: Eugenia Elizabeth, born in 1888, and Christian Adrian, born in 1889. The family moved to Colorado about 1890 or 1891, Mr. Hyrup having gone ahead in search of work. He was employed by the Colorado Midland Railroad as an engineer and sent to Aspen where that railroad was completing a branch from its main line at Aspen Junction.

Mr. and Mrs. Hyrup established a home on the east end of Main Street in Aspen Junction. The house was built by the carpenter, John Auld, who also built the A. M. Danielson home next to it. Four children born to the Hyrups in Basalt were: Otto Murmann, born July 18, 1891; Annie Murmann, born a few years later, and who died in infancy of spinal meningitis; Walter Joseph, born February 28, 1896; and Alfred Peter, the baby who arrived on September 22, 1899.

When Alfred was just two months old, the father of the family was killed in a runaway train wreck at Spring Gulch near Cardiff. A loaded coal train out of Sunlight on the Cardiff Coal Branch, with engine number 32, got out of control at mile post No. 10 and went eight miles to mile post No. 2 over a 4 percent grade before becoming derailed. When the engine struck the bank, it exploded, killing Fireman Peryan. The cab of the engine was found up the mountainside and parts of the engine in the fields. Engineer Hyrup either fell out of the cab or jumped just before the explosion. His skull was fractured from hitting his head on the big boulders. (Clarence Dearing gave this information about the tragedy.)

Walter, then a three-year-old child, only vaguely remembers his father, whom he pictures playing chess with Uncle Rhodie Hyrup. He has a hazy picture in his mind's eye also of his father with a wound on his head lying in his casket. However, he remembers his mother's telling of a more pleasant time when she and her husband were sitting on their front porch with little Walter playing nearby. "Mamma said to Papa, 'Pete, do you know that Walter just can't seem to be able to pronounce the letter L?' (Wise little guy, me) I turned to her and said, 'Hell, I can't say L' ".

Anna Regina Murmann Hyrup, the wife and mother, was born in Canada on August 18, 1854. It was during the troublous time of Bismarck in Germany that her father became a political exile. As such, he was a member of a German colony in Canada. Eventually all of the group returned to Germany where Anna grew up. She was not entirely happy there and so, at about age 30, she crossed the Atlantic again. In the boarding-house of a friend she found work as a cook and housemaid. It was there she met Pete Hyrup.

Neighbors recall her as an energetic, intelligent, slender lady prematurely gray and of medium height. They attest to the excellent job she did of managing her husband's property and rearing her children alone. To her sister, Mary Murmann, who lived with them, she continued to speak German. Her loyalty to her German forebears was strong. Her religion was Roman Catholic, as was that of most of her children. Mr. Hyrup was a Protestant

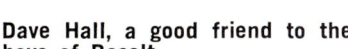

A Basalt picnic at Castle Creek, July 4, 1910.

photo from Fred Carlson

Dave Hall, a good friend to the boys of Basalt.

photo from Roy Mills

and had been helpful in building the Methodist Church of Basalt.

Anna Hyrup possessed natural financial ability and common sense. She rented properties and also ran the ranch at Seven Castles which her husband had bought just before his death from John Maylin. She had good help from her son Otto. She died September 9, 1921 at the age of 67 and is buried beside her husband and their infant daughter, Annie, in Fairview Cemetery. Walter has this to say in her memory: "My mother was a real honest-to-God mother and father to us children. She could cook as only a German woman knows how. Very staunch,—when she made a decision she stuck to it. She kept a very neat home with plenty of love, kindness, and understanding. All of us thought the world of her. She was a wonderful model to guide us by and she succeeded in making us know right from wrong."

The first-born of the family, Eugenia Elizabeth, "Genie", married Charles Murray, an engineer on the Midland June 1, 1909. When the Midland closed they moved to Long Beach, California, where he worked for the Richfield Oil Company for many years before retiring. He died September 21, 1955 in Long Beach. Their five children are: Raymond H., Walter James, Vincent I., Charles F., and Ruth Anne. The daughter, at age 17, entered the Teaching and Nursing Community of "The Immaculate Heart of Mary" Order in Hollywood, California. Genie writes of Ruth Anne: "She gave herself to God and His works on August 26, 1946. After five years of study and preparation she took her final vows and became a nun on May 19, 1951".

Christian Adrian, "Chris", was a fireman on the Midland until it closed. He then bought the Shehi Park Ranch on Taylor Creek. In 1921 he married Hazel Mount who still lives in Basalt. Their four children are: Eugene, Annabel, Patricia, and Robert. His brother, Walter, says that at one time Chris found and accumulated a large collection of Indian arrow-heads on his ranch, but gave them away one by one.

Otto Murmann Hyrup, married Fay Fuhrman. They had one son, Larry, who was killed in an automobile accident on Loveland Pass in 1960. Larry left a widow and six children. Otto was struck by lightning while stacking hay and his health was never good after that.

Walter Joseph Hyrup, worked as a youth at the Basalt Supply Company Store when it was owned by W. A. Simmons. Then he became a fireman on the Colorado Midland. He was on active duty with the United States Armed Forces in France in 1918 when the Midland closed. On his return from World War I, Walter rented the old Sam Cramer farm from its new owner, Mr. Sam Letey, and married Yvonne Marie, daughter of Mr. Letey. He and his wife continued farming until he retired. Walter and Yvonne ("Eva"), now live in the original Hyrup home, his birthplace. They both are community-spirited. Their activities include work in the American Legion, and active support of St. Vincent's, the Basalt Roman Catholic Church built in 1918, and dedicated in 1924. Their four children are John V., Josephine Anna, called Joanne, Eugenia Marie, and Mary Rose. John works with heavy machinery such as bulldozers, in Basalt and Aspen. Joanne is a graduate nurse and lives in California. Eugenia is a teacher in the Aspen schools. Ever ambitious, she is working toward her Master's degree in Education in Greeley during the summers. She and her husband have several children. Mary Rose married a Mr. Peuser, a farmer in Iowa; they have six children. She is a registered nurse also.

Alfred Peter Hyrup married Mrs. Rachel McNeil Sloan, daughter of Tom McNeil. She had four children by her first marriage, Arthur, Bob, Norma and Madeline. Three are dead and only Madeline survives. She is married and has one child, Susan, and lives with her husband in San Diego, California. Alfred and his wife had no children. He was employed by the Shell Oil Company many years until his retirement. He died in January, 1963. Just a few weeks before he passed away he sent a most friendly letter to R. W. D. reminding him of their Basalt boyhood experiences together sorting potatoes and in handling a runaway team.

Rhodie Hyrup

Rhodie Hyrup, an engineer on the Midland, was a brother of Jens Peter. He married Mayme Cook, a teacher in Leadville, Colorado. They had one daughter, Dora Elizabeth. Before 1918 they left Basalt and he went to work for the Chicago, Minneapolis and St. Paul Railroad. Rhodie died of tick fever in 1922. His widow and daughter now live in La Canada, California.

(Information from Walter Hyrup and Genie Murray)

E. B. KELLY

In 1900 Aspen Junction's best building was erected. It was of brick with a stone foundation. Through the years it has remained in good condition. The owner, Mr. E. B. Kelly, kept a saloon on the lower floor, and he and his wife rented the upstairs rooms to railroad men.

courtesy of Zella Luchsinger

Grandma (Mrs. Gabe) Luchsinger, (l.) and Gabe, with irrigating shovel.

photo from Mrs. Ben Ashlock

Marcus Luchsinger in 1941.

Mr. Kelly, a notary public for many years, was a stocky, heavy-set man of a naturally generous nature. If there was need or distress of any kind he was one of the first to give or to lend a hand. In his later years he homesteaded 160 acres in the mountains on the north side of Little Basalt Mountain. He had a lake built on his place and stocked it with rainbow trout. For over a year he furnished the diner on the Colorado Midland Railroad with fish.

When age came on and his health was failing, he left for the south and never returned. The farm land was purchased by Emery Arbaney, and the building in town by Mr. and Mrs. Lamb. The Lambs started a restaurant there and rented the rooms upstairs.

The building is now owned by Ben Darien who runs a general merchandise store in it, The Basalt Supply Company. It is the only such store in town. The Dariens live upstairs.

(Information supplied by Walter Hyrup and Jake Lucksinger)

KIBBY

In the spring of 1886, Arthur J. Kibby, a railroad agent at Alden, Kansas, was transferred to Aspen Junction, Colorado, to be station master for the Colorado Midland. He was also a storekeeper and postmaster.

He and his wife, Ellen, and small son, Earl, lived in the rooms upstairs over the depot and eating-house, later named the Harvey House. This building and a small hotel, a general grocery store, and two or three saloons made up the business section of the little community.

A two-room school building was built a few years after the Kibby family's arrival. There was no church at first, but Ellen and Arthur saw to it that a minister from Aspen was brought in to hold occasional divine services in the school house. Earl recalled the name of the minister as the Reverend Carnine. Ellen started a Sunday School.

Earl always remembered the din caused that spring by the raging, swirling waters of the two rivers, the Frying Pan, and the Roaring Fork which joined forces at Aspen Junction. One could scarcely carry on a conversation morning, noon, or night for a time.

Earl married Edith Caldwell in 1906 in Colorado Springs. They had a daughter, Dorothy Ellen Wood, of Bay City, Michigan, and a son, Robert Dale Kibby, of Denver. Earl passed away October 16, 1961; Edith still lives in Denver.

(Information by Earl and Edith Kibby)

LIGHT

Fred Light homesteaded one of the first good cattle ranches in the Basalt region up on the Sopris Creek in 1880. He had arrived in Leadville from New York state in 1879. He and Mrs. Light had eight children: Effie, Edith, Leo, Fred, Jr., Helen, Ray, Howard, and Mildred.

Mrs. Light died rather young but when all of the children were of school age or older. Mr. Light was elected to the State Legislature in 1890.

During an unusual electric storm the Light home was struck

from Jake Lucksinger

Elsie Lucksinger Baxter.

Below: (l. to r.) India Reeves Luchsinger, Mrs. Gabe Luchsinger and Iona Rutherford. The next two people are unidentified. Charles Luchsinger and Zella Luchsinger on right.

Photo from India Reeves Luchsinger

Fred Carlson (l.) and Jake Lucksinger.

from Fred Carlson

by lightning. Ray was killed. The four girls were struck and knocked unconscious. Mildred, then about nine years old was hurt the least, and although so young, she took a horse from the barn and rode it bareback for help in the darkness. She had to go about four miles to a neighbor's place. Her brothers, Leo and Fred, Jr., were not at home that evening. Howard had died several years before.

All the Light children attended high school in Aspen. Effie (Killey), Ray, and Helen (Grover) are now deceased. Edith (Mrs. Bob Killey), and Mildred (Mrs. Howe Thayer) live in Long Beach, California.

In 1917 Mr. Light moved his family to Aspen. Fred, Jr., operated the ranch until his death in 1930. Leo took over its operation, and his father came back to stay, but died there the next year.

In 1962, Leo's son, Ray, bought the place and continues there. After selling it, Leo and his wife built a new modern home in Basalt on the old A. M. Danielson homesite. However, after living 75 years of his life on the ranch, Leo is unhappy in town. Every day he has gone back and helped his son with the cattle. He and his wife now plan to move again to the old Light homestead on Sopris Creek.

(Information from Mr. and Mrs. Leo Light)

LUCHSINGER (LUCKSINGER)

The members of the Luchsinger family played such a prominent part in the settlement and continued development of Basalt that the town might very properly be called Luchsinger. Perhaps

260 *Families of Basalt*

loaned by Jake Lucksinger

Jake Lucksinger, Jr., Jake Lucksinger, Sr., and Bill Lucksinger, in 1919.

a school, a road, a building, or a park might even yet be so designated.

Four brothers of this family came to Colorado: Jacob (Jake), Gabriel (Gabe), Ottomar (Otto), and Marcus (Mark). Jake and Gabe and their descendants remained in Basalt. Otto and Mark lived there for a time, but later moved away. There was also a John Luchsinger, probably a cousin, but we have been unable to get specific data about him.

The Luchsinger brothers were born in Mitlodi, Glarius, Switzerland. The date of their arrival in America is not known, but Otto reached Colorado about 1883, Jake and Gabe in 1885, and Mark in 1887. They were hardy pioneers, differing in their interests, but all willing and able to turn a hand to whatever work was needed in the new country. As described elsewhere, they took up much of the land occupied by the town of Basalt. They were farmers, ranchers, and dairymen. Jake's son, George, relates that his father was primarily interested in farming and ranching, while Mark spent much time hunting. Gabe and Otto, in addition to farming, were enthusiastic fishermen.

In those days the Basalt area was a fisherman's paradise. There were no regulations, and unlimited numbers of trout could be caught. Many of the fish were very large, as our photograph proves. Often Otto and Gabe each took twenty to forty pounds of fish in gunny sacks over their shoulders and carried them on foot twenty miles over poor trails to the mining town of Aspen. Sometimes they sold them to the Jerome Hotel and restaurants. With the cash they would buy much-needed groceries and return to Frying Pan Junction (this was before the railroad came in), again carrying the load on their backs. Such an expedition is a far cry from today's practice of driving an automobile two blocks to a supermarket.

(Information from Jake and George Lucksinger)

Gabriel Luchsinger

Gabe Luchsinger went first to Minnesota when he arrived in America. Later he homesteaded in Kansas. His wife, Julia Sneider, was from Germany; they were married about 1868. Gabe not only ran a dairy, but he and Julia also ran a "halfway" house for travelers before the railroad went through. It later was used as a milk house. They had wild game for meat for the table and had many vegetables from their large garden for serving their guests. There were trees to provide fruit for the winter. They later ran the most active dairy in Basalt, where we boys both worked for them.

The old "halfway" house is still standing, though in poor condition. It seems to the authors that this building has great historic interest, and should be preserved, but, as yet, funds and the necessary enthusiasm are lacking in Basalt.

Gabe died in 1927, at the age of 86. He and Julia had four children, a son and three daughters. The son, Charlie (1871-1918), married India Craig (Reeves). His widow lived in Rifle, Colorado, until her death in 1963. Charlie was always very obliging about furnishing a team when needed for funerals and other emergencies. Their daughter, Zella, lives in San Mateo, California, where she is secretary-treasurer of the building material firm which she joined in 1925. Speaking of her grandparents, Gabe and Julia Luchsinger, Zella has written "They were always farmers since I can remember them, but they rarely talked of their early days. I do know that I respected and admired them a great deal for their solid, honest, and tranquil life. They were a completely devoted couple."

Gabe's three daughters were Anna, Frances (Fanny), and Julia. Anna (Mrs. Beulah Burgin) (1872-1956) had one child who died in infancy. Julia (Mrs. Pete Frison) had no children. Frances (Mrs. Jake Rutherford) had a daughter, Ione, who married Robert Smith of Colorado Springs. Their son, Jack, now lives there with his father since Ione's death in 1951. Julia

Frison lived in Basalt on the Gabe Luchsinger ranch until her death in 1963. Her husband, Pete, who worked on the railroad, is remembered by C. L. D. as a good clog dancer and blackface comedian in his youth, frequently entertaining the crowd at dances in the I.O.O.F. Hall.

(Information—Zella Luchsinger)

Jacob (Jake) Lucksinger

Jacob Lucksinger came to the United States in 1872. Working first in Minnesota and Kansas, he came to Aspen Junction in 1885. After proving up on a homestead for dairying, he returned to Switzerland for his bride in 1892. She was Christine Genner, fifteen years younger than he, who was born in Ober Hallow, Switzerland, in 1873. Their marriage took place in Mitlodi, Glarius, where Jacob had been born.

Christine is the only surviving member of the older generation, and now lives in Basalt with her nephew, John Genner, whom she reared from babyhood. She celebrated her ninetieth birthday on February 10, 1963. When interviewed in the summer of 1962, the small slender lady had happy talk of early days in Basalt and supplied some useful information. In the busy days of rearing her large family, she seldom came to town from the ranch the family occupied at a short distance from Basalt. Therefore, the authors have, unfortunately, only a vague recollection of her at that time.

Her husband, Jake, Sr., was a small, slender, wiry man with a thin, wrinkled face. Although we always remember him as wearing an old slouch, out-of-shape hat, he, nevertheless, had a very dark complexion from being out in the open so much. Too, we picture him with boots almost always on, because he did so much irrigating. The shovel and the man seemed inseparable. He spent but little time down town, being on the job to provide for a large family.

Ten children were born to Jake and Christine. They were Jake, Jr., John, Elsie, William (Bill), Marcus, Theodore (Teddy), George, Carl (Tuffy), Agnes, and Raymond (Mike).

John and Marcus died in infancy. William never married and died of burns received in a fire in 1945. Teddy also remained a bachelor and died of pneumonia in 1926.

Jake, Jr., 70 years old in 1963, like many of the family, is a short, slender man who walks erect and with considerable vigor. He has always been robust and strong. He used to pitch on the baseball team, with R.W.D. as the catcher. He also rode several times in the bicycle road race from El Jebel to Glenwood Springs. This was run for eighteen miles over dirt roads in the remarkable time of a little over an hour.

Jake has been Eagle County Commissioner of District No. 3 for many years. He wrote to the authors on July 1, 1961, after his reelection as County Commissioner, "Thank you for your congratulations. I never had any thoughts that I would enter politics; it is enjoyable, and also a headache at times. I could write a book about it if I ever feel inclined to do so. You soon learn that the human has many complexes, as you have no doubt found in your professional career. The difference is maybe that those who climb aboard our backs are generally healthy".

Jake married Maybird Norris, of Aspen. (Her sister, Dorothy, is the wife of Bramblet Willits.) They have three children, Phyllis, Patricia, and Dorothy. Phyllis married Robert D. Roberts, of Grand Junction, Colorado. Patricia is now Mrs. Lee T. Kimmel, of Albuquerque, New Mexico. Dorothy is the wife of Tom Gabbert, of Azusa, California.

Regarding the change of name from "Luchsinger" to "Lucksinger" Jake wrote to me recently, "You asked about the difference in the spelling of the name. That came about when some of the townspeople misspelled the name and it gradually was spelled with the "k" instead of the "h", as it should be. I always

Mrs. Christina Lucksinger and sons, (l. to r.) Raymond "Mike", Jake, Carl and George.

photo from Jake Lucksinger

said that if we ever got so rich that we could put on the dog, we could take the "h" back and make it sound dignified. But the way it looks now, we will always remain Lucksinger." All other branches of the family have retained the original spelling.

Jake's sense of humor is further illustrated by another letter in which he wrote, "I was born here at the ranch. I tell people when they talk about how they arrived in this valley that I came here *bareback*—some came on the Midland, some walked in, some by covered wagon, but me,—bareback! But I will have to admit that I had more suits of clothes than I have ever had since. I had twelve suits of bird's-eyes, so I did not fare too badly."

Jake has written other comments for which we are grateful. He called to my attention that in the early days at Aspen Junction many homes had their own milk cows and each morning the cows would be gathered together as the "town herd" and driven up the hillside to graze by some boy hired at a dollar a cow per month. It was not only quite a sight, but quite a sound, for each cow wore a bell.

Now back to the remainder of the Jake, Sr. family. Elsie married Frank Baxter of Slater, Colorado and lived there many years but has now moved to Palisade. Her husband died two years ago. They have one daughter, Reba (Mrs. George Sheehan), of Dixon, Wyoming. Elsie was a tall, good looking girl who usually wore a hat, and always a long skirt, a much longer one than the other girls wore. Quite a life it was to be reared with eight brothers and a sister!

George Lucksinger married Louise Peterson, the oldest daughter of one of Carbondale's pioneer families. He has been the water commissioner and the town clerk of Basalt for many years and also helps his brothers, Jake and Raymond, in running the Lucksinger ranch. George and his wife were very helpful in making the town records available to the authors. Louise has made it a labor of love to get the minutes of the meetings of the Town Council into better shape. They have one daughter, Joan, now the wife of Lee Casto, of Gateway, Colorado, who has helped her mother in the restoration of the town records. George appears in some of the Basalt school pictures; in fact, it would be difficult to find a picture up to about 1918 that did not have a Lucksinger.

Carl married Nellie Renshaw, of Basalt; they are living in Carbondale and have two children. The son, Jimmie, is a petroleum engineer in Liberal, Kansas. Mrs. Bob Alexander, the daughter, lives in Boulder. Carl was short and stocky, but with a ruddy face and dark complexion that gave him a cherubic appearance. His smile in the pictures you can hardly miss noticing.

Agnes became the wife of Dr. Anand Brevik and lives in Fair Oaks, California. A daughter, Unadel, is married to Lt. Col. Leslie Shopton, of Great Falls, Montana.

Raymond married Margaret Donegan, daughter of old timers of Emma and Sopris Creek. Their daughter, Mary Ellen, is living in Littleton, and two sons, William and Raymond are high school students in Basalt. Raymond, Sr., with the help of his brothers, runs the original Jake Lucksinger ranch.

John Genner, who has been raised like a son and brother, never married and lives with his aunt, Christine. He has always been in partners with the brothers on the ranch.
(Information Jake Lucksinger, Jr., and the George Lucksinger family.)

Marcus Luchsinger

Youngest of the four brothers from Switzerland who pioneered in the Frying Pan Valley was Marcus Luchsinger. After working in Denver to help build the Tabor Grand Theatre, he arrived in Basalt about 1887. He homesteaded his ranch 9 miles east of Basalt where he became an expert hunter, fisherman, and a crack shot with a rfle. When he got ready to marry he wrote to his parents in Bern, Switzerland and asked them to choose a wife for him. They decided upon Annie Shearer, a childhood neighbor of Marcus's family. He sent money for her passage and she came to America to become Mrs. Marcus Luchsinger.

Nine children were born to the couple,—five on the ranch, and four after they left it. Annie, the first child died at age two, and Frank, the fourth one also lived only two years. The others were: Fannie, Jake, Susie, Julia, Marguerite, Rachel, and Marcus Jr. (Buster). According to daughter, Rachel, Mr. Luchsinger sold his ranch and moved to Slater, Colorado. He sold to the Slosses, and purchased the old Hunt place where he raised cattle.

Mrs. Annie Shearer Luchsinger died in December 1915, age 46. Marcus never remarried, and reared his large family by himself. Of the children, those living today are: Susie, who is Mrs. Thomas Lee Baxter of Palisade; Rachel, widow of Garland Ben Ashlock, an airplane mechanic of Rawlins, Wyoming, who died June 4, 1960; and the youngest, Marcus Jr. (called Buster), born

Feb. 26, 1905 who married Pearl Bedell of Hahn's Peak, Colorado, and now lives in Jeffrey City, Wyoming. Julia, Mrs. Elmer Beeler died December 5, 1953. Marguerite was Mrs. Roy Fleming and passed away in August 1932 at age 31. Mr. Fleming is a car salesman and car lot owner in Grand Junction.

There are now 54 direct descendants of Marcus and Annie Luchsinger, counting the children, grandchildren, great grandchildren, and great, great, grandchildren.

Marcus was a small, wiry man and a very determined one when it came to his rights. Many colorful stories of pioneer life in Basalt have been handed down and remembered by his family,—with Marcus as the central character. He told this one to Susie's husband, Lee Baxter: "One morning Ottomar Luchsinger caught a nice string of fish in the Frying Pan. Two hoboes came along and tried to get them away from him for their dinner. He finally gave the bums the trout after they had pelted him with rocks. Next they accosted Marcus in his cabin doorway and asked him to cook the fish. When he said he didn't have time to, they began to get tough with him also. Marcus took his rifle from above the door and told them to go. Then they picked up a bucket in his yard and began digging some potatoes in his field for their dinner. This time he took and aim and shot a hole through the bucket. They left in a hurry. When Ottomar returned and told of his treatment by the hoboes, and learned that they had also tried to get tough with Marcus and failed, he was so angry that he said he wished Marcus had shot them."

Marcus' daughter, Susie, says her dad often told the following incident which happened when the railroad was being built: "Dad lived on his homestead, and was alone at the time. The man who had the contract came to Dad's place and started work there. There wasn't much loose ground to work with and they had to haul the dirt for quite a distance. The contractor told the men to use some off of Dad's land, so they started to dig in Dad's meadow. Dad went down there and the boss told him to go back to 'grubbing his brush,'—he was running the men. This man was a big six-foot-tall Irishman. When Dad left and went back to his cabin the men all laughed at him; but when he returned with his rifle they got off the property in a hurry. The big boss called the men back to work,—saying that he didn't want a 'little sawed-off Dutchman telling him what to do.' He wanted his men to see how tough he really was. He told Dad to go back to his cabin or else. Dad said he wasn't going back until he settled it. He had nothing against the men, only the boss. Dad shot at his feet when he started toward him. Of course then the boss ordered his men off the property; he was through arguing. Later, when Dad was piling brush not far from the spot, he piled all the green brush on top of a big mound to let it dry. Later when he worked around the heap, getting ready to burn it, he noticed a burlap sack underneath, and reached under and pulled it out. He had already set a match to the trash on the other end. There were 8 or 10 sticks of dynamite fixed up with fuses and caps, in the sack. He figured that the boss of the railroad crew did it to get even with him for humiliating him before his workers."

Another story Susie remembers hearing about her father is that one time two Negroes came to Basalt and worked at odd jobs in the town. "Some section hands and others hanging around a saloon got to arguing that they didn't want any Negroes in Basalt. The more they talked and drank the more they came to agreement that the Negroes should be hanged. Someone who overheard the planning warned the two colored men, who gathered up their belongings and left, but the inebriated fellows didn't want to be cheated out of their 'fun' and ran up the Frying Pan after them. Marcus Luchsinger gave the two Negroes refuge in his cabin and questioned them as to whether they had done anything wrong. When he found that they hadn't, and that the mob of men only wanted to keep Negroes out of Basalt, he gave each a gun to guard the windows. Marcus guarded the door. The leader of the mob told Dad to send 'the black devils' out. He replied that they had done no wrong and he would defend them. As the leader approached closer, Dad shot in front of him and ordered him back saying that the next bullet wouldn't just throw up dust but would spill blood. The leader stepped back and told the others to dismount from their horses and rush the place. But none of the rest wanted to face the gunpowder, and they talked together about what to do. As they became more sober they decided they had better go back home. As they turned to go Dad found that the Negroes had thrown down their guns and were on their knees praying for their lives and had left him to face the gang by himself. This angered him somewhat, but he gave them food to take as they went on their way."

(Information from Susie Luchsinger Baxter)

Ottomar (Otto) Luchsinger

Otto took up his land in 1885, according to information from his grandniece, Zella, granddaughter of Gabe. He was past 80

This picture was taken in February, 1953 in the George Lucksinger home in celebration of the 80th birthday of Mrs. Christine Lucksinger.
Back row (l. to r.): Margaret Lucksinger (Mrs. Raymond), Joan Lucksinger Casto (George's daughter), Mrs. Ermine Chatrain, Louise Genner Shoemaker, Mrs. Vera Patterson (mother of Mrs. Geo. Lucksinger), Mrs. Jake Baumli, Jr.
Front row: (standing) Maggie Shay Renshaw, Julia Frison,. Seated are Annie Olson, Mrs. Christine Lucksinger, Nellie Lucksinger (Mrs. Carl), and Louise Lucksinger (Mrs. George).

photo from Harry Hanson

All dressed up.

when he died. His wife was never in Colorado. His son, another Jake, died in Grand Junction about 1933.

(There were three Jake Luchsingers in Basalt at one time.)

DANIEL W. LUPTON

Daniel W. Lupton and his wife, Nancy Riggs Lupton, were quite early settlers in Basalt, Colorado, coming there in April 1891 from Red Cliff and Leadville, Colorado. They built their home and also a business block and were quite active in the industrial and social advancement of the little town. They had one daughter, Jessie, who was born and grew up in Basalt.

After the town was incorporated, Mr. Lupton was one of the first members in the Town Council and was on the Town Board many times. When first coming to Basalt, Daniel and his brother, E. B. (Bruce) Lupton engaged in the saloon business for a few years, and Daniel, who was a meat cutter, also ran a meat market. After selling the saloon, Bruce Lupton went to California where he passed away several years later.

Mr. and Mrs. Lupton owned and operated a small fruit farm across the Roaring Fork river just south of town until 1917. Returning to their home in town, Mr. Lupton continued in the grocery business until the time of his death in March 1930 at the age of 75.

Mrs. Lupton was a member of the Methodist church and quite active in all its work. After Mr. Lupton's death, she continued to live in her home where she passed away in April 1935 at the age of 79. Both she and Mr. Lupton are buried in Basalt Cemetery.

Their daughter, Jessie, went to school in Basalt and was quite an accomplished pianist and took part in much of the church and school social activities, and also had a piano class. She was a telephone operator there for a few years before her marriage, after which she lived away from Basalt for many years. She now is a widow and living in her home in Basalt.

(Information from Jessie Lupton Rogers)

McCABE

Peter McCabe, a rancher near Emma, married Olive Gillespie, daughter of George Washington Gillespie, a very early settler on a homestead half a mile west of Emma. They had a family of nine children: Oma, born November 24, 1891, and Elbert, born September 15, 1895, these first two at Emma. Then Emmet, born January 6, 1897 at El Jebel; Vera Grace born June

24, 1901 at Basalt, and Vern born September 19, 1903 also at Basalt. Harold B., Annabelle, Warren H., and Flo Maxine were all born in Aspen. The youngest, Flo, became Mrs. Ainsworth.

The first daughter, Oma, married Frederick W. Seybold who worked for the Western Colorado Power Company. On June 23, 1932 at Montrose, Colorado, he was killed when high voltage electricity went through his body. Oma now lives in California.

The eldest son, Elbert, died in 1961 and is buried in Aspen. The next son, Emmet, died in 1963 and is also buried in Aspen. Both Vera Grace, who married Mr. Matis and the father, Peter McCabe, are buried in Hotchkiss Cemetery.

The McCabes were a closely-knit family. They were very companionable with their Gillespie relatives. Mrs. Annie Gillespie Grey, wife of Elbert H. Grey, Mrs. Gertrude Gillespie Allen, and Mrs. Cora Gillespie Tennis were sisters of Mrs. McCabe. Henry B. Gillespie of El Jebel was Mrs. McCabe's uncle. Mr. McCabe's brother, Hugh, was a much admired uncle. Born blind, he did not "vegetate" but applied himself diligently in grade school and then in the Institute for the Blind. A fine musician, he gave both vocal and instrumental concerts. He taught music and tuned pianos. Late in life he moved to Aspen and ran a men's furnishing store. He died there in 1944.

How widely the closely-knit McCabes are separated in death! Mrs. McCabe, the mother, and one son, Warren H., are resting in the Inglewood California Cemetery beside the grave of Aunt Cora Gillespie Tennis, mother of Voyle Tennis of Basalt. Cousin Earl Tennis, who was killed in an accident in Honolulu, had started to write the family history but died before he was able to finish it. Another cousin, Edwin B. Allen, is an employee of the Armored Service in Denver, Colorado.

(Information from Mrs. Oma M. Seybold and Edwin B. Allen)

DANIEL McCARTHY

Daniel McCarthy was born in Limerick, Ireland, where his father was a veterinarian. Daniel was a miller by trade. His wife, Maria Wills, was born in Stradbally, Ireland, her father being an attorney there, and related to Lord Cosby. Daniel and Maria were married in Denver and originally built a home near Carbondale. Later in 1903 they bought the Lloyd Grubb ranch for the fabulous sum (at that time) of $20,700. The modern house had twelve rooms, and a private spring.

They had five daughters, Eleanor, Anna, Josephine, Alice, and Grace. One son, Arthur, died in infancy.

George McLaren, Clarence and Lucy Danielson, and Mrs. McLaren.

Eleanor married Dee Hibner, who was the principal in the Basalt schools, and the teacher in the high school from 1910 to 1913, where he taught all the subjects in the freshman and sophomore years (the only ones in Basalt at that time). Mr. Hibner was an accomplished violinist. He tried to teach R.W.D. how to play the violin. His failure was due to the pupil's lack of musical ability.

From Basalt, Professor and Mrs. Hibner moved to Safford, Arizona, and later to Ray and to Coolidge, where she and her daughter, Eleanor Evelyn Hunt, still reside. Their son, Clayton, is a dentist in Tucson. Mr. Hibner died about thirteen years ago. Eleanor is a receptionist at Pinal General Hospital at Florence, Arizona.

Tom McNeil.

courtesy of Rachel McNeil Hyrup

Anne first married William Bogue. After his death she became Mrs. Frank Paddock. She was postmistress at Basalt for many years. They lived at Phippsburg for many years where Frank ran a helper engine on the old Moffat Road, now a branch of the Rio Grande.

(Information furnished by Anna McCarthy Paddock).

McLAREN

George McLaren, a native of Canada, served four years as an apprentice carpenter before emigrating to the United States as a young man. He married Minerva E. Rose who was born in Pennsylvania, February 23, 1851. They had two sons, John, who was born in Kansas, and George W. who was born in Walsenburg. They lived first in Kansas, and then moved to Walsenburg, Colorado, where Mr. McLaren continued as a carpenter. He also spent some time prospecting in the Frying Pan district.

In July 1893, the family moved to Thomasville where Mr. McLaren developed a most promising vein of ore just at the wrong time. The demonitization of silver and the disastrous Panic of '93 put a damper on any expectations of success along that line of work. However, as he continued ranching and logging in Thomasville, he never lost interest in doing some prospecting on the side. The last summer of his life, at the age of 79, he spent on the west slope of Mt. Massive, looking for a claim. When he returned and found that the Colorado Midland Railroad was preparing to tear up the rails at the east boundary of his ranch (November 1920) he gave up all hope of development on the Frying Pan and his health failed rapidly. He died December 23, a month later. His wife survived him twenty years, passing away on January 4, 1940 at the age of 89.

Mr. McLaren was a life-long Republican and the only Democrat he ever voted for in a national election was William Jennings Bryan who ran for President on a platform of free silver and the remonitization of silver. The school at Thomasville was called the Bryan School at that time. A sister of Mr. McLaren, Kate, and her husband, Russell La Pree, operated a store and post office in Thomasville during the eighteen nineties.

John McLaren, the first son, born March 23, 1878, entered the forest service as one of the first men working in the Holy Cross area with headquarters at Norrie, Colorado in 1906. A short time later he was transferred to Glenwood Springs as Assistant Supervisor. About 1909, the Sopris National Forest was created, and John went to Aspen as Supervisor. His next promotion was to the Denver District Office. In the early 1930's, he was made Liaison Officer for the Forest Service in the Civilian Conservation Corps (C.C.C.) in Chicago, remaining in that position until his retirement. He died October 23, 1946. He and his wife, the former Kathryn Skinner, native of Ohio, and teacher at Norrie, are buried in Aspen, as are his parents, in Red Butte Cemetery. Their one son, John Howard McLaren, is a building contractor in the Basalt and Aspen area.

The second son of the pioneer McLarens is George William, born November 23, 1889. He married Grace E. Parker of Aspen who was born April 6, 1885. Her pioneer parents had made many trips in the early days, taking their small daughter by covered wagon through northern and western Colorado. Like his father, George engaged in logging and lived near Thomasville. After the Midland closed, they became ranchers. In 1943, he started driving the first school bus from Muckawanago (near Biglow, east of Lime Creek) to the Basalt School. Three years later he purchased the first custom-built school bus in the Basalt area, continuing in this work for twelve years in all. The couple moved to Basalt May, 1955, and are still in good health and are great boosters for the town. Grace's sister, Amanda, and her husband, William Henderson, were also early residents of the Frying Pan area, where at one time they had a mining claim at the foot of Fool's Peak and mined some gold nuggets. They sold the claim to a mining company which packed in and set up a concentrating mill but were unable to continue development of the claim because of lack of funds. They later ran a cattle ranch at Ruedi.

(Information supplied by George William McLaren)

McNEIL

Tom McNeil, oldest engineer on the Midland, was born at Manchester, in New Hampshire, October 15, 1852, and when barely seventeen years old went to braking on the Chicago and North Western Railroad out of Chicago. He soon went to firing out of Janesville, Wisconsin to Fond du Lac, and stayed there until 1870. He then went to Kansas City and hired on the Kansas Pacific. In the spring of 1871 he was promoted to engineer. Twelve years later, in 1883, he started work for the Denver and Rio Grande at Gunnison, Colorado.

In 1884 he was made traveling engineer of the First District and remained on that job for one year. He left to take charge of the Lone Pine mining property at Aspen. He and his partners could not agree on location. He believed that if they had taken his advice they all would have become wealthy, as the Mollie Gibson mine afterwards turned out to be one of the best mines in Aspen. He sold out his share and ranched a few years before going back to railroading.

His first wife was Ann Goddard whom he married in Hugo, Colorado. She died three weeks after the birth of their daughter, Ann. The baby was taken to live with her maternal uncle and aunt in Janesville, Wisconsin. There she grew up, married, and now has two boys and two girls of her own.

After more than four years Mr. McNeil married Rachel Wiggins. They lived on a ranch at Rifle Falls. Three sons and one daughter were born to them. Rachel died in 1886. It was then that Tom left the ranch and moved to Leadville, keeping the two older boys with him while the parents of his wife took the daughter, named Rachel for her mother, and the youngest boy to Denver to live with them.

This daughter by his second wife knew her father only from infrequent trips to Leadville from her grandparents' home in Denver. She married Mr. Sloan and had four children, only one of whom—Madeline—is now living. The girl is now Mrs. C. E. Terry of San Diego, California. Rachel McNeil Sloan lived in Basalt for a while after her husband's death. She then married Alfred Hyrup of Basalt. They made their home in Long Beach, California, where Alfred died recently.

The eldest son by his second wife was Malcolm McNeil. He died in Alaska. Mr. McNeil went there in 1904.

Tom's third wife was Mrs. Faith Roe Downer, widow of Edward M. Downer Jr. She had three daughters by her former marriage: Martha, Mary, and Virginia Downer. Tom and Faith had a son, Tommy, who became 2nd Lt. Thomas Roe McNeil in World War II. He was killed at the Battle of Saipan. He was unmarried.

It was the youngest son, Tommy, who went with his father in a two-wheeled buggy drawn by a gentle horse to see McNeil's mining claim called the "Crown" between Sopris and The Roaring Fork. The boy was small, about nine years old. Mr. McNeil toppled over the cart and died of a heart attack. Tommy walked to the nearest farm for help.

Old timers remember the fine Masonic funeral for Tom McNeil in Basalt. The head of the engineers' lodge, Mr. Gilpatrick, came up from Grand Junction.

Mrs. Faith McNeil survives her husband and makes her home in Fruita, Colorado.

It is fitting that we quote from a letter Mr. McNeil wrote to a friend, Mr. Creagan:

". . . March 1887 I made a trip to Colorado Springs to investigate the Midland's possibilities. I saw Mr. William Fuller, the superintendent of machinery, with but very little encouragement, as he showed me a list of sixty-one engineers who had applied for work; but he asked me to leave my address. I told him I didn't want a job on the Midland behind sixty-one engineers. As he insisted, I did leave my name and address and gave two references, one being Mr. John McKenzie, formerly superintendent of machinery on the Kansas Pacific Railway . . . I found out afterward that Mr. Fuller and he were old friends . . . I could not have spoken a name more pleasing.

"A few days later Mr. Fuller came to Denver, asking me to show him around the machine shops where he expected to buy some machinery for the Colorado City shops then building . . . He told me of trouble they were having in handling trains down their three and four percent grades, and said he might want me to come to Colorado City and try and locate the trouble. A few days afterward I was called to Colorado Springs as traveling engineer, until the trouble could be located. I found the train

Roy Mills. from Roy Mills

crew knew nothing about retainers, and of course they were not being used down the heavy mountain grades. At each recharge of the engineer's brake valve the train would have gained such speed that the engineer could not help being a little rough in using air to check the accelerated speed of the train.

"About May 1, 1887 the Midland Company arranged to send an engine and a track-laying outfit over the South Park Railway to Leadville to start laying track west of there. They had an especially heavy car made to carry the engine to Leadville from Hill-top on the Midland. I was assigned to this engine with orders to place her in service as soon as possible. On June 10th we commenced laying track west of Leadville. During July we built what was called the Big Trestle, 1,100 feet long and 85 feet high. We also built another trestle 600 feet long and 30 feet high, and laid track through Hagerman Tunnel and on down the western slope near Ivanhoe Lake before the main track-laying gang overtook us. In due time we reached Aspen Junction, now Basalt, then went on up the Roaring Fork Valley to Maroon Creek bridge, where the trains stopped for some little time on account of the high iron trestle bridge being built over Maroon Creek. The first scheduled train was put on November 5th, 1887 west of Leadville—from Leadville to the Maroon Creek bridge three miles east of Aspen—Frank Farquahar and I being assigned to the runs, with Riley Miller as conductor.

"Engineer Farquahar and I were on these runs at the finish of the road, August 5th, 1918, and neither of us had ever injured a passenger seriously in all these years. Each one had one bad accident—Frank's one account of a loose wheel, and mine on account of two engineers' miscalculating the time order on my train. In mine we came together at Hell Gate along a granite wall, and were rounding a 16-degree curve when we struck. My fireman was badly injured and barely lived to reach Leadville before he died. As to myself, I was at work in about three months after the accident. None of the engine men on the light engine was hurt badly, only bruised up some."

(Information obtained from Mrs. Faith McNeil, Mrs. Rachel M. Hyrup, and Clarence L. Danielson)

MALLORY

Fred Vernon Mallory with his pretty young wife Ella Jane Reid Mallory and their infant daughter, Nettie, came in 1902 from Carthage, Missouri, and settled on the Hook Ranch at El Jebel.

The next year their son Frank Vernon was born, and three years later another daughter, Violet Ima came to them, both born in Basalt.

The family moved to Aspen where they lived until Mr. Mallory's death in 1912. His widow moved back to Basalt to rear her three children. She homesteaded a place up Cattle Creek and worked very hard there. A log cabin was built and the land cleared as required. She and the children raised some stock.

After the three years of "proving up" she sold her ranch to Mr. MacLaughlin who lived on the neighboring ranch. His daughter Ima MacLaughlin Renftle still lives on the old Mallory's homestead.

Nettie married Sie Lawrence in 1918. They had a family of twelve children. Nettie lives in Salinas, California.

Frank's wife is Opal Green of Missouri Heights. They and their three children also live in Salinas.

While attending school in Basalt, Violet lived with the Grace family, the Atkinsons and then the Marvin Slosses. After two years of high school in Glenwood Springs, she took nurses training in Beth-el Hospital, Colorado Springs. In 1925, she married Eugene P. Morley of Pueblo. They live in Denver and have no children.

Mrs. Mallory's second husband was John Patrick of Carbondale. They married in 1925 and lived at Satank. He died within seven years. She lived until 1961.

Violet pays this tribute to her mother: "She had a life of hard work, yet a good life spent more in doing for her loved ones and friends than in spending any thought on her own enjoyment."

We regret being unable to get anything about the Enoch Mallory family.

(Information from Violet Mallory Morley)

MILLS

The parents of Roy A. Mills moved from Colorado City to Basalt in 1900. Three or four years later they left Colorado for San Bernardino, California where they stayed only about three years. They moved east to Coolidge, Kansas and remained there and in Holly, Colorado until 1936.

Roy Mills worked as an engineer for four years during World War II in Nevada, running a diesel for the government at Hawthorne.

Lydia Jakeman Newkirk.

from Mrs. Newkirk

The three children of the Mills family were: Fred E. born August 27, 1863 in Topeka, Kansas. Married Mary Alice Summers on June 12, 1887 in Jetmore, Kansas. He died April 10, 1938 in San Francisco. His wife, Mary, died November 1951 in Arlington, California. She was born June 11, 1864 in Minnesota; Roy Arthur Mills was born December 16, 1895 in Staffordville, Kansas. He married Dora Rose Towne on December 16, 1917. She was born January 16, 1899 in Holly, Colorado; Ethel Marie Mills was born September 16, 1900 in Colorado City, Colorado. She married Leslie Wonn on October 23, 1921.

NAEFE

August Naefe's family located on a ranch near Emma, Colorado in 1886. They raised fruit, small and large, and their farm was known as Pioneer Fruit Bee and Honey Farm.

August Naefe was very prominent in the Odd Fellows and Knights of Pythias.

August's father was Fredrick Naefe, who married Caroline Beck in January, 1860. To this marriage three children were born, Annie, Julia, and August. August Naefe's mother took care of Mrs. Danielson when Ralph was born.

CHARLES NELSON

The family of Charles Nelson were farmers and ship builders in Nova Scotia.

After having been shipwrecked in the East Indies, he was returning home on the "Atlantic" when she went down off the coast of Newfoundland with the largest loss of life ever recorded up to that time—some 500. Still in his early twenties, he determined to get as far from the sea as possible and came to Colorado; first to Georgetown, then to La Junta and, finally, to Basalt and employment on the Midland.

He married Florence E. Collins in 1889. Her Father, Louis H. Collins, returned, blinded from the Civil War, to the plantation home where he was raised in Southern Missouri to find himself disinherited for having joined the Federal forces. He brought his family first to Salida. Believing the Midland would build down Piceance Creek, he homesteaded there and began raising cattle. He later built a home on a three-acre site, just across the old bridge on the south bank of the Frying Pan and commuted seasonally between there and his ranch.

Charles Nelson died in 1912 from a heart ailment; Florence passed away as a result of injuries received in a hotel fire in Amarillo, Texas, in 1927.

Their one son, Wallace, is now credit manager for the Kistler Stationery firm in Denver.

(Information supplied by Wallace Nelson)

NEWKIRK

The parents of Lydia Newkirk were John and Jeanette Henning who lived on a farm near Oelwein, Iowa. Forbears of the Henning family were early colonists in America from England.

Her two maternal uncles, Charles (Cap) Noble and George Noble, came into the Frying Pan Valley before the railroad. "Cap" had served in the Civil War and was a 32nd degree Mason. Then Lydia's two brothers, Charles and Lester Henning came west. Charles, a stone mason, came for his health. He became foreman of the Lime Quarry in Thomasville in 1893 when Mr. Beard owned both the Meredith and the Thomasville quarries. They in turn urged the rest of the family to join them.

Lydia was 15 when her parents brought her and her three sisters, Flora, Ida, and Martha to Thomasville by the Midland in 1892. The family ran a boarding and roominghouse. The youngest girl, Martha, was an invalid requiring much care from the mother. The other three daughters worked very hard helping with the work. Mr. Henning, a retired cabinet-maker and farmer, did chores such as splitting wood, carrying water, and many other tasks necessary in a pioneer home where there were no conveniences.

Flora married Paul Billow. Ida married Will Ross. Lydia continued running the boardinghouse by herself until at 19 she married Fred Jakeman, who was also from Iowa. He was a surveyor and had homesteaded a place west of Thomasville. He is mentioned in the "Hough" family as he was a brother to Christine (Mrs. J. T. Hough) and an uncle to Gladys Hough Wachob.

The creek there still bears his name on government maps. Mr. Jakeman was one of the first Justices of the Peace. He held court in a special little building built for the purpose on his ranch. The main crops they raised were hay and potatoes. They also raised cattle.

Lydia and Fred had three children: Blanche, Maude, and Fred Jr. According to a daughter, Lydia begged her husband to give up the position as Justice because there was so much controversy, and many people disregarded government rules. Some people who wanted to haul logs through his ranch and over a bridge to the railroad siding became angered when he asked if they would help strengthen the bridge so it would not break under the heavy load. One man under the influence of liquor returned and shot Mr. Jakeman. The bullet hit him near the temple but was not fatal. Soon after this narrow escape, Fred died of heart trouble following an appendectomy performed in the hospital at Aspen. The widow and her children had to keep the ranch alone with some help from old Mr. Myers. They irrigated the hay fields, fed the stock, milked the cows, and did very heavy work. It was a hard life for any woman.

Two years later, Lydia married Swan Nelson, a timber man, who then moved on the ranch to help her. A son, Frank Eddy, was born to them. They sold the ranch and moved to Meredith where Mr. Nelson supplied timber for the mines in Leadville. There a second son, James Albert, was born. They bought another ranch west of Meredith, but lived there only one summer.

Forest and Lydia Newkirk with grandchildren, Earl and Linda Nelson and baby.

from Lydia Newkirk

Mr. Nelson went to Norrie to work at logging, and the family followed him. The next seven years were difficult ones for them. Two more sons, Leon Odell and Earl Vernon, were born to the Nelsons, so they now had four sons. In 1918, when the Midland was junked, most families had to leave the towns. The Nelsons went to their ranch once more. Swan never overcame his dislike for ranch life, and decided to leave. A few years later Lydia obtained a divorce. One of the sons, Leon, still lives on the place. When the Ruedi Dam is built he will have to leave, for the ranch will be under water.

In 1927, Lydia married Forest Newkirk, a widower and former railroad man. He was born September 18, 1887 in Pennsylvania. His boyhood was spent there and in Montrose, Colorado, but he came as quite a young man to Basalt. Going to work for the Midland until it closed down, he spent 50 years of his life in our town. Later he became the mail carrier from Basalt to

Mr. and Mrs. John Ould with favorite horse.

photo from Irene Ould

courtesy of Jake Lucksinger

Alvin Ould, Clifford Rhodes and George Ould.

Meredith. An avid fisherman, his favorite pastime was trying to catch the "big ones" which he frequently did. At the age of 82, while fishing on the Frying Pan, he suffered a fatal heart attack and was found by John Hyrup, with the line and net still in his hands. Mrs. Anna Olson, another Basalt pioneer, died on the same day. How we regret that we had no opportunity to interview these old timers before writing this story.

Mrs. Newkirk is a remarkable woman of whom Basalt is justly proud. She is known for her good cooking and makes excellent jelly from fruits she raises, and freezes and cans all her surplus garden vegetables. Mrs. Newkirk has made beautiful handpieced quilts, crocheted rugs, and embroidered articles. In her youth she had no time for these activities. She now lives with her daughters, Blanche and Maude Elmont in the old Fahey residence.

Lydia and Fred Jakeman's daughter, Blanche, started nurse's training in Denver but gave it up to marry William Elmont, who was an invalid for several years before he died. He is buried in Basalt.

Blanche Jakeman Elmont's six sons are: William Alfred, a Technical Sergeant in the Air Force, who is married and has one son, and is presently stationed in Germany; Fred, the second son is a mechanic, married, with three children, living in Englewood, Colorado; Raymond, a designer, married, with one daughter, is living in Southhampton, Pennsylvania; Walter, married and living in Upland, California; Earl, a student at present at Brigham Young University in Provo, Utah, married to a Denver girl who is teaching first grade in Provo; Clifford, a carpenter, working for the Aspen Foundation and living in Basalt with his mother.

James Phelan.

loaned by Ruth Phelan Hallock

Another daughter of Lydia and Fred, Maude, was sent to Greeley to High School because her mother thought a lower altitude would cure her rheumatism and persistent tonsillitis. She says that teachers were scarce because of the war, and she easily obtained a position in Deer Trail after graduation. There she met and married Herbert Elmont, brother of her sister's husband. He was a bachelor farmer. He died in June 1946 and is buried in Basalt. They had twin daughters, Ruth Blanche and Alice Flora who grew up and married brothers from Woody Creek, George and Allen Vagneur; they still live there. The Vagneurs' grandfather, a pioneer, came to the Roaring Fork Valley in a covered wagon. The third daughter of Maude and Herbert Elmont, named Maude also, was born on her mother's birthday, married Stanley Usel, son of Leonis Usel. Stanley is now a teacher in Greeley, and his wife is a school secretary there. Maude and Herbert Elmont's only son, Albert Elmont, was graduated from Basalt High School, enlisted in the U. S. Navy during the Korean War, and afterward attended the Colorado State College at Greeley. He married a class-mate, Myrna Borchert of Denver. He received a Master's Degree in Speech Therapy. Both he and his wife now teach in the Jefferson County schools. They live in Englewood, next door to Maude's nephew, their double cousin, Fred Elmont, Blanche's second son.

Fred Jakeman, Jr., married Rhoda Price of Byers, Colorado. Her parents were pioneer cattle ranchers there. Fred and Rhoda have no children. They own a few acres of land in Pomona, California, where they now reside.

(Information from Lydia Newkirk and Maude Elmont)

photo from George Lucksinger

Back row (l. to r.): Charley Peterson, Anna Peterson, Christine Genner Lucksinger, Jacob Lucksinger, and John Genner.
Front row: Johnny Peterson, Jake Lucksinger, and Jake Genner.

Enoch Olson.

photo from Mrs. Vernon Eiswerth

OULD

John Ould had the barber shop in Basalt. In conjunction with it, he and Mrs. Ould had accommodations for baths, one day a week being reserved for ladies. Mr. Ould was also the town marshal for a long time.

Mr. Ould was born in Cornwall, England, April 13, 1859. He died February 17, 1934. Mrs. Ould, whose maiden name was Elva Jane Moon, was born in Joplin, Missouri, June 6, 1868. She and her family came to Leadville during the mining boom in a covered wagon. She attended school in Leadville and married there. She died March 23, 1937. Both she and her husband are buried in Glenwood Springs.

The Oulds had four sons. Three were born in Leadville. Will became a dentist. Rialto (Rye) was a gasoline station owner. Alvin is a real estate salesman, and George is the superintendent of road maintenance at Glenwood Springs. They have all lived in Glenwood since the Midland closed in 1918.

In the summer of 1963, we had the privilege of attending the 50th wedding anniversary of Rye and Irene where we visited with their many relatives and friends.

John Ould's children recall that he decided to leave Leadville because it was "too tough" a place in which to rear children.

We remember Mr. Ould as a rather large man with a luxuriant mustache. He always wore a large hat. How pleasant he was when he cut our hair!

PADDOCK

Fred Paddock was born in England about 1853. After his graduation from a boys' school (probably an Anglican church school) he joined the British navy and sailed around the world. He had always excelled in penmanship and delighted in writing a beautiful hand. At an early age he emigrated to the United States. In Indiana, he married Margaret O'Connell of Terre Haute, who was born September 13, 1860, a Roman Catholic.

The family came to Basalt about 1890. Fred Paddock ran the first switch engine for the Midland in Basalt and worked in that capacity for many years. Originally the switch engines would help the trains get started rolling out of town by pushing them up beyond "Graveyard Hill" near the present ranger station.

When ill health forced Mr. Paddock to retire from the Midland he started a pool-hall and cigar store and operated it for many years.

Fred and Margaret had one son, Frank, who started employment for the Colorado Midland as a call boy at the age of sixteen. Then he worked as a fireman until the railroad closed in 1918. He then went to the Moffat Road where he ran a helper engine at Phippsburg for many years. He married Mrs. Anna McCarthy Bogue, widow of William Bogue. He retired March 15, 1963.

(Information from Anna Paddock)

PHELAN

Mr. James Phelan was a locomotive engineer who spent most of his active railroad life running a pusher engine out of Basalt. He and Andrew Danielson were on hundreds of trains together up the grade to Ivanhoe and were always very friendly.

He was born December 29, 1867. He was married in Leadville on February 19, 1903, to Agnes Shea, who was born in Blackhawk, Colorado, on June 6, 1879.

He first started railroading on the Denver & Rio Grande, but when the Tennessee Pass tunnel caved in and the D. & R. G. trains had to be routed over the Midland, he went to work for the latter railroad as the Terminal Superintendent at Basalt. He soon transferred to running helper engines, however.

When the railroad closed down in 1918 he went out on the last train to run. The family moved to Denver, where he was Secretary of Division 186 of the Brotherhood of Locomotive Engineers until the time of his death. He died November 9, 1949, and she on January 16, 1948, both in Denver.

The Phelans had three children, Ruth, Mayme, and Maurice. Ruth Phelan Hallock and Maurice Phelan live in Denver; Mayme Phelan Sanchez lives in Littleton.

(Information from Ruth Phelan Hallock)

PETERSON AND OLSON

Mrs. Anna Olson was a very prominent figure in Basalt because, besides caring for a large family, she took an intense interest and active part in the life of the community. It was she who knew and remembered all the lore and history of the area. We regret that we did not begin to write these pages in her lifetime, for she could have added much to them.

Born Anna Rush in Mitlodi, Switzerland, Christmas Day, 1872, she came to the United States at the age of seventeen in order to join her four uncles, the Luchsinger brothers. At first she was employed in a cheese factory in Carbondale and continued there until her marriage to Charles Peterson who had emigrated from Sweden. They then lived on a ranch just above El Jebel. In 1902 they moved to a ranch two miles west of Basalt.

Mr. Peterson was a small man but worked much harder than the average person. He was an active Odd Fellow. He worked in the Midland roundhouse, but after his hours there he labored at the almost superhuman task of digging a long ditch by hand from the Jake Luchsinger pond to his own place. This ditch included a tunnel through a hill. R.W.D. could not remember whether it ever carried water, but a daughter, Zella Eiswerth, testifies that it did and that crops were irrigated from it and were very good. Eight children were born to the Petersons, five sons and three daughters. They were: John, Leonard, Charlie, Clara, and Oscar who are now deceased, and Alice, Hazel and Edward. Alice and Hazel married the Templeton brothers, Harry and Robert. The Harry Templeton family lives in Twin Falls, Idaho. Mr. and Mrs. Robert Templeton reside in Glenwood Springs, Colorado. Oscar Peterson and his wife also lived in Glenwood. Ed Peterson married Beulah Eiswerth Gearhart and they live in Jerome, Idaho.

After her husband's death, Mrs. Peterson married Enoch Olson in about 1905. He was born in Hogerud in the province of Varmland, Sweden, October 18, 1874. He too emigrated to the United States at a youthful age. He was only 19 years old. After working in various places in Colorado he came to the Roaring Fork Valley. After marrying the widow Peterson, he worked at the Tie Camp at Shehi Park, the Peach Blow Rock Quarry, and also helped on the ranch. Enoch was a big strong man with very masculine features. He belonged to the Woodmen of the World Lodge.

Anna and Enoch had four children: Fred, Alma, Henry and Zella. Zella married Vernon Eiswerth and lives in Basalt. Alma is Mrs. Chester Stewart of Denver, Colorado. Grandma Olson, as she was affectionately called, was a small woman with a ready wit and pleasant smile. She was a faithful member of the Rebekah Lodge and a charter member. Our mother and she were close friends. She passed away August 15, 1960 and was buried in Basalt Cemetery.

(Information furnished by Zella Eiswerth and Alma Stewart)

RENSHAW

Alvin Renshaw was born in South Dakota in 1891. He lived in Camp Point, Illinois until he came to Carbondale, Colorado in the spring of 1912. He married Maggie Shay in Aspen April 27, 1913. They farmed in Carbondale for three years. He then went to work as a fireman for the Midland in March 1918. He fired for Arthur Bates on the helper engine of the last passenger train east out of Basalt. (Claude Harris says he was the fireman). Tom McNeil was the engineer and Frank Paddock the fireman on the other engine. (Some say the last fireman was Sam Phillips).

After helping junk the Midland Alvin Renshaw returned to farming and raising sheep for a while. Since then he has been a school janitor and a stone mason.

For 37 years the Renshaws lived in the log house across the Frying Pan built by Frank Snell. Then they purchased the lots where the Stiffler roominghouse used to be from Grandma Lucksinger, and they built their home there.

Alvin and Maggie had three daughters. Frances passed away in 1959. Nellie, who was born in Carbondale in 1916, is married to Carl Lucksinger, and they have two children. Anna Lois, third daughter of the Renshaws, lives in Hampton, Virginia.

Mr. Renshaw was elected councilman five times, beginning in 1938. In 1950 he was elected mayor, and held that office continuously until 1964.

(Information from Alvin Renshaw)

RHODES

Oscar Gerton (Gert) Rhodes was an engineer on the Colorado Midland for a number of years. He was born December 4, 1870 at Fountain, Colorado. He married Addie Mae Roszell, who was born near Vinton, Iowa, March 22, 1869; she was a niece of Samuel Cramer.

They had two sons, Clifford Marle, born in 1897, and Melvin Ellis, born February 15, 1910 at Glenwood Springs, Colorado. Clifford became an inspector at the Ordnance Depot at Avondale near Pueblo. Malvin was employed by the Southern Pacific Railroad. He died September 22, 1952 at Fresno, California.

Mr. and Mrs. Rhodes also reared Anna Wilson of Meeker, Colorado, from the time she was a girl of twelve years. She later married Alfred Sloss.

Mrs. Rhodes was a niece of Tillie Kester of Aspen. Gert died at Pueblo at the home of his son, Clifford, July 25, 1954.

Mrs. Addie Rhodes was always active in the Methodist Church serving in many capacities. She was a very jolly person. If there happened to be a local-talent play being put on at the I.O.O.F.

Hall, one could bank on it that she would be in it. She passed away June 6, 1949 at Basalt.

(Information given by Anna Sloss)

RUEDI

A man who enters vitally into the early history of settlement of the Frying Pan area is John Ruedi. He not only bought a tract of land in the south part of the Basalt neighborhood, but about 1897 he took up a homestead in the valley which was known as Ruedi. It was a water-tank stop for the Midland Railroad. The dam which in the near future will be constructed for the Frying Pan-Arkansas River Project will be located in his valley. Thus his name will be preserved in a monumental manner.

Born in Switzerland, and coming to Colorado from Missouri, Mr. Ruedi was a pleasant but quiet man, almost a recluse, about whom very little was known. He was six feet tall and had very black hair. A bachelor, he lived alone except for the time his nephew, Hugo Miller, stayed with him before settling in Meredith.

John Ruedi was kind and obliging to those who lived in the vicinity. He picked up the mail which was dropped off the train at the water tank, and took it to his neighbors, the Hough family. In return they loaned him their books and magazines. Gladys Hough (Mrs. Frank Wachob) remembers that he read all of her parents' books with great interest in the five years the family homesteaded near him. The Houghs always felt grateful to him because at the time Gladys' birth was imminent and there was not time for Mrs. Hough to go to the hospital in Glenwood Springs, Mr. Ruedi told them he knew of a woman "up the river" who could "help out," and he went for her.

In addition to ranching he conceived the clever idea of turning the swampy part of his acreage into fish ponds from which he sold trout to the diningcars on the Colorado Midland. At times his customers included disappointed fishermen who were reluctant to return home with empty creels. The latter market for his trout increased in the late nineties when the Will Smiths from Iowa settled at Ruedi and built a two-story fishermen's lodge nearby.

Truly revealing of the personality and character of the man is the following incident which Gladys Hough Wachob remembers her father's telling. One time a boy about twelve years old, who was stealing a ride on the train, was put off at the water tank at Ruedi. The kindly bachelor took him home, fed him and kept him, meanwhile trying to find out who he was and why he was "bumming" a ride. The child was quiet and taciturn, but helped willingly with whatever tasks he was asked to do. Then he would slip off into the hills, returning each evening dirty and exhausted. One day the neighbor, Mr. Hough, caught a glimpse of him digging on a hillside. Although he usually was friendly enough, this time he ran quickly and hid among the rocks. When Jonce Hough happened to mention it to Mr. Reudi, the latter looked for his money box in its hiding-place in his bedroom and found it gone. He cautioned Hough to say nothing to the boy. Later he tactfully and in a kind way made more effort to get his small guest to talk. Slowly he learned from the lad that his father had been killed in a Leadville mine accident. His mother was doing washing for the miners and the boy picked up the laundry and delivered it. He said he wanted to go farther into the mountains and find a gold mine for himself so that his mother would not have to do washing any more. Finally he also told his name.

Mr. Ruedi wrote to the mother in Leadville. By return mail the lonely boy received a letter from her saying how worried and sleepless his mother had been over him. She needed his help and could scarcely get along without him. She sent his train fare, and wrote that she and his little sister would meet the next day's train from the west. John Ruedi, busy all day at his fish ponds, found his young guest happy and gay that evening. No mention was made of the lost money-box, but later, when he went to his room Mr. Ruedi found it, with the contents intact, in its hole underneath his bed.

The *Basalt Journal* of September 29, 1906, says that John Ruedi had sold his homestead to Loren Brown and moved to Baggs, Wyoming, where he continued ranching. He was found dead there, presumably of a heart attack, soon afterward. The cattle ranch was sold to Ford and Henderson in 1910, and they in turn sold to Frank Neal about 1935. The present owners are Mr. and Mrs. William Framm.

John R. Smith, son of Mr. Ruedi's neighbors the Will Smiths, furnished the information that John Ruedi arrived in Leadville in 1890. With Charles (Cap) Noble and Will Smith, Ruedi prospected the Frying Pan country when they were on hunting trips from Leadville. They sold the game they shot to the construction crews of the Midland. Livestock was the principal income of those living at Ruedi until about 1905 when the Roaring Fork Plaster Company built a mill there. The Smiths and the Browns each built a log hotel for the mill-workers. In 1918 the mill was dismantled and sold for scrap. Mrs. Smith bought the station and converted it to a tearoom.

Charles Curtis, present owner of the hotel, dismantled the tearoom and built cabins. The Will Smith ranch is now owned by Leon Nelson who operates it in conjunction with his father's adjoining place. Mr. Smith died in 1942 at their home in Basalt. His wife passed away two years later. Their son, John R., left Ruedi in 1920, trying his luck in the oil fields of Texas, Arkansas, and California, but always yearning for the Frying Pan. He and his wife, Florence Olson, whom he met in Grand Junction, now live in Minturn, Colorado. They have three children: John, now with the F.B.I. in Denver; Roy, 24 years old, with the F.A.A. in Denver; and Iva Jean, who married Lynn Kanikas of Minturn and has one boy.

Hugo L. Miller, the nephew of Ruedi, was an Oxford University graduate. He had some very educational books. His mother had left him some Suez Canal bonds and the interest on them furnished his living. During World War I he had to go to work on a farm because the French Government paid him none of this interest, but after the war he received all back interest in full. Perhaps some of this was a pension; he was in the French army before coming to the United States. Like his uncle John, Mr. Miller never married. He died in Meredith about 1935.

Sam Phillips and John Scandlan.

from Fred Carlson

Jake Lucksinger remembers that John Ruedi was an excellent shot with a rifle. On one occasion Ruedi saw a section foreman lazily sitting on a chair tipped back against the section-house. He procured a rifle, took aim and fired, striking the two back legs of the chair. The foreman took a sudden unexpected dump on the ground, but never knew until later how it happened.

Another nephew, Peter Ulysses Ruedi, worked in Aspen as a miner. He was born in Bern, Switzerland. His son, George Ruedi, has an army book of military training in Switzerland which belonged to his father. George Ruedi lives at 605 Fillmore Street in Denver. He was born in Aspen, October 15, 1910. He was educated in Cleveland, Ohio, and moved to Denver in 1928. He is in electrical construction work and has one daughter, Cathy, who teaches at Colorado State University in Fort Collins.

George remembers that his great uncle, John Ruedi, had a brother who was a physician and who specialized in the treatment of tuberculosis. George says this Dr. Ruedi was one of the founders of Denver General Hospital.

Mrs. Peter Ulysses Ruedi, who was Catherine Prechtel, of Cleveland, Ohio, before her marriage, lives in Denver. Her grandfather came to Aspen in the early 80's, and was a mine blacksmith.

The Rocky Mountain News of July 18 and 19, 1964, contains accounts of the official start of building the Ruedi dam as part of the Arkansas-Frying Pan Project. This dam will undoubtedly help many people, but it would have given a great heartache to John Ruedi, as it does to the present owners of the land, to see their beloved ranches covered up by water.

(Information from many sources).

SCANDLAN

One couple that did a tremendous amount of good for Basalt was the Scandlans. John R. and Electa Mather Scandlan came from New York state to our little town about 1900. From then on until the fateful year of 1918 Mr. Scandlan worked in various capacities in the railroad depot.

John was one of the most inconsistent men we have ever known. He was a close friend of our family. At the time that he became mayor of Basalt he was in our home frequently to plan meetings of the city council with our father who was a councilman. We remember hearing them talk about prohibition and local option especially. On these occasions he seemed affable

Anna Sloss, Mrs. Price Sloss, Mayme Barker, Alvin Sloss, Price Sloss, Alfred Sloss, Baby Mary Lou Barker, and Edith Sloss. Taken about 1915.

and able to hold up his end of the conversation. Furthermore through experience we knew him to be an ideal hunting and fishing companion,—a very pleasant friend. One time when a group of townspeople went to Hopkins on a picnic, he and R.W.D. became so absorbed in their fishing that they missed the helper engine home. "Borrowing" a hand-car from the section men they rode the 13 miles to Basalt, at times pushing it across mud slides, and arrived home at the unusual hour of 3 A.M.

However, when Mr. Scandlan was on duty at the depot he was glum, uncooperative, and just plain sour. Words could scarcely be dragged from him. When asked the most straightforward question, especially about whether an expected train were on time or not, he would allow the questioner to wait interminably long before deigning to pay any attention to him; then his answer would be gruff and short. Gruffness was not too unusual among depot men, conductors, and brakemen in those days; railroads were not then competing with air lines or buses. John was a good-looking man of medium height with exceedingly well-built shoulders.

Mrs. Scandlan, from an old colonial New England family, was a direct descendant of the famous preacher, Cotton Mather. In speaking of Mather, Benjamin Franklin in his Autobiography said that as a child he read "De Foe's *Essay on Projects,* and Dr.

loaned by Dr. Cuthbert Powell

Alfred Sloss.

Mather's *Essays to do Good* which perhaps gave me a turn of thinking that had an influence on some of the principal future events of my life".

Electa Scandlan certainly inherited Christian virtues from her renowned forbear. A very intelligent woman, kind and gracious to everyone, and most energetic and hard-working for one so small in stature, she took an active part in the affairs of the community. She taught Sunday School, was organist in the Methodist Church for a time, and also worked in the Ladies Aid.

When the Midland closed, the Scandlans moved to Tolland on the Moffat Road where John became station agent and telegrapher. After his health failed about 1929 they moved to Denver. They came to visit us in turn, for a time, in our homes. On February 15, 1931 Mrs. Scandlan died from pneumonia. Her two sisters requested that her body be sent to New York for burial near the graves of her parents. Two years later Mr. Scandlan passed away and is buried in the Masonic plot in Crown Hill Cemetery in Denver.

(Information from Ralph & Luverne Danielson)

SHAY

Mike Shay (Shea) and Kate Driscol were married in New York and came to Colorado in 1887 where Mike's first assignment was work as foreman on the section at the Hagerman Tunnel. Kate was one of the very few women ever to live in the "all men" town of Hagerman. Perhaps she was the one who had the garden described in the Midland chapter.

In 1889 they moved to Aspen Junction but soon afterward to Leadville. Mike was transferred back to Busk to care for the Busk-Ivanhoe Tunnel in 1893. Their son, John, was born there, probably without benefit of doctor or nurse. The family moved back and forth from Busk to Leadville several times. In 1897 their daughter, Maggie, was born in Leadville.

From 1904 they lived in Basalt where Mike was the section foreman for seven years. He then worked at Woody on the Rio Grande, then moved to Marble and worked seven years for the Crystal River Railroad.

His last move was back to Leadville where he worked for the Colorado and Southern Railroad until he retired in 1927. They made their home in Glenwood at that time and he died there February 25, 1929. Mrs. Shay died in Basalt in 1942. Both are buried in Leadville.

(Information from Alvin Renshaw)

SLOSS

The Sloss families have had an important role in the development of the Basalt region. Anna Sloss is nobly carrying on the work and interests they began.

Sterling Price Sloss, born in Missouri October 25, 1862, started working at the age of twelve as a farm hand at Silver Cliff for $25.00 a month and board. Later he moved to South Park and worked for his brother-in-law, A. J. Bates, husband of Ellen Sloss.

In 1882 he and George W. King had a dairy business at Ashcroft. They sold milk for fifty cents a gallon. Sometime later Mr. King sold the property to Sterling Price Sloss and his brother John W. Sloss who were in partnership until 1885. Price then took up a ranch on west Sopris Creek in 1887. He married Edith Alwilda Bogue who was born in Nebraska February 3, 1870. Twin boys were born to them: Alfred and Alvin, on January 10, 1890 at Emma.

Price Sloss was a cattle inspector between Leadville and Glenwood Springs for many years. From 1895 to 1898 he was County

Commissioner of Pitkin County. With Fred Light and others he was active in the fight to prevent range fees for grazing on Government land. In the West at one time this land had been free, and this caused many inter-ranch fights and even murders. He served also on the committee that traveled to Washington, D.C. to try to block the junking of the Midland. He was a charter member of the Carbondale I.O.O.F.

In 1902 Mr. Sloss bought a ranch at Sloane on the Frying Pan from Ottomar Luchsinger. Within four or five years the name of Sloane station was changed to Sloss. The Slosses raised registered cattle and ranged them up Lime Creek to Wood's Lake.

Mrs. Sloss died March 6, 1922 at Glenwood Springs. Price later married Amanda Parker Henderson, a widow from Ruedi.

Price and his boys were not ordinary men. They stood out among ranchers as most enterprising. Although while haying and irrigating and doing other heavy work they wore overalls, they preferred ranch suits with colorful shirts, cowboy boots, and ranch hats, especially when they went to town. They were leaders in community affairs and were proud to do their part. Price was an Odd Fellow and his wife Edith was active in the Rebekah

John A. Smith, with Belgian bay stallion, "Neron."

photo from Hilda Stager Peet

Clifford Smith, about 1925.

Fred Carlson photo

Lodge. They belonged to the Methodist Church at Basalt. Son Alfred was a Mason and his twin, Alvin, joined the Elks and the Masons. For almost thirty years the father and two sons cooperated in raising Hereford cattle.

Many people could not tell Alfred and Alvin apart, but we could. Like their father they were large well-built men. Alfred was more on the serious side while Alvin's nature was more fun-loving and of a jovial bent.

After Mr. Sloss's death on January 26, 1931, his sons ran the ranch until 1941 when they sold it to Tucker McClure of Los Angeles, California. Mr. McClure also quieted title to 1360 acres in old mining claims, so people in that area will probably notice that item in their abstracts of title for years to come.

Mr. McClure died in October 1954 and his wife died in December the same year. The estate sold the ranch to Miller Nichols and Joe Gregg of Kansas City, Missouri, who now operate the property under the name of the "Cap K Ranch".

Alfred Sloss married Anna Wilson on January 15, 1911. They lived on a ranch below Sloss Station. She was born in Meeker, Colorado, March 14, 1890. She was brought up by the Rhodes family, where she went to live in 1902 at the age of twelve. Anna and Alfred had two children, Edith Winona and Sterling Andrew. For over twenty years Alfred was an Eagle County Commissioner, representing the southern part of that county. In March 1950 they sold their ranch to Kendall Sloan and his wife, Marjorie. Two years later the Sloans sold it to Mr. and Mrs. Murdock, who later split the property, selling the part north of the Frying Pan to Adelbert Bowles and his wife, Thelma. Adelbert Bowles died in 1947 and his wife, Thelma, sold their part to Jack C. Jackson, who still owns it. The south half of the

Clifford and Greta Pottinger Smith (right), and Virgil and Blanche Smith Holcomb (above) taken in 1960.

photos from Virgil Holcomb

ranch the Murdocks sold to Robert King from Texas. He has a resort there.

Alfred and Anna Sloss's daughter, Edith, married Walter Lawrence, a rancher near Carbondale. He died in 1963. Alfred and Anna's son, Sterling, is employed in the Post Office in Aurora, Colorado near Denver.

Alvin Sloss, twin to Alfred, always lived on the main ranch at Sloss, Colorado. He married Clemence Bryer on July 10, 1917. They had no children. Alvin stayed four years on the place as manager after it was sold to the McClures. He then moved to Glenwood Springs where he is in the real estate business.

The brother of Sterling Price Sloss who had been his partner in the dairy business at Ashcroft, John W. Sloss, later worked for Price on his ranch at Sloane (Sloss). His uncle, Jack Bates, of Arkansas, gave him the "Nesbit" ranch which he also ran for a time. He married Emaline Bogue. They had four sons: Walter, Carl, Bates, and Paul. Mr. Sloss, a Justice of the Peace at Basalt died in Utah in 1901, and his wife, Emaline, died the same year in Basalt.

Another brother of Sterling Price Sloss was James Fillmore Sloss who came to the region in 1900. For two years he worked for his brother on Sopris Creek, then purchased the Pinger Mercantile Store at Emma which he ran for three years. Then he bought the Tierney General Store at Basalt. He managed it with the help of a son, Marvin, until the 1918 temporary disaster to the community when the Midland closed. Besides Marvin, he and his wife Emma had two other sons, Conson and Archie B., and a daughter, Mable. Archie B. went to California to work for an oil company. He later became an engineer for a wire company at Bakersfield, California. Conson became an engineer for the Union Pacific on the Rawlins-Green River, Wyoming run. He lives at Rawlins, Wyoming and has a son, James F., and a daughter, Constance. Mable married Mark Kellerup, a Midland engineer who later worked for the Union Pacific. He was killed in an accident a few years ago.

Marvin, son of James Fillmore Sloss, married Edna Long and had three children: Clyde who became a dentist; Erlo a pharmacist; and Ellis who died at the age of 49. After Edna's separation from Marvin he married Goldie Lawrence. He closed his store and worked for the State Highway Department on the western slope for six years. He then ran a drug store and a package liquor store in Denver until he retired.

(Information from Anna, Alvin and Marvin Sloss)

SMITH

J. A. Smith arrived in Basalt in 1892 and had a general store with his brother, B. L. Smith, on Railroad Street and later on First Street below the Odd Fellows Hall. J. A. Smith was born in 1855 and died at Glenwood Springs October 23, 1929. Mrs. J. A. Smith (Adelaide Wilson) was born March 7, 1858, and died at Carbondale July 10, 1939. They were married December 20, 1883 at Kimbolton, Ohio. The couple had one daughter, Blanche, and two sons, Phil and Clifford. Blanche and Phil were born in Dillon, Montana, and Clifford at Aspen Junction.

John Smith was well known and was a very prominent person in the town. Whenever anyone was in trouble, one could be sure John Smith would be there to help out. In case of a funeral, he would always furnish a team. The reins from the harness would be used to lower the casket into the grave.

Besides the general store, John Smith also operated a slaughterhouse between Lucksinger's fish pond and what was called the Emma bridge and swimming hole. Later he bought the ranch up Toner Creek and he and his sons ranched there for many years. It was there we used to visit the Smith children frequently.

John Smith was always dealing with horses. Clarence Danielson remembers how Lou German had a buckskin he couldn't get anything out of. He wouldn't pull the hat off your head. It seems one of the ranchers had got the best of John Smith on a trade and John was laying for him. This fellow spotted the buckskin and told John he sure would like to get that buckskin to team up with the one he had. Of course, John pretended he didn't want to arrange the trade with Lou and got some "to boot". The rancher had difficulty in even getting the horse to pull him out of town.

At one time John Smith took his stock for the summer range to Ashcroft, but later took his cattle up on Black Mountain where they ranged from Toner Creek reservoir over to Taylor Park Rim. In later years he had a stallion, Neron, that he kept on the ranch, but he would also make money by taking the stallion on regular trips around the countryside. Neron went on foot; today the mare or the stallion is hauled in a horse trailer.

Mr. and Mrs. John Perry Snyder.

photo from Fred Carlson

When John died his son Phil took over the place on Toner Creek. Harry Woodward informs us that the State Fish and Game Department bought the property from Phil Smith September 3, 1940.

He gives the added information that the original owner was Patrick Toner, his patent having been issued to him January 30, 1895. Toner was a prospector as well as a rancher. No one knows of any mine named for him, although he may have been interested in the small mining operation as indicated by the tumbledown shacks on Basalt Mountain over by the Taylor Creek Rim, known as the Copper Spar.

The Smiths' first child, Blanche, born July 18, 1885, married Fern Stager by whom she had three daughters: Hilda, now Mrs. Archie Peet of Denver; Helen, who is Mrs. Harold Perkins of Denver; and Irene, who married Herman Thelin and lives in Boulder, Colorado. Blanche named Hilda for Rev. Hole's daughter, Helen for Helen Clarke Smith, and Irene for Irene Clarke Ould. The girls remember how they used to drive the "stacker" horse at haying time. One summer, their grandfather, John Smith, gave them small wrist watches for their help. Blanche's second husband is Mr. Virgil Holcomb and they now live in Denver. Mr. Holcomb was a forest ranger with headquarters at Taylor Creek for 10 years, then a lineman for the Public Service Company. They have one daughter, Lois, who married Clinton Reynolds and lives in Arvada, Colorado. Virgil was a Mason and Odd Fellow.

Phil Smith was born September 13, 1888 and married Helen Clarke. They purchased the Dan German place about 1918; it is now owned by the Armstrongs. Oscar Peterson worked for Phil for many years. Phil died April 17, 1943. His wife, Helen, died June 9, 1947. They had no children.

The last of the Smith children was Clifford, born July 8, 1894. He worked with his father on the Toner Creek, or J Diamond A, Ranch. Ralph Danielson describes in another chapter the many happy trips made with Clifford; in fact, the Smith home in Basalt and their ranch up the Frying Pan were frequently visited and the Smiths made him feel very much at home. Clifford married Gretta Pottinger who died July 2, 1941. They had no children. Clifford died in Glenwood Springs February 27, 1935.

An unusual experience Phil Smith had will not be forgotten. While riding across a field above his place, a field that had recently been thoroughly irrigated, he felt the whole muddy ground begin to slip down the Toner Creek valley. It was with the greatest difficulty that he and the horse extricated themselves. He said it was frightening in the extreme. Phil told me several times—and this is not to his discredit—that he dreaded the horse-breaking time. He was the one in the family to whom the unwanted duty usually fell.

B. L. Smith, brother of John Smith, arrived in Basalt in 1889 when it was still called Aspen Junction. In 1894 he became the Postmaster, a position he held until December 1897. He also taught school for two years.

A sister of Mrs. Smith married John McMillan. She died shortly after their arrival in Basalt. Mr. McMillan then married a school teacher, Lora Cooke, cousin of Virgil Holcomb's father. Mr. McMillan worked for J. A. in the store. Later he was elected County Assessor for Eagle County. He and Cliff Wilson each took up a homestead above the place which John Smith bought from John Lucksinger. Later both McMillan and Wilson sold their homesteads to Mr. Smith.

The family of Col. and Mrs. Henry Stiffler, about 1891. Standing, (l. to r.) are Charles, Fred, Mathew and Erwin. Seated are Mattie, Susan, Harriett (Futtrell), Rachel, Henry and Lydia.

photo from R. Ewing Stiffler

SNYDER

The following information was given by Ruth Snyder Carlson:

"John Perry Snyder was born at Millertown, Ohio, July 26, 1853. In 1872 he came to Colorado as a young lad. He went back to Ohio for a while but returned to Colorado in April 1879. He was in Denver, Leadville, Fairplay, Black Hawk, Central City, Silver Plume, Georgetown and Aspen. Many times he told about crossing the high mountain ranges on snowshoes from Fairplay to Leadville, from Leadville to Aspen and of the short provisions and the cruel, cold weather.

"He was in Aspen before even one house was built. He was a miner by trade and worked in the various mines, the Smuggler and Molly Gibson at Aspen. He was elected County Commissioner of Pitkin County, November 3, 1885. The cabin, which he built in Ashcroft in 1885, still stands. He also built a house in Aspen and as far as I know it is still occupied.

"He and a few of his friends got the Klondike fever. He returned to his native state for a brief visit, then left the States in May 1894 for Alaska. October 25, 1894, a mine accident at the Tredwell Mine, Douglas City, Alaska, caused him the loss of his right eye. He was hospitalized in San Francisco. He returned to Aspen March 9, 1895. On June 17, 1896 he married E'Mila Luella Zimmerman of Altamont, Kansas, and brought his bride to Aspen. In 1904 they moved to a small ranch, three miles from Basalt which they purchased from John McKnight. He passed away in 1929. Their two children were Floyd C. (deceased) and Ruth E. Snyder.

"Following mother's death in 1944, the place was sold to Verne Harris who is living there now.

"Am sorry I don't know too much about my people. My father kept a diary for many years when he was young, but two volumes are missing—one of which tells so much about Leadville and Aspen and his activities there.

"J. Perry Snyder was a member of the I.O.O.F. Aspen Lodge No. 59, Ozias Encampment No. 29, Aspen Canton No. 8, and Esther Rebekah Lodge No. 9—all of Aspen, Colorado. He was an active member of the Odd Fellows for 47 years."

(Written by Ruth Snyder Carlson)

STIFFLER

"Colonel" Henry Stiffler, the son of Frederich and Martha McCormick Stiffler, had seven brothers and one sister. He and his wife, Harriett Futtrell Stiffler, in their turn, also had a very large family—seven boys and four girls. He was born May 7, 1838, and he served all through the Civil War as a corporal in the Second Indiana Cavalry, where he developed a great love for horses. The family moved to Leadville in 1880, where he established a successful livery business, renting horses and selling them; he obtained the animals in Missouri. Among his "carriage trade" customers were the Walshes, Nicholsons, Tabors, and Boettchers. He was of a jovial nature and was nicknamed "Colonel" in the fast-growing and booming mining city.

About 1892 Mrs. Stiffler's health failed. They moved to the lower altitude of Basalt. The change evidently benefited her, for she outlived her husband thirteen years and died in Basalt August 1, 1925.

In Basalt Colonel Stiffler ran a grocery and candy store and also rented rooms in his large rectangular house which had a hallway down through the center. This home and rooming-house was located a few houses west of the Smith store on the north side of First Street. The Stifflers were Christian Scientists. Henry was a strong Republican and an ardent member of the G.A.R. He was instrumental in promoting the incorporation of Basalt and the establishment of the town's water system.

Their children, in order of birth, were: Matthew (Mack); Frederich; Lydia Belle; Daniel; Charles May; Martha (Mattie); Irwin Barr; Louis; Susan; Henry; and Rachel.

Four of the boys died in childhood: Daniel, Irwin Barr, Louis, and Henry.

Mack was a cowboy and then a Colorado Midland conductor. Later he was superintendent of an oil company. He and his wife, Bessie Kelly Stiffler, had no children.

Fred was a locomotive engineer. Later he went into mining. He married Sadie Mallory and they had four children. Fred was killed in a snowslide at Twin Lakes.

Lydia Belle married Horace M. Shepherd. They had two daughters, one now deceased, and the other, Helen, who is married to Mr. F. W. Davis of Denver. She held office as Assistant Secretary of the Midland Federal Savings Company when she retired a short time ago. Lydia Belle and Horace Shepard left Leadville and moved to Denver in 1921. He was a good friend of Sam Nicholson, of Leadville, who later became a United States Senator. Mrs. Sheherd was very active in the Ladies of G.A.R.

Charles May was a conductor on the Colorado Midland for many years until it closed; he then worked in Denver until his death in 1942. His first wife was Mary Hoffinger. After her death he married Mrs. Elizabeth Heaps.

Martha (Mattie) graduated from Leadville High School in 1894. She was the postmistress at Basalt many years. Later she spent a few years in California, then went to Chicago where she sold real estate, mainly in the Hettie Green addition to Chicago. Mattie was a practitioner registered in the *Christian Science Journal,* who later resigned but continued to teach *Truth* in Chicago, until her death in 1929.

Susan became the wife of a southerner, John F. Stender, originally of Birmingham, Alabama. They first made their home in Wisconsin. Then they bought a pecan grove near the small town of Grand Bay, Alabama. They later sold it and moved into the town, which is 25 miles from Mobile. She has been a state officer in the Alabama Federation of Women's Clubs. They had no children.

Rachel, the youngest of the Stiffler family, born in Leadville in 1888, was graduated from the East Denver High School, and, in 1913, from the State Teachers' College in Greeley, Colorado. She taught school in Basalt and in Ruedi, then married Charles Ellis, clerk of the Midland Railroad in Basalt. They had one son, Robert Ellis, who now lives in California, is married, and has two children. Rachel divorced Mr. Ellis and later married Mr. Weir. They separated, and she carried on a successful magazine business for a number of months before moving to Los Angeles, California, where she now resides.

(Information from Mr. J. Ewing Stiffler, Mrs. Helen Davis, and Susan Stender.)

TEMPLETON

Lorenzo Dow Templeton, a rancher, was born at Fountain, Colorado, October 27, 1864. He was married for 61 years to Minnie Etta Casteel, who was born at Knoxville, Iowa, November 23, 1866. She died August 23, 1946. He was buried May 30, 1946 at Jerome, Idaho.

They came to Basalt in March 1904. The couple had seven children: Katie Goldsmith, born December 19, 1884, and now lives in Seattle; Earl, born April 30, 1886, was a forest ranger at Boise, Idaho until his retirement; Harry, born November 1888, married Alice Peterson and is now a retired farmer living at Twin Falls, Idaho; Don, born October 7, 1890; Prue, Mrs. Jess Bogue, born July 16, 1892, was the postmistress at Woody Creek for 15 years, now a widow living in Basalt; Rob, born October 7,

1899, married Hazel Peterson and lives near Glenwood on a farm; and Win, who was born March 13, 1901 is a consulting engineer and lives with his wife, Lillian, at Salt Lake City, Utah.

Prue's husband, Jess, was an Odd Fellow and, at the time of his death, he and Bramblet Willits were the oldest members of the lodge.

Mr. and Mrs. Templeton belonged to the I.O.O.F. and Rebekahs. They never owned a ranch, but rented various ranches in the vicinity.

(Information from Prue Templeton Bogue)

TENNIS

Voyle Tennis is one of the old timers still living in Basalt, having come back there to retire in a very attractive home which he built. He is full of Basalt history and passes it on to the listener in a very interesting and energetic fashion. It would be a great favor to the community if he would write down for some group or society all he knows about the Basalt region. He has given us much information on various subjects.

His father was A. L. Tennis who located a mining claim nearby in 1886. He was also a freighter in the building of the Denver and Rio Grande branch from Glenwood to Aspen, and worked for a while on the Colorado Midland. His father and several other men in the early days incorporated a Stage Line from Carbondale to Aspen, not with the primary idea of making money operating it, but to get the right of way and to sell it to the Denver and Rio Grande who were planning to build there. This they did quite successfully financially.

His mother was Cora D. Gillespie, the niece of the famous H. B. Gillespie, who had so much to do with the founding of Aspen, and who built the fabulous home and farm "El Jebel" which is discussed under the Willits story.

Voyle, who never married, had six brothers and one sister, Wilma T. French, who is dead. The living brothers are Edgel H., Allen O., Ardith L. of Inglewood, California, and Stanley K. of North Hollywood, California. Earl G. was killed in Honolulu and Dean W. has passed away.

(Information from Voyle Tennis)

TIERNEY

The Tierney history begins with an account interestingly written by Dr. James Tierney:

"To start these notes, my father, William Tierney, was born in New York; I think it was about 1850. His father died when he was six and his mother died when he was twelve. He had just a few short years of school, but became rather well self-educated. He was a real pen-man, a mining man, and took a special course in Harvard University when he was 27 years old in Chemistry, Assaying, etc., and, from what I can gather was what might be classed as a mining engineer today.

"He was a roamer and a boomer by nature. He traveled all over the world as a merchant seaman. Mother said his one regret was that he never got to visit Ireland, the land of his ancestors. He mined and prospected all over the United States and Alaska. He made and lost several fortunes before Mother met him in Leadville during the great Leadville boom.

"When a gold mine was discovered in Independence, he went there and had charge of the mine before the old stage line over Independence was completed. Through some method of refining they processed the ore partially and carried it to Leadville on jack or donkey trains, later by stage coach. I have heard my mother say that one time she carried the gold into the halfway house, where they stopped for lunch. The old halfway house is still there, about half way up the modern pass. She carried the gold in a hand bag so no one would notice that there was gold on the stage coach, because of so many stage coach robberies in that time.

"My father went in partnership with Dr. De Avene (probably not spelled right), a famous Leadville doctor at that time and for whom I am named—the Frederick part of my name. They bought a large ranch on Woody Creek when Aspen started to boom. They raised horses instead of cattle, mostly draft horses, that were used for heavy hauling of ore and timber in the mines of Aspen and Leadville. My father's brand was T-W Bar, and his horses became well known in that part of the country. The big gray fire team of Aspen's early days were T-W Bar horses as well as some of the great teams of the mines. He had the first draft horse stallion in that region.

"Soon after the Colorado Midland Railroad was built into Aspen in 1887, my father leased out the ranch and went to Basalt, which was then Aspen Junction. He was, I guess, the pioneer merchant of that town. He had a general store; everything from castor oil to boots, shoes, farming equipment, dry goods, fresh meat. He had a slaughter house down by the river, near the old Cramer place on the Aspen branch.

C. L. D. photo
Oscar Riebel, uncle of the authors.

R. W. D. photo
Ralph Danielson (l.) and Leonis Usel, in the yard of the Usel home in Basalt, 1961.

"There was a tremendous business going on at that time with the Colorado and Midland booming. Aspen was shipping train load after train load of ore. The stone quarries up the Frying Pan River and saw mills at Thomasville were active and all were getting their supplies from Basalt. I have heard my mother tell how sometimes on a Sunday morning someone would come to the house to get my father to open the store for a pair of gloves or work shoes and before they left another one would come and then another and by noon they had sold from two to five hundred dollars worth of merchandise.

"The silver panic of 1893 closed down Aspen, Leadville, and, of course, Basalt, to some extent. That was a little before our time. Anyway, Basalt was never the same.

"Father died of pneumonia, which was nearly always fatal at that time; that was before you boys got your penicillin, etc. He died on Easter Sunday, April 18, 1897.

"The bell had just been installed in the little Methodist Church, where you and I went to Sunday School, and I understand it was rung for the first time at my father's funeral. He was quite a civic-minded person and was interested in politics (Democrat—which I am not). The late Edward T. Taylor, of Glenwood Springs, was the congressman from that district and at the time of his death was the oldest member of Congress in point of service. I have heard him say that when he was a young man in Leadville I think my father was the first man to sponsor him and to electioneer for him for public office. Father was a charter member of the Basalt Odd Fellows Lodge, as your father was also."

Mrs. Ella Tierney was born about 1858 in Chelsea, Massachusetts. She came to Leadville as a young woman with an aunt and uncle, who had a boarding house where she met and married Mr. Tierney. Soon after, they moved to Independence, and then to Woody Creek, and then to Aspen Junction. Fortunately, Mrs. Tierney had considerable managerial ability so that after her husband's death she carried on the store and cared for several rental properties, thus supporting her five children. Furthermore, she went ahead aggressively and built a better store, a brick building opposite the I.O.O.F. Hall, later owned and operated by Marvin Sloss and his father.

Editor Hildreth of the *Basalt Journal* had this to say under the heading of The Tierney Block on Jan. 7, 1899: "Notwithstanding the non-arrival of prosperity, Mrs. Ella Tierney has

The Willits and Clarke families. The two children on the ground are Ruth Norstrom and Marion Mitchell. Second row, (l. to r.): Ruby Clarke Hubbard, Cornelia Willits holding Baby Dudley Mitchell, Mary Willits, John Clarke, and Ruth Hildreth. Third row: Mrs. Edith Clarke, Helen Clarke Smith, Irene Clarke Ould, Marcia Willits Mitchell, Baby Roger Mitchell, Lee Willits and Lucy Clarke Danielson.

C. L. D. collection

L. R. WILLITS.

Candidate for Representative From Eagle County.

L. R. Willits was born in New Boston, Mercer county, Illinois, in 1848. He received his education in Keithsburg, Ill., moving westward in 1867. Locating in Riley county, Kan., he remained there until 1873, when he moved southward and settled in Montaigne county, Texas. Here he was married and remained a citizen of the "Lone Star" state until the splendid opportunities offered by Colorado attracted him hither in 1887. He located in the immediate vicinity of Basalt and has since been engaged in farming and stock raising.

Mr. Willits is blessed with a most estimable wife and a family of three handsome daughters and one son. He enjoys the confidence and respect of every class, especially among those who know him best as a neighbor and associate.

An uncompromising Democrat for years, Mr. Willits joined the great popular protest against both old parties which resulted in the birth of the Peoples party. In 1896 he was asked by his party to accept the nomination for county commissioner. He did so and was elected by a large majority.

Mr. Willits' record as commissioner proved to be so acceptable to the people of Eagle county that in 1899 he was re-nominated for the office upon a ticket comprising the Democratic and Peoples party voters. From a total of 1,157 votes he received the very large plurality of 508 votes. This constitutes a fair evidence of the confidence of the people of Eagle county in Mr. Willits.

When the conventions of the Democratic and Peoples party delegates were held at Red Cliff on October 1, Mr. Willits was the choice of the two conventions as the nominee for representative. Robert E. Palmer has since contested the nomination, claiming that he himself was the nominee for the same office in the Democratic convention. By a decision from the supreme court, which has filled the Democrats of Eagle county with indignation, Mr. Palmer was declared the Democratic nominee. Therefore, Mr. Willits will appear on the ballot as only the Peoples party candidate for representative from Eagle county. The opinion appears to be very prevalent in the said county that Mr. Palmer has received substantial aid from Mr. Wolcott and much encouragement from local Republicans, in carrying on his contest. Be that as it may, the vote Mr. Willits will receive on November 6 will illustrate that he is the choice of the two parties' rank and file.

1900 Rocky Mt News

loaned by Bramblet Willits

Taken from the Rocky Mountain News, Oct. 31, 1900.

begun and completed within our midst during the last six months of 1898, a store building which for workmanship, material used, and modern convenience is not outclassed in three counties adjoining. The structure is built of brick, with foundations of Peachblow sandstone."

William and Ella Tierney had five children. Bertha married Mr. I. T. Starbuck and died in California several years ago. Gladys became Mrs. Frank Clavel; she lives in San Diego, California. Mable, the wife of Mr. Joe McBurney, resides in New Castle, Colorado. William Tierney recently died in California. Dr. James Tierney has practiced dentistry in Tyler, Texas, for many years and recently has had some luck in finding oil on his property.

Gladys Tierney Clavel has given some additional interesting facts as follows:

They moved from Woody Creek to Aspen Junction in 1888 or 1889, her father having previously gone down and had a building erected, the lower floor for a store and the upstairs for living quarters. They built a home near John Smith's on First Street in 1892, both residences being precut and similar.

She recalls her whole family caught the measles from Laura Hammond. Earl Kibby took them to school the first day, the teacher being Ida Miller, Mrs. Kibby's sister. At that time the "High School" was up on the north side of town, where Mr. Ruland was the principal. Among the ministers, she remembers the Rev. Ashby. She recollects with horror the screaming of the

Irene Willits Randall (opposite).

R. W. D. collection

Dorothy Willits, Clarence and Lucy Clarke Danielson, and Bramblet Willits, 1961.

C. L. D. collection

passengers at the time of the wreck on the Y to Aspen, when so many people were scalded by live steam. Seeing the big snow plows pull into Basalt after the big snow blockade made an indelible impression on her.

It gave her a thrill to have Flavine Arbaney visit her in 1961 in California while home on a vacation from Italy to visit his father in Basalt. It had been 50 years since he had been home and it was amazing how many names he remembered.

Jim Tierney, Hun Hartson, Gus Thurston, and Fay Eiswerth were the first to go to World War I.

Sometime later, after Mr. Tierney's death, Ella married Mr. Elbert Gray and moved to the old ranch on Woody Creek. They had no children, but Mr. Gray had three children by a previous marriage, Ernest, Harold, and Beulah Gray.

Elbert Gray and the Tierneys were staunch members of the Odd Fellows and the Rebekahs and were strong supporters of the Methodist Church.

(Information from Dr. James Tierney, Gladys Clavel, and Mable McBurney.)

USEL

Joseph Usel was a native of Aosta, Italy, and emigrated to the United States in 1898. In 1904 he purchased the ranch originally homesteaded by Charles Kester. Kester had sold the place to Edwin McMillen, who, in turn, sold it to Alexis Arbaney, and, in turn, sold it to his son, Leonis, in 1930. Leonis operated the ranch alone until 1950 when he went into partnership with his son, Stanley, until 1958, when the property was sold to the present owner, Johnnie Hoagland. Leonis and his son raised Hereford cattle, hay, and potatoes.

Joseph Usel was married to Genevieve (maiden name unknown).

Leonis, born January 24, 1901, married Pierina Betemps of Aosta, Italy, December 19, 1922. They have three children, Stanley, Laurie, and Rosina. Stanley married the younger Maude Elmont and they have three children, Leroy, Joyce, and Carolyn. Laurie married Galen Mullins and they have one daughter, Sandra Kathleen. Rosina is married to Eldon Johnson.

Leonis has been a member of the Basalt School Board for nine years; he and Pierina live near the Ranger Station at Basalt. They are active in the Basalt Methodist Church. He is a member of Mt. Basalt Lodge No. 83, I.O.O.F. Pierina and Leonis are members of Free Silver Rebekah Lodge No. 47.

(Information from Leonis Usel)

WILLITS

(Related families: Gillespie, Shehi, Robinson)

Although the Willits family lived in Basalt only briefly, they and their relatives have always played such a prominent part in the affairs of the community and of Eagle and Pitkin Counties that considerable space should be devoted to them.

Lee Willits came from Texas to the headwaters of the Roaring Fork in 1887, by way of Taylor Park into Ashcroft. Ashcroft at that time was more prominent than Aspen. On this first trip he had several teams and a herd of horses. The oldest daughter, Pearl, then 12 years of age, has told of her frightening experience as a driver the last day. Due to the clearness of the air, when they came in sight of Ashcroft, they were sure they could make it before dark, but, because of slow travel over atrocious roads, this little girl had to drive on in the dark until eleven o'clock at night.

Accompanying Lee on this trip were Charles M. Robinson, Cornelia Ann Robinson (his wife), and three children, Pearl, Marcia, and Bramblet. In addition, was "Grandma" Willits (nee Mary Catherine Frick), widow of John Elias Willits. She had three sons and three daughters, but only Lee and two of the girls, Edythe Maye and Ada, came to Colorado. The family of Edythe is written up under Clarke.

The children of Lee and Cornelia have also been intimately identified with the Basalt region. Pearl Willits, the little girl who drove the team to Ashcroft, married Will Shanks, who was a conductor for the Colorado Midland until 1918. They had two sons, Rollin and Kenneth, and a daughter, Dorothy. Pearl died in Montrose. Will recently moved to Fruita to live with his son, Rollin, an employee of the Telephone Company. Kenneth is a County Agent in eastern Colorado. Dorothy became Mrs. Bud Stewart and lives in San Angelo, Texas.

Irene Willits, after teaching in Basalt a few years, went to Eagle to teach where she married Dr. O. W. Randall, a dentist. They had no children of their own. Irene and Grace Hallock were great friends and lived in a house next to the Danielson's residence.

Marcia married Ira Mitchell, likewise a conductor on the Midland. Ira has died, but Marcia is still living in San Angelo, Texas, with her daughter, Marian Dahle. Dudley lives in Grand Junction, Colorado, but Roger died a few years ago.

Bramblet married Dorothy Norris, of Aspen, a sister of Maybird Norris, wife of Jake Lucksinger. They still live in semi-retirement on the original 160 acre ranch that his father purchased in 1892. Bramblet has sold off nearly all the surrounding land in the ranch, leaving the home and historic buildings. Only recently they have installed central hot water gas heating so that they can have the winter comfort they deserve.

Bramblet, like his father, has been extremely active in the Odd Fellows and the Methodist Church. Elsewhere in this book is an account by Bramblet Willits of the history of the local Odd Fellows Lodge. Dorothy has followed in the footsteps of Cornelia in the ladies work of the church, in the Rebekahs Lodge, and in the Literary Sorosis Society, one of the oldest ladies' clubs in Colorado.

Bramblet and Dorothy have only one son, Lee, who is no longer a boy. He has worked with his father on the farm for many years, but now is employed in a store in Aspen, and commutes back and forth to his parents' home near El Jebel each evening and weekend. He, too, is carrying on the tradition of activity in the Basalt Community Church and the Odd Fellows Lodge.

The Willits family have always been great readers. In addition to the usual magazines, they have a large library of books which they read and not just place on the shelves.

Bramblet has been a very successful farmer—the word farm is used to indicate a place that raises crops primarily for sale, while a ranch uses the farm products largely to feed livestock. A ranch usually has range rights for grazing purposes. Bramblet recalls that when they were only boys, he and Ross Long were hired by the surveyors of the region to climb to the tops of the mountains around, — especially Sloane's Peak, Little Basalt Mountain, Big Basalt Mountain, the foothills to the south, and Sopris,—to plant flags to be used as triangulation points for surveys.

Dorothy is widely known as quite a cook and has passed on many excellent recipes.

Lee Willits was a slender man of medium size with dark hair and a large dark mustache, as worn in that day. He did not use liquor or tobacco and was active with our father and others in "local option". He was the County Commissioner for Eagle County for many years. He was also in the State Legislature of the 13th General Assembly. He was industrious, calm and friendly; the only time he became angry was his reaction to dishonesty; in that regard Bramblet has the same disposition as his father. Lee and Cornelia are buried in Basalt.

George Gillespie

A very early settler in the region, George Gillespie homesteaded 160 acres a half-mile west of Emma, Colorado. He was a brother of Henry B. Gillespie, owner of El Jebel and famous in mining circles.

Of George Gillespie's four daughters, Annie, the eldest, married Elbert Gray. She died in 1896, leaving two sons and a daughter, Beulah, (who is now Mrs. Woods and lives in Basalt). The second daughter, Cora, married Will Tennis. They had a large family; Voyle, the oldest boy, lives in Basalt. The third daughter, Ollie, married Pete McCabe. They also had a large family. Oma McCabe, the oldest girl, lives in Grand Junction. Some of the McCabe boys has always lived in Aspen. One died in 1963.

The youngest Gillespie girl, Gertie, married Frank Allen and has always lived in Denver.

Henry B. Gillespie

Another member of the Robinson family, Liss, became the wife of H. B. Gillespie. Lee Willits homesteaded ground in 1887 north of their present ranch between Carbondale and Basalt. Soon after he proved up he sold it to his brother-in-law, Henry B. Gillespie, the famous mining tycoon of Aspen, who also purchased several adjoining farms to assemble the country estate known as El Jebel. The name was chosen because Gillespie was very much interested in the higher degrees of Masonry. Lee then stayed on as manager of El Jebel for about five years, before buying the land from Harvey Dalton that now belongs to Bramblet and Dorothy Willits and where they live.

Mrs. Gillespie was a Robinson, and a sister of Cornelia Robinson Willits and Emma Robinson Shehi. Henry and Liss had two sons, Ken and Bert. Henry had three brothers, George, John, and Will.

A few paragraphs about El Jebel are now in order. Hall wrote in his *History of Colorado* in 1895:

"Twenty-two miles below Aspen, on the Roaring Fork, in Eagle County, Mr. H. B. Gillespie has one of the finest ranches in Colorado, comprising 1280 acres of the best land in the valley, upon the improvement of which he has expended, according to his own statement, $185,000. The results are seen in a beautiful summer residence, superbly furnished and supplied with water and electric lights from independent power plants, and capacious enough to accommodate scores of guests. This lovely home is surrounded by green lawns, adorned with shrubbery and flowers, supplemented by greenhouses, where a great variety of plants are propagated.

"At convenient distances are immense barns, stables, and corrals for the accommodation of large herds of blooded horses and cattle, and at other parts are fruit orchards in bearing, embracing apple, pear, apricot, and plum trees. There are gardens devoted to small fruits and vegetables. Upon hundreds of acres of well-watered meadow lands vast crops of hay are harvested. From the porches of his mansion delightful views of neighboring ranges, including Maroon, Castle, and Sopris Peaks, are obtained."

The house still stands and is now owned by Mr. and Mrs. Floyd Crawford, who are much interested in the history of its gardens and other glories. The fine woodwork of the interior remains, as well as the stone fountain in the bay window off the dining room, scene of so many brilliant gatherings of prominent in the great days of the mining camps. The large, beautiful pavilion nearby which was used for recreation, parties and dancing, still has the original piano. What a place for their children to play, and pick up the lore of the past!

Shehi

Mr. and Mrs. Dan Shehi arrived in 1885 when the town was on the south side of the river and was known as Frying Pan Junction. Mrs. Shehi's maiden name was Emma Robinson. Her tart and lucid opinions about saloons have been quoted elsewhere in this book. She was a sister of Mrs. H. B. Gillespie and Cornelia Willits. They had one son, Fred, by adoption. Dan Shehi originally homesteaded the Hough ranch across the river from Basalt.

Fred Shehi, the son, married Tessie Lamareaux, but they were divorced after a few years; no children. He originally took up a homestead just south of his father's place up toward the foothill now owned by Joe Firon. He then purchased the ranch from a Mr. Taylor at the head of Taylor Creek, on the north side of the Frying Pan. Fred ran this place for many years and the name Taylor Park gradually changed to Shehi Park.

This park is a beautiful one to visit not only from the road and the residence, but is even more entrancing when seen from the edge of the cliffs above. It is here that Clarence Danielson describes the almost disastrous accident where some of them came close to going over the cliff.

The park was later sold to Chris and Hazel Hyrup who raised alfalfa, potatoes, oats, and cattle there for a long time. The oats were cut green and made excellent hay. Chris then sold the property to Dr. Schweppe, and we certainly envy him and his family this enchanting view where deer and elk can be seen almost every day in the year.

Robinson

The Robinson family was related to the Willits, Gillespie, Clarke, McCabe, and Shehi families.

Cornelia Robinson was the wife of Lee Willits, and the sister of Al Robinson. Al Robinson was married to Ada Helen Willits, the sister of Lee Willits. Al and Ada originally took up a homestead a mile south of the present ranch, but sold out to A. B. Foster about 1897 and moved to Aspen. Albert was killed in a mine accident. He had two other sisters in addition to Cornelia. They were Emma (Mrs. Dan Shehi) and Liss (Mrs. H. B. Gillespie). Also in the region were Al's parents, Mr. and Mrs. E. W. Robinson, and two brothers, Ed and Charles. The latter married Milda, Wm. Gillespie's daughter.

The Al Robinson children were double cousins of Bramblet Willits and his sisters.

Mr. and Mrs. E. W. Robinson were the parents of Mrs. Willits, Mrs. Shehi, and Mrs. Gillespie. His full name was Elhinen Winchester Robinson; Bramblet wishes he knew where that name came from. He was born in Kentucky, near Abe Lincoln's birthplace, and fought in the Black Hawk Indian War. He came to Colorado in 1885 and settled on the land later to become the El Jebel Ranch. The Robinson Ditch was named for him. He died in 1897, but his wife passed away in 1887.

(Information from Bramblet and Dorothy Willits)

WHEATLEY

John Edward Wheatley, born in County Wexford, Ireland, October 6, 1851, was the third child of the eleven children born to James and Ellen Dorcey Wheatley. James was English, Ellen was a native of Ireland. One of the sons and the only daughter in the family died in infancy. The remaining nine sons had all emigrated to America by the year 1879.

John Edward, the first of the brothers to cross the Atlantic in 1875, found work in the coal mines of Pennsylvania that winter at ninety cents a day. He had already been married, May 5, 1874 to Catherine Moore in Cleatormoore, Cumberland County, England. When the mine shut down in the spring he returned to her in England.

Still thinking America had great opportunities, he crossed the ocean again 1879. His eight brothers who had gone to Leadville, Colorado had written to him that they were making $2.75 a day there in the mines. He decided to join them.

Soon he was able to send for his wife and three small daughters. After a turbulent three-week voyage aboard a condemned vessel (although she was not aware of that fact until they put out to sea), Mrs. Catherine Wheatley with the children arrived in New York. To her dismay, the ship was not allowed to dock for two days because of the funeral of James A. Garfield, President of the United States, who had been assassinated.

In 1882, because of the high altitude of Leadville and his wife's poor health, John Wheatley moved the family to Aspen. Catherine was not sorry to leave booming Leadville because of the frequent lynchings that took place. It shocked her to know that even women attended these ghastly affairs. John had preceded the family to Aspen to find work in the mines and to homestead a ranch on the Roaring Fork River, fifteen miles from the town.

In a stage-coach drawn by six horses, Mrs. Wheatley, the three girls, and the baby, Richard, who had been born in Leadville, traveled over Independence Pass to the new town to remain until her husband could complete the log cabin he was building on his ranch. The trip was a very frightening experience for them. Today one can still see the zig-zag, sharp-cornered trail of the stage coach. It was both steep and narrow.

John Wheatley had already bought a horse in Leadville and also five hens and a rooster. He had quite a ride carrying the chickens all the way over Independence. One wonders how he was able to do it, but the effort was worthwhile. He soon had a flock of chickens to help with food for his family, and horses were in short supply where his ranch was located.

Their home was in a gulch still known as Wheatley Gulch. The small family cemetery is there. One evening they looked out the window to see a wolf looking in. After that, when the children were outside playing, Catherine lived in constant fear that wild animals might wander near.

When John's brother, Richard, was killed in a snowslide in Aspen, the Wheatleys adopted his baby son to add to their large family. Ellen, their oldest child, grew up and married Miles Sweeney of Aspen. She died at twenty-four. Margaret, a registered nurse, was the first to enlist from Pitkin County in World War I. She served until the Armistice in 1918; she died October 21, 1954. Marie married Frank Daywalt who worked on the Colorado Midland and later in the mines in Aspen where he was killed in a cave-in. They had five children: John, Frank, William, Catherine who is Mrs. John Carson, and Margaret who is Mrs. John Hatch. All five are living in or near Los Angeles. Marie died August 17, 1956.

The Wheatley's first son, Richard, died at eighteen. Catherine (Cassie) married Paul Bourg of Woody Creek; they had three children: Benoit (Chub) of Denver, Vernon of Fremont, California and Gretta, now Mrs. Forrest Tritchka of Fallbrook, California. Cassie died September 22, 1962.

Georgina married Arthur Bates of Basalt; their family is written up under Bates.

Blanche, who is Mrs. John Florida, lives in Prescott, Arizona. Esther married Dr. J. J. Sinton and they live in Colorado Springs. William lives in Fallbrook, California. There were also three Wheatley children who died in infancy.

One of the first things Mr. Wheatley did on his ranch was to donate a piece of land to Pitkin County for a schoolhouse. The first building for the one-room school was made of rocks gathered from the surrounding land. Later it was replaced by a brick one. Two of the Wheatley girls taught there. It was the second school built in the county, Aspen's was the first. There were eight grades taught by one teacher. It still stands at the Bates spur on the Rio Grande railroad tracks between Aspen and Basalt.

Catherine Moore Wheatley died at the age of fifty-two.

A great lover of education, John Wheatley studied long hours by the light of tallow candles and coal oil lamps. In spite of his hard pioneering life, he lived to be ninety-one years old, dying in Denver in 1942.

(Information given by Georgina Wheatley Bates)

BASALT WEEKLY NEWSPAPERS
(information provided by State Historical Society)

		Editors	Publishers
Eagle County Examiner	1894-1896	W. H. Hildreth 1894-1896 (see *Eagle County Examiner*, Aspen and Eagle, Colo.)	W. H. Hildreth 1894-1896
Basalt Tribune	1896-1898*	B. L. Smith 1896-1897 Editor Unknown 1898-1898	B. L. Smith 1896-1897 Tribune Publ. Co. 1898-1898
Basalt Journal	Jan. 7, 1897* 1910* *The authors question the time overlap of the *Eagle*, the *Journal* and the *Tribune*.	Editor unknown Jan. 7, 1897-1898 R. H. Zimmerman Jan. 7, 1899- May 5, 1900 H. F. Kane May 12, 1900- Jan. 5, 1901 J. R. Newman Jan. 5, 1901- Mar. 22, 1902 M. V. Crockett Mar. 29, 1902- ——, 1902 Grant Ruland Mar. 29, 1902- Aug. 22, 1903 W. H. Hildreth Aug. 27, 1904- Dec. 14, 1910	Journal Publ. Co. Jan. 7, 1897-1905 W. W. Hildreth 1906-1910
Basalt Eagle	1909*-1912	Fred Stiffler 1909-1911 Daniel Barker 1912-1912	Fred Stiffler 1909-1912 Daniel Barker 1912-1912
Frying Pan	1922-1924	Roy S. Shadle 1922-1924	Roy S. Shadle 1922-1924
			There is no record of a newspaper in Basalt during the period of 1912 to 1922.

The State Historical Society also has the following Carbondale newspapers:

(1) *Carbondale Avalanche*   July 20, 1889-May 31, 1891
(2) *Carbondale Item*   Jan. 12, 1911—Feb. 24, 1921
(3) *Crystal River Empire*   April 17, 1924

CHAPTER 8

Newspapers

There were several newspapers published in Basalt at various times as shown in the list of papers, managers, and editors furnished by the State Historical Society. Many editions of the Basalt Journal can be found there. Unfortunately, many issues of the newspapers were lost when the printing office was torn down. Because no one had enough interest to turn the volumes over to some responsible depository, they were taken out and burned!

Bramblet Willits intends to give some copies to the State Historical Society and it is hoped that other people who have newspapers, photographs, or other data of historical interest will do the same—you will find the officers most cooperative and grateful.

To read the old editions of the Basalt Journal is a most interesting experience for one who lived at the time and remembers some of the incidents. It is also entertaining reading, however, for those interested in journalism. The editorials, the advertisements, and the news are presented in a pungent fashion and several pages in this book are devoted to excerpts of news items and to examples of editorials.

For anyone interested in the outspoken, fiery, pithy, and even libelous editorials that were common in that day, one can do no better than to read the articles by Betty Wallace in the Westerners Roundup for January 1963. She also tells how very many small papers were started, many of them to last only a few months or for a few issues.

An interesting sidelight recalled by Bramblet Willits was the shortage of newsprint paper during the big snow blockade in 1899. He was working as a "monkey" in the printing shop at the time and the emergency was solved by his suggesting to the editor that he use wrapping paper from the grocery store, which was successfully done. A few copies of these rare editions are still extant.

Favorite items in the paper were school and church programs and birthday parties. Not only were the names of the people attending the party given, but also what gifts were given by whom. The programs consisted largely of recitations; we well remember giving them.

Quotes and Notes from Basalt Journal
1899

Jan. 20 There are rumors of a smelter at Basalt.

Jan. 21 "The coal famine in town had become a serious matter especially to those who are in the habit of buying coal. Had not Supt. Bryant of the Colo. Mid. come to the rescue and let Mr. Hull, the genial dispenser of black diamonds, have a car, many of us would be well frozen."

Feb. 4 This is one of the snowbound editions of the Journal printed on wrapping paper procured by Bramblet Willits for R. S. Zimmerman, the Manager. It said, "Again we are compelled to print the Journal on wrapping paper. We propose to keep our files complete and to furnish our readers a paper of some kind, each and every Saturday, blockade or no blockade.—We are getting our mail from Emma".

Feb. 11 "Lucky Turn Over — Mesdames Sloss and Willits, while driving around the grade opposite Emma, were thrown from the cutter by the shying of the horses. The ladies were not hurt in the least and walked back to town. The horse returned to Newt Henry's ranch."

Mar. 4 "A committee has been formed to protest the tailing of the mills from Aspen into the Roaring Fork River—because of danger to livestock and killing of trout."

Mar. 18 Regarding two men caught in the snowsheds in the blockade the paper then said "Engineer (Pete) Hyrup and Fireman Fields arrived home from Hagerman first of the week over the D. & R. G. (via Leadville). The boy's whiskers had grown entirely out of our knowledge. They tell a thrilling story of this experience, while imprisoned in snow shed No. 9 about 44 days. The snow shed is 52 feet high, the snow on top of the shed was 15 or 20 feet making it 37 to 42 feet deep. The boys (sic!) made two trips daily through the tunnel to Pepper's boarding car."

Mar. 25 (a)—Andy Wilson to be married; he is brother-in-law of J. P. Smith and J. P. McMillen.

(b)—Mrs. A. J. Robinson of Aspen died—three sisters are Mmes. Shehi, Willits, and Gillespie, of El Jebel.

(c)—J. P. Hyrup has purchased Maylin Ranch 5 miles east of Basalt.

(d)—Jake Freiler killed a bobcat by throwing rocks at it.

Apr. 1 The I. O. O. F. had a big 4th anniversary, the lodge having been founded March 28, 1895. All indebtedness reported paid.

Apr. 15 "One of the most welcome sights around Basalt was the evening of April 15, 1899, when the snow plow came into town with red fusees burning, everyone shouting, and, I think, some guns fired after there hadn't been any trains over the hill since January 27, 1899."

May 13 Otmar Luchsinger bought out Maylins at Sloane.

July 21 Regarding the big fire the paper states that it started in Nell Smith's restaurant by the explosion of a kerosene lamp. The men fought the fire with a hose from a boiler of an engine, but the pressure was too low. A bucket brigade was formed to no avail. The other buildings burned and their losses were as follows: Kelly $7,000 ($1,300 insurance); John Dooling $2,000 (insurance $700.00); Frank Snell $700.00 (no insurance); Mrs. Kate McCormac $500.00; Joe Tillison $1,200.00 (no insurance); Mrs. Nell Smith $500.00 to $1,000 (no insurance); Lupton Bros. Saloon $300.00 ($300.00 insurance); J. A. Smith coal sheds and coal $125.00.

Aug. 12 Engine No. 33 ditches. "About 2:05 A. M. Friday, freight No. 48 ran into a slide about 30 yards west of the little bridge which spans the small stream which is the outlet of Jacob Lucksinger's fish pond, just west of town. A curve in the track prevented Engineer Danielson from seeing the slide until he was within less than 50 yards of it. Fortunately, he had just put down his seat and was standing at the throttle. In an instant he was down in the gangway following Fireman Braman in a hasty leap on the fireman's side. The head brakeman was sitting on top of the cab and escaped in the same manner as Engineer Danielson and Fireman Braman.

"Engine 33 ploughed into the slide a little way, and was hurled over the embankment into the surging river, bottom side up, followed by a car of coal. The coal car was broken squarely in twain and left hanging bottom side up. Had Mr. Danielson and Fireman Braman been sitting in the cab, or had the accident occurred while the train was running full speed, they would have, no doubt, fallen under the powerful engine and been drowned or crushed. Their escape seems miraculous. The wrecking-train from Leadville was early at the scene and is busy preparing to lift the engine on the track."

Sept. 9   Reverend & Mrs. Hollenback are housekeeping in Mrs. Tierney's property adjoining her family residence.

Sept. 11   Hon. W. J. Bryan is to speak at Peach Day in Grand Junction.

Oct. 13   Susie Stiffler is calling a meeting for Friday, Oct. 20 of the Valley Literary Society in the High School Building.

Nov. 24   J. P. Hyrup killed in runaway on engine No. 32 at Cardiff.

Dec. 7   Telephones installed in town.

1900

Feb. 10   Rev. Tom Leland is to give his famous lecture Sunday.

Feb. 24   Ad inserted by Dan German for Asst. blacksmith.

Aug. 8   R. H. Zimmerman sold drug store to M. E. Carlson & Co.

Dec. 29   "A. M. Danielson, of Basalt, is the first subscriber to pay in advance for the new year, his receipt reading from January 1, 1901 to January 1, 1902. Mr. Danielson was also first in the field last year. We incline to the opinion that the recording angel smiles leniently at the faults of such a person."

1901

Mar. 2   (a) Cowboys from Capitol Creek "shot up the town".

(b) President Theodore Roosevelt had permission to ride the engine on the President's Special.

May 11   Mr. Frey has received a carload of wagons and buggies for sale.

June 20   Notice of election to incorporate the town.

July 13   John Beard of Fruita won the bicycle roadrace from Peterson's to Glenwood in the time of 1 Hr.; 16 Min. and 25 seconds.

July 20   Election Notice. Notice is hereby given that an election will be held in John Auld's carpenter shop on 12th day of August A.D. 1901 in Basalt Eagle Co., Colo.
Commissioners:
W. W. Frey
John Auld
Wm. Conerty
B. W. Burgin
C. L. Benbow

Aug. 24 (a)—Rev. F. R. Hollenback left Monday morning for Canon City where he is in attendance at the annual conference of the M. E. Church.

(b)—Levi Hatfield had a very serious accident by running into a tree while riding a bicycle. His face was badly cut.

Dec. 7 A drum corps has been organized consisting of Al Clegg, Harry Prime, Geo. Davis, Joe King, Elmer Huff, Will Bogue, Roy Bancroft.

1902

Feb. 2 Oil fever from a reported strike on Sopris Creek.

Feb. 8 Pushers at Thomasville discontinued.

Spring "J. G. Ould, always solicitous of the welfare of Basalt, has fixed Friday as Ladies Day at the bath rooms. Mrs. Ould will have charge. 10 A.M. to 6 P.M."

Summer "Three rooms are being added to the Old School House and will be occupied in the fall."

June 7 "Art Bates has recently trapped three bears on Basalt Mountain and is distributing the meat among friends."

July 26 The Journal reports that Dr. Rucker delivered tiny Marion Mitchell prematurely (about 2½ pounds). He has placed her in a pasteboard shoebox surrounded by cotton and kept warm by a hot water bottle. (It can be reported that she survived and grew up to be a beautiful girl—quite an accomplishment for a town doctor without incubators.)

Aug. 25 Adlai Stevenson Sr. gave a talk at Glenwood Springs.

Sept. 20 Rich Thompson won the rodeo.

Sept. 27 Edith Bailey is now Supt. of Schools of Eagle County.

Oct. 11 Game Warden Harris shot by Indians in Rio Blanco County.

Nov. 1 Mrs. Ruland in a runaway accident.

Nov. 8 The engines damaged in the big wreck at Rifle have arrived in Basalt.

1903

Jan. 10 (a) Water works to be completed soon.

(b) Rev. Leland is the minister.

(c) Carlson Bros. now in drug business 2 years.

(d) Dr. Gill and Dr. Rucker are the physicians in town.

Jan. 17 "The parents of Clarence Danielson plan a sleigh ride for his birthday."

Mar. 28 Engineer Conerty's daughter died.

Apr. 8   "Clarence Danielson (12 years old), who lately became an apprentice at the Journal office, is showing wonderful proficiency in the art of typesetting."

Apr. 25 (a) Water schedule drawn up.

(b) Write-up of Glenwood Springs Wheel Club which had been started in 1897.

Aug. 1   John Hanson won second in bicycle race. Jake Lucksinger also placed.

1904

June 6   At the Council meeting a motion was made and passed for saloon keepers to keep a certain person out of the saloons because he was a drunkard.

June 20 Motion passed to keep the saloons closed on Sunday.

July 19 A baseball game was played between the married men and the single men.

Contestants were:

Married men: George Norris (c); Jessie Schmeiser (p); Dan Denton (1b); Fred Stiffler (2b); Charlie Andrus (ss); Clint Benbow (3b); Grant Ruland (rf); W. A. Irwin (lf); Rhode Hyrup (cf).

Single men: Charlie Giersch (c); J. Nolan (p); W. H. Lowry (1b); M. Warner (2b); Dean Sutcliffe (ss); W. Jones (3b); B. Tobey (rf); Frank Howard (lf); Bert Barton (cf).

Umpire: Walter W. Frey.

Aug. 27 "Notice to Parents and Pupils: The Basalt P. Schools will open on Monday, Sept. 5th. All pupils who wish to attend should be present on the first meeting in order that he may start under the most favorable circumstances. Be on hand bright and early on the first day, and on every other day of the term. Come with a determination to do the best that can be done by you, and do not be satisfied with anything less than your full share of success.

J. H. Troendly, Principal"

1905

Jan. 14 "The editor and family are obligated to Mr. and Mrs. W. P. Bates for a well-filled basket of apples and pears and a jar of cherries on New Year's morning."

Jan. 21 Chancellor Buchtel of Denver University preached at the Methodist Church.

Apr. 1   (a) Appropriation by the General Assembly of

$5,500.00 to build the Basalt-Ruedi road. Pushed by Senator Taylor and Rep. Gordon.

 (b) Sam Cramer deeds right of way to Cemetery Association.

 (c) "King's" addition to Basalt established.

Apr. 8 Teddy Roosevelt's Special went through Basalt.

Apr. 22 (a) Mr. Frey started building store.

 (b) To send a committee to see Vallery to try to prevent moving terminal to Cardiff.

Sept. 30 (a) Mr. Ikeler of Glenwood Springs is building a big water tank for Basalt.

 (b) Cowboys from Capitol Creek again rode into town shooting and yelling.

 (c) Clarence Danielson promoted to Sergeant at the Kearney (Nebr.) Military Academy.

1906

Jan. 27 "Chancellor Buchtel, of Denver University, will deliver his famous lecture on 'Theodore Roosevelt' at M. E. Church on Tues. Eve., June 30."

Feb. 3 "At the close of the lecture, the Chancellor presented the cause of Denver University and asked for subscriptions for the running expenses. Over $27.00 was quickly given in cash and pledges. All who have heard and become acquainted with Dr. Buchtel will gladly welcome him whenever he comes to our town."

Feb. 24 (a) A bank for Basalt is being discussed (none was ever established)

 (b) The Washington's birthday party at School was as follows:

Primary grades.
  Recit.—Alvina Dickson
  Recit.—Mildred Carlson
  Recit.—Wallace Nelson
  Recit.—Edgar Hilton
  Recit.—Ruby Hough
  Dialogue—Alvin Ould and Ralph Danielson
  Recit.—Irene Bates
  "Fishing"—Alfred Brittain
  Solo—Geo. Norris
  Recit.—Fay Decker
  Recit.—Thomas Foley
  Recit.—Maggie Shea

Recit.—Frances Hole
Recit.—Jack Folger
Recit.—Jessie Lupton
Recit.—Stephen Bogue
Recit.—Earl Hilton
(c) S. P. Sloss continues to fight the grazing fee.

Mar. 3   O. B. Cain shoots Thos. J. Heuston at Emma.

Mar. 31   Red Rocks Dancing Club
Pres.—J. C. Thompson
V. P.—John Eckwall
Secty.—E .M. Marks
Treas.—Marvin Sloss
Other officers also—Charles Richardson.

Mar. 31   "Engr. A. M. Danielson and Fireman R. D. Hammond and Conductor Dan Needham almost met death in the Busk-Ivanhoe Tunnel while on train No. 41 last Tuesday afternoon. The train broke in two near the west end of the tunnel and they were held 40 minutes in the smoke and gas. Fireman Hammond became unconscious and it required very hard work to revive him after they got out. Engineer Danielson and Conductor Needham were quite sick for several hours after the fearful experience. Both Engr. Danielson and Fireman Hammond had to give up their engine and were brought to Basalt in the 41's caboose, where a physician was called to attend them. The two brakemen suffered from severe headaches but were not knocked out."

Mar. 31   Apple trees advertised for sale, 2 years old, 12 cents. Cherry and plum trees, 20 cents each.

June 2   "A. M. Tatum and Thos. Lamoreaux are entitled to first honors for driving the first team and heavily-loaded wagon over the Basalt-Ruedi road from Castles to Basalt.

June 24   "Dr. Gill entertained friends on his gramophone."

June 30   "Wild gooseberries are plentiful this year."

Aug. 11   (a) Geo. Washington Warner killed accidentally in saloon by his friend, Louis St. John.
(b) At the home of Grace Stewart, the Rev. J. Wilson Currens married James I. James and Miss Garnet M. Thompson, of Thomasville. Garnet is the daughter of Mr. and Mrs. Elijah Thompson.
(c) The Women of Woodcraft were entertained by Eugenia Hyrup and Gladys Hough.

BASALT JOURNAL

Grant Ruland, Prop.

Journal Publishing Company

(J. S. WARNER)

PUBLISHER

Address all Business Communications to J. S. Warner

Issued Saturday of Each Week.

Entered at the postoffice at Basalt, Colorado, as second-class matter.

Subscription, $2.00 per year.
Display advertisements, 50 cents per inch, single column, per month.
Local reading matter, 5 cents per line insertion.

Cattle Market.

Kansas City Mo. May 11

Cattle receipts at Kansas City last week amounted to 27,940 head as compared with 16,667 head the corresponding week last year. At this time a year ago receipts at all all the markets were small and prices advancing. This year all the markets have had heavy supplies, and prices are from $1.75 to $1.90 lower than a year ago on fat steers. Light and medium to thin heifers declined sharply last week, but stockers and feeders showed little change. Western fed steers brought $4.60 to $4.96, and western stockers and feeders from $4 to $4.45. Some Colorado cows last week weighing 1096 sold Tuesday at $4.50. Receipts since the middle of last week have been light, with a beneficial effect on prices.

Today the run is light at 5000 head, and the general market was from strong to 10 cents higher than Friday. This puts steers almost equal to a week ago, but the stuff is from 20 to 35 cents under a week ago. Most sales of stockers and feeders were steady today, some good stockers strong and some heavy feeders weak. Western fat steers brought up to $4.85 today and 100 Colorado stockers weighing 466 brought $4.00.

GREATLY ALARMED

By a Persistent Cough, but Permanently Cured by Chamberlain's Cough Remedy

Mr. A. P. Burbage, a student at law, in Greenville, S. C. has been troubled for four or five years with a continuous cough which he says "greatly alarmed me, causing me to fear that I was in the first stage of consumption. Mr. Burbage having seen Chamberlain's Cough Remedy advertised, concluded to try it. Now read what he says of "I soon felt a remarkable change and after using two bottles of the twenty-five cent size, was permanently cured. Sold by M. E. Carlson & Co.

WANTED — Local organizer, lady or gentleman, for the Highland Nobles, a fraternal benefit order admitting both sexes. Best fraternal insurance policy in the field. For contract, literature and terms write J. F. Manning, State Agent, 925 Eighteenth Street, Denver, Colo.

For Sale Cheap

A good second hand lounge. Suitable for single bed. Inquire at Rulands.

QUICK ARREST

J. A. Gulledge of Verbena, Ala., was twice in the hospital from a severe case of piles causing 24 tumors. After doctors and all remedies failed Bucklin's Arnica salve arrested further inflamation and cured him. It conquers aches and kills pain. 25c. M. E. Carlson & Co.

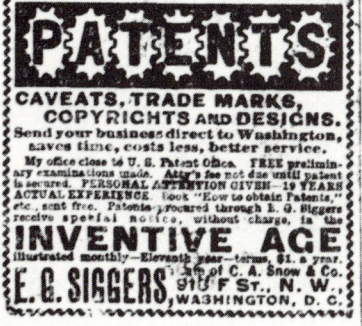

JOHN G. OULD,
Barber Shop. Hot and Cold Baths.

THE BASALT NOVELTY,
Dealer in Cigars, Tobaccos and Confectionery

MRS. N SMITH,
Furnished Rooms.

THE BASALT DAIRY.
Jacob Lixxxxger, proprietor.

DR. P. T. RUCKER,
Physician and Surgeon.

W. W. FREY,
Dealer in Dry Goods, Groceries and Meats.

CLARK & HANSON,
Dealers in Dry Goods, Boots and Shoes and Gents' Furnishings.

M. E. CARLSON & CO.
Dealers in Drugs, Medicines, Toilet Articles, Oils, Paints and Stationery.

H. W. BOYCE,
Painting and Paper-hanging. Samples of Wall Paper to show at any time.

THE MANHATTAN
Restaurant. Only Short Order House in Basalt.

DEPOT HOTEL
and Lunch Counter.

DR. A. E. GILL,
(Successor to Dr. M. McNeilan), Physician and Surgeon.

W. H. HARRIS,
Justice of the Peace. Collections given

BASALT SHOEING SHOP,
Blacksmithing and General Repairing Horseshoeing, Carriage Work a specialty. C. Vandeventer, proprietor.

THE BASALT JOURNAL,
All kinds of Job Printing.
We do all kinds of job work. Give us a call.

LUPTON BROS.
Dealers in Wines, Liquors and Cigars

JOHN AULD,
Builder and Contractor.

BASALT EXCHANGE,
Wholesale and Retail Wines, Liquors and Cigars. E. B. Kelly, proprietor.

Taken from the "Basalt Journal", May 16, 1903.

(d) The L. L. Collins and R. G. Freeman families went on a camping trip to Cattle Creek and took their milk cow with them.

1906

Nov. 3 "To Basalt voters:
I notice that the official ballot contains my name as a candidate for justice of the peace in this precinct. I am not a candidate and never authorized the Democrats to put my name on the ballot. I consider it a slur and would suggest my friends vote the straight Republican ticket, thus avoiding voting for me.
This is only one of the many dirty little tricks practiced by the Democrats of Basalt.
Signed
W. W. Frey"

Dec. 8 The paper records the injury of Mary Rose Fahey by falling out of a high chair. She died Dec. 2.

1907

Nov. 30 Cement bridge across Frying Pan completed.
Dec. 7 Death of John Auld
Dec. 14 Kindergarten started

1908

Feb. 8 The old school house to be used as pest house for smallpox and scarlet fever.
Apr. 29 Editor Hildreth of the Basalt Journal has purchased the Eagle County Blade at Red Cliff and has yet not found a successor for the Journal.
May 2 "By instruction of the Town Council, notice is hereby given that fast driving or riding through the streets of Basalt will no longer be tolerated, and in all cases, on and after this date, the Town Ordinance will be strictly enforced! A word to the wise ought to be sufficient.
—John G. Ould, Marshall, Basalt, Colo., Apr. 10, 1908."

1918

Dec. 11 Minutes of a special meeting of the town council of Basalt. Meeting called to order by Mayor "protem" Maltingly with Lamb, Tucker and Whitenack present. Absent, Mayor Scandlan and Trustees Drake and Jarvis.
The purpose of this meeting was to take some further action to prevent the spread of the Spanish "flu".

On motion by Lamb and recorded by Tucker it was resolved that all business houses of Basalt, including the Drug Store, Frey, Atkinson, Mrs. Bogue, Basalt Supply Co., and Sloss, keep their doors closed, allowing no one to enter, but are to serve their customers at the door. And the barber shop to allow no more than one customer in the shop at any time. Any violation will mean the closing of your business for such time as the Committee may see fit.

This resolution was followed by a motion by Lamb and seconded by Whitenack that signs be placed at four entrances to town worded "Quarantined; if you enter, do not stop".

W. E. Reid
Clerk

Editorials from *Basalt Journal*

Jan. 7, 1899 "We blow for Basalt, The Roaring Fork, and Frying Pan Valleys."

Feb. 16, 1903 "Certain unmarried persons living in adultery must marry, leave town, cease living together, or go to jail."

Apr. 22, 1905 "Every man in every town during the course of a lifetime has to ask a favor of an editor—not an exception to this rule. A man may escape a doctor, keep clear of the courts, but once in a life-time, at least, every man has to go to the newspaper to have a certain piece put in—a death notice, a marriage notice, etc., to have a certain piece kept out or to have his name printed in, or omitted from, some item. It is, therefore, to your interest to treat the editor fairly. He desires to be fair; he would rather do the right than the wrong thing, but if you give him a kick, the dent of it may be found in the top of your own hat some day and you will never know how it got there. Don't think that you are immune; don't think that providence has especially favored you. Your time will come. It will be a fine investment if you have a friend in the editor's office."

Jan. 23, 1906 "It has fallen to the lot of the writer to travel up and down this broad commonwealth to a considerable extent, both in search of business and pleasure, and without an attempt to flatter the good people of this section it can be truthfully said that no town of equal size has yet been found that equals our own little city."

July 14, 1906 "Next to the wife beater comes the horse beater and it is to be regretted we have one or two in this community. A horse is the most noble and faithful of animals and the man who would abuse his horse has something lacking in his manhood."

Aug. 4, 1906   "We do not need money ourselves, but the fellow we owe wants us to pay. Pay your subscription and help the other fellow out."

Aug. 11, 1906   "Barney Flynn, an old timer in Basalt, is lying quite ill in a dugout back of the section bunk house. It would be well for our charitable people to look into his condition and surroundings."

Sept. 1, 1906   "The man who gets mad at what the newspaper says about him should return thanks three times a day for what the newspaper knew about him and suppressed."

Oct. 6, 1906   "We almost fell over a couple of lovers while on our way home last Tuesday night. They were "spooning" on the town bridge and did not notice us, so deep were they in their "swap-spit" affair. He had hold of both her hands and as we passed we heard him say: "Oh, dear, darling little pet, I hate to leave you!" Wouldn't that make you throw up your grandmother's preserves—and we went home and kicked a duck into the Frying Pan."

Date (?)   "On several occasions, persons have narrowly escaped serious and probably fatal injury, from coasters on the hill from J. A. Smith's corner to the depot. Sleds go down this hill at a frightful rate of speed and pedestrians turning into the alley at the lower end of the street are liable at any time to have their feet knocked from under them with such force as to break a limb. On the other hand, horsemen or team and sled turning abruptly around the same point, when the children are coming down, would produce disastrous results, for the coasters would, in all probability, be killed. Parents, we would suggest that you think this matter over seriously and see if you do not love your children too dearly to permit them taking such chances."

Date (?)   "Here are a few things that Basalt people should "cut out". Going around with a gloomy face, fault finding, nagging, and worrying. Taking offense where none is intended. Talking big things and doing little ones. Dwelling on fancied slights or wrongs, scolding and flying into a passion over trifles. Carping and criticizing. See the worst rather than the best in others. Dreaming that you would be happier in another place or circumstances. Belittling those whom you envy because you feel that they are superior to yourself."

Daily Herald Democrat
Leadville, Colo.
April 30, 1886

A Busy Camp

Two saloons, six boarding houses and a grocery store are being erected at the mouth of the Roaring Fork and Frying Pan, on the other side of the range. The valley of the Frying Pan has been stripped of rock and timber for several miles, and the grading has commenced. Railroaders are traveling towards the camp daily by stage, wagon, and on foot, with their blankets and knapsacks on their backs. The camp presents a lively appearance, and the presence of 150 mules fills the air morning and evening with that discord so familiar to old soldiers, who were wont to travel with wagon trains. The valley is covered with tents for a quarter of a mile and the new men are accommodated with pleasant quarters and good board as soon as they arrive. The force of men is being added to by the daily arrivals from Pueblo, Denver, and even Nebraska, all of Orman, Crook and Company's old employees being anxious to come to work for them again.

Those who have not experienced the pleasure of working in the open air in such a delightful climate as that of Colorado, cannot appreciate the pleasure with which old railroaders, men who work on the grade, go into camp for the summer. These advance men consist of a class of laborers who do not like any other kind of work, and they are the jolliest, most muscular, and easiest pleased people in the world. While there is no red tape about the system in vogue with contractors, the men have an ethical code of their own, which is strictly enforced. For this reason these railroad towns that grow up in a week are well governed, and there is generally very little need of a justice of the peace to settle disputes between the men. Men that work for contractors know, too, that a good day's work is expected of them, and there is generally very little of what is called "soldering" among them.

June 19, 1886

"'. . . But about Frying Pan City, Mr. Wigglesworth?", said the superintendent (George W. Cook), taking up the catechism.

"I don't see much to make a city of any dimensions of it, although it's of 6,600 feet in the altitudes, and at the confluence of the Roaring Forks and Frying Pan. Then, surrounding it, is a small strip of agricultural land, and if a man wanted a park or summer residence, he might fancy this a desirable locality. At present everything is tent-roofed and gabled, and I suppose the natives will pull up stakes so soon as the construction forces move camp.' "

Carbonate Weekly Chronicle

August 19, 1901

Basalt, Aug. 19—Sheriff Flick was down from the county seat on Thursday for the purpose of summoning jurors for the petit jury. Court will convene next Tuesday. Several cases are set for trial.

During a severe rainstorm Thursday afternoon a large portion of Frying Pan scenery slid on to the track at Castles, about five miles above Basalt. A gang of workmen was sent up from here to clear the road.

Engineer Danielson, while wiping the headlights on his engine Tuesday evening, slipped and fell on the flagstaff, fracturing two ribs.

Wednesday morning about 1:15 o'clock Louis Valiquette, night caller, when passing the post office noticed that the rear door was open. He came to the conclusion that something was wrong and immediately aroused several of the citizens, who started to investigate. They found the safe had been tampered with. The combination had been broken off, but the robbers had left suddenly without accomplishing their object. Valiquette with his lantern probably frightened them and they left in a hurry. A heavy sledge hammer and chisel were left behind by the would-be safe robbers. The hammer was taken from the round house and the chisel from John Auld's carpenter shop. They first attempted to enter through the front door as they drilled a hole in order to slide the latch aside, but the plan failed, and they started for the rear door, where they forced an entrance without much effort. A posse of armed citizens immediately started out to hunt for the robbers, but they had made good their escape, and no clue could be obtained of them.

Dec. 12, 1892

Aspen Junction Depot Burned

The Midland depot at Aspen Junction burned to the ground on Tuesday night. The building took fire in the upper story in the eating manager's room and the flames spread so rapidly that the fire was well under way before it was discovered. The building comprised the eating house, freight house, telegraph office, waiting rooms, and employes' rooms. The loss will approximate $15,000. The company, it is thought, carried an insurance policy of $5,000. Only the strenuous efforts of the people of the place kept the main part of the town from burning down, and the available water was used to keep the fire from burning. Mr. E. B. Kelly's and Mr. J. C. Eberson's saloons, both of which were on the opposite side of the street, took fire several times, but were extinguished before any great damage was done. The windows in the fronts of both buildings were all broken out and a part of Eberson's saloon was torn down to prevent the fire from spreading.

September 21, 1891

A Progressive Town

Aspen Junction, on the Colorado Midland, is coming quickly to the front as a progressive town, and boasts a weekly paper called *The Pusher*. In the last issue it states that Aspen Junction possesses "two general stores carrying large stocks of goods to supply almost any demand, a hotel, several restaurants, and lodging houses, a drug store, two saloons, a lumber yard, post office, telegraph and express offices, etc. Good openings for business still exist, which it is certain will soon be supplied". In addition, it has a handsome school house, which is also used as a church, and the town has a population of 300 inhabitants, nearly all railroad employees. There is some talk of putting in a new round house and repair shops, and the town is destined to become an important point. The employees of the road, in a great many instances, have built substantial and comfortable homes. Before the Midland made its advent, Aspen Junction was not known, and the progress made in the last few years is entirely due to the Colorado Midland.

May 22, 1893

Mr. and Mrs. J. B. Danielson, 202 West Sixth, will leave Sunday morning for Aspen Junction to attend the marriage of their brother, Mr. A. L. Danielson, and a young lady of that place. When the couple start for Chicago on their wedding tour, Mr. and Mrs. J. B. Danielson will accompany them.

January 1, 1894

A forthcoming social event of interest to the people of Aspen Junction, and especially to the employees of the Midland, is the first annual ball to be given by Mount Sopris Lodge No. 503 Brotherhood of Locomotive Firemen, which will take place at Epperson's Hall on New Year's night. Judging from the preparations already made, and the character of the committees having them in charge, it will be a truly brilliant affair.

January 8, 1894

A new locomotive firemen's lodge, organized a year ago at Aspen Junction, gave its first ball on New Year's night. It was a brilliant success, socially and financially, there being one hundred and twenty-five couples in attendance. The lodge is composed of Colorado Midland firemen exclusively.

(These excerpts from the two Leadville papers were furnished by Don and Jean Griswold)

The Crystal River Empire
Sat. Dec. 13, 1924

Early History of Carbondale, Roaring Fork Valley and Garfield County by Charles H. Harris.

"We landed on the Roaring Fork in May, 1880, we came as far as Bowman at the head of the Taylor River in Taylor Park, and pushed to Aspen, then a town just started.

"Others came in 1881. Built road to Aspen. In 1883 Pitkin Co. started to build a road down Roaring Fork from Aspen to Emma.

"Coal was discovered at Spring Gulch in 1884. Coal was wanted badly at Aspen. A company was formed and a road built from Emma to Carbondale, afterwards made a toll road, where the present roadbed of the D. & R. G. now is. This road left the farmers west of Basalt on the north side of the river without a road, only to ford. We decided to have a road. We could not get the counties to help us. There were seventeen of us in all when we started on the 14th of October 1884, and in three weeks we had constructed a good road about 2.5 miles around the base of Basalt Mountain, also bridged the Frying Pan River. With this job completed most of all the travel from Aspen to Glenwood Springs was on the north and east side of the river, and still is."

CHAPTER 9

Residents of Basalt

1880-1918

When the idea of such a list occurred to us, we naively thought it would be a simple job, but it has turned out to be a very heavy chore. For source material, we called on not only our own memories, but those of people in the region. Furthermore, our correspondence has yielded many more names. The reader should also refer to our chapter on occupations and our lists of teachers, ministers, ranchers, and Midland employees. "The quilt" helped greatly. Corrections and additions have been graciously provided by many friends, but particularly by painstaking work of Jessie Rogers, Anna Sloss, Walter Hyrup, Arthur Bates, Virgil Holcomb, Clarence Dearing, and Prue Bogue.

We are, of course, aware that inevitably there will be omissions and errors, for which we apologize in advance; we would appreciate the reader's corrections.

For the construction of the list, we have placed a colon after the family name. The first names of parents have been given where known; otherwise they are listed as ——————— and wife. A wife's maiden name, where known, has been put in parentheses. The children have been placed after the semicolon. In the case of daughters, married names, when known, have been added in parentheses (indicated by "m."). We have tried to put down the children's names in order of birth. Where a name stands by itself with no given name, it is to be assumed that it is a man. The trainmen who worked in and out of Basalt, but did not live there, can be found under the chapter on "Occupations".

We trust that this list will recall many names for those former residents still living, and will be source material for history-minded descendants.

A

Ammerman: Amerzette (m. Sam Cramer)
Anderson: Annie
Anderson: Anton
Andrus: Charlie, Jennie; Blanche, Charles, Jr., Jennie, Ted

Arbaney: Alec, Clementine; Alice, Alver, Emery, John, Edith (m. Shiff), Lena (m. Gerbaz)
Arbaney: Alexis, Felicity (Gerbaz); Flavine (Flalie), Isabeline (Isabelle)
Arbaney: Emery, Lottie (Clavell); Fredrick, Sue Ann, Lucille (m. Boyd Carlson and Albert Nelson)
Arbaney: Peter
Arondale: John, Elizabeth (Williams); Squire, Harriett
Ashby: James, Sadie; Hope
Ashby: Rev. W. R. and wife
Atkinson: Will, Mattie (Harvey); John, Tommy
Atwater: Dutch, Ellen
Augustine: Clarence, Irene (Stratton); Clara
Auld: John

B

Bailey: Edith (m. Reed)
Balcom: W. D., Nell (Smith)
Bancroft: Charles S. and wife; Blanche, Glener, Guy, Harry, Roy
Bancroft: George and wife; Orlie
Barker: F. C.
Barnes: John
Barnes: Newton
Barnes: Ralph, Walter
Barrett: John
Barton: Bert, Anna May (Griffith)
Batches: Della
Bates: Arthur L., Georgina (Wheatley); Norma (m. Kleve Sheare; Herbert Minor), Barbara (m. Dick Jones), Katherine (m. Art Abbey), Ester (m. James Delaney)
Bates: William Pridham, Jennie (Herrick); Arthur, Ralph, Irene (m. Harry Wilson)
Baumli: Jacob, Marie; Eddie, Fred, Jake, Jr., Louise, Bob
Bear: D. G., Rachel
Beckenstein: B. A.
Bedford: Fred, Jennie (May); Phyllis
Bedford: M. L.
Beggerman: Earnest
Bell: F. H.
Benbow: Clint, Mollie
Bennet: Rev. Will E. and wife
Berthod: Fred
Biglow: Victor
Binnings: Albert, Lutie; Ernest, Albert, Richard (see Cramer)
Blair: Frank, Anna
Blane: C. E.
Bogue: Charles E., Clara (Smith); Clifford, William, Jesse, Essie (m. C. N. Kinney), Josiah, Steven, Frank
Bogue: Jesse, Prue (Templeton); Viola, Arlie, Aloha, Beulah, Buford
Bogue: Will, Anna (McCarthy) (later Mrs. Frank Paddock); Arthur Bryan
Boniger: Mrs.
Borneman: H. G., Anna
Bourg: Venoit, Ursulla; Frank, Nettie (m. Smith), Louis, Ursulla, Paul, Lillian (m. Gavin), Victor, Alex, Alice, Mayme, Eva, Anthony
Bowler: W.
Bowles: James T., Luetta (Jacobs); Oliver, Gertrude, Adelbert, Clarence
Boyce: H. W., Elizabeth
Bradley:
Braman:
Brickle: Louis, Gertrude
Brittain: Jim and wife; Alfred, Edith, Hester
Buffer: Charles

Bun: R. H.
Burch: Mary
Bureman: John, Daisy (Sheward); Erwin, Harold, Eric, Elston
Burgin: Beulah, Anna (Luchsinger)

C

Cadwell: Madge
Caffery: ———— and wife; Nellie, Will
Cahill: William and wife
Cain: O. B., Jewel; Earl, Guy, Roy, Nelson, Lizzie
Carey: T. J.
Carlson: Anthony, Neva (Cox); Emma, Adolph, Anthony, Eunice, Dwight, Cherry, Boyd, Loyal
Carlson: Oscar and wife; Fred
Carlson: Victor, Myra (Johnson); Everett, Pearl, Mildred (m. Botoroff), Lyon
Case: Charles
Case: Joseph
Catt: Mrs. Bell
Cerise: John and wife; Ella (m. Francis Stapleton), Alvin, Anita (m. Dewell Hatch), Deanna
Cerise: John, Ermine (Blanc) (m. Eugene Chatrion); Eva J. (m. Kelly Cerise), Georgina (m. Terliamis)
Cerise: Joseph J., Emily (Tisseur); Kelley, John
Cerise: Kelley, Eva (Cerise); John, Aleda
Cerise: Mela, Margaret; Reno, Lola Mae, Telio B.
Chandler: Mr. and Mrs.
Chatfield: C. S. and wife; Arthur, Clark, Mable, Marjorie, Levi, Willard, Ora, Jacqueline
Chatfield: I. W., Elizah; Charles, Elmer, Jacqueline, Callia
Christian: Robert
Clark: ———— (Father of Carrie Clark (Hanson))
Clarke: John, Hazel (Chapman); Anna Maud (Neil), Conway
Clarke: Dr. Virgil, Edith May (Willits); Lucy (m. Clarence Danielson), Irene (m. Rialto Ould), Helen (m. Phil Smith), Ruby (m. Erle Hubbard), John
Clavell: Fred, Hilomine (Brier); Mary, Frank, Adell, Lottie (m. Emery Arbaney), Henry, Louis, Hattie, Ollie
Clavell: J. F., Gladys (Tierney); Leona (m. Sisely)
Clay: Abe, Henry (brothers) (Sister was Jennie Crawford)
Clegg: Jack and wife; Florence, Albert
Coe: S. D.
Coffin: Harry, Molly
Collins: C. M.
Collins: E. C. and L.L.; Oscar, Russel, ———— (m. Grant), Florence (m. Charlie Nelson)
Collins: J. B.
Collins: Louis H. and wife
Collier: E. F.
Comrie: Kenneth, Ella; Harry, Katie
Conerty: William and wife
Connel: Dan and wife: John, Annie, Mary
Cook: Lora (m. John McMillen)
Cook: Mamie (m. Rhodie Hyrup)
Cookman: Gid
Corbin: Dr. E. S.
Craig: F.
Craig: George
Craig: Will
Crain: ————
Craine: Mrs. ————
Cramer: Samuel, Amerzette (Ammerman), (first wife); Frank, Maude, Lutie (m. Albert Binnings) (second wife); Clementine (m. Bryant)

Crane: ———
Crauser: ———
Crawford: Clara
Crawford: Henry, Effie; Guy, Margaret (m. Bert Rosey)
Crenshaw: ———
Cridon: Mary
Cronin: John, Jessie (Lupton); John L.
Cummings: Clyde

D

Danielson: Albert, Emma (Hillgren); Carl
Danielson: Andrew, Clara (Hillgren); Clarence, Ralph, Myron
Danielson: Clarence, Lucy (Clarke); Lois (m. Clarence Batcheller), Edith Louise (m. Arthur Vaughn)
Danielson: Jake, Josie; Laura (m. Fennell) and (m. Carey), Florence (m. Means)
Danielson: Myron, Nina (Willard)
Danielson: Ralph, Luverne (Langley); Philip, Marjorie (m. Leonard Kowalski)
Darien: Ben, Margaret; Shirley, Alvin, Jerry, Robert
Darien: Roger, Lucille; Henry, Ben, Gus, Jim
Daugherty: Dan and wife; Dan, Annie
Davis: ———, Gladys I.
Daywalt: Frank, Marie; Jack, Frank, Jr., Will, Katherine
Dean: Jack W.
Dearing: Clarence, Ethel (Fipps); Howard
Decker: Jess, Gwendolyn; Faye, Shorty, Lena (m. L. Heller)
DeGroot: Dan, Pearl (May); Helen, Edna
Denison: G. C.
Denman: George, Pauline
Denton: Dan, Olive (Troendly)
Denton: Fritz
Denton: Walter and wife
DeWeese: J. W.
Dibble: William
Dibble: Ralph
Dickson: August and wife; Alvina (m. Harris), Rosella
Dobson: William and wife; Eva, Lloyd, Blanche, Mamie, Vera, Bessie
Donegan: J. J. and wife; Charles
Donegan: S. A. and wife; Margaret
Dooling: Jack and wife; Glenn, Ruth (m. Forrest), Paul, Eugenia, Raleigh
Downey: Dave and wife; Alex, Albert (Bert), Elmer (Em), Clyde, Austin (Chub), Charles (Tod)
Downey: Chub, Carrie (Furman)
Downey: Dave, Eva; Herbert, Merril
Drake: Ray, Esther
Drake: Sam and wife
Driver: Silas
Duggan: Red
Duncan: Mike, Harry, Emma, Carl, Eva
Dunn: John, Coria; Earl, David, Ardith, Daisy
Dunn: Percy
Durkin: Duke and wife
Dwyer: Bob

E

Earley: Ed
Eckwall: John
Edeinborg: Fred
Egar: S. S.

Eiswerth: William Fayette, Fern (Collins); Betty Jane (m. Kenneth Marsh), Wm. F. Jr., Addie Fern (m. Joe Tarrington)
Eiswerth: William Franklin, Addie (Roberts); William Fayette (Fay), Helen (m. Earl Cain), Anthony, Bessie, Juanita (m. Clavell), Pauline (m. Clavell), Naomi, Beulah, Mary, Phoebe, Robert, Arthur, Vernon, Bessie Marie
Eldridge: H. B.
Ellingwood: ───────
Ellis: Charles (Slim), Rachel (Stiffler)
Ellmaker: ─────── and wife
Elmont: Maude (m. Albert Elmont), Blanche (m. Wm. Elmont); (sisters)
England: Al, Sophie; Myrtle
Englebright: Pete, Alice (Woods); Ralph, Pearl
Epperson: John C., Bridget; Nellie, Mary, Raymond
Erickson: Ida
Erwin: Horace

F

Fahey: Jim, Anna (McCahey); James, John, Stephen, Thomas, Rosemary
Farquhar: D. B.
Fagan: Barney
Fastabend: F. J.
Fay: Walter F.
Fennemore: Mamie, Fechtig, Louise (brother and sisters)
Fields: Milton
Fields: Ira
Flynn: Barney
Folger: A. T. and wife; Jack, Mildred
Ford: Tom
Forrest: Catherine
Forrest: Harry, Ruth (Dooling)
Foster: A.B., Ollie
Fouse: Charles, Viola (Graham)
Fraser: James E., Ida Louisa (Murray) - (First marriage to George Stewart— see children under Stewart)
Freeman: G. R.
Freiler: Henry and wife; Jake, Harry, Fannie
Freiler: Jake, Julia (Shay); Harold, Katherine, Barbara
Frey: Walter W., Ora; Edna (m. M. C. Fuller), Josephine, Caroline (m. Smith), Walter, Jim, Dorothy, John
Frick: (Mrs. Edith Clarke's mother)
Frison: Jake and wife; Ann Ell, Paul, one other boy
Frison: Pete, Julia (Luchsinger)
Fuhrman: ─────── and wife; Carrie, Fay (m. Otto Hyrup), Nettie, Nellie, William
Fuhrman: Will, Kate
Fulghum: ───────
Fuller: Bert and wife
Fuller: Charles, Edna (Frey)
Fullman: Frank

G

Gabory: Louis, Roy, Ollie, Josic (brothers and sisters)
Gaddis: William
Garrison: J. M.
Gavin: J. C.
Genner: Jake, Anna (Kramer); Elsie (m. Ruther), Gladys (m. Feeley), Ellen (m. James), Evelyn (m. Ficco), Louise (m. Shumacker), Josephine (m. Sovis), Charlotte (m. Stewart), Clara, Robert
Genner: John (nephew of Jake)

George: R. C. and wife
Gerbaz: Auzel, Clonia (Corbin); Delbert
Gerbaz: Edmund, Albena (Tekovich); Cherie, James
Gerbaz: Harvey (Mike), Eva (Arbaney); Dolores (m. Stutsman), Douglas, Jerry
Gerbaz: Homer, Mabel (Hoaglund); Jerry, Mae, Epeneter
Gerbaz: Olive, Lena (Arbaney); Ted, Ernest, Fred
Gerbaz: Orest, Helen (Evans); Beverly
German: Dan, Elizabeth (Farthing); Louis, Emma (m. Dick Mizer), Lillie (m. Jim O'Brien), Dan, Jr.
German: Dan, Jr., Bertha (Hand)
German: Louis and wife
Gilbert: C. F. (Pug), Louise (Nixon); Carl, Ford
Gilbert: Van
Gill: Dr. Arthur, Florence
Gillaspie: John
Gillespie: H. Bert, Liss (Robinson); Ken, Bert
Gillespie: George, ——————— (Robinson); Annie (m. Gray), Cora (m. Tennis), Olive (m. McCabe), Gertrude (m. Allen)
Gillespie: William, ——————— (Robinson); Tom, Harvey, Milda (m. Robinson)
Goff: Walter
Gonzales: A. M.
Gordon: Sam
Gowan: L. E.
Grace: Gustavus G. and wife; Claude, Mable, Georgia, Gerald, Austin, Nina
Graham: Charles, Mattie (Griffith); Viola
Graham: E. B.
Graham: H. G.
Grant: ———————, Henrietta; Ruby, Cassie
Gray: Elbert Henry, Annie B. (Gillespie); Beulah (Wood), Ernest, Harold (second wife was Ella Tierney, widow of William Tierney)
Gray: C.
Green: William R.
Gregory: ———————
Griffith: Richard, Margaret (Doherty); John, Martha (m. Graham), Anna May (m. Barton), Grace (m. Shafer), Maggie (m. Smith), Nina (m. High), Jeannette, Dick, Jr.
Gritman: Ed

H

Hagbloom: Albert
Hall: ——————— and wife; Teller, Josephine, Roy, Grace
Hall: Dave and wife; Nelson, Ned
Hall: Joe and wife; Julia, Flora, Clarence
Hall: Judge William and wife; Dave, Doc, William, Ted, Tiny (m. M. P. Nobbe), Edna (m. Morris Kramer)
Hallock: Grace (m. Frederick Pike)
Hammond: Rube D., Laura (Storer)
Hancock: Tommy
Hanlan: ———————; (sister of Mrs. Duykin)
Hansen: Harry (Name originally Hanson)
Hanson: Charlie, Alice (Hanson)
Hanson (Hansen): Matt, Carrie (Clark); Harry, Alice (m. Charlie Hanson)
Hancock: Tommy
Hardcastle: ———————
Hardesty: ——————— and wife
Hargis: ———————
Harniff: J. B.
Harris: Asa, Bertie; Thelma (m. Vernon Tiller), Wilma (m. Walter Shideler)
Harris: Rev. C. F. and wife; (several children)

Harris: Charlie, Rose; Vern, Beth
Harris: Claude, Zella; Ethel, Ardith
Harris: William, Rose; Albert, Ralph, Raymond
Hartson: Claude and wife; Hubert, Fannie, Hazel, Doris, Hortense, Claude, Jr., John
Harvey: John, Pet; Jessie, Georgia, Charles, Frank
Harvey: Mattie (m. W. Atkinson)
Harvey: Sam, Jennie; Harlan, Zona, Leslie
Hayes: Grace
Hayward: W. A.
Hazleton: R., Jennie; Harold, Irma (m. S. R. Brandt), Lucille (m. Ira C. Jordan)
Healy: M. V.
Heap: F.
Hedges: William
Heid: L. A.
Height: Bertha
Heller: Leo, Lena (Decker); Leo Francis, Bernard Leroy, Robert Earl
Henry: Newton
Henry: Jim
Henry: S. N.
Henston: T. J.
Hess: C. W.
Hibner: Dee, Eleanor (McCarthy); Clayton and a daughter
Hildreth: W. H., Lulu (Scudder); Will, Lambert, Ruth, Fay, Frank, Hoffman, Bert
Hill: ―――――
Hilton: John, Maude; Hazel, Edgar, Earl
Hoffman: Bert
Holcomb: Virgil, Blanche (Smith) (Stager); Lois (m. Clinton Reynolds)
Holder: ―――――
Hole: Rev. L. J., Cora (Burford); Frances (m. Underwood), Hilda (m. Parmater)
Holland: May
Hollenback: Rev. Frank R., Eva Mable (Schock); Frank Robert
Hollingsworth: Ross, Ida; Warren, Lillian
Hollingsworth: Walter, Lydia
Hollins: L.
Hollister: A. B.
Holmes: ――――― and wife; Ophelia
Hook: William, Olive
Hotz: George, Pansy
Hotz: Joe and wife; Martin
Hough: Johnston T., Christine (Jakeman); Ruby, Gladys (m. Frank Wachob), Walker
Houston: Tom
Howard: D. E.
Howard: Grace
Howard: O. E.
Howater: C. E.
Howie: Jim I.
Hoyt: Lee
Hull: George and wife; Clyde, Edna, Ethel
Hunt: S. G.
Hurtgen: Joe, Lillie; Lloyd, Joe, Jr., Nellie
Hynds:―――――
Hyrup: Alfred, Rachel (McNeil)
Hyrup: Chris, Hazel (Mount); Eugene, Robert, Annabel, Patricia
Hyrup: Otto, Fay (Fuhrman); Larry
Hyrup: Pete, Anna (Murman); Annie, Eugenia (m. Murray), Chris, Otto, Walter, Alfred

Hyrup: Rhodie, Mamie (Cook); Dora
Hyrup: Walter, Yvonne Marie (Eva) (Letey); John, Josephine, Eugenia, Mary Rose

I

Imler: J.
Ireland: Charles and wife
Irom: E. E.

J

Jacobs: Ed and wife
Jacobs: Ollie and wife
Jakeman: Christine (m. Johnston Hough)
Jakeman: Fred, Lydia (Henning); Blanche (m. Elmont), Maude (m. Elmont), Fred, Jr. (Fred, Sr. was the brother of Christine)
Jarvis: ———
Jarvis: George and wife
Jarvis: Ray
Johnson: August and wife; John, Carl, Louise
Johnson: B. and wife
Johnson: John
Johnson: ——— and wife; Elsie Emelia
Johnson: Roy
Jones: Annie
Jones: Thomas R., Jennie

K

Kalfus: J. W., Annie (Anderson) (second wife); Joe. First wife unknown. (Had son Milton)
Kastellic: 2 brothers
Kellerup: Mark, Mable (Sloss); Harold, Junior
Kelly: E. B. and wife
Kennedy: Dr., Erlo, Mable; Charles
Kibby: A. J., Ellen; Earl, Dale
Killian: D. B.
King: G. W. and wife; Joe, Jennie, Lizzie, Ella
Kinney: Frank
Kinney: John, Essie (Bogue)
Kinney: Tom
Kniphausen: Bob
Kopkey: Charles
Kopkey: Gus and wife
Kramer: Morris, Edna (Hall); Edward, Zella, Ruby

L

Lamb: James F. and wife; Nora, Jennie
Lamoreaux: Thomas and wife
Landin: Mrs. H. W.
Lannsberry: M. L.
Lapham: Fannie
Larson: Pete
Law: Charlie, Sylvia (Barker); Nina (m. Corbin), Bessie (m. Drath)
Law: Rev. Harvey M., Catherine (Rexroad); Charlie, Dickey
Lees: Bertha
Leland: Rev. T. S. and wife; Kate, Joe
Letey: Sam, Josephine (Clavell); Yvonne Marie (m. Walter Hyrup), Laura
Liddle: G. F. and wife; Arvid
Light: Fred and wife; Leo, Fred, Jr., Edith, Effie, Helen, Ray, Howard, Mildred

Light: Leo, Mary (Epperson); Ray, Jean
Little: Hattie
Locker: Ed, Annie
Lombard: Therisa
Luchsinger: Charlie, India (Reeves); Zella
Luchsinger: Gabe, Julia; Fannie, Anna (m. B. Burgin), Julia (m. P. Frison), Charles
Luchsinger: John
Luchsinger: Mark
Luchsinger: Ottomar
Lucksinger: Jake, Christina; Jake, Jr., George, Teddy, Elsie (m. Baxter), William, Raymond, Agnes, Carl. (Jake spelled his name with a "k", all the others with an "h").
Lumley: Rev. Stephen and wife
Lupton: Dan W., Nancy; Jessie (m. John Cronin) (m. Rogers), Gertrude
Lupton: E. Bruce
Luzi: John
Lydick: H. C. and wife; Clay, May, Pete, Nora, Oren, Emmett, George

M

Magnall: Sidney and wife; Sidney, Earnest, Herb
Mallon: Ed
Mallon: Jim, Jacqueline (Chatfield)
Mallory: Enoch G. and wife; Murray, Sadie
Mallory: Fred, Ella Jane (Reid); Nettie, Frank, Violet, Ima
Manning: J. T., Mary
Marks: E. M.
Martin: W. T.
Massell: Earnest, Maggie; Irene, Alex
Mather: C. H. and wife; George
Mattingly: J. P. and wife; Helen
May: Mrs. Cal
May: Jim, Jennie; Gladys
May: John, Jennie (Timberlake); Floyd, Pearl (m. Dan de Groot)
Mayhew: B. L.
Maylin: John and wife; Nell
McBurney: F. J., Gladys (Clavell)
McBurney: Mable (Tierney)
McCabe: Hugh
McCabe: Peter, Olive (Gillespie); Oma (m. Seybold), Elbert, Emmet, Vera Grace (m. Matis), Vern, Harold B., Annabelle (m. Unger), Warren H., Flo Maxine (m. Ainsworth)
McCaffry: ———
McCarthy: Dan, Maria (Wills); Anna (m. Frank Paddock), Eleanor (m. Dee Hibner)
McCarty: Hank and wife
McClave: A. K.
McClavin: George and wife
McCormac: ———
McDonald: T. M.
McFarland: ———
McGonagal: ———
McGranahan: ——— and wife
McKey: A. M.
McLaren: George W., Grace (Parker)
McLaren: George, Minerva (Rose); John, George W.
McLean: E. U.
McLewis: E. V.
McLewis: A. R.
McMahon: Mike and wife; Ina
McMillen: J. P., Lora (Cook); Martha

McNeil: Tom and (1) Ann (Goddard), Ann; (2) Rachel (Wiggins), three sons and one daughter, Rachel; (3) Faith Roe (Downer), Tom McNeil, Jr. (Mrs. Downer had Malcomb, Martha, Mary, Virginia by her first marriage)
McNeilan: Dr. ——————— and wife
Mead: John
Melborn: W. A.
Miller: K. and wife
Miller: S. H., Ophelia (Holmes)
Mills: Fred E., Alice (Summers); Glenn, Roy, Ethel (m. Leslie Wann)
Mitchell: Ira, Marcia (Willits); Marion (m. Dahle), Dudley, Roger
Mizer: Dick, Ena (German); May, Lewis
Morast: C. W.
Morrison: G. H.
Mount: ———————, Fannie; Hazel (m. Chris Hyrup)
Murray: Charles, Eugenia (Hyrup); Raymond, Vincent, Walter, James, Charles, Ruth Ann (became a nun)

N

Naefe: Fred, Caroline (Beck); August, Annie, Julia
Nash: William and wife; Nora, Frank, Fred, William, Jr.
Needham: Dan
Nelson: Charles, Florence (Collins); Wallace D.
Nelson: John, Lydia; Harry, John, Jim
Nesbit: Mrs.
Newkirk: Forrest, Lydia (Henning) (her other husbands were Fred Jakeman and Swan Nelson)
Nickol: J. A.
Nobbe: Paul, Tiny (Hall); George, Ray, Mary
Norris: George, Zada; Floyd, Mary
Norris: Henry, Mary; Dorothy (m. B. Willits), Juanita (m. Fred Simpson), Maybird (m. Jake Lucksinger), Elnora (m. Ernest Early)
Norstrom: Arthur, Clara (Denton); Ruth
Notkin: ———————
Nott: J. F.

O

O'Brien: Jim, Lillie (German)
O'Brien: William
O'Connell: John and wife; Kate, Tom, Reese
O'Connell: Tom
Olson: David
Olson: Enoch, Anna (Peterson); Freddie, Henry, Alma (m. Chester Stewart), Rozella (m. Vernon Eiswerth)
Omer: Ed
Ongemach: Louise; Claudia
O'Neil: Arthur and wife; Arthur
Opie: Harold, Doris (Hartson)
Ostrander: Richard and wife; Harry, Richard, Jr.
Ould: John, Elvie (Moon); Will, Rialto, Alvin, George

P

Packard: Fred
Packard: W. R.
Paddock: Frank, Annie (McCarthy) (Wm. Bogue—first husband)
Paddock: Fred, Margaret (O'Connell); Frank
Patrick: M.
Peck: J. F.
Pepper: J. D.
Peryan: ———————

Peterson: Charlie, Anna (Rush); Anna, Eddie, Oscar, Johnny, Alice, Hazel
Phares: B. G.
Phelan: Jim, Agnes; Ruth (m. R. J. Hallock), Maymee (m. W. L. Sanchez)
Phelps: Dr. E .M.
Phillips: Sam, Gladys
Phipps: Eva
Pottinger: B. W.
Powell: Mrs.
Powers: Grant
Priest: Tom
Prine: Harry

Q

Qualey: Orvis W. (Bill)
Quist: Oscar and wife

R

Ramsey: George
Randall: Joe, Jennie; Joe, Jr.
Randall: John and wife
Randall: Myrtle
Rasmussen: Victor
Ray: Victor and wife; Warren
Reeves: India (m. Charlie Luchsinger)
Reeves: John
Reid: William, Edith (Bailey)
Renshaw: Alvin S., Maggie (Shay); Anna Lois, Nellie, Bill
Reynolds: Shuford
Rhodes: Gert, Addie Mae (Rozzell); Clifford, Melvin, Anna (Wilson—before adoption)
Rice: Howard
Richardson: Charlie
Richardson: Jim
Riebel: Oscar, Josie (Hillgren); Chester, Iona, Clifford
Riley: Pete
Roberts: L. M. and wife; George, Wade, Susie
Robinson: Abbie
Roselle: Miss ———
Ross: Bert
Rother: Carl, May (Lydick); Lucille, Buster
Rother; Mary
Rucker: Dr. P. T. and wife; Allen
Ruland: Grant and wife
Russel: M. R.
Rutherford: Jack, Fannie (Luchsinger); Iona
Ryan: James
Ryan: Thomas

S

Salsbery: ———
Sandusky: Minnie
Sawyer: J. L. and wife
Scandlan: John, Electa (Mather)
Schmueser: Jess, Clara (Crawford)
Scudder: Ben
Sebring: Andy and wife
Shadle: E. S.
Shafer: Scott, Grace (Griffith)
Shanks: W. J., Pearl (Willits); Dorothy (m. Stewart), Rollin, Kenneth
Shannon: Pat

Shay: Mike and wife; Maggie (m. Renshaw), John, Julia
Shehi: Dan, Emma; Fred
Sheppard: Jack, Lydia (Stiffler)
Sherritt: Dad and wife; Jessie (m. Bill Finley), Bill
Sheward: David, Daisy (Bureman); Cora (m. John Dunn), Eva (m. Dave Downey)
Sheward: Ed
Sheward: Ervin
Shideler: Grover, Eva; Leora, Mildred, Helen, Frankie Jo
Shippie: Mark L., Gertrude; Leta, Lois, Lillie, Clyde
Simmons: Arthur and wife; one son
Simpson: Alex, Maggie; Alex, Tom, Floyd
Sizelove: Luretta
Slapp: J. M.
Sloss: Alfred, Anna (Wilson-Rhodes); Edith (m. Lawrence), Sterling
Sloss: Alvin, Clemence (Brier)
Sloss: J. F., Emma (Ditty); Marvin, Conson, Mable (m. Mark Kellerup)
Sloss: John, Emaline (Bogue); Walter, Carl, Paul, Bates
Sloss: Marvin, Edna (Long); Clyde, Erlo, Ellis
Sloss: Price, Edith (Bogue); Alfred, Alvin; Also had second wife (Henderson)
Smith: B. L. and wife
Smith: Clifford, Gretta Clark (Pottinger)
Smith: Edwin, Gladys (Hall)
Smith: Fair
Smith: John, Adelaide (Wilson); Blanche (m. B. F. Stager—m. V. Holcomb), Phil, Clifford
Smith: Nell
Smith: Phil, Helen (Clarke)
Smith: W. H., Kittie; John
Snell: Frank and wife; Roy, Lester
Snyder: John Perry, E'Mila Luella (Zimmerman); Floyd C., Ruth (m. Fred Carlson)
Spahr: J. W. and wife
Splettstoesser: Otto
Sprague: Perry
Stager: B. F., Blanche (Smith); Helen (m. Harold Perkins), Hilda (m. Archie Peet), Irene (m. Herman Thelin)
Stager: Morton and wife
Stapp: Carrie
Stauffer: Eddie
Steinberg: ─────
Steiner: Fred
Stettler: L.
Stewart: Chester and wife; Alma (m. Olson)
Stewart: George Hugh, Ida Louise (Murray); Winifred, William LeRoy, Bertram M., Mary M., John Arthur, George Hugh
Stewart: W.
Stiffler: Fred, Sadie (Mallory); Ethel (m. Stanley Smith), Lester, Harold, Henry
Stiffler: Col. Henry, Harriett (Futtrell); Matthew (Mack), Fred, Lydia Bell (m. H. M. Shepard), Daniel, Charles May, Martha (Mattie) (m. Pat Allen), Irwin Barr, Louis C., Susan (m. J. F. Stender), Henry, Rachel (m. Charles Ellis and later m. John Weir)
Stiffler: Matthew (Mack), Bessie (Kelly)
Stobbe: A.
Stockman: Fred H. and wife
Stockton: Ed and wife; Lottie, Harry
Stoker: Bill
Storer: Mrs. Laura
Stores: ───── and wife; Laura
Strong: R. D. and wife

St. John: Louie, Vern
Sullman: F. W.
Sutcliff: Dean, Claudie (Ohngemach)
Suttlemeyer: Tom
Swartz: W. E. and wife; Ed, Ben
Swisher: ———

T

Talmadge: Gladys
Tandy: ———
Tansy: J. W. and wife
Tatum: Alonzo M. and wife
Tatum: J. H., Hattie; Buster, Jessie, Geneva, Velma, Esther
Tatum: Wren
Taylor: S. K.
Templeton: Dow, Etta; Katie, Prue, Earl, Henry, Don, Rob, Win
Tenard: ———
Tennis: Voyle
Thomas: Charlie
Thompson: George
Thompson: Dr. J. C. and wife
Thompson: Lige
Thorp: ———
Thurbull: ———
Thurston: D.
Tidwell: Opa
Tierney: William, Ella; Bertha, Gladys (m. Clavell), Mable (m. McBurney), Will, Jim
Tillison: Joe
Timberlake: Stella (widow); Earl, Charles
Toner: ———
Trezise: ——— and wife
Triplett: Will, Edith
Troendly: John, Harriet; Olive, John, Jr.
Trout: Jess and wife ——— (Harvey)
Trout: Ray and wife
Trowbridge: Ed, Mina; Roland, Harry, Verna
Tucker: L. R. and wife
Tuggles: C.
Tully: Mrs. Elizabeth (widow); Grace, Maurice, Henry, Frank
Turner: Miss ———

U

Usel: Leonis, Pierina (Betemps); Stanley, Lauria Ella (m. Mullins), Rosina (m. Eldon Johnson)

V

Valine: John
Valiquette: John and wife; Louie, Blanche, Joe
Vandeventer: J. H. and wife; James, Hazel, Blanche
Venetish: Oscar

W

Waller: Arthur E. and wife
Walsh: John
Walters: Anthony, Harriett (Arondale)
Walters: Bobby
Watermeyer: ———
Wathen: F.

350   Residents of Basalt

Weaver: Jim and wife; Bessie, James
Wheatley: John, Catherine (Moore); Ellen (m. Miles Sweeney), Cassie (m. Paul Bourg), Georgiana, Blanche (m. Florida), Esther (m. Sinton)
White: W. A., Allie; Hazel
Whitenack: Ed (and his mother)
Williams: James J.
Williamson: J. S., Shermie (Smelling)
Williamson: ──────── and wife; Tookie, Wayne, Vesta (m. McQueen), Marvin, Iver
Willis: Fred and wife; Fred, Frank
Willits: Bramblet, Dorothy (Norris); Lee
Willits: Fred, Sophia
Willits: Lee, Cornelia (Robinson); Pearl (m. Shanks), Irene (m. Dr. Randall), Marcia (m. Ira Mitchell), Bramblet
Wilson: Anna (m. Alfred Sloss)
Wilson: Cliff
Wright: William

Z

Zimmerman: R. H.

CHAPTER 10

Geology of the Basalt Area

While arranging this book it occurred to us that such a varied display of rock formation as there is around the Basalt area should have something said about it. We, therefore, called Dean P. G. Worcester, our good friend, and former teacher at the University of Colorado, and asked him whether he could suggest someone to do this for us. With characteristic friendliness he said, "Why not let me do it myself?" We were elated, for no one is better qualified, and we are most grateful to him for writing the following account of the geology of this area.

The rocks of this area are igneous and sedimentary; there are no metamorphic rocks. Igneous rocks are formed by the cooling of molten rock material (magma) that is in some way forced out from the deep interior of the earth. Sedimentary rocks, usually found in layers, are fragments of older rocks that have been weathered and eroded and finally deposited by wind or streams in lakes and seas or, much less commonly, on land.

The ages of the rocks in this region represent portions of the Paleozoic (early life), Mesozoic (middle life), and Cenozoic (recent life) eras of geologic time. Translated into years (approximately) the oldest rocks of the region, those of the Minturn formation, were deposited some 250 million years ago. The youngest rocks, the Basalt and Felsites of igneous origin, were spread out on the earth's surface from volcanic centers only 10 or 15 million years ago. The other formations, named below, except for recent alluvial deposits from the present streams, are intermediate in age. They are described in ascending order from oldest to youngest.

Sedimentary Rocks

The *Minturn* formation belongs to the Pennsylvanian Period of the Paleozoic era. The rocks are red, buff, yellow, and gray sandstones and siltstones with some gray anhydrite and gypsum. The total thickness is not known but near Glenwood Springs it

352 *Geology of the Basalt Area*

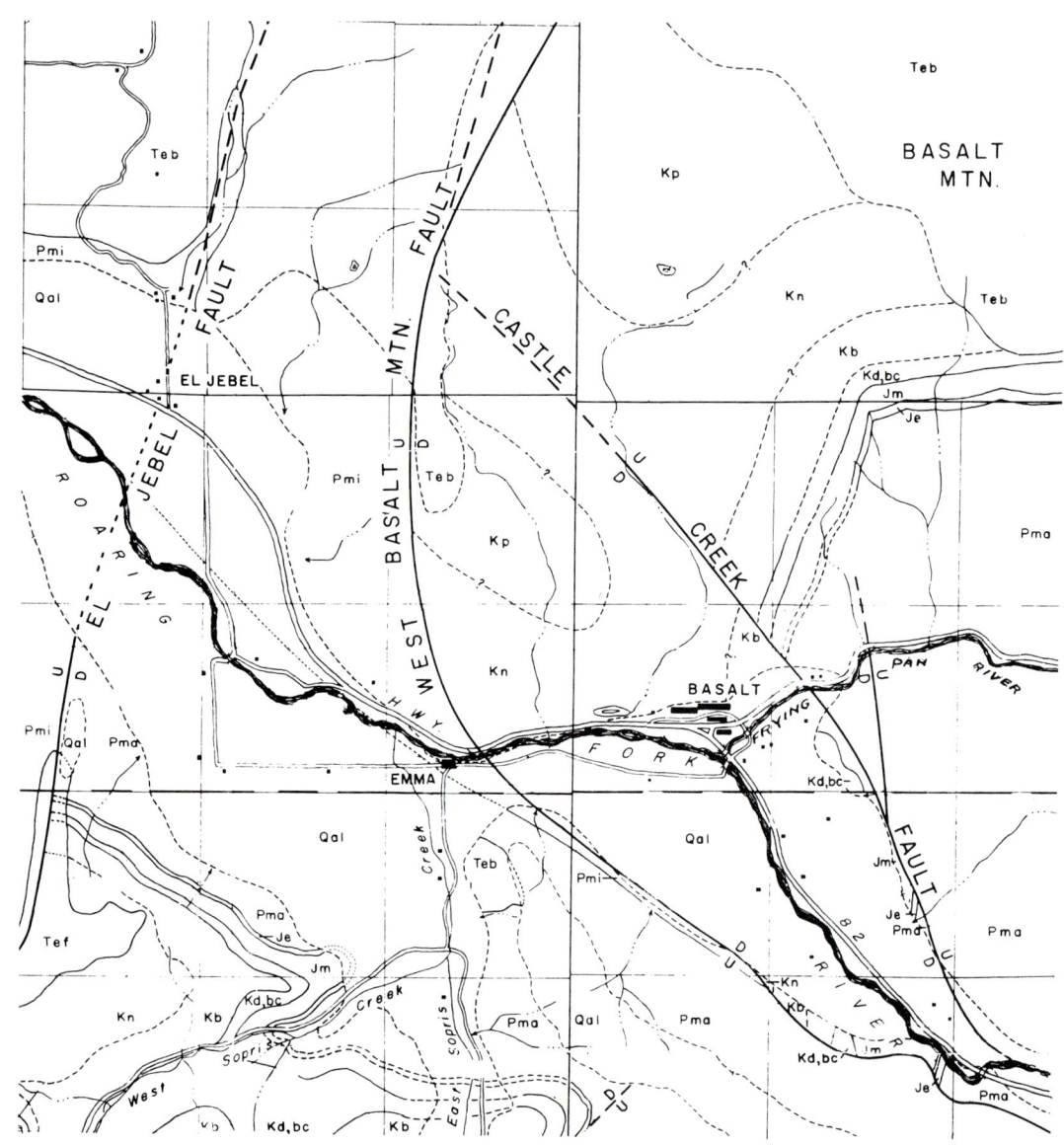

Drawn with permission from Master's Thesis
University of Colorado, 1954 by G. E. Welder

Geologic Map of the Basalt Area

Geologic symbols: Pmi = Minturn; **Pma** = Maroon; **Je** = Entrada; **Jm** = Morrison; **Kd.bc** = Dakota Group; **Kb** = Benton; **Kn** = Niobrara; **Kp** = Pierre; **Qal** = Alluvium; **Teb** = Basalt; **Tef** = Felsite; **r50** = dip and strike. **U/D** = Up-throw and Down-throw sides of a fault.

is about 6,000 feet. The reader should refer to the geologic map for outcrops in the Basalt area.

The next younger formation is the *Maroon*. Normally the Maroon is of the Permian age but here, due to indefinite boundaries, a thick section of Triassic rocks is included in the Maroon that is shown on the map. This is the most colorful formation in the area. It is exposed on both sides of the Frying Pan River for many miles east of Basalt. The principal rocks are red shades and sandstones, with some conglomerates. The total thickness ranges from 6,000 to 8,000 feet. Fine sections may be seen a few miles east of Basalt on Toner and Seven Castles Creeks.

Overlying the Maroon is the *Entrada,* a massive, white, gray and pink sandstone 35 to 180 feet thick. This is believed to be a wind deposited sandstone which means that in upper Jurassic time, perhaps 150 million years ago, the Basalt area was a desert.

Immediately above the Entrada are the gray limestones, white sandstones, and green, red, and gray shades of the *Morrison* formation. This also is upper Jurassic in age and is about 400 feet thick. This formation is noted for dinosaur bones that are found in many Colorado, Wyoming, and Utah localities. It also is the chief uranium and vanadium bearing formation in the plateau region of western Colorado, but, so far, neither these minerals nor perfect dinosaur bones have been found near Basalt.

Next in order is the *Dakota Group* which consists of a lower massive and conglomerate sandstone and shale series of lower Cretaceous age and an upper series of sandstones, conglomerates and gray or reddish brown shales that represents the true Dakota, one of the most wide-spread formations in western North America. The Dakota represents a transition from the lower to the Upper Cretaceous. The thickness of the Dakota Group is about 200 feet. After extensive erosion, the massive sandstones and conglomerates tend to make cliffs that stand conspicuously above the multicolored shales of the Morrison formation.

The youngest sedimentary rocks of the region are in ascending order the *Benton, Niobrara and Pierre* formations. They consist chiefly of gray and black shales but the Niobrara contains a thick, massive limestone member. The combined thickness of the Benton and Niobrara is 600 to 700 feet. The thickness of the Pierre cannot accurately be determined because of erosion and alluvial covering. All these formations were deposited in shallow epi-continental seas that covered much of western North

Ampitheater at the head of Seven Castles Creek. Geologic formations: Kd, Kbc, Dakota Group; Jm, Morrison; Je, Entrada; Pma, Maroon.

America in Upper Cretaceous times. These three formations are correlated by fossils with the same formations that occur extensively east of the mountains in Colorado. Where they are not separated in western Colorado they all are included under the term *Mancos* formation which is beautifully exposed in the Book Cliffs east of Grand Junction.

Igneous Rocks

A tremendous mass of *Olivine Basalt* caps Basalt Mountain immediately north of the town of Basalt. It extends northward to the south rim of Glenwood Canyon. Typically this rock is dark gray in color but in some places it is reddish-brown. It is dense in texture or is vesicular (that is, a sponge-like texture) in many places. It shows indistinct layers which represent repeated lava flows from an unknown volcanic vent. There are no criteria in the local area to determine the age of the Olivine Basalt but similar occurrences in central Colorado are Miocene in age. Because the lava flowed onto a well eroded land surface the thickness is quite variable with a maximum of about 500 feet. A small detached mass of the same rock occurs about one mile southwest of the town of Basalt.

About three and one half miles westerly from Basalt there is a mass of Felsite some 200 feet thick and more than a mile in length that was extruded from a volcanic vent. This flow lies on uptilted Jurassic and Cretaceous beds. Its occurrence is unusual in a region where the prevailing volcanic rocks are basalts.

Structures of the Rocks

The many folds and faults in the region around Basalt reflect the tremendous forces that produced the Rocky Mountains. The Sawatch Mountains on the east and the Elk Mountains and Grand Hogback on the west were uplifted thousands of feet during mountain growth which began about 70 million years and ended around 5 million years ago. In between, the Basalt area was subjected to squeezing and buckling that produced the present structures. The town of Basalt is situated between two great faults, Castle Creek on the east and West Basalt Mountain on the west. On the east, the upthrow side of Castle Creek fault, beds have been raised as much as 1000 feet. On the west, upthrown side of the West Basalt Mountain fault, Minturn beds are in contact with Niobrara, indicating a vertical displacement of at least 6000 feet.

Economic Geology

In spite of the fabulous deposits of lead and silver at nearby Aspen these metals are not found in the Basalt region. Neither are there other metals of economic importance.

Acknowledgements. Considerable information in this article was obtained from a master's thesis entitled "Geology of the Basalt Area, Eagle and Pitkin Counties, Colorado", submitted by George E. Welder to the Graduate School, University of Colorado, in 1954.

Old Timers' Reunion

The authors planned and held on Sunday, August sixteenth, 1964, a gathering of many Basalt old-timers and their families. The party was at Ralph's home and the response was heart-warming.

Assistant hostesses were Clarence's two daughters: Lois (Mrs. Clarence Batcheller) and Edith Louise (Mrs. Arthur Vaughn), and Ralph's daughter, Marjorie (Mrs. Leonard Kowalski); also Mrs. Arthur Bates (Georgina Wheatley), Mrs. Frank Wachob (Gladys Hough), Mrs. Earle Bryant (Clementine Cramer), Mrs. Clarence Dearing (Ethel Fipps), Mrs. George Denman (Pauline Pearce), and young Barbara Abbey, grandaughter of the Arthur Bateses.

Besides many from the Denver area, Mr. and Mrs. Bramblet Willits and their son, Mr. Lee Willits, drove over from Carbondale; Mr. John Genner and Mr. Cecil R. Shoemaker both came from Basalt; Mr. and Mrs. Fred Carlson made the trip from Montrose; Mr. Leo Heller, Mr. and Mrs. Dave Cuthbert, Mr. and Mrs. Richard C. Jones (Barbara Bates), Mrs. Mabel M. Kellerup, Mr. and Mrs. Arlington Cuthbert, and Barbara Abbey all drove from Cheyenne, Wyo.; Mr. and Mrs. John R. Smith came from Minturn; Mr. and Mrs. Paul W. Dooling travelled on the train from Grand Junction; Mr. and Mrs. William H. McBurney (Mabel Tierney) arrived from New Castle; Mr. James H. Larsh from Leadville; Mr. and Mrs. Herman Thelin from Boulder; and Dr. and Mrs. Joe Sinton (Esther Wheatley) drove from Colorado Springs.

Among the hundred guests some had travelled a long distance to be present. The Reverend and Mrs. Ford L. Gilbert came by train from their home in Henderson, Nevada. Also making the trip by train was Mrs. Mae Dorine Fahey, widow of Stephen Fahey. From farthest away were Mr. and Mrs. Carl W. Gilbert of Long Beach, California. Among those greatly missed was Mr. Claude E. Harris who had planned to fly from Seattle, Washington. Although at 88 he is still very active, his physician thought he should not attempt the trip. Mrs. Anna Sloss and Mr. and Mrs. Walter Hyrup who have contributed information most generously toward the writing of the authors' book on Basalt, had made definite plans to drive over from their home town for the gathering but were prevented from coming at the last minute much to everyone's regret.

Old friends spent the afternoon reminiscing, viewing a name quilt of true historical interest and beauty made in 1905 by the Ladies' Aid of Basalt and owned and exhibited by Arthur and Georgina Bates, looking over old iron relics of the Midland, reading many letters from old-timers who could not come to the party, looking over some of the photographs that will be included in "the book", and enjoying projected colored slides taken in and around the Basalt area. Some friends had not met for forty years.

Basalt, Colorado Midland Town 359

R. W. D. Collection

Old friends meet, (l. to r.) Charlie Dentner, Arthur Bates, Dave Cuthbert, Clarence Danielson, Gus Hotz, Clarence Dearing, James Larsh, Sterling Sloss and Ralph Danielson.

Former Midland Engineers and their wives, left to right: Clarence and Ethel Dearing, Arthur and Georgina Bates, George and Pauline Denmen, Clarence and Lucy Danielson.

R. W. D. Collection

Memorabilia

Recently, we have received much additional information, interesting and pertinent to the Basalt story, and we include here as much as space permits.

Some Railroad Miscellanea

In the section devoted to railroad jargon (page 71) the authors were unable to explain the derivation of such terms as "tallow-pot," "Big O," "stinger," and "snake." Dudley Mitchell, who once worked for the Midland, advises us that firemen were referred to as "tallow-pots," because in the early days they had to lubricate the slide valves on locomotives with hot tallow from a spouted can known as a tallow-pot. The other terms were derived from the emblems of the various railroad labor unions.

Another term meriting some explanation is "switchback," frequently used to describe a series of reverse curves on a road or trail. However, in reference to railroads, Clarence Danielson and Ed Haley have pointed out that where the Midland is concerned it is more accurate to use either "horseshoe" or "reverse curve" rather than "switchback." There are, of course, true railroad "switchbacks," which consist of multiple, alternating spurs, but these were never used on the Midland.

The term "whistle-stop" also originated with railroading and was used to describe a very small village. "Whistle-stops" were so small that an approaching train would stop only if flagged down or if a passenger signalled from the inside. In either case, the engineer would indicate that he had received the signal by answering with two short blasts of the whistle.

For those who have known both the diesel and steam engines, the difference in attraction between the two is worth noting. The former possesses a distinctive personality that makes it unique in its own right. But to many, there will always be something very special about the steam engine. The old Iron Horse had certain facial-type characteristics that made it appear almost human. The spinning drivers and wheels reminded one of an athlete's churning legs. Indeed, between the smoke, steam, and the shrill blast of the whistle, there were times when it seemed to be a living, breathing creature.

Missouri Heights

The Missouri Heights region, although not contiguous to Basalt, is sufficiently close and has had so little written about it that we include a brief mention of it here.

The region was settled somewhat later than the other communities in the area and was homesteaded by a group from Missouri, one of whom was a prominent Jamestown, Missouri physician by the name of Clagett. His son, Doctor O.T. Clagett, is now on the staff of the Mayo Clinic in Rochester, Minnesota.

In the early days, the area was nicknamed "Misery Flats," because of the difficulty in obtaining water. Nevertheless, Missouri Heights was able to boast of some small but productive farms. In recent years, these farms have, more and more, become the property of "gentlemen" farmers and ranchers. No other spot offers such a superb view of Mt. Sopris.

Additional Histories of Early Basalt Residents

Cox

Albert J. Cox, his wife, Catherine Yingst Cox, and four children came to Colorado from Pennsylvania sometime prior to 1890 and purchased a farm near Number 2 Bridge on the Roaring Fork River, two miles from Basalt.

Mrs. Cox was a thrifty, hardworking woman who raised flowers and vegetables in her conservatory-greenhouse. She also sold farm produce, eggs, encyclopedias and a face cream of her own making.

Their youngest child, a daughter, Verne, married Frank Atkinson (related to the Barnes family) of Basalt. After the death of another daughter, Alkey Jane (Mrs. Charles F. Graham), Mr. and Mrs. Cox raised both of her children, Violet and Charles.

Violet Graham married Charles Fouse, who had come from Carbondale to work on the Midland. After the railroad closed down, the Fouses moved to a 640 acre farm near Eckart.

Charles Graham married Martha Griffith, eldest child of the Richard Griffiths. He was employed for a time by the railroad but gave that up to become a prosperous rancher at Eagle.

Darien

Roger Darien came to Basalt from Italy in 1899, and was employed on the Arbaney Brothers ranch at Wingo. When one of the Arbaney brothers died, Roger purchased the ranch and sent for his family, which arrived in 1904. They had five children.

In 1909, the Dariens sold their Basalt ranch and purchased another one at Carbondale. In 1915 they sold that ranch, and bought the old Harris place at El Jebel, under the firm name of the Darien Brothers. It was sold to Bruce Arlean of Woody Creek in the spring of 1945. The Dariens also operated a store in Basalt for many years.

Dearhammer

The Dearhammers have run the store and post office at Meredith since 1887. The son, Howard, was one of those forced to move, because of the construction of the Ruedi Dam and Reservoir. He is very critical of the actual cost of the project, as compared to the original estimates.

Frey

Walter William Frey, a native of Nashville, Tennessee, worked on the railroad in Leadville. He and his wife, the former Ora May Howe of Peoria, Illinois, were married in Denver. They lived for a short time in Como, Colorado, where he was employed by the South Park and Colorado Southern Railroad.

In 1888, the Freys came to Aspen Junction, where Mr. Frey served two terms as mayor and later operated a general merchandise store. Caroline Frey Smith still lives in Basalt.

Hurtgen

Joseph Hurtgen, Jr. was born in Florissant, Colorado in 1890. His wife, Lillie Harrietta Christensen was a native of Nebraska. They were married in Glenwood Springs in 1912 and lived there for fourteen years.

In 1926, they moved to the Diamond G Ranch at Ruedi. In 1940, the Hurtgens moved to the Bill Smith ranch, remained there for two years before returning to the Diamond G, and finally settled in Basalt.

Lillie Hurtgen was the town clerk of Basalt for a number of years. Both she and Joe were active in the Odd Fellows and Rebekahs.

Hall

Mrs. Flora E. Hall taught school in Basalt in 1908 and 1909, and in Emma, Colorado from 1909 to 1910. In 1910, Mr. Joseph W. Hall, the husband and father, returned from Alaska, and the family moved to Fort Collins where they purchased a farm.

One son, Teller Hall, became a very successful inventor and manufacturer. He and his wife live in California. Ralph Danielson remembers with gratitude that it was Teller who saved him from drowning at the Emma Bridge.

Hyrup

Whenever we "Basalters" return for a visit, one of the first persons we hunt up is Walter J. Hyrup, one of the few old-timers still there. It is a joy to talk to a man so friendly, with such an excellent memory, keen wit and pungent vocabulary. He has definitely "kept his marbles."

On March 20, 1968, Walter's beloved wife, Eva, died suddenly and unexpectedly of a heart attack. Since then, our pleasure at seeing Walter is muted by the ever-present atmosphere of loss that pervades his home.

Walter's recollections of the "old days" and his philosophy of life form a rare combination, one we want to add to the story of Basalt. . . .

Reminiscences of my Youth

by
Walter J. Hyrup

"When school was out for the summer we boys worked at clearing the sagebrush and oak brush and other growth off our land. Then came the never-ending job of picking rocks off the fields. . . . It seemed to us that we labored many summers before the ranch began to pay. . . .

"Mother had a small herd of about forty cattle to be fed by ranch hay, as well as six work horses. When we grew old enough Mother stopped renting out the place and we ran it ourselves. We raised hay, grain, and potatoes. I remember flailing out the grain to get seed for planting.

"We owned no machinery. It was a great help for the people of the Frying Pan in later years when the fanning-mill and the horse-powered threshing machines were brought in.

"One must admit that in those days people were more congenial when they traded work. Threshing would usually last three weeks. Getting the job done took quite a number of helpers. I do not remember that any money was paid out except to the owner of the threshing-machine, who received so much cash for each bushel threshed.

"After finishing the eighth grade and a year helping to run the ranch, I worked as delivery boy for Art Simmons' Basalt Supply Company Store at $60 per month. However, railroading was always in my mind, and I went to Leadville and worked in the Colorado Midland roundhouse on the twelve-hour night shift at $52.50 a month. I'll never forget how excited I was when I got promoted to locomotive fireman. My engineer was Leo Heller, a mighty fine man. I fudged a bit on my age. I joined the Brotherhood of Locomotive Firemen and took my oath from Claude Harris.

"In 1916 Woodrow Wilson was elected President. People said, 'He kept us out of war.' Nevertheless, our country in time became involved in World War I. Being single and with no dependents it was not long before I was inducted into military service. I wound up in the Field Artillery, Battery B, 125th. After intensive training we went to France. At the end of the war, although I had the opportunity to change outfits and to be in the Army of Occupation in Germany, I chose to go back home.

"The Midland had closed down and there was no job for me! Through a tip from an old friend, Oscar Quist of Grand Junction, I landed work on the Uintah narrow-gauge railroad out of Mack as a 'travelling fireman' and on a salary. When the boss found out that an engineer and I had helped the men to join the Brotherhoods, and that they were asking for scheduled pay, I was out of a job!

"Back in Basalt again, I married my girl, Eva M. Letey, the one I couldn't forget since the time I returned from the war. At her father's invitation, we ran his ranch for twenty-four years. Our four children were born there. With our savings, we soon bought three ranches of our own.

"We then moved to my childhood home in Basalt and offered the fine ranch of 320 acres at Snowmass to our son, John, as a gift when he returned from duty in World War II. However, his great interest in life was heavy machinery, so he turned it down! The eventual owner of the place, Evans Milton, sold it not many years ago at an enormous profit to the Aspen-at-Snowmass Corporation.

"All our children have done well, are married and have families. John is superintendent of heavy equipment at a nice salary at Aspen-at-Snowmass. Our eldest grandson was a helicopter pilot in Vietnam. He is back in this country, but still in the service.

"In the fall of 1967 our home, the place of my birth, burned. We guessed that a fault in the electric wiring was the cause. Another one had to be built on the place. We moved into it on

New Year's Day, 1968. March 20 was the saddest day of my life. A sudden heart attack took my beloved wife from me.

"I now live here alone and very lonely. I have time to think a great deal about the changes that have taken place in this small community. Gone is the railroad and so are the horse and buggy and one-room school. Today we have two large schools with about 500 pupils. These boys and girls enjoy a gymnasium, a football field, and an auditorium. Basalt has become quite a lively place. I recollect the time when there were two saloons and each one paid an annual $500 fee to the town. What a contrast now! There are two package liquor stores, two bars at present, and the City Market sells beer. I am not certain, but I doubt that the revenue to Basalt from all of them exceeds $75 yearly. The state seems to grab most of the profits.

"My viewpoint is that we are gradually losing our freedom in this whole country through legislation. Each year bundles of new laws are passed. The public gets rooked. Just what is the matter with man? He surely seems to be making a poor showing at being able to live with himself. You may mark me down as a real 'doubting Thomas!' This Basalt boy, born in 1896, believes we should try harder to abide by the Ten Commandments the Lord gave to us, and we would then need less legislation!"

Lucksinger

Fortunately for Basalt, Mr. and Mrs. Jake Lucksinger, Jr. still reside there. Besides keeping very active painting landscapes and portraits, he has written an interesting history of events in his life. We have encouraged him to publish it or at least give a copy to the library. During the past year he has contributed many articles to the local newspaper, the *Sopris Sun*, some of which are entitled: "Desperado Days," "Pioneer Women," "Early Diaries," "Fishing," and "Evolution of a Hot Biscuit."

His parents also had a dairy, and Jake, Jr. remembers branding cows and delivering milk in cans. He recalls how one time a housewife brought out a chamber pot to receive milk. When a look of astonishment came to his face, she said "What's the matter? You act is if you have never seen one of these before, and besides there is nothing the matter with it. I've just bought it from the drugstore this morning."

Jake says that, believe it or not, not long ago he read in *Time* magazine where chamber pots were being used now as antique jardinieres and as soup tureens.

Although there were a couple of other dairies in town, the Lucksinger's was the largest. According to Jake, sometimes the delivery boy would get short of milk and then would stop at the

Frying Pan to add a little water. Folks used to say jokingly that the milkman's favorite song was 'Shall We Gather at the River.'

Mount

Hazel Mount, Mrs. Chris Hyrup, sister-in-law of Walter Hyrup, still lives in Basalt. Her four children are living and doing well.

Eugene Hyrup lives in Byers, Colorado and runs a bulk plant for Standard Oil. Annabelle is a stenographer in Colorado Springs, has six children and one grandchild. Robert is in the Air Force. Patricia is a registered nurse, lives in Buena Vista and has four children.

Boyhood Days in Basalt:
Some Reflections by the Authors

On Bicycle Race Days the drum corps from Leadville would come in on Number 3 and play on the station platform before going on to Glenwood. Their uniforms were very impressive, with short blue jackets, red pants, white leggings, white socks, and red caps. They later moved to Denver and were known as Cook's Drum Corps.

We remember well how worried Mother used to be when Father rented a horse and buggy from John Smith to drive down the valley. When going over that very narrow part called the "grade," opposite Emma, Mother would say, "Andy, be careful." There were few turnouts and one might have to back the horse and buggy to get by another vehicle.

On Hallowe'en we were sure that we "scared the daylights" out of the inhabitants by rotating a notched empty spool over windows. Careful householders always took their fence gates indoors for safekeeping. There were instances when pranksters even went so far as to put their neighbors' buggies astraddle of house roofs.

Clarence vividly remembers the time when he really became frightened as he lost his footing in the swift current on the German stretch of the Frying Pan. Harry Nelson and Arthur Bates stood laughing at him as he floated down the river. Fortunately, in those days we wore no boots and one could swim out if necessary.

On one occasion our uncle, Oscar Reibel, was returning home from courting one of the Lucksinger daughters and encountered a skunk. Uncle Oscar came out second best, and all of his clothes had to be burned.

We never go past the huge pile of stones on the Willits place near El Jebel without feeling tremendous admiration for the men and boys whose back-breaking work was responsible for the removal of the rocks from the land. Today this would be done mechanically. *The younger generation can enjoy improvements and inventions, but can they ever deeply appreciate them?*

Points of Interest in the Basalt Area

There is a great temptation to write at length about the wonders of the Basalt area. Unfortunately, space will not permit more than a brief review. Suffice it to say that it is possible to spend many pleasant and rewarding hours, travelling by jeep, horseback, or on foot to such places as the historic Midland tunnels; Woods Lake and the many small but beautiful little lakes on the headwaters of the Frying Pan and White Rivers; Ruedi Dam; Sloane's Peak; Basalt Mountain; and the Red Tables.

There is a map accompanying this enlarged edition, which shows these and other points of interest. More detailed maps of the area can be purchased from the U.S. Geological Survey, Building 41, Denver Federal Center, Denver, Colorado 80225.

Busk-Ivanhoe and Hagerman Tunnels

Two trips that railroad buffs would enjoy are to each end of the Busk-Ivanhoe and Hagerman tunnels, particularly the latter. At the ghost town of Hagerman, one is able to view the caved-in portion of the historic old tunnel, dilapidated cabins, the rock dump, and countless pieces of old iron. At Douglass City, one can see the remains of the east construction camp used in the building of the tunnel; also the remains of the air compressor, and the pipe leading up to the tunnel entrance. There is also a structure that appears to be an old bake oven. The views from here are magnificent.

A couple of years ago, Ralph Danielson was returning to Leadville from Basalt. Noticing where the Public Service Company's recent road over Hagerman Pass had cut across the old Midland grade, he parked his car, and walked out to search for the abutments of the famous old trestle, but finally grew reluctant to proceed too far because of age, altitude, and being alone. He then returned to his car and continued on to Leadville, where he arranged for Dick Anderson to drive him back in a jeep the next day.

Interesting Local Projects

The Ruedi Dam and Reservoir, the Pan-Ark Collecting Channels, the tree nursery at El Jebel, and the Red Tables are among some of the more prominent points of interest in the Basalt area.

Virgil Holcomb says that the ridge along the Red Tables was once an Indian trail, which he converted to a horse trail. He said there is evidence that the Indians even made improvements by constructing rock walls.

About 15 or 20 years ago, when the beetle infestation was killing off so many Englemann spruce trees, the Forest Service built a road on the top in order to get spraying equipment into the area to kill the beetles and destroy the larvae. It is really an education to strip the bark from a dead tree and see the channels made by the beetles. A most obliging ranger demonstrated this to me some fifteen years ago.

On this trip, one has a magnificent view in all directions, the most beautiful being the snow-capped peaks of the Elk Range to the south, the top of Basalt Mountain, and the Cattle Creek area close at hand.

Wilderness Trail Trips

The most impressive trips of all are those sponsored by the Forest Service, known as Wilderness Trail Trips. There are about ten conducted through the Western states annually. One in the Basalt area, for example, starts at Maroon Bells, takes a circle through the Elk Mountains, over to Gothic and back. The views are magnificent, especially the one from Buckskin Pass (elevation 12,100 feet) between Carter Lake and Snowmass Lake. For those who can endure some rain, don't object to fussing with a tent, and are able to spend most of the day in the saddle, this is a most satisfying and memorable way to see the country.

Other interesting, recently developed areas worth seeing are the campuses of Colorado Mountain College at Glenwood Springs and Leadville, the Colorado Rocky Mountain Outward Bound School at Crystal, and the Colorado School at Carbondale.

Please don't take any of these trips at high speeds. Slow down! Stop! Look around, observe, and drink in the beauty of this great country. You will find it more rewarding than you ever imagined.

For trail rides, contact the Whittleseys, Horseshoe Bend Ranch, the Riley Quest Ranch, Seven Castles Lodge, Woods Lake, Otto Creek Cabins, and the King Guest Ranch at Basalt. Dick Anderson runs Timberline Jeep Tours out of Leadville.

Chronology

Relative to Colorado and the Basalt Area

20,000 years ago	Sandia men.
8,000 B. C.	Eden people.
1-1300 A. D.	Mese Vedre Indian culture.
1541	Coronado touched Colorado.
1761-1765	Juan Maria de Rivera expedition into San Juan and Sangre de Cristo Mountains.
1776	Friars Escalante and Dominguez traverse western Colorado (and probably down the Roaring Fork from Aspen or Carbondale).
1803	Louisiana Purchase—(no portion west of Continental Divide).
1806	Pike reached headwaters of Arkansas River near Leadville.
1820	Stephen H. Long expedition.
1825	Opening era of fur traders, trappers, and Mountain Men.
1842	Lt. John Fremont made first of several trips.
1851	San Luis established; oldest settlement of Colorado.
1853	Capt. Gunnison trip.
1854	Kansas-Nebraska Territory established May 30.
1858	Capt. Randolph Marcy explored Eagle River Valley. Arapahoe County (as part of Kansas Territory) formed.
1859	Discovery of gold at Idaho Springs in January, and by Gregory at Gregory Gulch near Central City in May.
1860	Start of Leadville rush—placer discoveries in California Gulch. Capt. Sopris trip to Glenwood Springs and Roaring Fork Valley. Berthoud and Bridges trip to northwest Colorado.
1861	Colorado Territory established in February.
1867-1869	Survey expedition by Ferdinand V. Hayden.
1868	Establishment of Ute Reservation.
1876	Colorado admitted to the Union.

Basalt, Colorado Midland Town   371

1877	University of Colorado opens classes.
1878	Leadville incorporated.
1879	Aspen started.
	Fort Defiance built.
	Meeker Massacre and Major Thornburgh Ambush.
	First Post Office built in Leadville on Harrison Avenue.
	July trip by Wm. Markt to Defiance over Frying Pan Trail.
1880	Chief Ouray dies.
	June 15—Ute bill for exclusion of Utes from western Colorado signed by President.
1881	Pitkin County established.
	Aspen incorporated.
	Road to Glenwood from Aspen started.
	Grand Junction founded.
	U.S. Troops escort Uncompaghre Utes to reservation in Utah, August 28.
1882	Construction of Fort Defiance begun.
	Ute Reservation declared public land, August 10.
	Charcoal ovens at Frying Pan Junction built and village started.
	Grand Junction incorporated July 26.
1883	Colorado Midland Railroad organized November 23.
	Defiance incorporated February 10.
	Carbonate City incorporated.
	County seat Garfield County moved from Carbonate City to Glenwood in October.
	Satank post office started June 27.
1884	Eagle County established.
1885	Emma post office established.
	Glenwood Springs incorporated.
	Hagerman Tunnel started.
	Luchsinger (Lucksinger) brothers applied for land.
1886	Colorado Midland surveys completed.
	Gabe Luchsinger and Jake Lucksinger sold right-of-way to Colorado Midland.
	Hagerman Tunnel finished late 1886—early 1887.
	First railroad buildings in Aspen Junction.
1887	Colorado Midland reached Leadville in Spring.
	Colorado Midland reached Aspen Junction and edge of Aspen and of Glenwood Springs in Fall.
	Aspen Junction mail handled by station agent.
	Rio Grande Railroad into Aspen.
	Charcoal ovens no longer used; replaced by coke ovens at Cardiff and Carbondale.
1888	Carbondale incorporated January 30.
	Band of Utes from Utah under Colorow make last Indian raid into Colorado.
	Colorado Midland into Aspen February 4.

	Colorado Midland reached Newcastle October 20.
1889	Gabe Luchsinger sold lots for homes.
	Otmar Luchsinger acquired title, by purchase, to Tract 45 on April 2.
1890	Busk-Ivanhoe Tunnel started July 26.
	Post Office established at Aspen Junction Feb. 13th.
1891	Gabe Luchsinger gets final title to land by purchase of Tract 47 on November 20.
	Bob Womack discovers gold at Cripple Creek.
1892	John Ruedi obtained title to Tract 48 by purchase February 23.
1893	Busk-Ivanhoe Tunnel finished October 18; trains began going through December 17.
	Sherman Act repeal strikes silver mining industry and enhances effect of '93 panic in Colorado.
1895	Name of Aspen Junction changed to Basalt June 19.
1897	Dan German acquired title by purchase of Tract 51 on April 6.
1899	Snow blockade from January 24 to April 17.
1901	Basalt incorporated August 26.
1907	Division moved to Cardiff November 2; pushers left at Basalt.
1914	Beginning of World War I.
1917	A.E. Carlton and associates purchase Midland, April 21.
1918	Last passenger train east out of Basalt, August 4.
1921	Rails torn up and right-of-way made into highway; Carlton Tunnel used for autos.
1930	Carlton Tunnel closed to all traffic.

Bibliography

BOOKS

Athearn, Robert G. *Rebel of the Rockies: The Denver and Rio Grande Western Railroad.* New Haven, Yale University Press, 1962.

**Baker, James H., and Hafen, Leroy R. *History of Colorado.* Denver, Linderman Company, 1927. (Prepared under the supervision of the State Historical Society and the National Historical Society of Colorado.)

Bancroft, Caroline. *Early Glamour of Glenwood Springs.* Boulder, Colorado, Johnson Publishing Company, 1958.

Bancroft, Caroline. *Famous Aspen. Its Fabulous Past, Its Lovely Present.* Denver, Golden Press, 1957.

Beardsley, Isaac H. *Echoes from Peak and Plain.* Cincinnati, Curtis and Jennings, 1898. (See page 516)

Beebe, Lucius. *Mixed Train Daily.* New York, E. P. Dutton, 1947.

Beebe, Lucius, and Clegg, Charles. *Rio Grande: Mainline of the Rockies.* Berkeley, Calif., Howell-North, 1962.

***Berrey, Lester, and Van Den Bark, Melvin. *The American Thesaurus of Slang.* New York, Thomas Crowell, 1953.

Bollinger, Edward T., and Bauer, Frederick. *The Moffat Road.* Denver, Sage Books, 1962.

Bollinger, Edward T. *Rails That Climb: Story of the Moffat Road.* Santa Fe, N. M., Rydal Press, 1950.

Burroughs, John R. *Headfirst in the Pickle Barrel.* New York, Morrow, 1963.

Cafky, Morris. *Colorado Midland.* Denver, Rocky Mountain Railroad Club, 1965.

Carroll, Gladys Hasty. *Only Fifty Years Ago.* Boston, Little, Brown, 1962.

Clements, Edith S. *Flowers of Mountain and Plain.* New York, H. W. Wilson, 1915.

Colorado: *A Guide to the Highest State.* Writers of W. P. A. Project, New York, Hastings House, 1941.

Colorado: *Short Studies of It's Past and Present.* University of Colorado Semi-Centennial Publication.

Colorado Historical Association. *The Historical Encyclopedia of Colorado.* 2 vols. Thomas S. Chamblin, ed. Denver, 1960.

Colorado State Planning Commission. *Colorado Yearbook,* 1956-58.

Colorado State Historical Association. *Year Book, Centennial Edition,* vol. 2, Denver, 1960.

Crofutt, George A. *Gripsack Guide of Colorado.* Omaha, Overland Publishing Co., 1881.

Daniels, Helen Sloane. *Story of the Ute Indians of Southwest Colorado.* (Durango Public Library Museum Project). National Youth Administration, 1941.

Elston, Allan Vaughan. *Last Stage to Aspen.* Philadelphia, Lippincott, 1956.

Foote, Alvin. *The Fabulous Valley.* New York, A & T Company, 1950.

Griswold, Don L. and Griswold, Jean. *Colorado's Century of Cities.* Denver, Smith-Brooks, 1958. (See pp. 159, 161, 234, 244.)

**Hafen, Leroy R. *Colorado and It's People.* vol. 1 of 4 vols. Lewis Historical Publishing Co., 1948.

Hafen, Leroy R. and Hafen, Ann W. *Colorado.* Denver, Old West Publishing Co., 1943.

Hall, Frank. *History of the State of Colorado.* 4 vols. Chicago, Blakely Printing Co. for Rocky Mountain Historical Company, 1889-95.

Hayden, Ferdinand V. *Geologic and Geographic Atlas of Colorado and Portions of Adjacent Territory.* (Field work of 1873-76.) U. S. Department of the Interior. New York, J. Bien, 1877.

Kappler, Charles J. *Indian Affairs: Laws and Treaties.* 3 vols. Washington, D. C., U. S. Government Printing Office, 1903. (See vol. 2, p. 990.)

Le Massena, R. A. Ronzio, R. A. and Ryland, C. S. *Colorado Mountain Railroads,* vol. 1. Golden, Colo., Smoking Stack Press, 1963.

Ormes, Robert M. *Railroads and the Rockies.* Denver, Sage Books, 1963. (See pp. 133-139.)

Parkhill, Forbes. *The Last of the Indian Wars.* New York, Collier Books, 1961.

Portrait and Biographical Record of the State of Colorado. Chicago, Chapman Publishing Co., 1899. (No author)

Perkin, Bob. *First Hundred Years.* New York, Doubleday, 1959.

Rockwell, Wilson. *The Utes: A Forgotten People.* Denver, Sage Books, 1956.

Shoemaker, Len (Leonard C.) *The Roaring Fork Valley.* Denver, Sage Books, 1958.

State Museum Library. *Progressive Men of Western Colorado.* Chicago, A. W. Bowen and Co., 1905.

Thompson, Goldianne, and Halley, William H. *History of Clayton and Union County, New Mexico.* Denver, Monitor Publishing Co., 1962.

***Weseen, Maurice H. *Dictionary of American Slang.* New York, Thomas Crowell, 1934.

ARTICLES AND PAMPHLETS

***Bird, Horace A. *History of a Line.* (Colorado Midland Railway Promotional Pamphlets): *From Plains to Peaks; Fishing and Hunting in Colorado.* 1889.

Bogue, Lucille M. "The Irish Angel," *Colorado Wonderland,* Dec. 1955, pp. 13-15.

Borland, Lois B. "Ho for the Reservation (settlement of the Western Slope)," *Colorado Magazine,* vol. 29, 1952, pp. 56-74.

Borland, Lois B. "The Sale of the San Juan," *Colorado Magazine,* vol. 28, 1951, pp. 107-127.

Brandes, Ray. "Historical Materials in Limbo." Editorial in *Arizoniana,* vol. 8, no. 4, winter 1962, pp. 50-51.

Brandhorst, N. F. Colorado Midland *Railroad Stories,* Sept., 1933, p. 89.

Cafky, Morris. "Remember Hagerman Pass?" *Denver Westerners Monthly Roundup.* Sept. 1963, p. 8.

Colman, Sam M. "Bucking Snow on the Colorado Midland." *Locomotive Fireman's Magazine,* June, 1899.

**Colorado Fish and Game Department. "A Look Back—65-Year History of Colorado Fish and Game Department." 1961 Report.

***Colorado Midland Railway. Article on Hagerman Tunnel. Pikes Peak Route Publicity Pamphlet, 1887.

***Colorado Midland Railway. *Heart of the Rockies.* (A promotion book). Charles S. Lee, 1890.

Cormack, Bob. "Will James: A Cowboy for Fifty Years." *Denver Westerners Monthly Roundup*, vol 18, no. 12, Dec. 1962, p. 5.

"Early History of Carbondale, Roaring Fork Valley, and Garfield County." *Crystal River Empire*, Dec. 13, 1924.

*County Commissioners of Eagle County. *A Descriptive History of Eagle County, Colorado*. Sept. 1899. (Courtesy Bramblet Willits.)

Dunklee, Ivah and Dinkel, Wm. M. "A Pioneer of the Roaring Fork," *Colorado Magazine*, July 1944, p. 133 and Sept. 1944, p. 184.

Foster, Jack, and Beckwith, Ruth. Answer to query by Ray S. Eldridge on the Colorado Midland, in "The Colorado Question Box." *Rocky Mountain News*, Feb. 10, 1952.

Frazier, J. L. "Prologue to Colorado Territory," *Colorado Magazine*, July 1961, p. 161.

Graves, Carl F. *The Colorado Midland Railroad*. Bulletin No. 36, The Railway and Locomotive Historical Society, The Baker Library, Harvard Business School, Cambridge, Mass.

Hafen, Leroy R. "Claims and Jurisdictions Over the Territory of Colorado Prior to 1861." *Colorado Magazine*, May 1932, p. 95.

Haley, E. J. Historical Map of Colorado Railroads. For the Rocky Mountain Railroad Club. Hotchkiss, Inc.

Hay, Keith. "A Look Back." *Colorado Outdoors*, January-April, 1959.

Heatley, Elaine H. "Ernest E. Lee, Big Game Hunter." *Arizoniana*, vol. 3, no. 4, winter 1962, pp. 36-39.

Jackson, William S. "Railroad Conflicts in Colorado in the Eighties." *Colorado Magazine*, Jan., 1946, p. 7.

Jackson, William S. "The Record vs. Reminiscence." *Denver Westerners Brand Book*. 1945.

Knight, McDonald, and Hammock, L. A. "Early Days on the Eagle." *Colorado Magazine*, Oct. 1963, p. 294.

Larsh, James. Reminiscence in *Herald Democrat* of Leadville, July 17, 1956.

Le Massena, Robert A. "Minturn Memories." *Trains Magazine*, April 1963, p. 20.

Lipsey, John J. "Hagerman Builds the Midland." *Denver Westerners Monthly Roundup*, Dec. 1954, pp. 8-20.

Lipsey, John J. "How Hagerman Sold the Midland." *Denver Westerners Brand Book*, 1956, pp. 265-86.

Lipsey, John J. "How Hagerman Sold the Midland in 1890." *Denver Westerners Monthly Roundup,* May 1956, pp. 6-15.

Lipsey, John J. "J. J. Hagerman, Building of the Colorado Midland." *Denver Westerners Brand Book,* 1954, pp. 95-115.

Marranzino, Pasquale. "Famous Pigpen Is Being Razed." *Rocky Mountain News,* Jan. 27, 1964.

Moody, Linwood. "The Old Colorado Midland." *Railroad Stories,* August 1936, pp. 29-54.

News Item on Colorado Midland (with photo of advertisement on side of California Building, Denver). *Denver Post,* Tuesday, Jan. 31, 1961.

Queal, Cal. "The Fishy Express," in "Outdoor Empire". *Denver Post,* Oct. 6, 1960.

Rogers, James Grafton. "Law and Order in the Early Days," in "Trails Through Romantic Colorado." *University of Colorado Bulletin,* April 26, 1935.

Ronzio, Richard A. "Fort Crawford on the Uncompahgre." *Denver Westerners Monthly Roundup,* March 1963, pp. 3-9.

Roth, Charles B. "Wild Meat for the Mines; Diary of Frank H. Mayer." *Denver Westerners Brand Book,* 1961, p. 363.

*Shehi, Emma Davis. Letter to *Kansas Agriculturist.* April, 1887.

Shoemaker, Len (Leonard C.) "Roaring Fork Pioneers." *Denver Westerners Brand Book,* p. 53, also in *Denver Westerners Monthly Roundup,* Oct. 1962, pp. 5-9.

Spring, Agnes Wright. Review of *Centennial Edition of Colorado State Historical Society Yearbook, Colorado Magazine,* April 1959, p. 82.

*Stewart, Omer C. Letter regarding Chief Colorow and the White River Utes.

Trask, Edgar P. "Toot Translations." *Trains Magazine,* Feb. 1964, p. 56.

United States Land Office. Maps of Basalt.

Wallace, Betty. "History of Early Newspapers in Western Colorado." *Denver Westerners Monthly Roundup,* Jan. 1963.

UNPUBLISHED MATERIAL

Basalt Methodist Episcopal Church. Record of the Official Board, Feb. 15, 1907-Aug. 1918. Courtesy Anna Sloss.

*Bogue, Randell. "A History of Basalt." Basalt High School Research Paper, 1942.

Boigegrain, Walter J. "The Methodist Church in the Eagle-Colorado River Valley in Colorado, 1880-1906." Master's Thesis, Iliff School of Theology, Denver.

**Borden, Harold L. "A Report on the History of Elk in Colorado." May 2, 1936.

*Brown, David R. C. "Account of a Trip from Black Hawk to Aspen, 1880."

*Chamber of Commerce of Aspen. "Community Book of Aspen, Basalt, and Carbondale." Courtesy Mrs. Joseph Hurtgen and Mrs. Anna Olson.

*Colorado Midland Railway Co. "Rules and Regulations of the Operating Department." May 1, 1906.

Crowner, Virginia. "Reminiscing." Glenwood Springs Public Library.

*Danielson, Luke. "The Colorado Midland." Research Paper, Boulder High School, 1962.

Danielson, Philip. Information on Basalt Patents. Personal Communication, 1962.

Eagle County Abstract Office. Records, 1888 to 1890, Gene Luby, Prop.

Edgerton, E. N. "History of Carbondale Methodist Church." 1948. Ira J. Taylor Library, Iliff School of Theology, Denver.

Iden, Thomas L. "A History of the Ute Indian Cessations of Colorado." Master's Thesis, Western State College, Gunnison, Colorado, 1929.

"Journal of the Thirty-fourth Session of the Colorado Annual Conference of the Methodist Episcopal Church (1896)." Ira J. Taylor Library, Iliff School of Theology, Denver. (See p. 52.)

*Kibby, Earl. Notes on Basalt; personal communication, 1962.

Ladies Aid Society, Basalt Methodist Church. Two books of minutes, Dec. 10, 1902 - Feb. 17, 1918 and Feb. 8, 1930-Dec. 9, 1954. Courtesy Anna Sloss.

Lloyd, John B. "The Uncompahgre Utes." Master's Thesis, Western State College, Colorado, 1932.

Lucksinger, George. "Minutes of Early Basalt Town Records." In possession of Jacob and George Lucksinger.

*McNeil, Tom. Letter describing his railroading career.

*Mosley, Earl. "The History of the Colorado Midland." Paper presented to Round Table Club, Colorado Springs, 1958.

*Rhodes, Addie. Poems about the Basalt region collected by Mrs. Rhodes.

Errata

Errata in the First Edition

We are most grateful to Len Shoemaker, a long-time forest ranger and resident of the area, also an author of books on the region, for going over our book with a fine-tooth comb and providing many of the following corrections.

Page

VI	Malcolm is sometimes spelled Malcum
IX	Peggy Coble instead of Cable
IX	Laura Ekstrom instead of Eckstrom
1.	Opal Harber instead of Harter
1.	Spring Gulch instead of Spring Park
3.	Sloane's Peak instead of Sloan's Peak
10.	Benedict Benoit Bourg instead of Bourg Brothers
10.	James Ashby instead of Ashbys
10.	Ferdinand Vevey instead of Vevie
18.	L.B. Mow instead of L.B. Maw
21.	Rock Creek instead of Willow Creek
22.	eight instead of eighty
24.	sanitarium instead of santarium
24.	Ed Koch instead of Ed Keough
24.	Charley Teas instead of Charley Thias
24.	Dorothy Falk instead of Dorothy Faulk
25.	Sellar instead of Sellars
25.	William Henderson instead of John Henderson
28.	Freiler is sometimes spelled Frieler
33.	Mrs. Hanthorn instead of Mrs. Hanthorne
61.	locomotives instead of locamotives
65.	fossils instead of fossiles
95.	Later investigation reveals that the Interstate Commerce Commission was established by the Federal Government in 1887 but did not receive the authority to examine engines until 1911.
135.	Walter Frey instead of Walter Fay
146.	William J. (Bill) Barker instead of William J. (Bill) Barber
146.	John McLaren instead of George McClaren

146. M.B. Louthau instead of M.B. Louthan
157. Caption under top photograph should read: Charlie and Sylvia Law.
177. cemetery instead of cemetary
179. Caffery instead of Caffeny
194. Pete Engelbrecht instead of Pete Engelbright
204. Clara Louise Hillgren, born January 4, 1860
220. Albena Tchoucich (later spelled Tekoucich) instead of Albena Tekowick
220. Olice Gerbaz instead of Alice Gerbaz
222. Roy Lee Williams instead of Leroy Williams
223. Clarence Danielson and Art Bates think that Riley Miller had the longest service record.
254. Chris Hyrup and Hazel Mount married October 20, 1914
262. The Jake Lucksinger ranch has been purchased by the State Fish and Game Department and has been named Christine Ranch after Mrs. Jake Lucksinger.
264. Louise Patterson instead of Louise Peterson
304. Shephard instead of Shepard and Shehard
313. four children instead of three
314. Pearl Shanks died in Elko, Nevada. Marion and Marcia Mitchell live in San Francisco.
326. 16 years old instead of 12
328. James F. Jones instead of James I. Jones
341. Cecil Shoemaker instead of Cecil Shumacher
343. Ambro Vern Harris instead of Vern Harris
361. Mesa Verde instead of Mese Verde